GRE
BIOLOGY

How to Prepare for the Graduate Record Examination in Biology

Third Edition

John A. Snyder, Ph.D., and C. Leland Rodgers, Ph.D.
Furman University
Greenville, South Carolina

BARRON'S

Barron's Educational Series, Inc.

All inquiries should be addressed to:
Barron's Educational Series, Inc.
250 Wireless Boulevard
Hauppauge, New York 11788

Library of Congress Catalog Card No. 89-6468

International Standard Book No. 0-8120-4199-2

Library of Congress Cataloging-in-Publication Data

Snyder, John A., 1943-
   Barron's GRE biology: how to prepare for the graduate record examination in biology/
by John A. Snyder, and C. Leland Rodgers. — 3rd ed.
   p.   cm.

   Rev. ed. of: Barron's how to prepare for the graduate record
examination/C. Leland Rodgers. 2nd ed. © 1983.
   ISBN 0-8120-4199-2
   1. Biology — Examinations, questions, etc. I. Rodgers, C. Leland
(Charles Leland), 1918-   . II. Rodgers, C. Leland (Charles
Leland), 1918-   Barron's GRE biology: how to prepare for the graduate record
examination in biology. III. Barron's Educational Series, inc. IV. Title.
V. Title: GRE biology: how to prepare for the graduate record examination in biology.
QH316.S64   1989
574'.076 — dc19   89-6468
                                                               CIP

PRINTED IN THE UNITED STATES OF AMERICA

56   100   987

Table of Contents

Part One Information About the Biology Test

Purposes of the Biology Test

The primary purpose of the *Biology Test* is to evaluate the accomplishment of biology majors. Both the student and the school may use the score as a basis for comparing the individual's performance with the performances of a large number of other people at the same educational level. Such a comparison can be useful to ascertain a person's qualifications for pursuing certain types of advanced study and the probability of success in a particular course of study. It is often used as a basis for preference in the granting of awards such as fellowships.

Although a minimum score for eligibility to graduate school has been set by most universities, the score is seldom if ever used as the sole criterion for acceptance, but is used in conjunction with the scholastic records, recommendations, a personal interview, motivation, or evidence of improvement. Similarly, the examination score alone will not necessarily qualify a person to receive a fellowship.

The Biology Test is also useful to show strengths and weaknesses. This is possible because the grade includes subscores for major subject-matter areas. Students may use the subscores to evaluate their own qualifications, or the graduate school may use them for counseling and placement.

Undergraduate biology departments with a large number of majors will benefit if their students have their scores sent back to the department. Sometimes the department uses them to compare the performance of its students with those in other schools or with the norm for all examinees. Such comparisons may tell something about the comparative effectiveness of different curricular programs and teaching competence. Obviously, students are seldom immediately concerned with these objectives but can do a service for their major department by providing the appropriate information on the Registration Form, authorizing the sending of a transcript back to the department.

Content of the Biology Test

Presumably the test covers the content of undergraduate biology curricula. The content is ever changing to keep pace with developments in science. At the same time, it includes a core of information that is considered basic to the field.

The questions are divisible into three categories representing different levels of organization. They are *cellular* (and *subcellular*), *organismal*, and *population*, each represented by approximately one third of the questions.

The cellular and subcellular level covers the cell as a functional and structural unit as well as its chemical composition. Obviously this includes the atoms, molecules, macromolecules, and organelles that comprise the cell. A study of this level of organization of necessity involves energy transformations in photosynthetic and respiratory pathways plus the replication of cellular components and cells. Other related topics are molecular genetics, viruses, unicellular organisms, and cell types of multicellular organisms.

The organismal part deals with all aspects of the biology of individual organisms. Among the subjects covered are function, structure, Mendelian inheritance patterns, growth, development, life cycles, homeostatic mechanisms, animal behavior, diseases, and aging. Emphasis is placed on vertebrate animals and seed plants.

The population level deals with the responses of groups of similar (interbreeding) organisms to genetic and environmental influences. Despite the population label, the level also encompasses relationships within communities and ecosystems. Major topics are evolution and systematics, energy flow and cycling, community homeostasis, and human impact on the ecosystem.

Student Preparation

Because curricula in colleges differ so much throughout the country and students almost always have some latitude in selecting courses in their major, each student has a highly individualized course of training. Furthermore, each reaches a certain level of competence in relation to his or her ability and dedication to achievement. Therefore each student approaches the examination uniquely trained.

Considering the broad coverage of subject matter and the unequal preparation of candidates, no biology student can expect to answer all of the questions on the test: Students may even fall short of achieving the goals they have set for themselves. Since so much is at stake, many students try to improve their chances by reviewing material not completely mastered and studying subjects to which they have had little or no exposure. One thing is certain — the more information a student possesses, the better he or she will do. Information included in this book is one way to help increase knowledge.

Whatever preparation is attempted, students will find the subject too large and the time too short. They should not get mired in needless review of subjects already known, or in new material that requires more time than is available. Instead they should concentrate on clarifying topics about which they have some knowledge but which they do not fully understand. If time is left, they can then look at unfamiliar or difficult material. Certainly it is worthwhile to review lecture notes from introductory biology courses and from broad-based courses in such subjects as genetics, physiology, and ecology. Perusal of a good, recently published textbook in introductory biology can help ensure that no major area of biology has been left unstudied.

By the time students have the test in hand, they can do no more to prepare for it but may be able to make the most of what they already know. One ingredient contributing to maximum recall and application of information is confidence — or, at least, freedom from anxiety. Although it is sometimes easier said than done, students can often find a measure of calmness by remembering that they have a considerable amount of training, that no one can achieve perfection, and that success in life is not dependent on a single event such as the Biology Test. Each student should remember that, even if he or she fails to achieve a specific goal, life offers many alternatives that may be more interesting and suitable. Some people have accepted this philosophy and experienced an unexpected serenity.

Where to Obtain Additional Information

The Educational Testing Service, P.O. Box 6014, Princeton, N.J. 08541-6014, will supply upon request a booklet entitled *GRE Biology Test*. It will be sent unsolicited along with the admission ticket to those who apply for the examination. Inquiries can be made by telephone to the Educational Testing Service: (609) 771-7670 (Princeton, N.J.) or (415) 654-1200 (Berkeley, Calif.). These calls must be made between 8:30 A.M. and 9:00 P.M. (local time) to Princeton or 8:30 A.M. and 4:30 P.M. (local time) to Berkeley.

Application forms and additional pertinent information about the Subject Tests and General Test are contained in the *GRE Information Bulletin*, available from most colleges' career planning offices and from the Educational Testing Service.

Prospective graduate students in biology may be interested in obtaining Volume A of the *Directory of Graduate Programs*, which covers the biological sciences, health sciences, and related fields. This book contains a wealth of information about graduate schools such as addresses, size of departments, programs offered, departmental emphasis, science prerequisites, language requirements, and financial aid. It can be ordered at the time of registration for the test or at any other time. A check or money order for $13.00 (subject to change) should accompany the order and be addressed to *Graduate Records Examinations*, ETS, P.O. Box 6014, Princeton, N.J. 08541-6014. The sender should allow three weeks for delivery.

Nature of the Questions

Questions cover the broad content of undergraduate biology curricula. Questions are about equally divided among the cellular (and subcellular), organismal, and population components. Questions are also designed to test the student's ability to apply information, interpret observations and data, and understand scientific methods, among other things. Some of the questions are based on graphs, diagrams, and experimental data. In short, the test is designed to measure knowledge and skills that the examination committee considers most important for graduate study.

The test contains typically 210 questions of the multiple-choice type, each with five possible answers from which the student must select the most suitable one. The format of the questions varies, however.

Some questions are straightforward and deal with a single item of information. Possible variations in this type of question follow:

1. In which of the following pairs are the animals most closely related?
   A. snake and fish
   B. frog and salamander
   C. bird and mammal
   D. nematode and annelid
   E. starfish and clam

   1. A **B** C D E

2. When stained with Gram's solution, gram-negative bacteria will appear
   A. blue
   B. brown
   C. black
   D. purple
   E. pink

   2. A B C D **E**

Sometimes groups of questions are based on certain information given. For example, the next six questions are based on the drawing below:

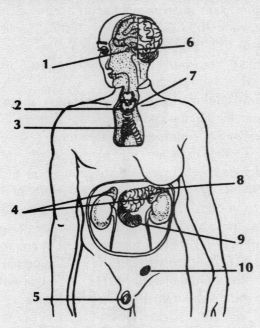

Locations of endocrine glands in the human.

1. This organ secretes both a hormone and enzymes.
    A. 1
    B. 2
    C. 4
    D. 8
    E. 10

1. A B C D E
   ‖ ‖ ‖ ▌ ‖

2. If this organ were removed, calcium and phosphorus metabolism would be drastically upset.
    A. 1
    B. 3
    C. 4
    D. 7
    E. 9

2. A B C D E
   ‖ ‖ ‖ ▌ ‖

3. There is a distinct homeostatic relationship between organs 4 and
    A. 1
    B. 3
    C. 6
    D. 7
    E. 8

3. A B C D E
   ▌ ‖ ‖ ‖ ‖

4. Radioactive iodine is concentrated in
    A. 1
    B. 2
    C. 5
    D. 6
    E. 10

4. A B C D E
   ‖ ▌ ‖ ‖ ‖

5. The only gland influenced by the nervous system is

A. 2
B. 3
C. 4
D. 8
E. 9

5. A B C D E

6. The only gland whose function is entirely hormonal is

A. 5
B. 7
C. 8
D. 9
E. 10

6. A B C D E

In another type of question there is a group of five lettered headings (answers) designated A, B, C, D, and E. These are followed by several questions whose answers must be selected from the lettered headings. Any one of the lettered headings may be used more than once or not at all. The letter preceding the correct heading (answer) is then recorded on the answer sheet. A sample group of questions follows:

A. bugs
B. beetles
C. flies
D. aphids
E. butterflies

1. have larvae called caterpillars

1. A B C D E

2. have only two wings

2. A B C D E

3. are the largest group of insects

3. A B C D E

4. have chewing mouth parts

4. A B C D E

5. are most closely related to cicadas

5. A B C D E

Length of Test The time allowed for the biology test is 170 minutes. From reporting time to dismissal the testing period is about 3 hours, some of which is used for necessary preliminaries and for collecting materials when the test is finished. The three categories of subject matter—cellular (and subcellular), organismal, and population biology—are randomly scattered through the test, so an examinee may proceed from start to finish of the entire test without interruption.

Taking the Test

Most examinees probably do better and save time by answering one question at a time instead of scanning the test first. Directions and questions should be read carefully. Since all questions count the same, the easy ones should be answered first just in case time runs short. This is particularly important for the last portion of the test, which involves analysis of readings. Examinees should not spend an inordinate amount of time on a reading that is outside their area of expertise if there are other readings further on that will be easier for them. Rechecking questions is always advisable if time permits.

Before taking the test students should realize that many questions will be based on information to which they have never been exposed. They can leave some of the questions unanswered and still make a good score. The average score is based on correctly answering approximately half of the questions.

With respect to guessing, the examinee should keep in mind that a fraction of a point is deducted for each incorrect answer. It is probably unwise to guess if the subject matter is completely unknown, whereas it is probably advantageous if the material is somewhat familiar. Guessing is recommended when, by eliminating one or more answers, the student can arrive at what might be considered an "educated guess."

Understanding exactly how the score is calculated will show how much risk is involved in guessing. All correct answers count one point, unanswered questions count zero, and incorrect answers are deducted at the rate of a quarter of a point each. This evaluation is based on the fact that random guessing of five-choice questions results in one correct answer to four incorrect ones. Thus, if the examinee answers 160 right and 40 wrong, the raw score will be 160 minus 10, which is 150. In general, if one or two of the five possible answers can be eliminated, it is advisable to guess among the remaining possibilities.

Who Prepares the Biology Test

The Educational Testing Service with the help of the American Institute of Biological Sciences, the Botanical Society of America, and the American Society of Zoologists appoints a six-member committee to plan and prepare the examination. The members represent different branches of biology, types of colleges, and geographical sections of the country. Their tenure is on a rotating basis, an arrangement that constantly brings in fresh ideas by new appointees and at the same time insures a continuity of policies.

In addition to determining the content and scope of the test, the committee of examiners writes questions. The examiners are assisted in this task by other subject-matter specialists. Testing experts from the Educational Testing Service provide statistical information and expertise in the construction of tests. Before any question is approved, it is reviewed and, if necessary, revised to meet certain standards. Before the entire test is released for use, it must be approved by the committee.

Continuity and Uniformity of Tests

Although the Biology Test is ever changing to incorporate new subject matter and to protect its security, the Educational Testing Service equates the different forms of the test by statistical procedures. This permits the comparability of test scores from different periods of time, so necessary to determine with accuracy the qualifications of students, the success of teaching, or the adequacy of a curriculum.

Scheduling Examinations

Most of the time the *General Test* and *Biology Test* are scheduled for the morning and afternoon of the same day for the convenience of students who have to take both of them. Students who feel that the two tests are too much to take consecutively can elect to take them on separate days. The reporting time for the General Test is usually 8:00 A.M.; for the Subject Test, 2:00 P.M. The first period ends at about 12:30 and the second at about 5:30.

Each year testing periods are scheduled on a nationwide basis. They occur in the months of October, December, February, April, and June. The Biology Test is available in all of these periods except June. To get the exact dates when tests are administered and the lead time necessary to meet all deadlines such as getting into a particular test and having the grades reported to the proper place, prospective candidates must consult the *GRE Information Bulletin* or a designated official in their college who advises on such matters.

The tests are given on Saturday except when that time conflicts with the religious convictions of a candidate. In that case the candidate can arrange without any additional charge to take the test(s) on Monday following the regular scheduled time.

The student must take two things into consideration in selecting a test date: the advantage of waiting as long as possible to learn more biology and the necessity of having scores ready at the proper time. To play it safe, a student might want to take the test one scheduled period early to allow for any emergency that might arise. Should he or she be unable to take the test at the regular time, it can as a last resort be taken at special testing centers on other dates than the five nationwide testing periods. Unfortunately the centers may not be close to home, and an additional fee is charged. Special tests are available in Atlanta, Georgia; Austin, Texas; Berkeley, California; Boston, Massachusetts; Evanston, Illinois; Los Angeles, California; Washington, D.C.; and Upper Montclair, New Jersey.

Graduate school applications that include requests for fellowships or assistantships often have an earlier date for all supporting data, including GRE scores. The fall months of the senior undergraduate year are the latest one should wait to take the GRE if such financial aid is to be requested. Be sure to consult current graduate school catalogs for the exact deadlines.

Applying for the Test

To obtain tickets for tests the candidate must submit an official Registration Form for each test date. If the General and Biology Tests are to be taken on the same day, only one form is used to register. Registration should be made in advance, not at the testing center. The Registration Form can be obtained from the Educational Testing Service or from college offices designated to handle testing or career planning.

Generally the applicant should send the Registration Form about 1 month before the scheduled test in order to reserve a place and avoid a penalty fee for late registration. A word of warning — deadlines established by the Educational Testing Service are times of receipt in its office and not postmark dates. Early registration may be especially important for a candidate wishing to take the test in June, the last scheduled time of the academic year. If he or she waits until all places are filled, the Registration Form will be returned without a ticket.

The completed Registration Form and the appropriate fee (check or money order) should be mailed to Educational Testing Service, P.O. Box 6004, Princeton, N.J. 08541-6004.

Walk-in testing may be permitted at the testing center only if test materials and sufficient space are available. Since standby registration by this procedure is uncertain, students should not attempt it except in an emergency. It is much less likely that a specific unreserved Subject Test will be available than that an unreserved General Test will be available. If this method is attempted, the student should take a completed Registration Form to the test center. Test fees and an additional standby fee are payable at the test center.

If a student who has preregistered for a single test later decides to take a second one on the same day by walk-in, he or she may do so without additional charge provided that test materials and space are available. Instead of submitting a second Registration Form, he or she must use the registration number on the admission ticket to mark the answer sheet of the second test.

Change of Registration

Changes in registration are permissible by sending a Test or Center Change Form and the appropriate fee. If the change is the addition of a test or a change in the center, a new Registration Form should *not* be sent, nor the admission ticket returned. In any case, the form should be sent to the same office to which the original Registration Form was sent and must arrive before the closing date of the test as given in the *GRE Information Bulletin*.

Transferring the test date requires the submission of a new Registration Form accompanied by a letter giving the date for which the student is registered, the one to which he or she wishes to transfer, and full test fees.

Places Where Tests are Administered

Numerous testing centers are located throughout the country, and new centers are continually established in response to increasing needs. Centers in the United States are close enough so that candidates seldom have to travel more than 75 miles from home. Prospective candidates can find the nearest center by writing to the Educational Testing Service, or by consulting the *GRE Information Bulletin*.

Some of the testing centers administer tests on all of the six nationwide testing dates, whereas others do not. Since some of them may add or delete testing dates, the current *GRE Information Bulletin* should be consulted.

The applicant for a particular test must indicate on the application blank the center of choice. The Testing Service assigns the applicant to that center if at all possible. If the candidate wants to change locations after having registered, he or she should complete a Test or Center Change Form (found in the *GRE Information Bulletin*) and include the appropriate fee.

Admission to Testing Center

For admission to the testing center an examinee must present an admission ticket from ETS and two means of identification. At least one should contain your recent photograph and signature; the other should have the same information or a physical description and signature. Social security cards are not acceptable because there is no way for the supervisor to know whether the person taking the test is the same person whose name is on the card.

Nobody (examinee or visitor) will be admitted to the examination room after the testing has started.

Regulations at Testing Centers

Examinees at all centers follow the same standard procedures and time schedules. The success of the testing process depends on cooperation with the supervisor and consideration for others. The supervisor has the authority to dismiss any person who engages in disruptive or irregular practices such as making noise, cheating, or failing to follow directions. The test of a person dismissed will not be graded.

For clarification of what is or is not permissible, the supervisor should be consulted. Figuring is allowed if it is done only on the margins of the test booklets. Examinees wishing to leave the room must secure permission. Smoking may or may not be permitted. Since smoking is offensive to many nonsmokers, people who are allowed to smoke should be considerate enough to isolate themselves as much as possible.

Bring:	Ticket
	Identification
	Eraser
	Three or four No. 2 (B or HB) pencils
	Watch

Do not bring:	Books
	Rulers
	Calculating devices
	Dictionaries
	Paper of any kind
	Compasses

Reporting Scores

Each examinee will receive a test score report unless requesting that the test not be scored. The scores are considered confidential and will not be sent to any place except those designated by the person taking the test. An examinee can allow or forbid the sending of the score to his or her undergraduate institution by checking appropriate blanks on the Registration Form. In addition, the examinee can indicate up to four other score recipients on the same form without paying an additional fee. Other recipients of scores can be designated at the time of registration or later by filling out a Request Form and paying a fee for each transcript.

Reports will be sent only to approved institutions of higher learning and to organizations granting fellowships. Most approved recipients are listed along with an identifying code number in the *GRE Information Bulletin*. Once a request for a transcript is made, it cannot be canceled. The reports will be sent to all recipients four to six weeks after the testing date.

The reports are cumulative, giving all scores on file for the current year and the five previous years. To prevent a score from being recorded in the cumulative file, a request not to grade the test must be made to the test supervisor at the time of testing or sent to and received by the Educational Testing Service within four days following the test.

Interpretation of Scores

Information on how to interpret scores will be sent to each examinee with his or her score report. The score report includes two total score items, the *scaled score* and the *percentile*.

The raw score is obtained by taking the total of correct answers and subtracting a fraction of the wrong answers. It is then equated by statistical procedures to the scaled score so that the performance of students taking different forms of the test can be compared.

The percentile is the relative standing of an individual with respect to a specific group: that is, the percentage of examinees who made lower scaled scores. Because percentiles are percentage figures, they vary from 0 to 100. Since the GRE percentile is derived by comparing one score with a large number of scores of other students from many institutions, it is not necessarily representative of the students in any particular college. In fact, some colleges may find the scores more meaningful by deriving percentiles from the performance of their own students. If a scaled score is compared to the scores of a smaller number of select students — for example, applicants to a prestigious department — the percentile will be lower than the national one.

In addition to a total scaled score and its percentile, a subscore will be reported for each of the three categories of biological knowledge. Subscores do not indicate a person's ability as reliably as the total score because each subscore is based upon fewer questions. Subscores do provide, however, some indication of where a person's relative strengths and weaknesses lie. Percentiles of the subscores are also given in the Score Interpretation Booklet.

The degree of reliance placed on the biology test in relation to other methods of evaluation such as recommendations and the college transcript is variable. Also the relative values attached to the General Test and Biology Test are not uniform. A specific graduate department may place more reliance on the General Test as a predictor of performance than on the Biology Test.

A passing or failing grade is not established by the Educational Testing Service. A grade may be passing or failing according to standards set by the institution requiring the score. Some institutions refer to a *cut-off score*, meaning that they will not accept students scoring below that level. The cut-off score varies considerably from institution to institution, and many do not adhere to such strict guidelines.

Reexaminations

Examinations may be repeated, but earlier scores are retained on record. Institutions receive a cumulative report. The scores earned anytime within the most recent five years are reported.

How to Use the Sample Tests

Part II of this book consists of four sample tests similar to the GRE Biology Test in style, content, and degree of difficulty. After each test is an answer key with explanations. The student should take each test under conditions simulating those of the actual Biology Test. He or she may calculate a raw score for each test as described on page 6. It is impossible to determine whether the sample tests are of the *same* difficulty level as any *particular* GRE Biology Test. However, if it is assumed that they are similar, a student may use the following table to make a rough estimate of the scaled score and percentile that would be calculated from the raw score:

Raw Score	Approximate Scaled Score	Approximate Percentile
175	900	99
120	700	75
100	630	50
75	550	25

Part III of this book is designed to strengthen a student's knowledge in areas of need, as diagnosed by his or her performance on one or more of the sample tests.

Part Two Tests in Biology

Sample Test 1

Directions for Taking Test: This sample test contains 210 questions or incomplete statements, and should be finished in 170 minutes. Each item will have five possible answers or completions. Choose the best and blacken its letter in the place provided. After finishing, you may determine your score by using the **Answer Key** at the end of this test. The Answer Key also contains comments and explanations that should clarify the concepts involved in each question.

Questions 1–90

For each of the following questions or incomplete statements there are five suggested answers or completions. Select the best choice.

1. The primitive atmosphere of the earth probably did NOT contain
   A. water
   B. methane
   C. ammonia
   D. oxygen
   E. hydrogen

   1. A B C D E

2. Plasmolysis of plant cells occurs when
   A. their walls collapse
   B. turgor pressure increases
   C. protoplasm dies
   D. extracellular fluids are hypertonic to intracellular fluid
   E. microtubules are closed

   2. A B C D E

3. Which of these is the most highly differentiated cell type?
   A. blastema cell
   B. blastomere
   C. erythrocyte
   D. neoblast
   E. zygote

   3. A B C D E

4. Cases are known in which certain animal crosses regularly produce litters that are about 25% smaller than normal. A logical explanation is that this results from
   A. sex-linked genes
   B. penetrance
   C. recessive lethal genes
   D. autopolyploidy
   E. chiasmatic interference

   4. A B C D E

5. Plankton lives near the surface of the ocean. The primary reason for this phenomenon is that deep oceanic areas are too
   A. cold
   B. dark
   C. dense
   D. unstable
   E. densely populated with primary consumers

   5. A B C D E

6. The killer T cells (lymphocytes) of the immune system function to
   A. destroy antibodies
   B. destroy foreign eukaryotic cells
   C. move antibodies to sites of antigenic invasion
   D. produce and release antibodies
   E. produce lymphatic fluids

   6. A B C D E

7. If all of the DNA contained in the nucleus of a typical human cell were stretched to full length and placed end-to-end, its length would be approximately
   A. one meter, composed of 46 separate pieces
   B. one meter, composed of thousands of separate pieces
   C. one micrometer, composed of a single piece
   D. one micrometer, composed of 46 separate pieces
   E. one micrometer, composed of thousands of separate pieces

   7. A B C D E

8. People who travel great distances by plane often have difficulty in immediately adjusting to the new location. The problem is related to
   A. pyrimidine displacement
   B. attunement to a circadian rhythm
   C. selection pressure
   D. behavior patterns of the people around them
   E. magnetic field variations

   8. A B C D E

9. Which of these is an oxygen carrier within the blood of some invertebrate animals?
   A. chlorophyll
   B. cytochrome c
   C. hemocyanin
   D. NAD
   E. prothrombin

   9. A B C D E

10. Sealing the stomates of leaves will slow or stop all processes EXCEPT

A. respiration

B. transpiration

C. photosynthesis

D. wilting

E. guttation

10. A B C D (E)

11. Acquired Immune Deficiency Syndrome (AIDS) is caused by defective

A. erythrocytes

B. genes coding for antibody production

C. T cells and macrophages

D. platelets

E. bacteria

11. A B C D E

12. The genotype of an individual showing a particular dominant trait can be determined by

A. crossbreeding

B. test-crossing

C. inbreeding

D. outbreeding

E. looking at the individual

12. A B C D E

13. The camel is unusually adapted to desert life because it does all of the following EXCEPT

A. tolerate dehydration up to 25% of its body weight

B. minimize exposure to heat by facing the sun

C. have long eyelashes that screen its eyes

D. tolerate a higher body temperature during the day

E. store water in its hump for emergency use

13. A B C D E

14. In the normal cell cycle the mitotic phase requiring the most time is

A. anaphase

B. leptonema

C. metaphase

D. prophase

E. telophase

14. A B C D E

15. Fatigue occurs when skeletal muscles accumulate which of the following products as a result of temporary deficiency of oxygen?

A. sugar

B. starch

C. glycogen

D. lactic acid

E. myofibrils

15. A B C D E

16. Which pigment is related to vitamin A?

A. carotene

B. xanthophyll

C. anthocyanin

D. chlorophyll

E. tannin

16. A B C D E

17. F. W. Went's classic experiment with stumps of coleoptiles involved placing upon them blocks of agar saturated with a growth stimulator. The experiment demonstrated that

17. **A B C D E**

   B. the stimulator is a fat-soluble substance

   C. growth is stimulated only when the light period exceeds the dark period

   D. bending is caused by a rapid increase in cell division on one side of the stem

   E. production of the stimulator depends on the presence of a high concentration of sugar

18. An antheridium is a plant organ that produces

18. **A B C D E**

   A. sperm cells

   B. spores

   C. eggs

   D. zoospores

   E. food

19. Which is a correct statement about photosynthesis?

19. **A B C D E**

   A. Oxygen generated from photosynthesis comes from carbon dioxide.

   B. Products of the light reaction of photosynthesis include ATP and NADPH.

   C. Oxygen is given off during the dark reaction.

   D. The fixation of carbon dioxide requires light.

   E. The color of light most used in photosynthesis is green.

20. In humans the major blood type differences are determined by multiple alleles designated I^A, I^B, and i. I^A and I^B are codominants and i is recessive. Gene combinations $I^A I^A$ and $I^A i$ produce type A blood; $I^A I^B$ produces type AB blood; $I^B I^B$ and $I^B i$ produce type B blood; and ii produces type O blood. Suppose that one parent having type A blood and the other having type B blood have a child with type O blood. What is the probability that their next child will have type AB blood?

20. **A B C D E**

   A. 0%

   B. 25%

   C. 50%

   D. 75%

   E. 100%

21. Some people believe that carbon dioxide in the atmosphere keeps the earth warmer by interfering with the reradiation of heat back into space. This phenomenon has come to be known as the

21. **A B C D E**

   A. heat trap

   B. Douglas theory of gaseous absorption

   C. principle of heat reflection

   D. carbon dioxide screen

   E. greenhouse effect

22. Which of the following environments is richest in free oxygen?

22. **A B C D E**

   A. warm fresh water

   B. cold fresh water

   C. salt water

   D. soil

   E. atmosphere

23. When ants follow the same route to a source of food, they are guided by
    A. visual tracking
    B. sun orientation
    C. landmark recognition
    D. pheromone marking
    E. frequency of body contacts

    23. A B C D E

24. Which of these is considered to be a "second messenger" for some hormones?
    A. cyclic AMP
    B. DNA
    C. estrogen
    D. glucose
    E. water

    24. A B C D E

25. Which of the following cellular substances or structures can be found in rabbits but NOT in *Escherichia coli*?
    A. enzymes
    B. genes
    C. ribosomes
    D. nuclear membranes
    E. semipermeable membranes

    25. A B C D E

26. Should the organ of Corti be damaged, the person could NOT
    A. hear
    B. feel pain
    C. see
    D. walk straight
    E. sleep

    26. A B C D E

27. If a freshwater protozoan did not have a contractile vacuole, it would NOT be able to
    A. breathe
    B. regulate water pressure
    C. excrete nitrogenous wastes
    D. move
    E. defend itself

    27. A B C D E

28. Which of the following statements is INCORRECT?
    A. Mutations cannot occur in viruses.
    B. Unlike the Protista, viruses do not contain organelles such as mitochondria, nuclei, or plastids.
    C. Respiration does not occur within viruses.
    D. Viruses do not have independent means of propulsion.
    E. Viruses have genes for enzymes, but do not produce enzymes within themselves.

    28. A B C D E

29. Of the various hormone or hormonelike substances that affect plants, which is used to ripen green tomatoes?
    A. indoleacetic acid   D. ethylene
    B. kinetin   E. 2,4-D
    C. gibberellin

    29. A B C D E

30. The phenotype of an individual can best be determined by
   A. crossbreeding
   B. backcrossing
   C. inbreeding
   D. outbreeding
   E. observing the individual

   30. A B C D E

31. Which of the following conclusions about evolutionary adaptations is based on sound logic?
   A. Animals living in cold climates tend to have longer appendages than those living in warmer places.
   B. Pollen of wind-pollinated plants should be large to give it buoyancy in the air.
   C. Since pollinating moths are most active at dusk and night, they depend heavily on bright-colored flowers to guide them to their target.
   D. On the basis of size, small mammals should have an advantage over larger ones in hot climates.
   E. Fishes tend to be darker on their lower surfaces, which are more shaded from the light that comes from above.

   31. A B C D E

32. The occurrence together of two or more morphologically distinct forms of a population is termed
   A. divergence
   B. hierarchical isolation
   C. morphogenesis
   D. polymorphism
   E. sympatric tolerance

   32. A B C D E

33. A major difference between a climax community and any subclimax stage of succession is that the former
   A. has an increase in net productivity
   B. is composed of a smaller number of species
   C. has more biomass
   D. cannot reproduce itself
   E. has a photosynthesis-respiration ratio (P/R) of more than 1

   33. A B C D E

34. Animals that live in caves are better fitted for survival if they
   A. have larger eyes
   B. are endothermic
   C. have larger bodies
   D. have larger intestines
   E. can perceive chemicals better

   34. A B C D E

35. According to the British political economist Malthus,
   A. populations tend to outgrow the ability of the environment to support them
   B. human populations have a faster growth rate than other populations
   C. the human population growth potential decreases in inverse proportion to its growth
   D. all populations have the same growth rate
   E. population growth can be checked only by starvation

   35. A B C D E

36. Genetic drift is a change in the gene pool caused by
    A. selection
    B. mutation
    C. migration
    D. hybridization
    E. chance

36. A B C D E

37. Down's syndrome has been shown to have a direct relationship to
    A. atrophy of the parathyroids
    B. brain damage
    C. hypoglycemia
    D. mother's age at conception
    E. vitamin K deficiency

37. A B C D E

38. Of which of these structures is pectin a major constituent?
    A. primary cell wall
    B. nuclear membrane
    C. middle lamella
    D. cell membrane
    E. plasmodesma

38. A B C D E

39. The two strands of nucleotides that compose the double helix of DNA are linked together by
    A. peptide bonds
    B. covalent bonds
    C. ionic bonds
    D. hydrogen bonds
    E. phosphate bonds

39. A B C D E

40. Blood vessels carrying blood under maximum pressure would normally
    A. have elastic walls
    B. be transporting deoxygenated blood
    C. be peripherally located in the body
    D. receive lymph from the lymphatic system
    E. have numerous valves

40. A B C D E

41. The glomerulus is a structure found in the
    A. lung
    B. kidney
    C. liver
    D. testis
    E. spleen

41. A B C D E

42. A person who is very energetic, perspires profusely, loses weight, and has bulging eyes has a disorder caused by the malfunction of which endocrine gland?
    A. pituitary
    B. adrenal
    C. thyroid
    D. parathyroid
    E. gonad

42. A B C D E

43. Lower primates have characteristics that especially fit them for life in

43. A B C D E

    A. deserts
    B. savannas
    C. forests
    D. tundras
    E. steppes

44. Phylogenetically speaking, which animal is more primitive than dinosaurs and more advanced than bony fishes?

44. A B C D E

    A. giant squid
    B. sea squirt
    C. shark
    D. frog
    E. whale

45. Mature plant cells originate from a tissue called

45. A B C D E

    A. parenchyma
    B. cortex
    C. meristem
    D. pericycle
    E. endodermis

46. Red tides that sometimes kill fish along the Atlantic Coast of the United States are blooms of

46. A B C D E

    A. seed plants
    B. bacteria
    C. krill
    D. dinoflagellates
    E. diatoms

47. Which of the following adjectives appropriately describes a particular type of autotroph?

47. A B C D E

    A. herbivorous
    B. chemosynthetic
    C. saprozoic
    D. holozoic
    E. phagocytic

48. Mapping gene locations on a eukaryotic chromosome is possible because of

48. A B C D E

    A. episomal proliferation
    B. transduction
    C. giant chromosome formations
    D. template matching
    E. crossing-over of chromosomes

49. In ecological succession

49. A B C D E

    A. the climax is always a deciduous forest
    B. the pioneers are always xerophytes
    C. except for the climax, each stage alters the habitat to make it less suitable for itself
    D. the number of species decreases up to and including the climax
    E. net productivity remains constant throughout

50. Vertebrate predators would be expected to have
   A. front-field vision
   B. grinding teeth
   C. a long digestive tract
   D. the habit of sleeping lightly
   E. long legs

50. A B C D E

51. Which of these skeletal muscle materials changes shape, thereby causing contraction movements?
   A. actin
   B. H zone
   C. myosin
   D. T system
   E. Z line

51. A B C D E

52. Which of these organelles is most closely associated with intracellular movement?
   A. endoplasmic reticulum
   B. Golgi apparatus
   C. lysosomes
   D. microfilaments
   E. mitochondria

52. A B C D E

53. The sinoatrial node
   A. functions as a pacemaker for the heart
   B. regulates the rate of breathing
   C. acts independently of the autonomic nervous system
   D. determines diastolic pressure
   E. ceases to function if the heart is removed from the body and kept in a nutrient solution

53. A B C D E

54. Impulses traveling through the nervous system are transmitted electrically in neurons and chemically across synapses. A well-known synaptic neurotransmitter is the substance
   A. angiotensin
   B. acetylcholine
   C. secretin
   D. cholecystokinin
   E. ecdysone

54. A B C D E

55. The temperature of endothermic animals may be increased by all of the following EXCEPT
   A. panting
   B. shivering
   C. curling up
   D. depositing fat in subcutaneous tissues
   E. reducing peripheral circulation

55. A B C D E

56. In most mammals, where are eggs fertilized if a successful pregnancy is to occur?

    A. vagina
    B. uterus
    C. lower portion of the oviduct
    D. upper portion of the oviduct
    E. ovary

56. A B C D E

57. If an organism that is heterozygous for two unlinked genes is bred with a homozygous recessive individual, the resulting genotype ratio is expected to be

    A. 16 : 0
    B. 9 : 3 : 3 : 1
    C. 1 : 1 : 1 : 1
    D. 3 : 1
    E. 1 : 2 : 1

57. A B C D E

58. Of the following habitats, which has the lowest rate of productivity?

    A. ocean
    B. moist forest
    C. moist grassland
    D. cornfield
    E. coral reef

58. A B C D E

59. A probable explanation for the vicious behavior of some dogs toward mail carriers and newspaper carriers is

    A. defense of territory
    B. training received from their master
    C. fright
    D. meanness
    E. reaction to human odors

59. A B C D E

60. In interrelationships among animals the greatest competition occurs between

    A. members of the same species
    B. males competing for a female
    C. members of two different species living in the same location
    D. predators and their prey
    E. members of young and old generations of the same species

60. A B C D E

61. The assembling of amino acids in a particular sequence to construct a polypeptide is known as

    A. peptide linkage
    B. ordination
    C. codification
    D. translation
    E. transcription

61. A B C D E

62. Nitrogenous bases of DNA are normally paired as

    A. T-T   **D.** C-C
    B. A-A   **E.** T-A
    C. G-A

62. A B C D E

63. Which of the following is NOT a component of blood?

A. monocyte
B. lymphocyte
C. erythrocyte
D. granulocyte
E. chondrocyte

64. The geologic period in which a large number of phyla appeared for the first time is the

A. Cambrian Period
B. Devonian Period
C. Jurassic Period
D. Pennsylvanian Period
E. Silurian Period

65. It has been found that the reproduction of a certain tree on the island of Mauritius may be dependent upon ingestion and chemical modification of its seeds by the dodo bird. Since the dodo is now extinct, the tree seems destined for extinction also. Presumably, the dodo birds obtained nourishment by eating the fruit that contains the seed. This is therefore a case of

A. coevolution
B. commensalism
C. Lamarckian adaptation
D. preadaptation
E. sympatric relationship

66. Which of the following is most likely to be common to plants that use C4 photosynthesis?

A. They are evergreens.
B. They do not use cyclic photophosphorylation.
C. They originated in tropical zones.
D. They tend to have slow photosynthesis rates in high O_2 environments.
E. They use a light-sensitive pigment other than chlorophyll.

67. In recombinant DNA technology, the first organisms used as hosts of artificially introduced DNA were

A. chicken embryos
B. fruit flies
C. monkeys
D. intestinal bacteria
E. slime molds

68. One danger of using massive doses of antibiotics is that they

A. cause emphysema
B. destroy the intestinal flora
C. accumulate in the bones
D. block the absorption of water by cells
E. crystallize in kidney tubules

69. Convergent evolution is illustrated by the
   A. rodent and dog
   B. starfish and fish
   C. fish and whale
   D. cactus and mistletoe
   E. bacterium and protozoan

69. A B C D E

70. All organisms that can share a gene pool are grouped together as a
   A. genus
   B. species
   C. deme
   D. community
   E. clone

70. A B C D E

71. In the rods located in the retina of the eye is a visual pigment called
   A. carotene
   B. chrome red
   C. photogene
   D. rhodopsin
   E. saffron yellow

71. A B C D E

72. A plant molecule responsible for photoperiodism is
   A. florigen
   B. gibberellin
   C. oxytocin
   D. phytochrome
   E. thyroxin

72. A B C D E

73. If a stem were cut as illustrated, roots would normally grow
   A. only above cut 1
   B. only below cut 2
   C. above cut 1 and below cut 2
   D. below cut 1 and cut 2
   E. above cut 1 and cut 2

apical end

73. A B C D E

74. In a partial chromosome region such as the one illustrated, the greatest amount of recombinations would be expected to occur between genes
   A. *C* and *D*
   B. *A* and *B*
   C. *A* and *D*
   D. *B* and *C*
   E. *B* and *D*

74. A B C D E

A   *B*   *C*   *D*

5 map units   8 map units   10 map units

75. How many different kinds of gametes can be produced by an organism with the genotype *AaBbCC*?
   A. 1
   B. 2
   C. 4
   D. 6
   E. 8

75. A B C D E

76. If you were looking for a high rate of cell division in plants, you would find it in

A. phloem
B. xylem
C. cambium
D. pith
E. fibers

77. Cryptic coloration is illustrated by

A. monarch butterflies
B. flounders
C. blue crabs
D. coral snakes
E. redwing blackbirds

78. The behavioral form that is responsible for a dog's trying to bury a bone indoors although the animal has never been outside where it could learn the experience is known as

A. fixed action pattern
B. imprinting
C. habituation
D. operant conditioning
E. insight

79. Which of the following effects of auxins, natural or synthetic, is a basis for commercial application?

A. induction of root formation
B. prevention of leaf abscission
C. destruction of plants
D. all of the above
E. none of the above

80. Which of the following statements best explains what causes a green plant to bend toward the light as it grows?

A. Green plants need light to carry on photosynthesis.
B. Light stimulates a more rapid growth of cells on the lighted side.
C. Green plants seek light because they are phototropic.
D. Cells divide faster on the shaded side.
E. Auxin accumulates on the shaded side, causing greater cellular elongation there.

81. Hollow trees can keep on living because

A. phloem takes on the function of the destroyed xylem
B. fibers develop into conducting tubes
C. growth is adjusted to the reduced amount of water and mineral nutrients that can be conducted
D. not all of the wood in a tree is necessary for conduction
E. the fungus that causes decay is itself a good substitute conductor

82. All of the following statements about a deme are correct EXCEPT:

    A. A deme is reproductively isolated from other members of the species.

    B. A deme is a small local population.

    C. Gene flow is possible between demes of a species.

    D. All members of a deme are identical.

    E. Demes are usually temporary population units.

82. A B C D E
|| || || || ||

83. The complex of thirteen species of finches that Darwin studied in the Galápagos Islands is a good example of

    A. Batesian mimicry

    B. Müllerian mimicry

    C. competitive exclusion

    D. adaptive radiation

    E. convergent evolution

83. A B C D E
|| || || || ||

84. If the terminal bud of a tree is removed

    A. the plant will regenerate another one by the following spring

    B. flower production will be inhibited

    C. vegetative growth will be accelerated

    D. the stem cannot elongate

    E. a lateral bud located near the tip will break dormancy and function as a terminal bud

84. A B C D E
|| || || || ||

85. Carrying capacity means

    A. the ability of an animal to store potential energy in the form of fat

    B. the amount of seeds or spores that can be transported from one place to another by a specific animal

    C. the total number of organisms that a particular place will support

    D. the total number of genes transferable by a sperm cell to an egg

    E. the maximum number of surviving individuals in a litter of placental animals

85. A B C D E
|| || || || ||

86. What kind of body symmetry is adaptive for sessile animals?

    A. asymmetrical   **D.** radial

    B. spherical   **E.** bilateral

    C. spiral

86. A B C D E
|| || || || ||

87. The young of some bird species will follow the first moving object they see and form a lasting attachment to it, even though it is such a thing as a toy. This kind of behavior is

    A. habituation

    B. conditioning

    C. imprinting

    D. trial and error

    E. taxis

87. A B C D E
|| || || || ||

88. Which of these is a function of cutin in a plant?

    A. to direct chromosomes during meiosis

    B. to form a barrier to water loss on a leaf surface

    C. to provide a cue for stoma opening and closing

    D. to store energy of photosynthesis in chemical bonds

    E. to transport minerals from the roots

88. A B C D E
|| || || || ||

89. Which of these could NOT be an isolating mechanism between species?
    A. infertility of offspring
    B. competition for resources
    C. mating behavior
    D. sperm-egg interaction
    E. time of mating season

89. A B C D E

90. A geneticist attempting to study the nucleotide sequence of a strand of DNA might use the class of enzymes called
    A. acetylcholine esterases
    B. cytochromes
    C. kinases
    D. proteases
    E. restriction endonucleases

90. A B C D E

The next five questions (91–95) consist of a group of lettered isotopes and five numbered phrases. For each numbered phrase select the lettered isotope that is most accurately characterized by the phrase, and mark the answer accordingly. Any one of the lettered isotopes may be used one or more times or not at all.

> A. strontium-90
> B. nitrogen-15
> C. cesium-137
> D. iodine-131
> E. carbon-14

91. behaves physiologically like potassium

91. A B C D E

92. accumulates like calcium in bone tissue

92. A B C D E

93. is not radioactive

93. A B C D E

94. is used to date organic remains

94. A B C D E

95. concentrates in thyroid tissue

95. A B C D E

The next five questions (96–100) consist of a group of five lettered tissues and five numbered phrases. For each numbered phrase select the lettered tissue that is most accurately characterized by the phrase, and mark the answer accordingly. Any one of the lettered tissues may be used one or more times or not at all.

> A. epithelial
> B. muscular
> C. nervous
> D. vascular
> E. connective

96. composes the cellular portion of blood

96. A B C D E

97. characteristically contains white or yellow fibers

97. A B C D E

98. has many of its cells produced by bone marrow

98. A B C D E

99. comprises the lining of the digestive tract

99. A B C D E

100. includes ligaments and tendons

100. A B C D E

The next five questions (101–105) consist of a group of lettered names of scientists and numbered scientific discoveries. For each numbered discovery select the lettered name(s) of the person(s) credited with making it, and mark the answer accordingly. Any one of the lettered names may be used one or more times or not at all.

A. Hardy and Weinberg
B. Watson and Crick
C. Fleming
D. Banting and Best
E. van Leeuwenhoek

101. discovered blood corpuscles and bacteria

101. A B C D E

102. isolated insulin

102. A B C D E

103. discovered the antibacterial action of penicillin

103. A B C D E

104. demonstrated gene frequency in a gene pool

104. A B C D E

105. built an accurate model of a double-stranded deoxyribonucleic acid

105. A B C D E

The next three questions (106–108) consist of a group of lettered phases in a cell cycle and numbered descriptions of these phases. For each numbered description select the lettered phase that matches it, and mark the answer accordingly. Any one of the lettered phases may be used one or more times or not at all.

A. anaphase
B. interphase
C. metaphase
D. prophase
E. telophase

106. Chromatids move toward poles of spindle.

106. A B C D E
|| || || || ||

107. This stage precedes metaphase.

107. A B C D E
|| || || || ||

108. Chromatids reach poles of spindle.

108. A B C D E
|| || || || ||

The next five questions (109–113) consist of a group of lettered animal phyla and numbered descriptions of these phyla. For each numbered description select the lettered phylum that matches it, and mark the answer accordingly. Any one of the lettered phyla may be used one or more times or not at all.

    A. Arthropoda
    B. Annelida
    C. Echinodermata
    D. Mollusca
    E. Platyhelminthes

109. includes barnacles

109. A B C D E
|| || || || ||

110. contains the largest number of living species

110. A B C D E
|| || || || ||

111. contains species that lack a coelom

111. A B C D E
|| || || || ||

112. contains species that are most closely related to humans

112. A B C D E
|| || || || ||

113. includes the earthworms

113. A B C D E
|| || || || ||

The next four questions (114–117) consist of a group of lettered molecules and numbered descriptions. For each numbered description select the lettered molecule that matches it, and mark the answer accordingly. Any one of the lettered molecules may be used one or more times or not at all.

    A. carbon dioxide
    B. ethanol
    C. glucose
    D. lactate
    E. ribose

114. is produced by fermentation in animal cells

114. A B C D E
|| || || || ||

115. is produced as a result of the Calvin cycle

115. A B C D E
|| || || || ||

116. is produced during the Krebs cycle

116. A B C D E
|| || || || ||

117. is starting material for anaerobic glycolysis

117. A B C D E
|| || || || ||

The next five questions (118–122) consist of a group of lettered molecules and numbered descriptions. For each numbered description select the lettered molecule that matches it, and mark the answer accordingly. Any one of the lettered molecules may be used one or more times or not at all.

A. chitin
B. cholesterol
C. collagen
D. cyclic AMP
E. phospholipid

118. is a polypeptide

118. A B C D E
|| || || || ||

119. is most closely related to nucleic acids

119. A B C D E
|| || || || ||

120. is most closely related to sex hormones

120. A B C D E
|| || || || ||

121. is most closely related to starch

121. A B C D E
|| || || || ||

122. is structurally related to adenosine triphosphate

122. A B C D E
|| || || || ||

The next four questions (123–126) consist of a group of lettered animal structures and numbered descriptions of these structures. For each numbered description select the lettered structure that matches it, and mark the answer accordingly. Any one of the lettered structures may be used one or more times or not at all.

A. alveoli
B. Malpighian tubules
C. sphincters
D. tracheoles
E. villi

123. are analogous to nephrons in function

123. A B C D E
|| || || || ||

124. serve for gas exchange in insects

124. A B C D E
|| || || || ||

125. provide large surface area for absorption of food in intestine

125. A B C D E
|| || || || ||

126. are important in both digestive system and circulatory system

126. A B C D E
|| || || || ||

The next four questions (127–130) consist of a group of lettered physiological or behavioral processes and numbered descriptions of these processes. For each numbered description select the lettered process that matches it, and mark the answer accordingly. Any one of the lettered processes may be used one or more times or not at all.

A. abscission
B. gravitropism
C. cohesion
D. cyclosis
E. translocation

127. explanation for solvent movement against gravity in plants, alternative to root pressure theory

127.A B C D E

128. loss of leaves from deciduous trees

128.A B C D E

129. movement of solutes within a plant

129.A B C D E

130. plant growth pattern influenced by position relative to the earth

130.A B C D E

The next five questions (131–135) consist of a group of lettered biomes and numbered descriptions of these biomes. For each numbered description select the lettered biome that matches it, and mark the answer accordingly. Any one of the lettered biomes may be used one or more times or not at all.

A. savanna
B. temperate grassland
C. taiga
D. tropical rain forest
E. tundra

131. Dominant trees tend to be cone bearers.

131.A B C D E

132. Few trees are present; hot and cold seasons alternate.

132.A B C D E

133. Few trees are present; hot year-round; wet and dry seasons alternate.

133.A B C D E

134. There are many tree species, forming dense canopy.

134.A B C D E

135. Winters are very cold; there are many trees but few species.

135.A B C D E

The next four questions (136–139) consist of a group of lettered ecological processes and numbered descriptions of these processes. For each numbered description select the lettered process that matches it, and mark the answer accordingly. Any one of the lettered processes may be used one or more times or not at all.

A. biological magnification
B. eutrophication
C. interspecific competition
D. intraspecific competition
E. succession

136. This process is accelerated by runoff of phosphorus into lakes.

136. A B C D E

137. As a result of this process animals at the top of the food chain are most affected by persistent chemicals.

137. A B C D E

138. This process often leads to a complex, stable ecosystem.

138. A B C D E

139. This process is produced by overlapping needs for a resource by two or more populations between which no gene flow occurs.

139. A B C D E

The next five questions (140–144) consist of a group of lettered neuronal activities and numbered physiological consequences of these activities. For each numbered consequence select the lettered activity that causes it, and mark the answer accordingly. Any one of the lettered activities may be used one or more times or not at all.

A. Permeability changes occur in adjacent membrane regions.
B. Exchange of potassium and sodium occurs simultaneously.
C. Potassium channels open.
D. Sodium channels open.
E. Sodium-potassium "pump" operates.

140. The environment outside the membrane becomes progressively more positive with reference to the cytoplasm.

140. A B C D E

141. Positive ions flow into cell by passive diffusion.

141. A B C D E

142. Nerve impulse is propagated along axon.

142. A B C D E

143. Resting potential is maintained.

143. A B C D E

144. A gradient of ions is held across membrane of neuron.

144. A B C D E

The next five questions (145–149) consist of a group of lettered plant types or parts and numbered descriptions. For each numbered description select the lettered plant type or part that matches it, and mark the answer accordingly. Any one of the lettered plant types or parts may be used one or more times or not at all.

A. cotyledon
B. endosperm
C. gametophyte
D. seed coat
E. sporophyte

145. embryonic leaf

145. A B C D E
|| || || || ||

146. part often important in maintaining dormancy of a seed

146. A B C D E
|| || || || ||

147. most easily observed portion of a fern's life cycle

147. A B C D E
|| || || || ||

148. plant form that is diploid and produces haploid reproductive cells

148. A B C D E
|| || || || ||

149. tissue that nourishes the embryo

149. A B C D E
|| || || || ||

The next five questions (150–154) consist of a group of lettered processes of embryonic development in animals and numbered descriptions of these processes. For each numbered description select the lettered process that matches it, and mark the answer accordingly. Any one of the lettered processes may be used one or more times or not at all.

A. cleavage
B. fertilization
C. gametogenesis
D. gastrulation
E. induction

150. chemically triggers differentiation

150. A B C D E
|| || || || ||

151. process that often results in formation of three layers of cells

151. A B C D E
|| || || || ||

152. programmed cell movements within embryo

152. A B C D E
|| || || || ||

153. rapid cell proliferation by meiosis

153. A B C D E
|| || || || ||

154. rapid cell proliferation by mitosis

154. A B C D E
|| || || || ||

The next four questions (155–158) consist of lettered groups of organisms and numbered descriptions of representative organisms. For each numbered description select the lettered group of which it is a part, and mark the answer accordingly. Any one of the lettered groups may be used one or more times or not at all.

A. angiosperms
B. bryophytes
C. ferns
D. fungi
E. gymnosperms

155. plants that produce flowers

155. A B C D E
|| || || || ||

156. organisms of kingdom Plantae, but not vascular plants

156. A B C D E
|| || || || ||

157. organisms NOT of kingdom Plantae if the five-kingdom classification system is followed

157. A B C D E
|| || || || ||

158. one of the two types of organism that enter into symbiosis with algae to be lichens

158. A B C D E
|| || || || ||

The next five questions (159–163) consist of a group of lettered animal embryo regions and numbered adult parts that develop from these regions. For each numbered adult region select the lettered embryonic region that matches it, and mark the answer accordingly. Any one of the lettered embryonic regions may be used one or more times or not at all.

A. archenteron
B. coelom
C. ectoderm
D. endoderm
E. mesoderm

159. an opening that becomes the cavity of the gut

159. A B C D E
|| || || || ||

160. the layer from which muscle is formed

160. A B C D E
|| || || || ||

161. the layer from which the brain is formed

161. A B C D E
|| || || || ||

162. the layer that induces spinal cord to differentiate

162. A B C D E
|| || || || ||

163. the region that becomes notochord

163. A B C D E
|| || || || ||

The next six questions (164–169) consist of a group of lettered terms from molecular genetics and numbered descriptions of these terms. For each numbered description select the lettered term that matches it, and mark the answer accordingly. Any one of the lettered terms may be used one or more times or not at all.

A. codons
B. histones
C. introns
D. messenger RNAs
E. transposons

164. genetic elements that are capable of moving from one chromosome locus to another

164. A B C D E
|| || || || ||

165. proteins that are a major component of eukaryotic chromosomes

165. A B C D E
|| || || || ||

166. regions of structural genes that are not translated into portions of polypeptides

166. **A B C D E**
|| || || || ||

167. products of transcription, containing complete codes for the amino acid sequences of proteins

167. **A B C D E**
|| || || || ||

168. three-base sequences of DNA or RNA

168. **A B C D E**
|| || || || ||

169. usually chemical symbols for amino acids

169. **A B C D E**
|| || || || ||

The remaining questions ask for analysis of experiments. For each set, read the descriptions and data carefully; then answer the questions or complete the statements by choosing among the lettered alternatives and marking your answers accordingly.

Questions 170–174

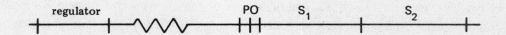

The diagram shown here represents the arrangement of DNA sequences making up two portions of a bacterial chromosome. All of the labeled areas are components of a repressible system. S_1 and S_2 are a pair of structural genes coding for two enzymes that work together to produce an amino acid essential for protein synthesis. P symbolizes "promoter," and O symbolizes "operator."

170. What would be the likely result of a large deletion occurring in the regulator gene?

170. **A B C D E**
|| || || || ||

A. One of the structural genes would be transcribed but the other would not.
B. Nothing would change except that the regulator's product would be different.
C. The amino acid could no longer be produced.
D. The amino acid would be continuously produced even if not needed.
E. The operator region would no longer influence the promoter region.

171. What effect, if any, does the amino acid produced by the action of S_1 and S_2 have upon the gene system?

171. **A B C D E**
|| || || || ||

A. As the end product, it has no effect.
B. It acts as a corepressor.
C. It acts as a repressor.
D. It acts as an inducer.
E. It stops the promoter's transcription.

172. Upon which region does a repressor have direct influence?

172. **A B C D E**
|| || || || ||

A. O
B. P
C. regulator
D. S_1
E. S_2

173. What would be the immediate effect of a mutation of the promoter region?

    A. A portion of a messenger RNA molecule would be translated incorrectly.

    B. DNA polymerase could not easily attach to it.

    C. RNA polymerase could not easily attach to it.

    D. The amino acid could not easily attach to it.

    E. The repressor could not easily attach to it.

173. **A B C D E**

174. If it were necessary to change the diagram so that it represented an inducible system rather than a repressible system, how would the diagram have to be revised?

    A. The regulator would have to be deleted.

    B. The P and O regions would have to be interchanged.

    C. The O region would have to be moved to fit between S_1 and S_2.

    D. The regulator would have to be moved to fit between O and S_1.

    E. No change of the diagram would be necessary.

174. **A B C D E**

Questions 175–177

Fibronectin is a protein found on the surface of many embryonic cells. It is believed that fibronectin may act as a "pattern" for the shaping of embryonic muscle when the protein is supplied by cells other than the muscle-forming cells. To help test this, an experiment was performed to determine whether an oriented fibronectin layer would influence the arrangement of myoblast cells (embryonic precursors to muscle) in a cell culture. A large drop of fibronectin solution was allowed to dry on a glass surface. Concentric rings of fibronectin formed on the plate. When chicken myoblast cells were spread over the surface, they quickly oriented themselves with their long axes parallel to the fibronectin rings.

175. This is an experiment in

    A. ecology

    B. developmental biology

    C. gross anatomy

    D. muscle physiology

    E. ornithology

175. **A B C D E**

176. What is the most important objection to the experiment as outlined above?

    A. An *in vitro* experiment does not tell much about the way the living organism works.

    B. Conclusions to be drawn from the results contradict the hypothesis.

    C. The experiment could lead to unforeseen dangers to human health.

    D. Since the experiment involves embryos, it could lead to ethical problems if done with human cells.

    E. There was not a control to determine whether materials other then fibronectin could also cause myoblast orientation.

176. **A B C D E**

177. What does the experiment demonstrate?

    A. Fibronectin is produced by myoblasts.

    B. Fibronectin orients embryonic muscle only under artificial conditions.

    C. Fibronectin is the most important factor in orienting embryonic muscle.

    D. Myoblasts always form concentric rings when cultured.

    E. Myoblasts can, under certain conditions, take orientation cues from underlying extracellular fibronectin.

177. **A B C D E**

Questions 178–181

The following graph illustrates an experiment in which two populations of the fruit fly *Drosophila* were raised in closed containers under identical conditions. Both food and space were limiting factors in the containers.

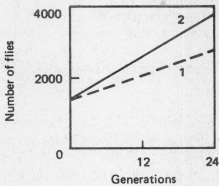

The population graphed as a broken line and labeled **1** had been derived from a single inbred line. The population indicated by a solid line and labeled **2** was begun by crossing two different inbred strains. Electrophoresis of tissue proteins from each population at the beginning of the experiment indicated that the genetic variability of population 2 was about twice as much as that of population 1.

178. What is the most that can be said about the populations from the data provided here?

    A. Both populations adapted to the conditions.

    B. If populations 1 and 2 had been allowed to interbreed, the resulting population would have done better than either 1 or 2.

    C. Neither population evolved.

    D. The population with more genetic variation adapted better to the conditions.

    E. The population with more genetic variation would have done better under ANY conditions.

178. A B C D E
    ‖ ‖ ‖ ‖ ‖

179. Why was electrophoresis used as a tool to determine genetic variability?

    A. It allows separation of genes for individual analysis.

    B. It can separate proteins in a complex mixture, making it possible to count the number of different ones present.

    C. It can be performed on every fly of the population without harming it.

    D. It is less expensive than the alternative method — cloning all of the flies' genes for individual analysis.

    E. It uses radioactive tracers and therefore is a very sensitive method for finding proteins in a tissue.

179. A B C D E
    ‖ ‖ ‖ ‖ ‖

180. Although this was not tested in the experiment described, population 2 probably

    A. eventually would have slowed its growth rate to match that of population 1

    B. had fewer visually observable abnormalities than population 1

    C. was closer to crashing to extinction soon after generation 24 than was population 1

    D. was less heterogeneous in generation 24 than in generation 1

    E. was more heterogeneous in generation 24 than in generation 1

180. A B C D E
    ‖ ‖ ‖ ‖ ‖

181. Which of the following helps explain why inbreeding of population 1 led to lack of heterogeneity?

   A. Genetic drift had necessarily occurred.
   B. Given the chance, individuals prefer to mate with their own kind.
   C. No new mutations can occur in an inbred strain.
   D. There was no opportunity for migration of new genetic variations from other populations.
   E. Two of the above phenomena contributed to the loss of heterogeneity.

Questions 182–185

Calmodulin is a protein that apparently plays a fundamental regulatory role in many organisms. It does not become active until after it accepts the calcium ion. In the starfish, oocytes do not continue meiosis until they receive a hormonal message. The final step in reception of this message is dependent upon the presence of calcium ions. An attractive hypothesis is that calmodulin, if activated by a hormonally induced calcium ion population, may then activate the several enzymes that induce meiosis. To test this, starfish were injected with two chemicals known to inhibit the activities of calmodulin. The ability of the treated starfish to produce mature gametes was monitored, and the results are graphed below.

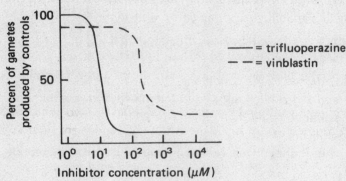

182. Which of these sequences is the one postulated for starfish gamete maturation control?

   A. calcium release → calmodulin activation → hormone production → enzymes activation → meiosis
   B. calcium release → hormone production → calmodulin activation → enzymes activation → meiosis
   C. calmodulin production → hormone production → calcium release → enzymes activation → meiosis
   D. enzymes activation → meiosis → calcium release → calmodulin activation → hormone production and release
   E. hormone arrival → calcium release → calmodulin activation → enzymes activation → meiosis

183. Which of the following is a correct statement about the experiment?

   A. At all doses vinblastin is a more effective meiosis inhibitor than trifluoperazine.
   B. At all doses trifluoperazine is a more effective meiosis inhibitor than vinblastin.
   C. At 10 micromolar concentration neither chemical is a meiosis inhibitor.

D. At 100 micromolar concentration vinblastin is a more effective meiosis inhibitor than trifluoperazine.

E. At 100 micromolar concentration trifluoperazine is a more effective meiosis inhibitor than vinblastin.

184. Which of the following is a correct statement about the experiment?

    A. Because the two inhibitory chemicals did not give identical results, no conclusions can be drawn concerning the regulatory role of calmodulin.

    B. The experiment definitely proved that calmodulin plays a controlling role in starfish meiosis.

    C. The experiment gave results opposite to those expected: calmodulin probably does not control starfish meiosis.

    D. The results were consistent with the hypothesis that calmodulin may play a controlling role in starfish meiosis.

    E. Since calmodulin was not used in the experiment, no conclusions can be drawn on its role in starfish meiosis.

184. A B C D E
    || || || || ||

185. Which of the following would be the most logical next experiment to perform on this system, to determine whether calmodulin is an important controller of starfish meiosis?

    A. Determine whether the starfish gonads contain calmodulin.

    B. Look for other calmodulin inhibitors to test in the same system.

    C. Remove calcium from the starfish gonads and find whether this inhibits meiosis.

    D. Repeat the experiment with higher and lower doses of the two inhibitors.

    E. Try the same experiment as shown in the graph with a different animal.

185. A B C D E
    || || || || ||

Questions 186–191

The following table shows the distribution of average weight in grams of seeds harvested from 1000 individual bean plants of the same species.

Average Weight (gram)

	Below 0.10	0.10– 0.15	0.16– 0.20	0.21– 0.25	0.26– 0.30	0.31– 0.35	0.36– 0.40	0.41– 0.45	0.46– 0.50	0.51– 0.55	0.56– 0.60	Above 0.60
Number of Plants	15	22	40	62	140	210	200	152	70	50	25	14

186. What is the best genetic explanation for these data?

    A. A single gene existing as many alleles is responsible for the observed variation.

    B. All of the plants had the same genotype; the observed variation is an effect of the environment.

    C. Seed weight is inherited via several genes that add their effects.

    D. The small numbers of plants surveyed does not allow one to feel confident about predicting the inheritance pattern.

    E. This is a case of pleiotropy.

186. A B C D E
    || || || || ||

187. What would be expected if a plant derived from the lightest seed were crossed with a plant derived from the heaviest seed?

187. A B C D E
    || || || || ||

A. All of the seeds would be identical, falling at the average weight of all of the seeds shown in the table.

B. Half of the seeds would be very light; the other half would be very heavy.

C. The resulting seeds would fall into all of the 12 categories listed in the table above.

D. The seeds would tend to be near the average weight of all of the seeds shown in the table, but would show some variation toward either extreme.

E. The result would be totally unpredictable.

188. What would be expected if two plants were crossed, each of which had been derived from seeds that fell exactly at the average weight for the population shown in the table?

188. A B C D E
|| || || || ||

A. Their seeds would fall at or very near the average weight of their parents.

B. Their seeds would fall into two distinct categories, very light or very heavy.

C. Their seeds would tend to duplicate the distribution of the table.

D. There would be a 3:1 distribution of seed weights in the next generation, with the largest category being the weight of the parents.

E. The result would be totally unpredictable.

189. This graph shows the distribution of the table:

189. A B C D E
|| || || || ||

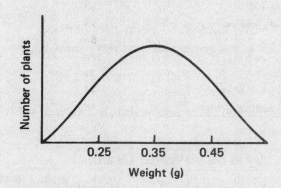

Approximately two thirds of the plants have average seed weights that fall in the range between 0.25 and 0.45 gram. Another way of expressing this is that 0.20 gram is

A. one degree of freedom

B. one standard deviation

C. the chi-square value

D. the mean deviation

E. one standard error

190. In humans, a similar inheritance pattern is seen with

190. A B C D E
|| || || || ||

A. adult height

B. blood types

C. cystic fibrosis

D. hemoglobin abnormalities

E. musical ability

191. In the inheritance mode illustrated by the table, what is the likely role of environmental factors such as rainfall, sunlight, and mineral availability?

191. A B C D E
‖ ‖ ‖ ‖ ‖

   A. at least as potent as any individual genetic factor
   B. negligible
   C. overridingly important, subjugating all genetic factors
   D. totally unpredictable
   E. variable, depending on which end of the weight range is being examined

Questions 192–195

The table on page 43 shows data obtained from a study of how coyotes search prey. For each trial, a coyote was released into a large pen in which a rabbit had been placed. Some trials took place on moonless nights to effectively eliminate visual cues. In other trials, the rabbit was dead to eliminate auditory cues. In some trials, the coyote's nasal passages were chemically treated to deaden smell perception temporarily. Some trials involved various combinations of these three sensory deprivations. In all tests, the unit of measure was the duration of search (in seconds) before reaching the rabbit.

Condition	Average Duration (seconds)
1. All cues absent	150
2. Sight, smell, and hearing present	20
3. Sight present	50
4. Hearing present	200
5. Smell present	80
6. Sight and smell present	30
7. Sight and hearing present	40

192. Which of the three senses appears to be most important in locating prey?

192. A B C D E
‖ ‖ ‖ ‖ ‖

   A. hearing
   B. sight
   C. smell
   D. All of them are equally important.
   E. This cannot be determined from the data.

193. From the data given above, which is the most accurate statement?

193. A B C D E
‖ ‖ ‖ ‖ ‖

   A. Hearing is the sense relied upon least by a coyote during hunting, but it can serve as a backup if other senses fail.
   B. If deprived of all of the senses tested, a coyote would be unable to find food.
   C. Some other sense, not tested in these experiments, is probably just as important as any of the tested senses.
   D. The artificial conditions of the testing site make these results invalid.
   E. The color of the rabbit used in each test is an important factor in determining search duration.

194. Which of these would be the most important factor in determining whether these data are significant?

194. A B C D E

A. the age of the rabbits used
B. the journal in which they were presented
C. the temperature during trials
D. the physiological condition of the observer
E. the number of separate trials of each category

195. Which of these would NOT have profoundly affected the results?

195. A B C D E

A. the hunger state of the coyote
B. the presence of coyote pheromones in the enclosure
C. the shape of the enclosure
D. the size of the rabbits
E. the wind velocity and direction

Questions 196–199

Human inheritance patterns can be described by a diagram in which a circle indicates a female and a square represents a male. An open symbol indicates a "normal" appearance, and a filled symbol represents whichever "abnormal" condition is being studied. Look at the diagram below showing four generations.

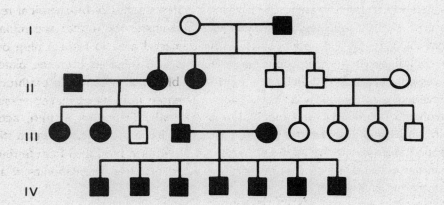

196. What is the best explanation for this inheritance pattern if the condition can be traced to a single gene?

196. A B C D E

A. The allele for this condition is sex-linked and dominant.
B. The allele for this condition is sex-linked and recessive.
C. The allele for this condition is autosomal and dominant.
D. The allele for this condition is autosomal and recessive.
E. There is not enough evidence to determine unambiguously the mode of inheritance.

197. Which generation(s) provided evidence to rule out one or more inheritance possibilities?

197. A B C D E

A. generation I
B. generation II
C. generation III
D. generations I and II
E. generations III and IV

198. Generation IV consists entirely of males. If an eighth child were born in this family, what is the probability that it would be a girl?

198. A B C D E

    A. 0

    B. .125

    C. .25

    D. .50

    E. 1.0

199. For this question only, assume that the mode of inheritance of the abnormal condition is through a sex-linked recessive allele, *b*. What are the genotypes of the parents that produce generation IV?

199. A B C D E

    A. Father is *b* and mother is *bb*.

    B. Father is *B* and mother is *BB*.

    C. Father is *bb* and mother is *b*.

    D. Father is *bb* and mother is *bb*.

    E. Father is *Bb* and mother is *Bb*.

Questions 200–203

    Blood clotting is a vital and complex process that requires the presence of several materials in their active form. If a blood platelet makes contact with collagen of a damaged blood vessel, and if a plasma protein called von Willebrand factor is present, the platelet initiates a series of biochemical reactions that leads to its release of ADP into the region of damage. ADP initiates the further accumulation of platelets, causing them to aggregate with each other in the damaged area to form a plug over the wound. Serotonin, a central nervous system neurotransmitter, is also released from the platelets. It causes nearby blood vessels to constrict, thereby limiting further bleeding. Meanwhile prothrombin, a plasma protein, is converted to thrombin by a "tissue factor" released from the damaged vessel wall. This reaction also involves calcium ions and other plasma materials. Thrombin, in turn, acts upon another plasma protein, fibrinogen, to convert it to fibrin. Thrombin has a second function, to stimulate further platelet aggregation and secretion of ADP and serotonin. The fibrin produced from fibrinogen is a tough, stringlike material that adheres to the plug of aggregated platelets, strengthening it and enmeshing erythrocytes to complete the clot.

200. Which of the following is a correct statement?

200. A B C D E

    A. Damaged tissue releases a material that becomes part of the clot.

    B. Platelets act both to stimulate clot formation and to become part of the clot.

    C. The central nervous system releases one of the materials that act to form a clot.

    D. Thrombin and fibrin combine to become a fibrous mesh that entraps red blood cells.

    E. All of the above statements are correct.

201. Aspirin interferes with the biochemical reactions that lead to secretion of ADP by platelets. The IMMEDIATE effect of treating platelets with aspirin would be

201. A B C D E

    A. lack of fibrin production

    B. lower concentration of von Willebrand factor

    C. production of "thin" blood that will not clot easily

    D. reduced aggregation of platelets

    E. slower conversion of prothrombin to thrombin

202. Hemophilia is a disease that involves lack of a plasma protein needed for the conversion of prothrombin to thrombin. However, an alternate pathway exists to produce reduced amounts of thrombin with help solely from tissue factor. It would be expected, therefore, that a hemophiliac would be able to

A. produce the fibrin portion of a clot, but not the platelet portion

B. produce no clots at all

C. produce the platelet portion of a clot, but not the fibrin portion

D. quickly produce small clots, but not large ones

E. release serotonin from platelets, but not ADP

202. A B C D E
|| || || || ||

203. Atherosclerosis is a deposition of fatty materials and endothelial cells within a blood vessel. Sometimes an atherosclerotic vessel triggers formation of a clot. Based only on what you have read here, which of the following is a logical explanation for this inappropriate clot formation?

A. Endothelial cells attract the white blood cells that initiate clot formation.

B. Erythrocytes attach to atherosclerotic areas; their presence attracts platelets that initiate clotting.

C. Fatty deposits cause a localized reduction in the concentration of von Willebrand factor; this in turn initiates clot formation.

D. If the turbulent blood flow causes damage to the endothelial cells, collagen is exposed and the clotting mechanism is activated.

E. Reduced blood flow through the constricted vessels is enough to trigger clotting.

203. A B C D E
|| || || || ||

Questions 204–207

The pores of bird egg shells are essential for maintenance of gas exchange between the developing embryo and the atmosphere. The two graphs shown here tell something about a comparative study of pore sizes in the eggs of many species. In Graph 1, "pore length" is the average length of an air passageway through the shell from outside to inside. In Graph 2, "pore area" is the estimated cross-sectional area of the egg shell that is actually openings (pores) rather than shell.

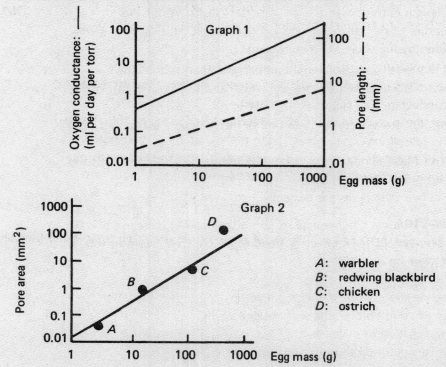

A: warbler
B: redwing blackbird
C: chicken
D: ostrich

204. Which of these is the most accurate statement about Graph 2?
   A. Pore area bears no predictable relationship to egg mass.
   B. Pore area is directly proportional to egg mass.
   C. Pore area is inversely proportional to egg mass.
   D. Pore area is directly proportional to the logarithm of egg mass.
   E. Pore area is inversely proportional to the logarithm of egg mass.

204. A B C D E

205. Which of these is the most accurate statement about comparing changes of oxygen conductance with changes of pore length?
   A. As egg mass increases, these two change at the same rate.
   B. As egg mass increases, these two do the opposite: one increases, the other decreases.
   C. As egg mass increases, oxygen conductance increases at a faster rate than does pore length.
   D. As egg mass increases, oxygen conductance increases at a slower rate than does pore length.
   E. These two changes cannot be directly compared.

205. A B C D E

206. From data presented here, which of these is the most accurate statement about ostrich eggs?
   A. Although their pore area is disproportionately high, its relationship to egg mass is not significantly different than that of other birds.
   B. Their pore lengths are at the upper range of lengths that have been measured.
   C. They do not conduct as much oxygen per gram of egg mass as do other birds.
   D. They do not obey Fick's law of diffusion.
   E. They seem to be operating under entirely different principles of oxygen conductance than do other eggs.

206. A B C D E

207. Why is pore length considered to be an important factor in this study?
   A. It is a measure of shell thickness, which determines the degree of protection afforded by the shell.
   B. It is easy to measure.
   C. It was the only factor that showed an increase similar to the increase of oxygen conductance as egg mass increased.
   D. The longer the passageway through which gases must pass, the slower will be the rate of exchange between the embryo and the atmosphere.
   E. Transport of materials through a semipermeable membrane depends particularly upon the shape of the membrane's pores.

207. A B C D E

Questions 208–210

The graph on page 44 shows the effects of environmental oxygen upon three biochemical activities of blue-green algae (cyanobacteria).

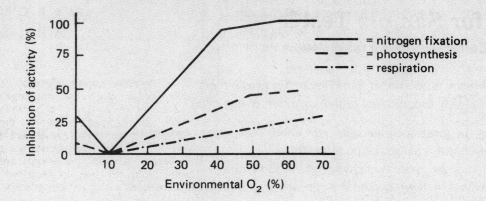

208. What does this graph say about the effect of oxygen upon ALL THREE processes?

A. Nitrogen fixation is least affected by a total lack of oxygen.

B. No generalization can be made, because each of the three responds in an entirely different way.

C. They all do better at higher oxygen levels.

D. They all do better at 10% oxygen than at 50% oxygen.

E. They all do worse at 10% oxygen than at 30% oxygen.

208. A B C D E
    || || || || ||

209. The earth presently has an atmosphere of which about 20% is molecular oxygen. What relation does this have to the information presented in the graph?

A. Blue-green algae do better under current atmospheric conditions than they would have in early earth history when there was less free oxygen.

B. Blue-green algae do not seem to be adapted perfectly to present earth conditions.

C. Since blue-green algae are prokaryotic, their performance in a 20% oxygen environment is probably explained by their chromosomal arrangement.

D. The evolutionary history of blue-green algae probably involves a common ancestry with oxygen-requiring eukaryotes.

E. There is no connection between the current earth value and the graph values, since the latter were derived under controlled conditions in a laboratory.

209. A B C D E
    || || || || ||

210. Which of these statements would seem to be a logical hypothesis, based on the data of the graph?

A. All prokaryotes evolved in an atmosphere that included 10% molecular oxygen.

B. Cyanobacteria would enjoy the greatest ATP availability at oxygen levels over 40%.

C. Nitrogen fixation is completely inhibited in all environments in which the oxygen level is above 60%.

D. Nitrogen fixation is inhibited by all levels of oxygen, because it occurs only in root nodules which are below ground level.

E. Some prokaryotes evolved in an atmosphere that included 10% molecular oxygen.

210. A B C D E
    || || || || ||

Answer Key
for Sample Test 1
(with Comments and Explanations)

1. **(D)** According to Oparin, the primitive atmosphere consisted of a mixture of all of the items listed except oxygen. Later work by Stanley L. Miller produced a variety of organic compounds, including amino acids, from such a mixture.

2. **(D)** Plasmolysis is the shrinking of protoplasm due to the loss of water. Water diffuses into and out of cells, but the net movement is from places of higher concentration to places of lower concentration. If the solution surrounding a cell is hypertonic (containing more solute), it is so diluted by the solute that the solution contains less water than the cell; therefore, the net movement of water will be out of the cell, causing the plant cell to plasmolyze. This effect will also be produced by drinking seawater, salting a ham, or overfertilizing plants.

3. **(C)** Erythrocytes, or red blood cells, are produced by mitosis of cells in bone marrow. Before they are released into circulation, they have become differentiated "bags" of hemoglobin and a few enzymes. Blastema cells and neoblasts are undifferentiated animal cells that participate in regeneration of body parts. Zygotes and blastomeres are undifferentiated cells of early embryos.

4. **(C)** If the genotypes of both parents are *Bb*, the gene combinations in the offspring will be *BB*, *Bb*, and *bb* (see diamond).

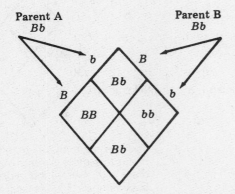

Parent A
Bb

Parent B
Bb

If *b* is recessive and lethal, the genotype *bb* will die. In the case suggested, death occurred early in development since there is no visible evidence of it. Of course the effects of a lethal gene might occur in a fetal or postnatal stage. You can see from the genotypes in the diamond that the probability of getting the lethal gene combination *bb* is 25%.

5. **(B)** Planktonic plants (phytoplankton) consist largely of chlorophyll-containing algae that require light to carry on photosynthesis. Naturally they cannot survive in the absence of light, and light of sufficient intensity to drive photosynthesis does not penetrate deeply in water. Planktonic animals (zooplankton) are also concentrated near the surface because they are primary consumers of the algae.

6. **(B)** T cells (so named because they are activated by residence in the thymus gland) are lymphocytes that comprise the cellular portion of the immune system. The variety called killer T cells can recognize foreign eukaryotic cells and engulf them by phagocytosis. The other portion of the immune system, the humoral system, consists of B cells (so named because they were first seen in the bursa of birds) that produce antibodies to recognize and attach to bacteria, viruses, and macromolecules.

7. **(A)** A typical human cell contains the diploid number of chromosomes, 46. Although it is difficult to prove, most geneticists agree that each chromosome is a single length of DNA. Astonishingly, the DNA of chromosomes is so compacted that it would stretch about one meter if all 46 chromosomes' worth was laid end-to-end. Coiling and supercoiling occurs to squeeze this DNA into a nucleus about 5 millimicrons in diameter.

8. **(B)** Many biological processes are cyclic. If they occur at intervals of approximately 1 day, they are known as circadian. Although they are internally operated, the cycles are apparently kept tuned by environmental cues such as the length of daylight. Travelers experience the jet lag phenomenon until the body has time to readjust to the different timing of a stimulus or stimuli.

9. **(C)** Hemocyanin is the oxygen-carrying pigment in horseshoe crabs (in phylum Arthropoda, class Merostomata) and in some molluscs and crustaceans.

10. **(E)** Respiration, photosynthesis, and transpiration are effected by exchanges of gases through stomates. Wilting results when the loss of water by transpiration exceeds the amount absorbed. All of these processes would be retarded or stopped if the stomates were sealed. Guttation is the loss of water in drops from special structures called hydathodes, which are usually located on the tips and margins of leaves. It occurs when absorption of water exceeds its loss by transpiration or use. Actually, sealing the stomates stops transpiration and increases guttation.

11. **(C)** AIDS symptoms can be traced to the inability of T cells (a variety of lymphocyte) to become active in immunity. The result is an inability to ward off infections or to recognize and destroy cancer cells.

12. **(B)** Test-crossing is crossing an individual showing the dominant trait (*AA* or *Aa*) with one that is homozygous recessive (*aa*) to determine whether the genotype of the individual showing the dominant trait is homozygous (*AA*) or heterozygous (*Aa*). If *AA* is crossed with *aa*, all offspring will be *Aa* and have the dominant trait. This indicates that only *A*'s come from the parent showing the dominant trait, and hence that its genotype must be *AA*. If *Aa* is crossed with *aa*, half of the offspring will be *aa* and have the recessive trait. This indicates that one of the *a*'s had to come from the parent showing the dominant trait, and hence its genotype would be *Aa*.

13. **(E)** Fat, not water, is stored in the hump. Of course, when fat is used to release energy, water is a byproduct of the process.

14. **(D)** Prophase usually requires more time than all of the other phases of mitosis combined, about 60% of the total. The time when the cell is not dividing, called interphase, is a preparatory period when DNA is duplicated. This phase, though part of a cell cycle, is not regarded as a phase of mitosis. Even in cells that divide repeatedly, interphase requires a great deal more time than all of the phases of mitosis.

15 **(D)** When glycogen is used as a source of energy, lactic acid is produced. If oxygen is available, some of the lactic acid is used for energy. The remaining portion is used in the resynthesis of glycogen. During normal muscular activity, oxygen can be supplied fast enough so that lactic acid does not accumulate; but with extreme exertion, lactic acid accumulates and causes fatigue. The deficiency of oxygen needed to oxidize the lactic acid is referred to as *oxygen debt*. We now know that the place most affected by fatigue is the junction of the neuron and muscle, where the neural impulse initiates muscle contraction.

16. **(A)** Carotene is a yellow-to-red hydrocarbon produced by many plants. It is present in foods such as yellow and green vegetables and the animal products butter, egg yolks, and liver. Carotene is converted to vitamin A in the liver.

17. **(A)** Went cut off the tips of oat coleoptiles and placed them on agar. After a short time he removed the coleoptiles and put little blocks of the agar on decapitated plants, which responded to light as if the coleoptiles had not been removed (without coleoptiles the plants would not respond to light). Clearly the coleoptiles produced a substance that diffused into the agar, and then from the agar to the growing tissues of the stem.

18. **(A)** An antheridium (pl., antheridia) produces sperm. In plants that have antheridia, these organs are unicellular in most plants below the level of bryophytes and multicellular in bryophytes and higher plants. The antheridial wall is a single cell wall in lower plants and a multicellular jacket (called a sterile jacket) in higher plants. Of course antheridia vary considerably in shape and size in the various plants.

19. **(B)** During the light phase of photosynthesis when light is trapped by chlorophyll molecules, light energy is converted into electrical energy; in turn, the electrical energy is converted into chemical energy and stored in the bonds of NADP (reduced) and ATP.

20. **(B)** Probability is based on possible gene combinations and not on what happened the last time. However, in the case given, knowing the genotype of the firstborn helps in determining the genotype of the parents. Since the first born has type O blood, its genotype must be *ii*, which means that each parent had to contribute one *i* by its gamete. The genotype of the parent with type A blood would then have to be $I^A i$; and that of the parent with type B blood would have to be $I^B i$. All possible gametes and genotypes that the parents can produce are shown in the diagram that follows:

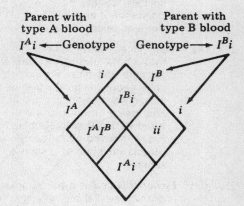

You can see from the genotypes in the diamond that these parents can produce children with four blood types and that the possibility is 25% for each type. The combination on the left corner of the diamond would result in type AB blood.

21. **(E)** Glass is transparent to light rays and not to heat rays. Sunlight enters a greenhouse and raises the temperature of objects such as soil and pots, which then emit heat rays that are trapped because they cannot escape through the glass. It is thought that carbon dioxide in the atmosphere may act like the glass of a greenhouse, interfering with reradiation of heat back into space.

Many scientists believe that the quantity of carbon dioxide in the atmosphere is increasing because of accelerated burning of fossil fuels. Some fear that enough heat may be trapped near the earth's surface to change the weather drastically and melt the polar ice caps, thereby overfilling the present oceanic basins. However, a large reservoir of carbon dioxide is dissolved in the oceans, much more than in the atmosphere. No doubt the oceans will continue to absorb and hold some of the additional carbon dioxide resulting from combustion.

22. **(E)** The atmosphere is 21% oxygen. The oxygen content of the soil varies greatly but is much less than that of the air. Much oxygen is consumed by soil organisms (including bacteria and the roots of higher plants), decreasing the amount of oxygen available to the point where many organisms die for lack of it. The same is true in aquatic habitats where the amount of oxygen is one twentieth to one fortieth of that in the air. Oxygen diffuses into water slowly. That is the reason for agitating water to increase the absorption of oxygen (the movement increases the surface area in contact with air). Temperature is an important factor in the oxygen-holding capacity of water; more can be held at colder temperatures.

23. **(D)** Ants leave chemical trails by secreting a pheromone. Pheromones are defined as chemical secretions that influence the behavior or development of other members of the same species. Besides their use for trail marking, pheromones are used for member recognition and sexual attraction.

24. **(A)** Most nonsteroid hormones cannot pass through the plasma membrane of their target cells and must act indirectly upon the cells' genes, via production or activation of a "second messenger." Cyclic AMP (cyclic adenosine monophosphate), manufactured in a cell only after such a hormone has interacted with components of the plasma membrane, is such a second messenger.

25. **(D)** *Escherichia coli* is a bacterium, and hence a prokaryote. Rabbits are, of course, eukaryotes. Eukaryotes have nuclear material surrounded by a well-defined nuclear membrane, whereas prokaryotes have the nucleus unenclosed. Many other eukaryotic organelles have membranes as well.

26. **(A)** The organ of Corti, the actual organ of hearing, is located in the cochlear canal of the inner ear. It contains five rows of sensory cells that are equipped with hairlike projections. Pressure waves (instigated by sound) in the canal are thought to lift hair cells against the roof (tectoral) membrane, thus initiating impulses in the dendrites of auditory neurons.

27. **(B)** In freshwater environments the percentage of water within protozoa is less than on the outside. Consequently the net diffusion of water (osmosis) is into the organisms. Excess water must, however, be eliminated, or the organisms will swell and probably burst. Excess water accumulates in the contractile vacuoles, which periodically contract, expelling the water to the outside.

28. **(A)** The constant appearance of new strains of influenza virus is ample evidence of mutation within a viral genome.

29. **(D)** Ethylene is a naturally occurring substance that promotes ripening of fruits. It causes color changes, softening of the tissues, and usually an increase in sugar content. These changes make fruits more attractive and palatable to animals that use them for food and incidentally disperse their seeds. Most market tomatoes, especially in the winter, are picked green and ripened with ethylene. Anybody can ripen fruits on a small scale by enclosing them in a plastic bag with ripe apples or bananas, which generate ethylene.

30. **(E)** By definition, phenotype generally means expressed hereditary characteristics, many of which, such as size and color, are visible. Certain physiological characteristics, for example, resistance to disease, or internal morphological characteristics, such as circulatory anomalies, may not be readily observed, although they are of hereditary origin. However, if caused by genes, the characteristic — visible or not — is a phenotype.

31. **(D)** Animals in hot climates may get too hot, especially since they also generate heat from internal metabolic processes. The smaller the size of a body, the greater is its surface area in proportion to its mass. An animal with a larger surface area in contact with the environment can dissipate metabolic heat faster than an animal with a smaller surface area. Animals in colder climates may need to conserve heat and would therefore be favored by having larger bodies with relatively small surface areas.

32. **(D)** Polymorphism is the occurrence of several distinct forms of a species. It may involve morphological differences (such as color or shape) or differences at the physiological or biochemical levels. Examples of polymorphism are the dark and light color forms of the peppered moth (subjects of a classic study involving industrial melanism) and the gray and black forms of the gray squirrel. Each form of the species may have a survival advantage at different seasons or in different locations. However, it is to the species' evolutionary advantage to maintain polymorphism even if there is no immediate advantage in having multiple forms.

33. **(C)** Climax communities are characterized ordinarily by being self-perpetuating and having species diversity, maximum biomass, complex food chains, and a low P/R (photosynthesis-respiration) ratio that approximates 1.

34. **(E)** To locate food in the absence of light for seeing, chemical senses (smelling and tasting) are useful. Being endothermic and having large bodies and intestines would actually be handicaps since these characteristics are related to heavy consumption of food and food is generally scarce in a cave habitat.

35. **(A)** The principle noted by Malthus became a fundamental part of Darwin's concept of evolution and an important consideration of population biologists. Almost without exception populations do increase beyond the carrying capacity of the places where they live. Thus individuals in a population must compete for limited resources, and as a consequence many individuals die, often because they are weaker competitors.

36. **(E)** Genetic drift is a change in the gene frequency of small breeding populations. The change is due to the chance assortment of genes in meiosis and fertilization or to random loss of individuals. When a change occurs in a small population, the percentage change is greater than if it occurs in a large population.

37. **(D)** Down's syndrome is the condition caused by the presence of an extra 21st chromosome, which is either separate or attached to another chromosome. The incidence of Down's syndrome increases with the mother's age at conception, particularly after the age of 35.

38. **(C)** The middle lamella, an intercellular layer cementing together adjacent cells, consists mostly of pectin (no cellulose). On each side of it are the primary walls of adjoining cells. Primary walls are composed mostly of cellulose but may contain other substances, including pectin. Secondary walls, deposited next to primary walls on their inside surfaces, are also composed primarily of cellulose but may contain other substances as well. All three layers may eventually become lignified.

39. **(D)** Hydrogen bonds are weak bonds that link hydrogen atoms to atoms of other molecules, usually oxygen or nitrogen. Each nucleotide pair is linked by two or three hydrogen bonds to either oxygen or nitrogen.

40. **(A)** Vessels with blood under maximum pressure have elastic walls that can stretch to accommodate surges of blood each time the heart beats. If a vessel loses its elasticity, as it often does in aging, it may rupture or balloon.

41. **(B)** The glomerulus is a cluster of capillaries that deposits filtrate from the bloodstream into Bowman's capsule, which surrounds it. It is a part of the nephron, the functional unit of the kidney.

42. **(C)** The thyroid gland secretes thyroxine, which increases the basal metabolic rate of the body. An oversecreting thyroid causes the symptoms described, and the disorder is called hyperthyroidism or Graves's disease. The condition may be caused by a thyroid tumor or by oversecretion of TSH (thyroid-stimulating hormone) by the anterior lobe of the pituitary gland.

43. **(C)** All lower primates have at least some limb extremities adapted for grasping, which facilitates climbing and swinging from branch to branch in trees. They also have stereoscopic vision, which permits more accurate judging of distance, a distinct advantage for leaping from tree to tree. In addition, all monkeys have tails that can be used for balancing, and some (the New World species) have prehensile tails that can be used almost like additional hands.

44. **(D)** The frog is an amphibian. Amphibians are more advanced than fishes and more primitive than dinosaurs, which were reptiles.

45. **(C)** Meristematic tissues differentiate into mature tissues. They may be classified as apical or cambial. Apical meristem is located at the tips of roots and stems, where it produces primary tissues that lengthen them. Cambial meristem is of two types, vascular and cork. Vascular cambium, located between the wood and bark, produces secondary xylem and phloem that increase the plant's girth; cork cambium produces cork that replaces epidermis in older roots and stems.

46. **(D)** Blooms are rapid increases in populations that are obvious to the eye. Some species of dinoflagellates make the ocean water red by their abundance. They are harmless to crustaceans and molluscs that eat them but are toxic to vertebrates that then eat the crustaceans and molluscs. When blooms are unusually large, countless fish are usually killed.

47. **(B)** Autotrophs are organisms that manufacture their own food. Most of them do this by photosynthesis, but some bacteria such as nitrifying ones are chemosynthetic, using the energy of chemical reactions (instead of light) to synthesize foods.

48. **(E)** If genes are linked together on the same chromosome, they should normally remain together when transmitted to offspring. For example, if the genotype of two parents is AaBb and the genes AB are on one chromosome and ab are on the other, there should be only two phenotypes. If the genes are on separate chromosomes, there

should be four phenotypes. However, because of crossing-over, or exchange of parts between chromosomes, cases occur when genes linked on the same chromosome produce four phenotypes instead of the expected two. The study of linkage and crossing-over has resulted in genetic maps of chromosomes.

49. **(C)** Succession is a series of community changes related to habitat changes that precede the development of a climax community. The climax is relatively stable since it is shaped by long-persisting climatic conditions. The successional stages are temporary because habitat conditions change from extreme to intermediate.

50. **(A)** Animals with front-field vision have eyes that simultaneously focus on the same objects ahead. This means that their vision is stereoscopic; that is, their vision is three-dimensional with the ability to judge depth. Such animals have good perception of distance, which makes it easier for them to capture prey.

51. **(C)** Under the influence of ATP and calcium, myosin molecules undergo a shape change that includes a pulling of attached actin molecules.

52. **(D)** Microfilaments are fibers that run through a cell's cytoplasm. Composed of actin or an actin-like protein, they can apparently contract, pulling together portions of the cell attached to them.

53. **(A)** Located at a point where the superior vena cava empties blood into the right atrium, the sinoatrial node initiates and regulates the heartbeat and is therefore called the pacemaker. A second node, the atrioventricular node, is activated by impulses from the contracting atria and transmits them through the bundle of His to the muscles of the ventricles, where it causes them to contract.

54. **(B)** Acetylcholine is one of the best known of the synaptic neurotransmitters. It is secreted in the craniosacral portion of the autonomic nervous system, probably in the central nervous system, and at junctions with skeletal muscle.

55. **(A)** Panting lowers the body temperature by evaporating water which absorbs heat. Panting is especially useful in reducing the body temperature of animals such as dogs that do not sweat.

56. **(D)** If a pregnancy is to ensue, the mammalian egg should be fertilized in the one-third of the oviduct nearest the ovary. If fertilization occurs elsewhere, the timing of embryo development and uterine wall preparation will be improper, and implantation in the wall will fail.

57. **(C)** The heterozygote is *AaBb*, and the homozygous recessive is *aabb*. When crossed, the possible combinations are as shown in the rectangular sections.

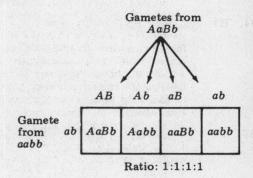

58. **(A)** Some people mistakenly think that the ocean is an unlimited reservoir of food. It is actually very unproductive when compared to forest land. The most productive parts of the ocean are in regions of upwelling and along the fringes of continents. Approximately half of the world's fish harvest is taken from about 1% of the oceans.

59. **(A)** Many animals, including domesticated dogs, establish territories which they defend with varying degrees of vigor against intruders. Because the territories of dogs do not always coincide with the property of their owners, problems occur when the dogs annoy or threaten people upon whose property their territories overlap.

60. **(B)** Members of the same species compete with one another more than with members of another species because intraspecies needs are the same. Within a species the greatest intensity of competition occurs between males competing for a female. Usually the period of intense sexual activity in male mammals occurs at specific seasons and is called rutting.

61. **(D)** Translation is the process; it occurs when tRNA, with its attached amino acid, finds its place on the mRNA strand, thus bringing the proper amino acid into a position where it can be bonded (by peptide linkage).

62. **(E)** The four nucleotide bases can be paired as A-T (or T-A) and C-G (or G-C).

63. **(E)** The suffix -cyte to all of the words means "cell." The first four listed are blood cells; the last is a cartilage cell.

64. **(A)** The rocks formed in Precambrian times (earlier than about 600 million years before the present) contain far fewer fossils than those of the Cambrian and later periods, both in absolute numbers and in numbers of represented phyla.

65. **(A)** Coevolution is the process whereby two species gradually adapt to each other's presence until each becomes somewhat dependent upon the other's characteristics. Commensalism, on the other hand, is a symbiotic relationship in which one species derives clear benefit and the other neither benefits nor is harmed.

66. **(C)** These plants are grouped together because they share certain anatomical features and perform photosynthesis in a unique way that involves production of a 4-carbon intermediate rather than the usual 3-carbon molecule of the Calvin cycle. Comprising over 100 genera, they have a common biogeographical history, originating in tropical regions. They can carry out photosynthesis in a high-O_2, low-CO_2 environment such as occurs in hot weather when leaf stomata close to retain water. Corn is a good example of C4 plants.

67. **(D)** *Escherichia coli*, a common inhabitant of the human intestinal tract, was the first organism used to clone genetic information that had been inserted via plasmids.

68. **(B)** Intestinal bacteria serve several useful purposes such as digestion of food, synthesis of vitamins, and regulation of fecal consistency. In humans, bacteria may comprise 25 to 50% of the bulk of feces. Obviously damage is done when antibiotics kill the bacteria.

69. **(C)** Convergent evolution is the development of similar adaptive characteristics by organisms with dissimilar origins. Fishes and whales, though in different vertebrate classes (whales are mammals), have similar body shapes that facilitate their movement in water.

70. **(B)** A gene pool is all of the genes in a population, and a population in the broad sense is all of the individuals in a species. Generally speaking, individuals of the same species can interbreed, thereby sharing genes with one another.

71. **(D)** Rhodopsin (visual purple) is a pigment in the rods of most vertebrates and in the retinal cells of insects. When triggered by light, it undergoes a chemical change that stimulates the receptor cell in which it is contained and sends an impulse to the brain.

72. **(D)** Photoperiodism is the phenomenon exhibited by plants when they change under the influence of day length. Spring flowering of fruit trees is such a response. A light-sensitive pigment, phytochrome, is the material that counts daylight time to trigger such changes.

73. **(E)** Plant stems have polarity; and no matter into how many pieces you cut a stem, each piece grows leaves at its top and roots at its bottom.

74. **(C)** The distance between *B* and *D* is 18 map units. The distances between *C* and *D, A* and *B,* and *A* and *C* are less than that. The distance between *A* and *D* is 23 units. A greater distance indicates that more recombination events have been observed between the two reference points. Map unit distances determined by recombination frequency are approximately equivalent to actual physical distances along the chromosome.

75. **(C)** The kinds of gametes that can be produced by an organism with the genotype *AaBbCC* are as follows: *ABC, AbC, aBC,* and *abC.*

76. **(C)** Plant cells divide in specific locations known as meristems. One such location is cambium. Vascular cambium, located between the xylem and phloem of roots and stems, adds annual rings of xylem (from which the age of the plant can be determined) and secondary phloem in the inner bark. Cork cambium, located in the bark, produces cork on the outside and other cells on the inside. Mature cells like phloem, pith, xylem, and fibers do not divide. In fact, all fibers are dead and most of the xylem also.

77. **(B)** Cryptic adaptations protect animals by making them difficult to see against their background locations. Flounders have the unusual ability to mimic the color patterns of the ocean floor where they rest.

78. **(A)** A *fixed action pattern* is innate and characteristic of a given species. Often it is expressed at birth or hatching, but it may occur later. Other examples than the one mentioned in the question are the tern's orientation of a fish head to facilitate its swallowing and the dog's turning around several times before lying down. Perhaps the latter is a lingering behavioral pattern used by dogs' ancestors to check the surroundings for safety before going to sleep.

79. **(D)** For a long time an auxin has been used to stimulate root growth on cuttings. It is available in a powder form into which the damp end of the cutting is dipped. An auxin can also be used to retard or prevent the formation of an abscission layer at the base of leaves. This is useful for preventing the shedding of leaves from Christmas trees. Synthetic auxins, called weed-killers, are also used extensively in agriculture and for clearing right-of-ways.

80. **(E)** Auxin is apparently destroyed by light; therefore, the shady side of a growing tip, where auxin is not destroyed, is stimulated to grow faster than the sunny side, where auxin is absent. The growth occurs in two phases, cell multiplication and cell elongation. The latter occurs because auxin somehow makes cell walls soften, allowing them to stretch as water is absorbed and pressure increases.

81. **(D)** Most of the water is conducted by the outer rings. Even in solid trees, heartwood is clogged and incapable of conduction. The vascular tissue in the leaves of the current year is directly connected to the outer ring of wood.

82. **(D)** A deme is a local, usually stable population. Since it is composed of a number of individuals that are sexually reproducing, individuals differ according to their genetic composition and expression.

83. **(D)** Adaptive radiation is the evolution of specialized types of organisms from a relatively unspecialized type. Darwin found thirteen species of finches in the Galápagos Islands, each having evolved adaptations fitting it for specific feeding habits. Their most obvious differences are in beak size and shape.

84. **(E)** Terminal buds dominate lateral buds so that their opening is delayed or prevented. If the terminal bud or whatever grows from it is destroyed by late frost, storms, insects, or other forces, one or more buds closest to the tip will begin growing.

85. **(C)** *Carrying capacity* is an ecological term for the size of a population that can be adequately supported in a particular location, for example, the number of people who can live on the earth or in a particular country, the number of eagles that can survive in Alaska, or the number of plum trees in a thicket. Carrying capacity is determined by fluctuations in biotic (competition, etc.) and abiotic (space, etc.) factors.

86. **(D)** Since sessile (attached) animals cannot forage for the things they need, they must obtain their necessities from the environment immediately surrounding them. Attached animals are not always radial, but that kind of symmetry is ideal for exposing their bodies in the most favorable way to the environment. On the other hand, bilateral animals are better adapted to venture into new places, searching for their needs.

87. **(C)** Imprinting is an especially strong response in hatchling ducks, turkeys, swans, and chickens. The behavioral attachment to objects other than their mothers occurs only within a short period of time after hatching, sometimes in a period of less than 1 day. Konrad Lorenz is responsible for much research on imprinting.

88. **(B)** The cuticle of a leaf is a noncellular layer over the surface cells. Cutin is the wax of this layer. It, like all lipids, is hydrophobic, and therefore forms a water-repellent sheath over the leaf surface.

89. **(B)** Competition for resources, such as food or oxygen, occurs among organisms of the same species as well as between species.

All of the other factors are well-known isolating mechanisms that can keep members of different species from successfully reproducing.

90. **(E)** Endonucleases cleave bonds between specific nucleotides of a nucleic acid. Biochemists can easily determine the nucleotide sequences of the short strands that are produced by treatment with these enzymes.

91. **(C)** Cesium-137 is a member of the alkali group of elements, and its physiological actions are similar to those of potassium.

92. **(A)** Strontium-90 is a product of uranium fission and is dangerous because it is deposited in bones like calcium. It accumulates in plants and is passed on to animals that eat them. Humans are likely to get it from cereals and milk.

93. **(B)** Nitrogen-15 is a heavy isotope of nitrogen, containing one more neutron than normal. It does not emit high-energy particles. Compounds containing nitrogen-15 are distinguishable from their normal counterparts by their greater density. The two forms are separable by use of an ultracentrifuge.

94. **(E)** Carbon-14, with a half-life of 5760 years, is incorporated into organic products and is used to date organic remains.

95. **(D)** Iodine is in the thyroxine molecule, which is produced by the thyroid gland. The isotope iodine-131, which is radioactive, will substitute for the stable form of the element and concentrate in the gland.

96. **(D)** Vascular tissue is the only tissue whose cells are not bound together, but flow through the circulatory system (erythrocytes, leukocytes).

97. **(E)** The cells of connective tissues are separated by a nonliving matrix in which there are varying amounts of fibers. The white fibers contain collagen, which can be converted to gelatin by boiling. They predominate in tough tissues like ligaments and tendons. Yellow fibers, also called elastic fibers, are much more elastic than white fibers and are found in the walls of arteries.

98. **(D)** Red bone marrow is responsible for producing erythrocytes and several types of leucocytes.

99. **(A)** Epithelial tissues cover surfaces, line cavities, and make up the secreting and excreting cells of many glands. Columnar epithelium lines most of the inside of the digestive tract.

100. **(E)** Connective tissues include the types adipose, areolar, cartilaginous, osseous, fibrous connective (such as ligaments and tendons), and lymphatic.

101. **(E)** Although he did not invent the microscope, A. van Leeuwenhoek (1632–1723) refined the instrument and used it to discover and describe many cell types and structures.

102. **(D)** Isolation of insulin was long delayed because the usual practice was to try to isolate it from ground pancreatic tissue. The problem was that pancreatic enzymes destroyed the hormone. Once that problem was understood, Frederick G. Banting and C. H. Best extracted it in 1922 in the laboratory of John J. R. MacLeod.

103. **(C)** Alexander Fleming discovered the antibacterial action of penicillin when he saw that the mold *Penicillium* on a culture plate destroyed the bacteria around it. Fleming, a bacteriologist at the University of London, reported the discovery in 1929.

104. **(A)** Hardy and Weinberg showed that, when mating is purely at random and there is no survival advantage of one allele over another, the percentages of the dominant and recessive genes in a population tend to stay the same.

105. **(B)** Working in England, James Watson and Francis Crick used X-ray diffraction data and other information to conclude that DNA can exist as a double helix with the two polynucleotide strands hydrogen-bonded at their nitrogenous bases.

106. **(A)** After chromosomes assemble at the equator of the spindle in metaphase, the two chromosome halves (chromatids) separate and move to the poles, apparently pulled by fibers attached at positions called kinetochores (centromeres). The cell is in anaphase when the daughter chromosomes are going to the poles.

107. **(D)** The chronological sequence of mitotic stages is as follows: prophase — metaphase — anaphase — telophase.

108. **(E)** In telophase the chromatids are at the poles of the spindle; the cell completes its division; and two new nuclei are formed. Once division is completed, the two new cells are in interphase, during which time DNA is reduplicated.

109. **(A)** Although a barnacle's shell might lead one to conclude that it is a member of the Mollusca, its jointed appendages place it within phylum Arthropoda.

110. **(A)** Insects make phylum Arthropoda the most diverse phylum. The number of identified insect species is over one million.

111. **(E)** Even though they possess three distinct layers of tissue (ectoderm, mesoderm, and endoderm), as do all of the others on the list, the flatworms lack any significant cavity within the mesoderm.

112. **(C)** Because the Echinodermata and the Chordata comprise the only major deuterostome phyla, they are placed (with some minor phyla) near each other on phylogenetic trees. A deuterostome animal builds its embryonic mouth after it has developed an anus; a protostome animal does the opposite.

113. **(B)** Phylum Annelida includes class Oligochaeta (earthworms).

114. **(D)** Lactate, or lactic acid, is the product of glycolysis under anaerobic conditions in many animals and some microorganisms. If a cell lacks molecular oxygen, it feeds pyruvic acid and reduced NAD to the fermentation reaction.

115. **(C)** Melvin Calvin won a Nobel Prize in 1961 for his work in elucidating the mechanism by which many plants convert 3-carbon molecules to glucose by the addition of CO_2 and hydrogen, using the energy of the "light reactions" of photosynthesis. The Calvin cycle is a set of "dark reactions," occurring with or without light if "light reactions" have previously supplied sufficient energy stored in bonds of compounds.

116. **(A)** The Krebs cycle, also known as the citric acid cycle or the tricarboxylic acid cycle, accepts 2-carbon molecules and yields 1-carbon molecules, CO_2. In the course of this activity bonds are broken and their energy is captured as bonds of ATP. Sir Hans Krebs received a Nobel Prize in recognition of his work on this nearly universal mechanism for transfer of energy to readily usable form in a cell that is operating aerobically.

117. **(C)** The word *glycolysis* means "splitting of glucose." This is the first series of reactions that a cell runs if it is to obtain energy by tearing apart glucose. It occurs whether or not O_2 is present, but its products are used differently, according to which of these conditions is in effect.

118. **(C)** Collagen is a protein of connective tissue. All proteins are polypeptides, although some proteins also include portions made of other material (like heme groups of hemoglobin).

119. **(D)** The letters AMP signify adenosine monophosphate. This is a nucleotide, being composed of a nitrogenous base (adenine), a 5-carbon sugar (ribose), and a phosphate group. Ribonucleic acids (RNA) are polymers of similar nucleotides. Cyclic AMP is an important intracellular messenger.

120. **(B)** The steroid cholesterol is a molecule that can be converted to other steroids, including sex hormones. Cholesterol is a major component of cell membranes.

121. **(A)** Both starch and chitin are polysaccharides. Chitin is used by many invertebrates as tough skeletal material.

122. **(D)** Adenosine triphosphate (ATP), is, like AMP, a

nucleotide, but it has two additional phosphates. It is an energy-carrying molecule.

123. **(B)** Named for the famous Italian anatomist Marcello Malpighi, these tubes receive nitrogenous wastes from an insect's coelom and transfer them to the intestinal tract. A vertebrate animal's nephrons (the functional units of the kidney) also process nitrogenous wastes.

124. **(D)** Tracheoles are tiny tubes at the end of larger tubes called tracheae. Continuous with the exoskeleton, they contain atmospheric oxygen, which diffuses into nearby cells.

125. **(E)** A cross-sectional view of a vertebrate animal's intestine reveals the presence of many fingerlike projections into the lumen (opening) of the tract. These villi enhance absorption by presenting a large surface area to contact digested food molecules.

126. **(C)** Sphincters are muscles encircling a tube, serving to close the tube when they contract. Sphincters are found at the arterial ends of capillary beds and at several positions along the digestive tract.

127. **(C)** Cohesion, the holding together of molecules that are alike, is a phenomenon that may explain how water can rise a significant distance in a terrestrial plant. According to this theory, as water evaporates from a leaf surface, it pulls other water molecules up to this surface because of the hydrogen bonds among them. Each molecule thus pulled is capable of pulling another one just beneath it. A previously advanced hypothesis was that water is pushed up from below by root pressure. This is based on observations that a fresh stump of some plants exudes water as if pushed up from the roots.

128. **(A)** Abscission is the development of a layer of cells at the base of a leaf, flower, or fruit. This makes the petiole weaken, eventually leading to a break. Abscission is under hormonal control.

129. **(E)** The products of photosynthesis, dissolved in water, may be redistributed in the process called translocation. This occurs principally in phloem.

130. **(B)** Gravitropism is the movement of a growing plant's shoot and roots, so that the former grows opposite gravity's pull and the latter grow toward gravity's pull.

131. **(C)** The northern coniferous forests include occasional deciduous trees, but annual plants are sparse.

132. **(B)** Both savanna and temperate grassland are characterized by a paucity of trees, but savanna is in an area of relatively constant temperature.

133. **(A)** See answer 132, above.

134. **(D)** Rain forest trees grow densely in their well-watered environment. To compete for sunlight, they tend to become quite tall with their leafy canopies near the tops.

135. **(C)** Needle-leafed evergreens of the taiga are well adapted for shedding snow before enough can accumulate to break branches. Much of Canada, Siberia, and Scandanavia is covered by taiga.

136. **(B)** Phosphorus, needed by organisms to make nucleotides, is the major limiting resource for green plants in lakes. If supplied in abundance to a lake via the runoff of agricultural fertilizer placed on nearby fields, an algal bloom may be expected. This increase of organic material is termed eutrophication.

137. **(A)** A stable fat-soluble chemical that tends to accumulate in low concentrations within simple organisms at the bottom of a food chain will be passed intact to animals that eat these organisms. Passage of the chemical will continue up the food chain; and since each animal in the chain eats many of its prey species, the concentration per animal of the persistent chemical will increase. Therefore, animals at the top of a food chain are most likely to contain an unhealthy concentration of the chemical.

138. **(E)** When fresh rock or soil is exposed in a particular biome, only certain plant species will be able to colonize here. These species eventually tend to change the area in such a way that they cannot compete with other incoming species. Thus, a predictable succession of species occurs. This displacement occurs several times in a predictable manner until certain species reach maturity and cannot be easily displaced. This stable climax condition often involves a large number of animal and plant species with complex interactions, all depending upon the ecosystem influenced by the larger plants that contribute most to characterizing the region.

139. **(C)** If two populations occupy the same territory but do not exchange genetic information by sexual reproduction, they are of different species. They may compete for certain resources.

140. **(C)** Just after sodium ions rush into a neuron as a result of the sodium-potassium active transport mechanism ceasing, positively charged potassium ions leave the neuron. This transfer leads to an increase of positive charge on the outside of the membrane.

141. **(D)** Much sodium (a positively charged ion) is held outside the cell until stimulation causes sodium channels to open, and sodium enters by diffusion.

142. **(A)** When the events of an action potential occur in a particular portion of the neuronal

membrane, these changes stimulate adjacent membrane, causing its sodium-potassium pump to cease temporarily. Thus, an action potential propagates a copy of itself. When repeated many times, the effect is of an action potential "flowing" along the elongated neuron.

143. **(E)** While the sodium-potassium active transport mechanism is operable, it ensures that more positive ions will be held outside the membrane than are present within the cytoplasm. The net effect of this is the maintenance of a small but significant potential difference (voltage) across the membrane.

144. **(E)** See answer 143, above.

145. **(A)** The cotyledons lie within a plant seed. As the seedling lifts out of the soil, the cotyledons often rise also.

146. **(D)** In some plant species, the seed coat must be altered before the embryo will begin development. This change may be brought about by mechanical or chemical abrasion, or by other environmental factors that alter or remove an inhibitor which may be stored within the seed coat.

147. **(E)** The diploid sporophytic stage of a fern is the familiar form of the plant, having large leaves. The far less conspicuous form in a fern's life cycle is the haploid gametophyte, which rarely exceeds 5 millimeters in its longest dimension.

148. **(E)** With any plant having alternation of generations between diploid and haploid, the diploid form may be called a sporophyte. It produces haploid spores by meiosis.

149. **(B)** Endosperm is specialized tissue within a seed. It is adjacent to the embryo and holds stored food.

150. **(E)** An inducer is a chemical produced in one group of embryonic cells that, upon diffusion to another group, triggers the differentiation of the latter.

151. **(D)** The single layer of cells of the blastula stage becomes a double or triple thickness of cells by the programmed movements of gastrulation.

152. **(D)** See answer 151, above.

153. **(C)** Gametes are haploid sex cells produced by the process of meiosis.

154. **(A)** The process of producing the hollow ball called a blastula involves many asexual divisions of cells by mitosis.

155. **(A)** Flowers, which are highly modified stems and leaves, are found only in angiosperms.

156. **(B)** The bryophytes, including mosses, do not contain tubes for internal transport. This limits their independence from an aquatic environment.

157. **(D)** Kingdom Fungi, according to the five-kingdom system first proposed by R. H. Whittaker, includes parasitic multicellular organisms with cell walls that are chemically unlike those of plants.

158. **(D)** A lichen is a pair of species living in a mutualistic relationship. One of those species is a fungus; the other is a photosynthetic protistan. The alga provides food for the fungus. The fungus reciprocates by catching water and providing a protected position for the algal colony.

159. **(A)** The archenteron forms as a result of gastrulation movements and is an opening that remains as the gut.

160. **(E)** Mesoderm can become a wide variety of materials, including muscle, bone, connective tissue, and blood.

161. **(C)** The brain is an anterior expansion of the neural tube, which is formed by an insinking of ectoderm along the embryo's mid-dorsal line.

162. **(E)** The presumptive notochord region, formed of mesoderm, has inductive influence upon the neural ectoderm lying dorsal to it. The ensuing differentiation results in neural tube, or spinal cord, formation.

163. **(E)** See answer 162, above. This portion of mesoderm is the archenteron roof, but the term *archenteron* refers to an open space, not the cellular material that forms its boundary.

164. **(E)** A number of genes are capable of moving from one site to another among the chromosomes. Transposons are DNA segments that carry these genes, and also have insertion sequences enabling the carried genes to be inserted into the new chromosomal locations.

165. **(B)** Occurring in multiple forms, histones are basic proteins that easily attach to nucleic acids. Their general effect is to inhibit the transcription of genes to which they reversibly bind.

166. **(C)** Some genes of eukaryotic cells have sequences that appear in the primary RNA transcript, but are cut out of mRNA before it leaves the nucleus. These introns contain information that is absent in the mature protein that results.

167. **(D)** Any RNA may be said to be transcribed as it is being produced under the direction of DNA. Messenger RNA is the type of RNA that carries instructions on the primary sequencing of a polypeptide.

168. **(A)** Sets of three bases are the smallest units that can be used to provide enough symbols for the 20 amino acids commonly found in proteins.

169. **(A)** The shapes of the nitrogenous bases comprising a codon are critical in determining which transfer RNA molecules sit side by side on a ribosome. Since each tRNA carries a specific amino acid, the codons are acting indirectly to determine which amino acids are given the opportunity to bond as neighbors in a polypeptide chain.

170. **(D)** The product of the regulator is a protein called a repressor. If the repressor is incorrectly produced, it cannot attach to the operator. The result of an open operator region is that all contiguous structural genes may be transcribed. Since the two structural genes in the illustrated region are catalysts for reactions to make an amino acid, this product would accumulate in the cell.

171. **(B)** Since the system is repressible, the end product of the structural genes can act as a corepressor. It does so by attaching to the repressor and therefore forms an aggregate shaped correctly to interact with the operator region.

172. **(A)** If a repressor is shaped correctly, it reversibly attaches to the operator region. The effect of this is to hinder the interaction of RNA polymerase with the nearest structural gene, thus preventing transcription.

173. **(C)** For RNA polymerase, the recognition site along a bacterial chromosome is the promoter region.

174. **(E)** An inducible system, in which an outside agent stimulates genes S_1 and S_2 to begin transcription, can be described by the same diagram as for a repressible system. The major difference is that the inducer modifies the product of the regulator to become active (in an inducible system), and the corepressor makes the product of the regulator inactive (in a repressible system).

175. **(B)** One of the concerns of developmental biology is to discover how patterns are formed in organisms.

176. **(E)** One might object that some other, yet undiscovered, material could perform the same function of pattern determination for overlying myoblasts.

177. **(E)** Although the experiment is too narrow to demonstrate that fibronectin is the pattern determinant *in vivo,* it does show that fibronectin can orient myoblasts in the artificial situation described here.

178. **(D)** Not only did both groups become better adapted to the environment (as shown by the fact that both increased in numbers although they were limited in food and space), but also one actually did better than the other. It would be pure conjecture to say that this would occur in ANY environment, or to say that interbreeding would lead to better organisms for this environment.

179. **(B)** Electrophoresis is a powerful tool to separate small quantities of macromolecules that differ in size and/or charge. The description of the experiment indicated that the macromolecules being studied were proteins, which are the products of genes.

180. **(D)** Any closed population with the relatively small number of individuals used in this experiment tends to lose some genes either by accidents or by natural selection. This is sometimes counteracted by the phenomenon of balanced polymorphism.

181. **(D)** Inbreeding is the controlled mating of closely related organisms, such as brother-sister matings.

182. **(E)** The first activity in the proposed sequence is release of calcium, which is induced by the appearance of a hormone from elsewhere.

183. **(E)** At 100 micromolar concentration, trifluoperazine inhibited about 90% of the gametes and vinblastin inhibited only about 10%.

184. **(D)** Although the results support the hypothesis that calmodulin plays a role in gamete maturation, it is possible that the inhibitors were acting on some material in addition to calmodulin, or that the inhibitors acted directly upon the oocytes. Further study would be necessary.

185. **(A)** The results outlined here are consistent with the hypothesis that calmodulin is present in the starfish, but it would be necessary to isolate the material from the gonads before any further refinement of the hypothesis could be attempted.

186. **(C)** If these results were graphed (see question 189), the resulting bell-shaped curve would be a clue pointing to multiple-factor (multifactor) inheritance.

187. **(D)** It may safely be assumed that one of the two extremes is homozygous dominant for as many genes as are operating, and that the other extreme is homozygous recessive. A cross between these produces organisms that are of identical genotypes, heterozygous for each gene. However, a characteristic of multiple-factor inheritance is that the phenotypes are determined by both genotypes and environmental factors. Therefore, one would expect some variation about the mean values.

188. **(C)** Since the likelihood is high that such parents would be heterozygous for all of the contributing genes, each could produce a large variety of gametes and every category of phenotype could be expected in the next generation.

189. **(B)** A standard deviation is defined as the range (centered about the mean) that includes 68% of the measured individuals. One standard error (standard deviation of the mean) is also 68% of a set of values, but the values in that case are all mean values

of different populations, rather than individuals.

190. **(A)** Adult height is determined partially by the additive effects of several genes (the exact number is unknown) and partially by nutrition, an environmental factor. Musical ability may have much, some, or little genetic basis; this has not been determined. None of the other possibilities are cases of multiple-factor inheritance.

191. **(A)** This is a characteristic of most multiple-factor cases, since each of the several involved genes makes a relatively small contribution.

192. **(B)** The animals hunted more efficiently when only sight was available than when any other single sense was available.

193. **(A)** Animals with hearing as their only sense took significantly longer to find prey than others with only a single sense.

194. **(E)** Whether an observer was tired would perhaps affect the timing accuracy, but the more important factor is whether a sufficiently large number of trials was run. In a study of complex behavior, any single trial may give quite different results from any other, but averaging a large number of trials run under identical conditions will validate any apparent trends.

195. **(D)** In a large enclosure, even doubling the size of the target would not make the search task significantly more easy.

196. **(E)** From the evidence of this pedigree, the mode of inheritance could be either sex-linked dominant or autosomal dominant.

197. **(C)** Generation III's results rule out either sex-linked recessive or autosomal recessive inheritance. Neither is possible because such a mode would not allow two affected individuals (therefore having only the recessive allele) to produce any normal children. As the pedigree shows, affected parents of generation II did produce one normal child (a male) in generation III.

198. **(D)** Unless cytological evidence is provided, it must be assumed that the seven males of generation IV were produced by a father who could just have easily produced a girl by providing an X-bearing sperm cell. Since normal meiosis leads to production of equal numbers of X-bearing and Y-bearing sperm, the probability of a girl developing from each fertilized egg is .5, regardless of the number of each sex already in the family.

199. **(A)** The evidence of seven affected children without a normal sibling leads one to suspect that neither parent could provide the normal allele. Assuming sex linkage, the father, carrying only one X chromosome

upon which the gene is carried, would have a single b allele. The genotype of the mother, with two X's, would be bb. Just as with answer 198, above, it cannot be ruled out that the eighth child would be normal simply because the first seven were affected. The appearance of any normal child in generation IV would require reassessment of the parents' genotypic analysis.

200. **(B)** Platelets release ADP, which attracts other platelets. All accumulated platelets become part of the clot.

201. **(D)** As stated in answer 200, above, ADP causes further aggregation of platelets.

202. **(D)** A hemophilia victim could produce a platelet plug. In addition, he could reinforce this plug with some fibrin made by the reduced amounts of thrombin from the alternate pathway.

203. **(D)** The trigger to clotting is damage to tissue such that platelets can make contact with collagen, a fibrous protein not normally present on the surface of the blood vessel walls. If atherosclerotic plaques include cells with exposed collagen, the platelets will react just as if there were a break in the vessel wall.

204. **(B)** Both axes of Graph 2 are scaled logarithmically. Since the line is straight and pore area also increases as egg mass increases, the relationship is direct.

205. **(C)** The slope of the oxygen conductance curve (solid line on Graph 1) is greater than the slope of pore length (dashed line on Graph 1) when both are plotted against egg mass. Therefore, oxygen conductance increases at a faster rate.

206. **(A)** The pore area value of ostrich eggs, when compared with egg mass, is somewhat higher than the values for the other plotted eggs, but not enough different to require a new theory. Fick's law, mentioned among possible answers, states that diffusion rate is directly proportional to the cross-sectional area available for the movement. No evidence is presented here that would contradict this fundamental assumption.

207. **(D)** The longer the passageway, the greater will be the time needed for a molecule to traverse it. Also, a longer passageway affords more opportunity for friction with side walls, with oxygen molecules slowing or even reversing direction after colliding with wall structures.

208. **(D)** The vertical axis of the graph shows inhibition of activity, not activity itself. Therefore, all three processes are at highest activity in a 10% oxygen environment.

209. **(B)** The facts of the graph — that blue-green algae in normal atmosphere do not operate any of these vital pathways at their theoretical maximum rates — indicate that these organisms' "heyday" is past. In other words, their biochemical operations are still geared for earth conditions that probably occurred billions of years ago.

210. **(E)** Blue-green algae are prokaryotic organisms. Other prokaryotes may also have maximum metabolic rates in 10% oxygen atmosphere, but the graph does not give this information. Of course, one could not be sure that blue-green algae evolved in a 10% oxygen environment; many more data would be necessary to make a more positive statement.

Tests in Biology

Sample Test 2

Directions for Taking Test: This sample test contains 210 questions or incomplete statements, and should be finished in 170 minutes. Each item will have five possible answers or completions. Choose the best and blacken its letter in the place provided. After finishing, you may determine your score by using the **Answer Key** at the end of this test. The Answer Key also contains comments and explanations that should clarify the concepts involved in each question.

Questions 1–90

For each of the following questions or incomplete statements there are five suggested answers or completions. Select the best choice.

1. Glycogen belongs in the category of molecules known as
   A. amino acid
   B. monosaccharide
   C. polysaccharide
   D. fat
   E. protein

   1.A B C D E
   || || || || ||

2. The middle lamella is a part of
   A. cell walls
   B. book gills
   C. skin
   D. Haversian systems
   E. membranes

   2.A B C D E
   || || || || ||

3. Barnacles are most closely related to
   A. clams
   B. sea urchins
   C. crayfishes
   D. insects
   E. brachiopods

   3.A B C D E
   || || || || ||

4. Myotomes of embryos give rise to
   A. endocrine glands
   B. reproductive organs
   C. the central nervous system
   D. the notochord
   E. muscles

   4.A B C D E
   || || || || ||

5. Which of the following sequences is INCORRECT?

5. A B C D E

A. cell — tissue — organ

B. blastula — morula — gastrula

C. individual — population — community

D. green plants — herbivores — carnivores

E. gametes — zygote — embryo

6. Auxins of plants correspond to what substance present in animals?

6. A B C D E

A. cytochromes

B. vitamins

C. buffers

D. enzymes

E. hormones

7. Angiosperms differ from gymnosperms in having

7. A B C D E

A. fruits

B. cotyledons

C. megagametophytes

D. broad leaves

E. tracheids in xylem

8. An herbaceous plant that dies back to the ground each winter but grows again from underground parts is best described as a(n)

8. A B C D E

A. annual

B. winter annual

C. deciduous annual

D. biennial

E. perennial

9. The function performed by the dermal branchiae of echinoderms is performed in birds and mammals by the

9. A B C D E

A. heart

B. lungs

C. feathers and hair

D. epidermis

E. skeleton

10. The Watson-Crick hypothesis is an explanation of

10. A B C D E

A. nitrogen fixation

B. fat synthesis

C. DNA structure

D. energy bonding

E. genetic drift

11. Of the following answers, which correctly explains why plants die when overfertilized?

11. A B C D E

A. causes flocculation of soil colloids

B. damages walls of delicate root hairs

C. upsets soil environment by poisoning soil bacteria

D. causes dehydration of plants

E. blocks absorption of nitrogenous ions

12. Lakes left undisturbed for a long time develop distinct marginal zones. Which of the following is the correct sequence from deep water to the shallow margin?
    A. rooted plants to floating plants
    B. emergent plants to floating plants
    C. rooted plants with floating leaves to emergent plants
    D. emergent plants to rooted plants with floating leaves
    E. floating plants to emergent plants

    12. A B C D E

13. Organic compounds having carbon, hydrogen, and oxygen in the proportion of CH_2O are
    A. carbohydrates
    B. lipids
    C. proteins
    D. carbonates
    E. nucleic acids

    13. A B C D E

14. Hypofunctioning of the thyroid gland will cause
    A. subnormal metabolic rate
    B. rapid drop in calcium content of blood
    C. sexual precocity
    D. enlargement of bones
    E. rapid heartbeat and nervousness

    14. A B C D E

15. One kind of tissue containing extracellular fibrils is
    A. nervous
    B. muscular
    C. connective
    D. epithelial
    E. reproductive

    15. A B C D E

16. In the binomial system, the name of an organism is composed of
    A phylum and class
    B. order
    C. genus and species
    D. species
    E. species and variety

    16. A B C D E

17. The colored structures associated with flowers of dogwood and poinsettia are
    A. sepals
    B. petals
    C. perianths
    D. bracts
    E. hypanthia

    17. A B C D E

18. What group of animals is totally marine?
    A. sponges
    B. flatworms
    C. cnidaria
    D. molluscs
    E. echinoderms

    18. A B C D E

19. The Krebs cycle is most directly involved in what process?
    A. digestion
    B. respiration
    C. excretion
    D. circulation
    E. synthesis of protoplasm

19. **A B C D E**
    || || || || ||

20. Which of these is the best-matched pair?
    A. autoimmunity—AIDS
    B. hybridoma cells—monoclonal antibody
    C. killer T cells—antibody release
    D. natural killer cells—allergy
    E. thymus tissue—plasma cells

20. **A B C D E**
    || || || || ||

21. The growth of pollen tubes to ovules illustrates
    A. thigmotropism
    B. chemotropism
    C. hydrotropism
    D. geotropism
    E. phototropism

21. **A B C D E**
    || || || || ||

22. The umbilical cord contains
    A. arteries and vein
    B. allantois and yolk sac
    C. arteries, vein, and allantois
    D. arteries, vein, and yolk sac
    E. arteries, vein, allantois, and yolk sac

22. **A B C D E**
    || || || || ||

23. The process by which genetic material is transferred from one bacterium to another by a virus is
    A. recombination
    B. translocation
    C. transduction
    D. contamination
    E. inoculation

23. **A B C D E**
    || || || || ||

24. The *AaBbccDd* genotype will produce what proportion of *aaBBccDd* individuals when self-crossed?
    A. 1/64
    B. 1/32
    C. 1/16
    D. 3/9
    E. 3/32

24. **A B C D E**
    || || || || ||

25. Lotic best describes the environment of a(n)
    A. freshwater stream
    B. freshwater lake
    C. swamp
    D. saltwater lake
    E. ocean

25. **A B C D E**
    || || || || ||

26. The practice of subjecting seeds to low temperatures for a period of time in order to break dormancy is called

26. A B C D E

    A. thermolysis
    B. winterizing
    C. acclimatization
    D. vernalization
    E. desensitization

27. In the ocean, where the following organisms live together, which has the LEAST biomass?

27. A B C D E

    A. phytoplankton
    B. zooplankton
    C. herring
    D. harbor seal
    E. killer whale

28. The hormone influencing the conversion of glycogen to glucose, enrichment of blood supply to muscles, and stimulation of heart muscles is produced by the

28. A B C D E

    A. thyroid
    B. adrenal
    C. pituitary
    D. parathyroid
    E. pancreas

29. Which of the following cells performs a function though dead?

29. A B C D E

    A. companion cell
    B. tracheid
    C. cambium
    D. sieve tube
    E. parenchyma of cortex

30. To which division do ferns belong?

30. A B C D E

    A. Chlorophyta
    B. Phaeophyta
    C. Eumycophyta
    D. Bryophyta
    E. Pterophyta

31. Of the following, which is NOT of the same sex as the others?

31. A B C D E

    A. archegonium
    B. oogonium
    C. embryo sac
    D. ascogonium
    E. antheridium

32. Which of the following is derived primarily from ectoderm in vertebrate animals?

32. A B C D E

    A. brain
    B. liver
    C. bone
    D. blood
    E. muscle

33. Green plants carry out cellular respiration
    A. only when photosynthesis ceases
    B. when the rate of photosynthesis is high enough to produce enough oxygen
    C. only when photosynthesis is in progress
    D. at all times
    E. only when stomates are open

    33. A B C D E
        || || || || ||

34. The part of the human brain having control over intelligence and personality is the
    A. cerebrum
    B. cerebellum
    C. pons
    D. thalamus
    E. medulla oblongata

    34. A B C D E
        || || || || ||

35. Which of the following is NOT an aneuploid?
    A. monoploid
    B. $2n - 1$
    C. trisomic
    D. $4n + 2$
    E. monosomic

    35. A B C D E
        || || || || ||

36. Because of its unusual adaptation, Venus' fly-trap is best described as
    A. herbivorous
    B. carnivorous
    C. insectivorous
    D. omnivorous
    E. parasitic

    36. A B C D E
        || || || || ||

37. Lacteals are
    A. ducts in the mammary gland
    B. tear glands
    C. lymph vessels
    D. lac-secreting glands of a scale insect
    E. latex-secreting tubes in plants

    37. A B C D E
        || || || || ||

38. The major function of a game management area is to
    A. exclude domesticated animals such as cattle and horses
    B. provide recreational facilities for vacation
    C. maintain fishing sites for local enthusiasts
    D. serve as a refuge for animals, both migratory and nonmigratory
    E. preserve the natural landforms

    38. A B C D E
        || || || || ||

39. Gibberellins affect plants by
    A. stimulating growth
    B. retarding growth
    C. causing leaf fall
    D. ripening fruits
    E. setting fruits without seed formation

    39. A B C D E
        || || || || ||

40. What is the best interpretation of the structure of skeletal muscles?

    A. acelluar

    B. cellular and uninucleate

    C. cellular and multinucleate

    D. coenocytic

    E. anastomosing and fibrous

40. A B C D E

41. Races, as in humans, and breeds, as in cattle, are categories

    A. equivalent to subfamily

    B. equivalent to genus

    C. almost equivalent to section of genus

    D. equivalent to species

    E. below the level of species

41. A B C D E

42. Lawn grasses ordinarily suffer little damage when cut because

    A. there are no apical meristems

    B. grass leaves quickly regenerate lost parts

    C. shorter plants can transport water and minerals better

    D. cutting increases rate of growth

    E. leaves grow from their bases

42. A B C D E

43. Which of the following is a name at the class level of taxonomic categories?

    A. Animalia

    B. Chordata

    C. *Homo*

    D. Mammalia

    E. Primates

43. A B C D E

44. Sex cells in ferns are produced by the

    A. frond

    B. prothallium

    C. rhizome

    D. embryo sac

    E. pollen

44. A B C D E

45. What field of biology might be especially concerned with the problems of biologically degradable products?

    A. taxonomy

    B. ecology

    C. paleontology

    D. histology

    E. dendrology

45. A B C D E

46. The chemical functional group $-NH_2$ is part of the molecule called

    A. ethanol

    B. glucose

    C. glycerol

    D. lactic acid

    E. urea

46. A B C D E

47. Feminine qualities are maintained by the hormone
    A. glucagon
    B. parathormone
    C. testosterone
    D. renin
    E. estrogen

47. **A B C D E**
    || || || || ||

48. In mitosis, chromosomes move to the poles of the spindle during
    A. interphase
    B. prophase
    C. metaphase
    D. anaphase
    E. telophase

48. **A B C D E**
    || || || || ||

49. If organisms are classified in kingdom Monera, they
    A. are uninucleate
    B. lack definite nuclei
    C. all are unicellular
    D. have coenocytic bodies
    E. all have sexual reproduction

49. **A B C D E**
    || || || || ||

50. Which group of animals does NOT share a common characteristic with the others?
    A. pterodactyls
    B. trilobites
    C. butterflies
    D. birds
    E. bats

50. **A B C D E**
    || || || || ||

51. Contractile vacuoles in protozoa are most important
    A. to store food
    B. for excretion
    C. to eliminate excess water
    D. for jet propulsion
    E. to circulate cytoplasm

51. **A B C D E**
    || || || || ||

52. The oxygen given off during photosynthesis comes from
    A. CO_2
    B. H_2O
    C. $C_6H_{12}O_6$
    D. $C_3H_6O_3$
    E. $NaNO_3$

52. **A B C D E**
    || || || || ||

53. Deoxygenated blood is transported in the
    A. aorta
    B. pulmonary artery
    C. pulmonary vein
    D. hepatic artery
    E. carotid artery

53. **A B C D E**
    || || || || ||

54. Materials enter cells against a concentration gradient because of
   A. active transport
   B. passive absorption
   C. turgor pressure
   D. diffusion pressure deficit
   E. membrane selectivity

   54. A B C D E

55. The fusion of two gametes ordinarily produces a cell that is
   A. haploid
   B. diploid
   C. triploid
   D. tetraploid
   E.. pentaploid

   55. A B C D E

56. The primary advantage of sexual over asexual reproduction is
   A. improvement of chances of reproduction
   B. involvement of two parents in the care of the young
   C. making possible reproduction in all types of environments
   D. introducing variations into the offspring
   E. speeding up the reproductive process

   56. A B C D E

57. Which of the following is NOT derived from mesoderm?
   A. thyroid gland
   B. bone
   C. blood
   D. kidney
   E. muscle

   57. A B C D E

58. Suppose a pure red-flowered four-o'clock is crossed with a pure white-flowered four-o'clock. The red gene and the white gene are incompletely dominant, producing a pink flower. Offspring of the F_2 will be
   A. all red
   B. all pink
   C. all white
   D. one-half red, one-half white
   E. one-fourth red, one-half pink, one-fourth white

   58. A B C D E

59. Convergent evolution is illustrated by
   A. clover and mimosa tree
   B. flies and mosquitos
   C. snakes and turtles
   D. cats and bats
   E. fishes and whales

   59. A B C D E

60. The role played by any kind of organism with respect to other organisms with which it is associated is the
   A. niche
   B. habitat
   C. ecotone
   D. ecosystem
   E. environment

   60. A B C D E

61. Bits of wood, cloth, grain, etc., found in cliff dwellings of the American West might be dated with
    A. ^{131}I
    B. ^{40}K
    C. ^{238}U
    D. ^{14}C
    E. ^{60}Co

61. A B C D E
|| || || || ||

62. Green moss growing on the bark of a tree is best described as a(n)
    A. parasite
    B. epiphyte
    C. saprophyte
    D. mimic
    E. mutualist

62. A B C D E
|| || || || ||

63. Sympatric populations CANNOT be isolated by
    A. behavioral barriers
    B. geographical barriers
    C. seasonal barriers
    D. habitat barriers
    E. structural (anatomical) barriers

63. A B C D E
|| || || || ||

64. The basic unit of nucleic acids is a
    A. nucleotide
    B. pentose sugar
    C. phosphate group
    D. purine
    E. pyrimidine

64. A B C D E
|| || || || ||

65. In what shape of cell is there the smallest external membrane surface in relation to volume?
    A. spherical
    B. spindle-shaped
    C. columnar
    D. fibrous
    E. flat

65. A B C D E
|| || || || ||

66. Distinction between a short-day and a long-day plant is based on
    A. time of flowering
    B. season of planting
    C. season of harvesting
    D. rate of growth
    E. size of plants

66. A B C D E
|| || || || ||

67. The most primitive mammals are
    A. monotremes
    B. marsupials
    C. whales
    D. rodents
    E. primates

67. A B C D E
|| || || || ||

68. Sucrose is digested to

    A. glucose

    B. fructose

    C. glucose and fructose

    D. galactose

    E. maltose

68. A B C D E

69. Which of these is a version of endoplasmic reticulum, found only in muscle cells?

    A. actin fibers

    B. Golgi complex

    C. intercalated disks

    D. sarcoplasmic reticulum

    E. T tubules

69. A B C D E

70. Blood flowing from the intestine to the heart returns by way of the

    A. kidney

    B. lung

    C. liver

    D. spleen

    E. pancreas

70. A B C D E

71. The pairing of homologous chromosomes in meiosis is known as

    A. syngamy

    B. synapsis

    C. synapse

    D. synergy

    E. syngenesis

71. A B C D E

72. The penetration of the egg by the sperm in humans occurs

    A. before ovulation

    B. after the first meiotic division

    C. after the second meiotic division

    D. after implantation

    E. during early cleavage

72. A B C D E

73. Which of the following is a generalized adaptation as opposed to a specialized adaptation?

    A. human foot

    B. horse's hoof

    C. bird's wing

    D. elephant's trunk

    E. human brain

73. A B C D E

74. The reason one cannot drink sea water is that the

    A. water content is less than the water content of cells

    B. salt content is less than the salt content of cells

    C. body is unaccustomed to certain salts in sea water

    D. unpalatable taste induces vomiting

    E. delicate acid-base equilibrium of body is upset

74. A B C D E

75. As a consequence of the removal of a submaxillary gland, the human would

    A. be unable to regulate calcium and phosphorus in the blood

    B. have a depressed rate of metabolism

    C. become obese

    D. be irritable and sleepless

    E. not be affected seriously

75. A B C D E
‖ ‖ ‖ ‖ ‖

76. The best way to separate two proteins that are very similar in molecular weight but differ in net charge is to use

    A. dialysis

    B. electrophoresis

    C. gel exclusion chromatography

    D. spectrophotometry

    E. ultracentrifugation

76. A B C D E
‖ ‖ ‖ ‖ ‖

77. Photorespiration is an inefficient form of photosynthesis Dark Reactions caused by

    A. very low chlorophyll level

    B. very low light level

    C. very low environmental temperature

    D. very high ATP level

    E. very high oxygen level

77. A B C D E
‖ ‖ ‖ ‖ ‖

78. Which cellular structure is NOT membranous?

    A. endoplasmic reticulum

    B. mitochondrion

    C. chloroplast

    D. chromosome

    E. Golgi complex

78. A B C D E
‖ ‖ ‖ ‖ ‖

79. The pollen grain is related to the embryo sac as the

    A. sperm is to the egg

    B. sperm is to the microgametophyte

    C. egg is to the megagametophyte

    D. microgametophyte is to the megagametophyte

    E. spore is to the gamete

79. A B C D E
‖ ‖ ‖ ‖ ‖

80. Color changes in such animals as the chameleon result from changes in

    A. melanin

    B. cytochromes

    Ç. phytochromes

    D. chromoplasts

    E. chromatophores

80. A B C D E
‖ ‖ ‖ ‖ ‖

81. A disease that should be of special concern to pregnant women because it often causes defects in the fetus is

    A. poliomyelitis

    B. rubella

    C. typhus fever

    D. malaria

    E. tuberculosis

81. A B C D E
‖ ‖ ‖ ‖ ‖

82. All of the following are true about oncogenes EXCEPT
    A. at least some oncogenes carry codes for building proteins
    B. oncogenes are related to initiation of cancer
    C. oncogenes never have normal functions in cells
    D. oncogenes may be present in cells without transforming them to the
       cancerous condition
    E. some cancer-causing viruses can carry oncogenes

82. A B C D E
    || || || || ||

83. The diploid number of chromosomes in humans is
    A. 23
    B. 24
    C. 46
    D. 47
    E. 48

83. A B C D E
    || || || || ||

84. The blastodisc of a chicken egg is equivalent to the
    A. egg nucleus
    B. zygote
    C. morula
    D. blastula
    E. gastrula

84. A B C D E
    || || || || ||

85. Which of the following structures are homologous?
    A. eye of squid and human eye
    B. human arm and wing of bat
    C. gill of fish and lung of dog
    D. leaf of moss and frond of fern
    E. rumen of cow and appendix of rabbit

85. A B C D E
    || || || || ||

86. Views on the origin of species most similar to Darwin's were held by
    A. DeVries
    B. Wallace
    C. Lysenko
    D. Lamarck
    E. Lyell

86. A B C D E
    || || || || ||

87. Which of the following is a pair of structures that do NOT have a direct
    anatomical connection with each other?
    A. urinary bladder and urethra
    B. lung and coronary artery
    C. gallbladder and bile duct
    D. metatarsals and phalanges
    E. epididymis and vas deferens

87. A B C D E
    || || || || ||

88. The body of a sensory neuron involved in a simple reflex is located in the
    A. dorsal root ganglion
    B. gray matter of the spinal cord
    C. white matter of the spinal cord
    D. brain
    E. effector organ

88. A B C D E
    || || || || ||

89. That the British came to be known as limeys resulted from an early practice of supplying sailors with lime juice to prevent scurvy. Now we know that lime juice contains vitamin

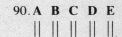

   A. C
   B. E
   C. D
   D. A
   E. B_1

90. There is a tendency among mammals living in the tundra and northern coniferous forests to have shorter limbs, tails, and ears than their counterparts in temperate and tropical biomes. This may be because

   A. random, neutral mutations have occurred
   B. low surface area causes reduction of body heat loss
   C. snow cannot cling as easily to shortened extremities
   D. these differences help the animals avoid interspecific mating
   E. longer structures are more noticeable to predators

The next four questions (91–94) are based on the five lettered graphs below. Any one of the graphs may depict the answer to one or more questions or none at all. The y-axis of each graph represents numbers (quantity); the x-axis, some other variable such as time or size.

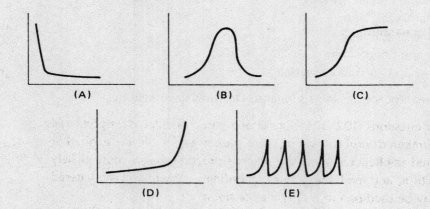

(A) (B) (C)

(D) (E)

91. Which graph indicates the typical growth of a population?

91. A B C D E

92. Which graph shows human mortality rates at different ages?

92. A B C D E

93. Which graph shows the weight of 1000 individuals?

93. A B C D E

94. Which graph represents the mortality of fishes?

94. A B C D E

The next seven questions (95–101) contain five lettered headings and seven numbered phrases. For each numbered phrase select the lettered heading that is most accurately characterized by the phrase, and mark the answer accordingly. Any one of the headings may be used one or more times or not at all.

A. ecosystem
B. biome
C. community
D. population
E. individual

95. is characterized by a predominant life form

95. A B C D E

96. will be altered most by a mutation

96. A B C D E

97. is a self-sustaining group of organisms and their physical environment

97. A B C D E

98. contains organisms all of which are capable of interbreeding

98. A B C D E

99. is composed of animals or plants but not both

99. A B C D E

100. is a balanced aquarium

100. A B C D E

101. is a desert

101. A B C D E

The next four questions (102–105) consist of a group of lettered properties of water and numbered implications of these properties for life on earth. For each numbered implication select the lettered property that is most closely associated with it, and mark the answer accordingly. Any one of the lettered properties may be used one or more times or not at all.

A. good solvent
B. high heat of vaporization
C. high heat capacity
D. high surface tension
E. relatively less density in solid state

102. A niche for some animals exists at the interface between a pond and the atmosphere.

102. A B C D E

103. Organisms in temperate lakes live through the winter.

103. A B C D E

104. People and dogs stay cool in the mid-day sun.

104. A B C D E

105. Ecosystems near large bodies of water are more uniform through the seasons than otherwise expected.

105. A B C D E

The next four questions (106–109) consist of a group of lettered molecule types and numbered descriptions. For each numbered description select the lettered molecule type that matches it, and mark the answer accordingly. Any one of the lettered molecule types may be used one or more times or not at all.

A. enzyme
B. prosthetic group
C. structural protein
D. substrate
E. vitamin

106. has an active site that might be changed by allosteric inhibition

106. A B C D E
‖ ‖ ‖ ‖ ‖

107. is the molecule that is changed by a catalyzed reaction

107. A B C D E
‖ ‖ ‖ ‖ ‖

108. is a material, not formed of amino acids, that becomes attached to a protein, thereby changing the protein in a fundamental way to allow it to perform normally

108. A B C D E
‖ ‖ ‖ ‖ ‖

109. is an organic molecule necessary for normal cellular activity, but not synthesized by the organism that needs it

109. A B C D E
‖ ‖ ‖ ‖ ‖

The next six questions (110–115) consist of a group of lettered names and numbered scientific accomplishments. For each numbered accomplishment select the lettered name of the person responsible for it, and mark the answer accordingly. Any one of the lettered names may be used one or more times or not at all.

A. Crick
B. Golgi
C. Koch
D. Pasteur
E. Schleiden

110. presented the theory that all living organisms are composed of cells

110. A B C D E
‖ ‖ ‖ ‖ ‖

111. described the membranous organelle that produces secretory vesicles

111. A B C D E
‖ ‖ ‖ ‖ ‖

112. worked on DNA structure and genetic code

112. A B C D E
‖ ‖ ‖ ‖ ‖

113. devised a series of steps that determines whether a particular microorganism causes a particular disease

113. A B C D E
‖ ‖ ‖ ‖ ‖

114. was the first to link bacteria with disease

114. A B C D E
‖ ‖ ‖ ‖ ‖

115. disproved the common belief of his day in the spontaneous generation of life

115. A B C D E
‖ ‖ ‖ ‖ ‖

The next three questions (116–118) consist of a group of lettered parts or accessories of a microscope and numbered functions or descriptions. For each numbered function select the lettered part or accessory that performs it, and mark the answer accordingly. Any one of the lettered parts may be used one or more times or not at all.

A. condenser
B. field micrometer
C. illuminator
D. diaphragm
E. objective

116. is a set of magnifying lenses placed beneath the stage

116. A B C D E

117. in an electron microscope, is replaced by an electron emitter

117. A B C D E

118. is of primary importance in determining resolving power

118. A B C D E

The next five questions (119–123) consist of a group of lettered vertebrate intestinal tract regions and accessories and numbered descriptions of them. For each numbered description select the lettered region or accessory that matches it, and mark the answer accordingly. Any one of the lettered regions or accessories may be used one or more times or not at all.

A. colon
B. gallbladder
C. gizzard
D. small intestine
E. stomach

119. in birds, serves the function of teeth

119. A B C D E

120. in terrestrial animals, is the chief area of water reabsorption

120. A B C D E

121. in cows, is the site of rennin production

121. A B C D E

122. in humans, is the principal digestion site

122. A B C D E

123. in humans, is the temporary storage area for a fat emulsifier

123. A B C D E

The next five questions (124–128) consist of a group of lettered cell structures and numbered functions of protein synthesis. For each numbered function select the lettered structure with which it is most closely associated, and mark the answer accordingly. Any one of the lettered structures may be used one or more times or not at all.

A. endoplasmic reticulum
B. messenger RNA
C. ribosomal protein
D. ribosomal RNA
E. transfer RNA

124. captures specific amino acid, brings it to protein synthesis site

124. A B C D E

125. is an organelle sometimes associated with the translation process

125. A B C D E

126. transcribed, then becomes part of a ribosome

126. A B C D E

127. includes a complete set of instructions for the primary amino acid sequence of a polypeptide

127. A B C D E

128. is the only material in this list that is directly made by translation

128. A B C D E

The next three questions (129–131) consist of a group of lettered probability values (1.0 = 100%) and numbered genetics problems. For each numbered problem select the correct lettered value, and mark the answer accordingly. Any one of the lettered values may be used one or more times or not at all.

A. 0
B. .125
C. .25
D. .50
E. 1.0

129. In humans, cleft ("dimpled") chin is traceable to the action of a single dominant autosomal allele. If a cleft-chinned man who is homozygous marries a woman without cleft chin, what is the probability that their first son will have the cleft?

129. A B C D E

130. Tay-Sachs disease is inherited via a single recessive allele. If two heterozygotes have a child, what is the probability that the child will also be a heterozygote?

130. A B C D E

131. If a heterozygote for both cleft chin and Tay-Sachs disease marries another person of the same genotype, what is the probability that their first child will be heterozygous for Tay-Sachs and not have a cleft chin? (Assume that the two genes are not on the same chromosome.)

131. A B C D E

The next five questions (132–136) consist of a group of lettered cell structures and numbered descriptions. For each numbered description select the lettered cell structures that match it, and mark the answer accordingly. Any one of the lettered cell structures may be used one or more times or not at all.

    A. chloroplasts
    B. microfilaments
    C. microtubules
    D. lysosomes
    E. mitochondria

132. Functional portions are thylakoids.

132.**A B C D E**

133. The structures can form basal bodies if arranged properly.

133.**A B C D E**

134. Protein strands are capable of contraction within a cell.

134.**A B C D E**

135. The structures are membranous vesicles.

135.**A B C D E**

136. The structures are contained within cilia.

136.**A B C D E**

The next six questions (137–142) consist of a group of lettered molecules that are important in the control of plant functions and numbered descriptions or examples of such molecules. For each numbered description or example select the lettered molecule that matches it, and mark the answer accordingly. Any one of the lettered molecules may be used one or more times or not at all.

    A. auxin
    B. cytokinin
    C. gibberellin
    D. ethylene
    E. phytochrome

137. is capable of bringing to full size plants that are genetic dwarfs

137.**A B C D E**

138. is related to control of photoperiodism

138.**A B C D E**

139. initiates fruit ripening

139.**A B C D E**

140. induces mitosis

140.**A B C D E**

141. is linked to phototropism

141.**A B C D E**

142. is the class of compounds that includes indoleacetic acid

142.**A B C D E**

The next five questions (143–147) consist of a group of lettered concepts and numbered descriptions. For each numbered description select the lettered concept that matches it, and mark the answer accordingly. Any one of the lettered concepts may be used one or more times or not at all.

   A. clonal selection
   B. competitive exclusion
   C. sliding filament model
   D. model of evolution by inheritance of acquired characteristics
   E. hypothesis of spontaneous generation of life

143. a model attempting to explain the formation of antibodies

143. A B C D E

144. an accurate view of skeletal muscle contraction

144. A B C D E

145. the hypothesis that if two species occupy one niche, only one will survive

145. A B C D E

146. an alternative to natural selection

146. A B C D E

147. a view of what may have happened at least once in the earth's history, but does not occur now

147. A B C D E

The next six questions (148–153) consist of a group of lettered men of science and numbered descriptions of their work. For each numbered description select the lettered scientist with which it belongs, and mark the answer accordingly. Any one of the lettered names may be used one or more times or not at all.

   A. Chargaff
   B. Darwin
   C. Lorenz
   D. Morgan
   E. Oparin

148. did his most important work before 1900

148. A B C D E

149. worked on chemical theories of the origin of life

149. A B C D E

150. showed the ecological importance of earthworms and the importance of the coleoptile for phototropism

150. A B C D E

151. was the first to recognize imprinting

151. A B C D E

152. examined sex linkage in fruit flies

152. A B C D E

153. found the first hint of specific base-pairing in nucleic acids

153. A B C D E

The next six questions (154–159) consist of a group of lettered molecules important in genetics and numbered descriptions of these molecules. For each numbered description select the lettered molecule that matches it, and mark the answer accordingly. Any one of the lettered molecules may be used one or more times or not at all.

    A. amino acyl tRNA synthetase
    B. anticodon
    C. DNA polymerase
    D. thymine
    E. uracil

154. is a nitrogenous base not normally part of DNA

154. A B C D E

155. is important in linking amino acids to specific tRNA molecules

155. A B C D E

156. is important in linking tRNA molecules to specific regions of mRNA

156. A B C D E

157. is important in linking nucleotides together with covalent bonds

157. A B C D E

158. forms hydrogen bonds with adenine of DNA during transcription

158. A B C D E

159. forms hydrogen bonds with adenine during DNA replication

159. A B C D E

The next four questions (160–163) consist of a group of lettered brain regions and numbered descriptions of the regions. For each numbered description select the appropriate lettered region, and mark the answers accordingly. Any one of the lettered regions may be used one or more times or not at all.

    A. cerebellum
    B. cerebral cortex
    C. hypothalamus
    D. olfactory lobes
    E. medulla oblongata

160. in mammals, tends to preempt control of functions from other regions of the brain

160. A B C D E

161. maintains balance and muscular coordination

161. A B C D E

162. is the brain region nearest the spinal cord

162. A B C D E

163. can control glandular functions via its release of hormones

163. A B C D E

The next five questions (164–168) consist of a group of lettered models or phenomena and numbered descriptions of them. For each numbered description select the lettered model or phenomenon that matches it, and mark the answer accordingly. Any one of the lettered models or phenomena may be used one or more times or not at all.

> **A.** adaptive radiation
> **B.** Cambrian explosion
> **C.** continental drift
> **D.** balanced polymorphism
> **E.** symbiosis model of eukaryotes

164. explains some floral and faunal distributions across oceans

164.A B C D E
|| || || || ||

165. describes a sudden increase in types and numbers of fossils in certain geologic strata

165.A B C D E
|| || || || ||

166. is related to possession of DNA by mitochondria and plastids

166.A B C D E
|| || || || ||

167. is a theory of speciation by natural selection

167.A B C D E
|| || || || ||

168. is linked to the observation that a population with genetic variability adapts better to environmental change than does a homogeneous population

168.A B C D E
|| || || || ||

The remaining questions ask for analysis of experiments. For each set, read the descriptions and data carefully; then answer the questions or complete the statements by choosing among the lettered alternatives and marking your answers accordingly.

Questions 169–174

In the fruit fly *Drosophila*, kidney-shaped eyes occur only in homozygous recessive individuals. The gene controlling eye shape is autosomal. A population was sampled and found to be composed of 100 kidney-eyed individuals and 300 normal-eyed individuals.

169. Assume that the population is in equilibrium. Which of these equations would be most appropriate for determining the number of heterozygotes in the population?

169.A B C D E
|| || || || ||

A. $(p + q)^2 = 1$
B. $(p + q + r)^2 = 1$
C. $p + q = 1$
D. $s = 1 - W$
E. none of them: simply count the heterozygotes by observation of the individuals

170. Assuming that the population is in equilibrium, what is the expected number of homozygous dominant individuals?
A. 100
B. 125
C. 200
D. 300
E. 400

171. If the number of homozygous dominant individuals were determined by actual count and found to be lower than predicted, what might be a good hypothesis to explain this variance from the expected?
A. A mistake was made in the census.
B. Some homozygous dominant individuals had changed to become heterozygous.
C. The fitness value (W) for homozygous individuals is higher than predicted.
D. The population is too large to expect equilibrium.
E. There is selection against the phenotype of the homozygous dominant individuals.

172. If the homozygous dominant individuals have the same phenotype as heterozygotes, how could one determine the actual number of the former in the population?
A. Cross each normal-eyed individual with a kidney-eyed organism.
B. It would be impossible.
C. Keep accurate records of the phenotypes of each individual's parents.
D. Since the proper equation always gives the exact number of each genotype, rely upon this calculated value.
E. Using a microscope, analyze the configuration of each organism's salivary gland chromosomes.

173. A pair of men, working in the first decade of the twentieth century, derived the rules used to predict the composition of a population in equilibrium. One of them was:
A. H. Spemann
B. M. Lyon
C. M. Meselson
D. T. Dobzhansky
E. W. Weinberg

174. What does the term *in equilibrium* mean when describing a population?
A. For each individual that has a forward mutation, a backward mutation of the same gene will occur in another individual.
B. Over a period of time, some individuals migrate out of the population, but they are replaced by an equal number migrating into the population from elsewhere.
C. Selection for one gene is negated by selection against another gene.
D. The birth rate equals the death rate.
E. The gene pool of the population remains unchanged from one generation to the next.

Questions 175–178

Organisms of a group of bacteria, the halobacteria, contain a purple material in their cell membranes. An absorbance spectrum of this fraction is shown in the graph.

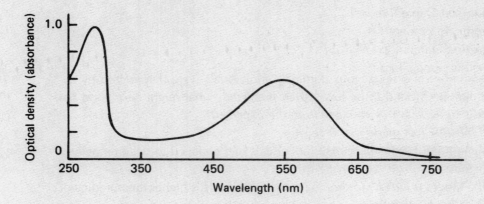

When workers attempted to isolate the purple membrane material by breaking up the membrane with detergent, the material retained the 280 nm absorption peak but lost the 550 nm peak. The material no longer appeared to be purple. Further work indicated that the molecule is rhodopsin, a prominent compound of the animal retina, whose changes in response to light are closely linked to vision. The intact purple membrane is reversibly bleached by visible light, just as is isolated rhodopsin. During bleaching, the bacterial material releases a proton. This, in a complex way, leads to the production of ATP within the cell.

175. Light whose wavelength is 550 nm is perceived by humans as yellow-green. Light at 280 nm is in the ultraviolet region. Which statement is correct about the purple membrane material?

    175. A B C D E

A. It is purple because it absorbs no light at 750 nm.
B. It is the 280 nm portion of its absorbance spectrum that makes it seem purple to us.
C. It is the 550 nm portion of its spectrum that makes it seem purple to us.
D. Its purple color is unrelated to its absorbance spectrum, since colors are a product of brain analysis.
E. Its purple color is a result of interaction between the absorbance peak at 280 nm and that at 550 nm.

176. Which of the following is the most logical statement about the fact that rhodopsin is found in both halobacteria and human eyes?

    176. A B C D E

A. It demonstrates that both organisms were created simultaneously.
B. It indicates an error of contamination in one or the other.
C. It is an example of little-related organisms using similar genetic instructions to perform different functions.
D. It is a clear-cut example of convergent evolution.
E. It shows that these two organisms are more closely related than previously suspected.

177. Relating the pumping of protons across a cell membrane to the production of ATP is a feature of a theory proposed for many organisms, called the

177.A B C D E

    A. chemiosmotic theory

    B. Davson-Danielli theory

    C. induction theory

    D. sliding filament theory

    E. sodium-potassium pump theory

178. From the evidence presented in this reading, how would one determine that protein comprises a portion of the purple membrane molecule?

178.A B C D E

    A. It absorbs light at 280 nm.

    B. It is part of the membrane.

    C. It releases a hydrogen ion when struck by light.

    D. It shifts a portion of its absorbance pattern when struck by light.

    E. It shows no absorbance of light at wavelengths above 750 nm.

Questions 179–185

During fertilization in sea urchins thousands of sperm cells may touch the egg, but only one will be accepted to contribute its chromosomes. Two barriers to polyspermy occur. The first happens within a few seconds of the first sperm contact and involves a flow of sodium ions into the egg, leading to a voltage change across the membrane.

The slower block to polyspermy begins 25–35 seconds after sperm contact and requires about 30 seconds to become complete. Approximately 15,000 vesicles stored just below the egg surface burst open. These vesicles, called cortical granules, contain an enzyme that changes the egg surface so that sperm cells bound to it fall away. A second granule enzyme helps the release of a separate membrane over the plasma membrane of the egg. This outer membrane, called the vitelline membrane, rises off the egg surface. Colloids released from cortical granules move into the space created by the rise of this membrane. They attract water, swelling this area into a protective jellylike region around the egg which repels late-arriving sperm cells.

A trigger to the cortical granule reaction is the release of calcium ions from intracellular depots. Demonstration of the importance of these ions comes from use of drugs called ionophores, which make cell membranes selectively permeable to calcium. When sea urchin eggs are treated with an ionophore, in the absence of sperm, they go through the normal sequence of fertilization reactions, including both cortical granule changes and mitosis to produce blastomeres.

Later activities, including synthesis of DNA and proteins, occur as a result of a rise in egg pH caused by loss of protons to the environment. This proton loss is linked to uptake of sodium from the environment. Treatment of eggs with amiloride, a drug that blocks sodium transfer across membranes, leads to loss of egg activation upon sperm contact.

179. What is the role of sodium in the early block to polyspermy?

179.A B C D E

    A. It causes a voltage change across the egg membrane that somehow affects sperm touching the membrane.

    B. It initiates cortical granule changes.

    C. It is linked to a change of intracellular pH.

    D. It enters cortical granules and is stored there.

    E. It produces a drug, amiloride, that acts on sperm.

180. Which of these is NOT an accurate description of cortical granules?

    A. Their bursting open leads to formation of a thick watery layer over the egg membrane.

    B. They are formed in response to contact by a sperm.

    C. They contain an enzyme that can cause release of unsuccessful sperm cells from the egg membrane.

    D. They do not change their structure until after the fast block to polyspermy has occurred.

    E. They help to separate the vitelline membrane from the plasma membrane shortly after fertilization.

180. A B C D E

181. Which of the following is a correct statement?

    A. Calcium is stored in cortical granules before fertilization.

    B. Calcium can initiate both cortical granule changes and later embryonic activities.

    C. It is likely that the sperm cell triggers egg response by providing calcium to the egg.

    D. The link between calcium and embryonic events is demonstrated by experiments involving the drug amiloride.

    E. The release of calcium within an egg leads to colloid production.

181. A B C D E

182. Which of these experiments shows the role of sodium in the activation of DNA and protein synthesis?

    A. amiloride treatment of fertilized eggs

    B. ionophore treatment of fertilized eggs

    C. ionophore treatment of unfertilized eggs

    D. measurement of voltage across the egg membrane

    E. treatment of cortical granules with sodium

182. A B C D E

183. What would be a likely consequence of polyspermy?

    A. a hybrid that would be a new species

    B. abnormal distribution of chromosomes during each mitotic event

    C. an animal that would be hermaphroditic

    D. normal embryonic mechanisms

    E. response of more than the normal number of cortical granules

183. A B C D E

184. Which of the following is the most valid statement?

    A. Since the sea urchin has already provided so many answers to questions about fertilization and early embryology, its future value to workers is limited.

    B. Since most animals erect barriers to polyspermy, the research described above may be a useful model for further work with other species.

    C. This research may be invalid because of the extensive use of artificial conditions, such as addition of synthetic drugs.

    D. The research on sea urchin development shows how early embryology of all animals is triggered.

    E. This research may have limited value for workers with other animals, since most animals do not normally produce as many sperm cells as do sea urchins.

184. A B C D E

185. Choose the correct statement.

    A. Amiloride is an ionophore.

    B. An ionophore triggers fertilization events only indirectly, by its action on plasma membranes.

    C. Cortical granules release their enzyme when they are touched by ionophores.

    D. Ionophores are normally released by sperm cells during fertilization.

    E. Ionophores mimic sperm action by providing genetic information to the egg.

185. A B C D E
    || || || || ||

Questions 186–190

Hemoglobin and myoglobin are proteins that share structural and functional features. Both are capable of reversibly accepting molecular oxygen (O_2). Both do this through the use of a nonprotein portion called heme. A myoglobin molecule has one heme group, capable of holding a single O_2; a hemoglobin has four hemes, each capable of holding an O_2. Myoglobin is found in muscle; hemoglobin is carried within red blood cells. The graph shows the ability of each protein to carry O_2 (be "saturated with oxygen") in a variety of environments that differ by their oxygen content. Both curves are for proteins isolated from adult humans.

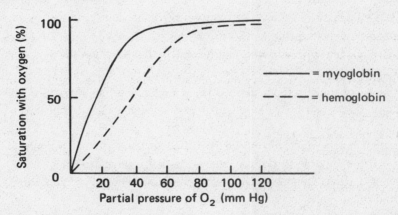

186. Which of the following is a correct statement?

    A. At 60 mm of environmental oxygen pressure, a given quantity of myoglobin carries twice as much oxygen as does the same quantity of hemoglobin.

    B. At 100 mm of environmental oxygen pressure, neither protein carries enough oxygen to be of value to an organism.

    C. Hemoglobin can release oxygen when it is in an environment with little oxygen, but myoglobin cannot.

    D. Hemoglobin releases oxygen more readily in a high-oxygen environment than does myoglobin.

    E. Myoglobin accepts oxygen more readily in a low-oxygen environment than does hemoglobin.

186. A B C D E
    || || || || ||

187. The shape of the curve described by hemoglobin shows the most resemblance to the curve describing

    A. the change in free energy of a system during a period in which an enzyme-mediated reaction is occurring

    B. the change in blood pressure as blood circulates around the body, beginning at the capillaries

    C. the growth of a population of bacteria within a confined area

187. A B C D E
    || || || || ||

D. the growth of a population of bacteria with no constraints of resources or space

E. the relationship between reaction velocity and substrate concentration during an enzyme-mediated reaction

188. Which statement best describes the relationship between hemoglobin and myoglobin?

    A. If hemoglobin were in muscle and myoglobin in red blood cells, the efficient transport of oxygen from lungs to muscle would not be adversely affected.

    B. If oxygen is not needed by a muscle at a particular time, myoglobin will release it back to hemoglobin to be carried elsewhere.

    C. Their structural similarities indicate that hemoglobin and myoglobin are made under the direction of the same gene.

    D. They compete for the same function; animals would do better to have only one or the other.

    E. They cooperate in transporting oxygen to muscles; as hemoglobin releases oxygen to the oxygen-poor muscles, myoglobin can accept it and hold it until needed.

188. A B C D E
    || || || || ||

189. Certain marine worms that live in the thick mud of the ocean floor have a variety of hemoglobin whose oxygen saturation curve looks more like that of myoglobin in the graph. Which statement is correct about these worms?

    A. The similarity of their hemoglobin curve to that of human myoglobin is purely coincidental, since the two organisms are not taxonomically similar.

    B. The shape of the hemoglobin curve is not important; all that matters is that hemoglobin be able to both accept and release oxygen.

    C. They are at a disadvantage since their hemoglobin holds oxygen more tightly than ours.

    D. They are ideally fitted to their environment since their hemoglobin can "load up" with oxygen even in the low-oxygen environment of mud.

    E. This similarity is good evidence that at least some human genes have been passed almost unchanged from ancient ancestors.

189. A B C D E
    || || || || ||

190. When hemoglobin of a variety of mammals is tested, the mammals' oxygen saturation curves vary considerably. In general, very large mammals produce curves resembling the one for human myoglobin, while very small mammals produce curves that are shifted to the right of the human hemoglobin curve. What is the most likely explanation for this?

    A. Large mammals are more insulated by fat, so they do not lose oxygen as easily.

    B. Large mammals have large lungs, so the hemoglobin does not have to carry as much oxygen.

    C. Small mammals are likely to have a higher internal temperature, which tends to cause oxygen to bind to hemoglobin more tightly.

    D. Small mammals tend to hide from danger rather than to fight; therefore, they do not need to transport as much oxygen to muscles during periods of stress.

    E. Small mammals use oxygen faster, and need to unload oxygen more readily to metabolizing tissues.

190. A B C D E
    || || || || ||

Questions 191–195

In birds, karyotype analysis shows that males have two Z sex chromosomes which are analogous to the X chromosome of humans or *Drosophila*. A cell of females contains one Z and one W, the latter being analogous to our Y chromosome. Feather color of canaries is a characteristic wherein the allele for green *(C)* is dominant over the allele for cinnamon *(c)*. Thirty green males whose mothers were cinnamon-colored were individually mated to thirty cinnamon virgin females. The offspring resulting from these matings were as follows:

Phenotype	Number
Green males	13
Green females	16
Cinnamon males	17
Cinnamon females	14

191. Which of these most accurately describes a female canary?

A. XX

B. XY

C. ZZ

D. ZY

E. ZW

191. A B C D E

192. The gene for feather color is best described as

A. autosomal

B. either sex-linked or autosomal: cannot be determined from the data

C. sex-linked, on the Z chromosome

D. sex-linked, on the W chromosome

E. difficult to analyze, since none of the four categories exactly matched in size any of the others

192. A B C D E

193. All of the green birds had black eyes; all of the cinnamon birds had red eyes. Which of the following terms best describes this phenomenon?

A. dihybrid cross: one gene sex-linked, the other autosomal

B. multiple alleles

C. multifactor (multiple-factor) inheritance

D. pleiotropy

E. position effect

193. A B C D E

194. If hypothetical gene A (or its allele, a) is a sex-linked gene, and if a canary is heterozygous for this gene,

A. a translocation must have occurred to produce this

B. the bird could be either male or female, depending on which chromosome carries the dominant allele

C. the bird must be female

D. the bird must be male

E. the bird must be aneuploid

194. A B C D E

195. To more accurately determine the mode of inheritance of the feather color gene, which of these tests should be performed?
    A. Cross some of the green males of the table with green females of the same generation.
    B. Cross some of the cinnamon males of the table with cinnamon females of the same generation.
    C. Cross some of the green males of the table with any females.
    D. Cross some of the green females of the table with any males.
    E. Repeat the described cross with larger numbers of parents.

195. A B C D E
|| || || || ||

Questions 196–199

Cytochrome *c* is a protein found almost universally among organisms. The complete amino acid sequence is available for this protein from many species of bacteria and algae. When compared, some regions of the protein are nearly identical from species to species, whereas other regions show considerable variation. Table 1 illustrates these variations for selected regions.

Table 1

Region	Number of Amino Acids Present	Number of Amino Acids Identical*
A	20	8
B	15	9
C	21	5
D	15	5

*From five species of bacteria of a single genus.

Table 2 compares those amino acids of the bacteria that are identical for all five species with the amino acids at the same positions of cytochrome *c* from the tuna fish, a eukaryotic organism.

Table 2

Region	Number of Positions Identical in All Bacteria	Number of Positions Identical in Tuna and All Bacteria
A	8	5
B	9	3
C	5	1
D	5	0

196. Which of these statements is supported by the data?
    A. Even though amino acid sequences are somewhat different from species to species, their genes for cytochrome *c* are probably identical.
    B. Mutation within the gene for cytochrome *c* appears to have occurred significantly more times in some regions than in others.

196. A B C D E
|| || || || ||

C. Mutation within the gene for cytochrome c appears to have been totally random.

D. The mutations within the cytochrome c gene that have been retained appear to have been significantly more numerous in some regions than in others.

E. The mutations within the cytochrome c gene that have been retained appear to be totally random.

197. Which region of the protein in the tuna is the LEAST like the corresponding region in bacteria?

    A. A
    B. B
    C. C
    D. D
    E. This cannot be determined from the data.

197. A B C D E

198. Which region of the protein is most alike among the bacterial species examined?

    A. A
    B. B
    C. C
    D. D
    E. This cannot be determined from the data.

198. A B C D E

199. What is the most biologically sensible explanation for the relationship between bacterial and tuna cytochrome c?

    A. Amino acid sequencing studies are not valuable for determining or confirming evolutionary relationships; this is shown by the data indicating more heterogeneity among closely related bacteria than between bacteria and fish.

    B. Although their proteins have diverged as have many of their other structures, the two organisms still use cytochromes in quite similar ways; this is reflected by the similarity of the amino acid sequences in certain essential regions of the molecule.

    C. Natural selection operates upon the whole organism, not its component parts; therefore, amino acid sequence studies say nothing about evolutionary relationships among organisms.

    D. The huge period of time since these organisms diverged from a common ancestor is reflected in the presence of many differences in amino acid sequences, scattered randomly through the protein.

    E. The two organism types compared here have developed entirely different ways of using cytochromes; this is demonstrated by their diversity in regions C and D.

199. A B C D E

Questions 200–202

The following three questions are based on the work of Engelmann, who devised a classic experiment in which he exposed an aquatic green algal filament to a minute spectrum of colors. He put the filament in a water medium containing bacteria that were known to be attracted to oxygen. After a period of time the bacteria congregated in spectral zones approximately as indicated in the sketch on p. 90.

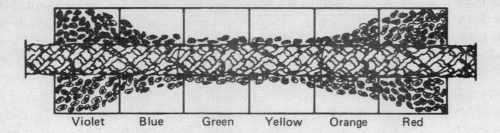

| Violet | Blue | Green | Yellow | Orange | Red |

200. The distribution of bacteria indicates that they
  A. are especially repelled by green light
  B. can be attracted by either high oxygen concentration or particular wave-
  lengths of light
  C. are more active under violet and red light
  D. congregate where photosynthesis is most active
  E. congregate where carbon dioxide is generated by the alga

201. Which of the following statements is true?
  A. If a blue-green or red alga had been used instead of a green one, the
  zones of photosynthesis would have been drastically altered because they
  contain the pigment phycoerytherin.
  B. All anaerobic bacteria will congregate in the same zones as the species
  used in the experiment.
  C. If the alga were kept in the dark, the bacteria would soon be uniformly
  dispersed.
  D. Viruses would be expected to behave like the bacteria because their oxygen and light needs are the same.
  E. If the alga were removed, the bacteria would soon die.

202. Which of these experiments would be most useful in the further clarification
  of this behavior of bacteria?
  A. Move the entire experiment to an area that includes a pure-nitrogen at-
  mosphere.
  B. Use a different species of alga.
  C. Use a narrower range of wavelengths.
  D. Use a more precise device to split light into its component wavelengths.
  E. Use the same physical apparatus but treat the alga with an inhibitor of
  Photochemical System II.

Questions 203–206

The interaction between mother and chick of a species of gull determines the mother's feeding behavior. When she returns to the nest after having swallowed a small fish, she points her red bill down-
ward and swings it from side to side. A hungry chick will respond by pecking at her bill in a particular
fashion. The response of the mother is to regurgitate the fish into the nest. The chick will peck at her
bill only when it is hungry. Observation shows that a chick pecks at the mother's bill on the day of
hatching, but its aim is poor; it misses on two thirds of its attempts. Within 2 days the chick can hit its
target on 75% of its attempts. By appropriate experiments, it was determined that this improvement of
accuracy is related to the amount of "visual experience"; that is, the amount of time the chick has used

its eyes to observe the world. A second component of accuracy improvement is the accumulation of experience at pecking. If a chick is too far away, the chick falls forward as it misses. If it starts its peck too close, it falls backward as a result of rebound off the mother's bill.

If a chick is taken from the nest before it hatches and then is presented with an accurate model of an adult female, it goes through the same pecking development as it would have in the nest. If such a chick is presented with a variety of models that differ in some features of shape and color from a real adult female, it has been found that the head is the most important feature in eliciting pecking, and the bill is the most important area of the head. An older chick is less likely to peck at any variant model than is a newly hatched chick. Chicks at any age respond best to a red-bill model that is placed vertically and moved back and forth horizontally.

203. Which of these features is an example of learning?
A. the chick's improvement of aim at the bill
B. the chick's recognition that the bill should be pecked
C. the greater likelihood that pecking will occur if the chick is hungry
D. the chick's recognition that the mother's bill is red
E. the mother's regurgitation of food

203. A B C D E
|| || || || ||

204. Which of these is instinctive?
A. the chick's improvement of aim at the bill
B. the chick's recognition that the bill should be pecked
C. the greater ability of an older chick to refrain from pecking at an inaccurate model
D. the mother's bill being red
E. the shape of the mother's head and bill

204. A B C D E
|| || || || ||

205. What is the most significant statement that can be made about these observations?
A. Only the instinctive portion of this behavior can be accurately assessed, since learning is more complex.
B. The observations show that this behavior is instinctive with a component of learning.
C. They are invalid because one cannot distinguish instinctive behavior from learned behavior.
D. They show that chicks communicate with their mother by a language that consists of pecking out a variety of messages upon her bill.
E. They show that the food-eliciting response is much simpler than it would appear upon first observation.

205. A B C D E
|| || || || ||

206. What would be an "appropriate experiment" to determine that pecking accuracy is related to the amount of visual experience the chick has?
A. Alternately place a chick in dark and light during testing.
B. Change the color of the model's bill during testing.
C. Keep chicks in the dark for various amounts of time from hatching until testing.
D. Move the model's bill at different rates during testing.
E. Permanently blind a newly hatched chick.

206. A B C D E
|| || || || ||

Questions 207–210

The following graph shows the population growth curves of two similar species of organisms that were grown either separately or mixed together. The beginning populations were the same size, and the abiotic conditions were identical. Assume that the food supply was a limiting factor.

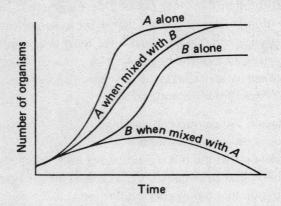

207. The typical growth curve exhibited by many populations is represented here by
   A. species *A* growing alone
   B. species *A* when mixed with species *B*
   C. species *B* growing alone
   D. species *B* when mixed with species *A*
   E. both species *A* growing alone and species *B* growing alone

207. A B C D E
   || || || || ||

208. When species *A* and species *B* are grown together,
   A. species *A* is benefited by the presence of species *B*
   B. species *A* is handicapped by the presence of species *B*
   C. species *A* and species *B* are both benefited by growing together
   D. species *A* and species *B* are both handicapped by growing together
   E. the results are atypical for competing organisms

208. A B C D E
   || || || || ||

209. These experiments illustrate what has become known as
   A. Hardy's law
   B. competitive tension
   C. population divergence
   D. Gause's principle
   E. incomplete dominance

209. A B C D E
   || || || || ||

210. The experiments confirm that
   A. species *A* and species *B* have different food requirements
   B. when two species compete, they quickly harmonize with each other
   C. when two species compete, only one is benefited
   D. when two species compete for the same resource, only one species survives
   E. growth curves *A* and *B* would be identical if both species had been of the same size

210. A B C D E
   || || || || ||

Answer Key
for Sample Test 2
(with Comments and Explanations)

1. **(C)** Glycogen is a polysaccharide (carbohydrate) composed of many linked glucoses, commonly stored in the liver and muscles.

2. **(A)** The middle lamella is a layer that binds adjacent cells together; it is a layer shared by adjacent cells.

3. **(C)** Both are crustaceans, gill-breathing arthropods.

4. **(E)** Myotomes lie between the dermatome and sclerotome (all derived from somites). They are segmentally arranged and give rise to all of the skeletal musculature except in the head and neck region.

5. **(B)** All sequences represent levels of increasing complexity or direction. The sequence of answer B should be morula — blastula — gastrula, stages in the early development of an embryo.

6. **(E)** Like animal hormones, auxins are produced in small quantities and produce large results. Plant responses thus produced are caused by growth.

7. **(A)** Angiosperms have seeds enclosed in fruits, whereas gymnosperms have naked (unenclosed) seeds. While most angiosperms have broad leaves and gymnosperms narrow leaves, there are many exceptions.

8. **(E)** Plants that persist indefinitely are perennials, whether they are herbaceous or woody.

9. **(B)** The function is gas exchange. Being on aquatic animals, dermal branchiae are in reality skin gills used to exchange carbon dioxide and oxygen directly with the water.

10. **(C)** DNA occurs in two strands, parallel to each other and twisted.

11. **(D)** In effect, the soluble salts in fertilizer dilute the water of the soil. If it is diluted enough, the plant will contain more water than the soil surrounding its roots. Since the movement of water by osmosis is in proportion to its quantity on each side of a membrane, the net movement will be out of the plant, thus dehydrating it.

12. **(E)** The complete sequence of zones is as follows: floating plants — rooted but submerged plants — rooted plants with floating leaves — emergent plants.

13. **(A)** Examples are glucose, $C_6H_{12}O_6$, and fructose $C_6H_{12}O_6$. Compound sugars like sucrose, $C_{12}H_{22}O_{11}$, are in the same proportion less one molecule of water.

14. **(A)** A hypofunctioning thyroid gland simply does not produce enough thyroxin to keep the oxidative energy-releasing reactions of the body at a normal level. In adults, a hypofunctioning thyroid causes such symptoms as goiter, physical lethargy, obesity, loss of hair, slower heartbeat, and mental dullness.

15. **(C)** The fibrils of connective tissue like cartilage, bone, tendons, and ligaments are located in the matrix, which surrounds the cells that secrete the fibrils.

16. **(C)** Linnaeus first devised the binomial system whereby any organism can be identified by its genus and species names.

17. **(D)** Any modified structure attached below the sepals is a bract. In flowering dogwood, for example, the four "petals" are bracts around (below) a cluster of small, relatively inconspicuous flowers.

18. **(E)** The phylum Echinodermata includes starfishes, sea urchins, and other animals that are all aquatic but never in freshwater.

19. **(B)** The Krebs cycle (also known as the citric acid cycle) is a multistep chemical event that provides usable energy to a cell by oxidation of certain food molecules. It requires the presence of molecular oxygen. Respiration refers, in this context, to the oxidation process rather than to the initial procurement of molecular oxygen by the act of breathing.

20. **(B)** A hybridoma cell is formed by fusion of a cancer cell with an antibody-producing cell. Thus, its descendants have the ability to reproduce indefinitely in culture (making a clone) and the ability to produce antibody of only one sort (monoclonal antibody). Killer T cells directly attack antigens after gaining competence by residing in the thymus. Plasma cells (B cells) release antibody and are not dependent upon residence in the thymus. Antibody of plasma cells, if of the IgE variety, can induce allergic reactions. The function of natural killer cells, although not fully understood, is most closely linked to defense against cancer cells.

21. **(B)** The tube unfailingly grows to the position of the egg, following a chemical gradient.

22. **(E)** At birth the umbilical cord is about 2 feet long and 3/4 inch in diameter. It contains the allantois, yolk sac, two arteries and one vein — all held together with a loose connective tissue. The allantois, a rudimentary

organ in mammals, outpockets into the umbilical cord from the posterior part of the primitive digestive tract. The yolk sac outpockets from the ventral part of the primitive digestive tract. Like the allantois, it is also rudimentary.

23. **(C)** Chromosome fragments of the host bacterium may become enclosed by new viral sheaths that form during viral multiplication. A virus containing such a fragment introduces it along with its own genetic material into the bacterium it enters.

24. **(B)** The genotype *AaBbccDd* can produce gene combinations: *ABcD, ABcd, AbcD, Abcd, aBcD, aBcd, abcD,* and *abcd*. The easy way to calculate the chances of the offspring being *aaBBccDD* is to determine the chance of each gene combination occurring individually and then multiply all of them together. The chance of it being *aa* is 1/4 (25%), *BB* is 1/4 (25%), cc is 1/1 (100%), and *Dd* is 1/2 (50%). Therefore, $1/4 \times 1/4 \times 1/1 \times 1/2 = 1/32$.

25. **(A)** Lotic means "of streams" (flowing water), and lentic means "of lakes" (standing water).

26. **(D)** Vernalization is the preconditioning of seeds, seedlings, or mature plants to induce physiological events such as breaking of dormancy and flowering. The preconditioning usually involves subjection to low temperatures for a certain period of time. It is often used to precondition winter wheat so that it can be planted during spring in regions that have winters too severe for fall planting and where suitable spring varieties are not available.

27. **(E)** In the order listed, the organisms represent successive trophic levels of the food pyramid. Being at the top of the pyramid, the killer whale has much less biomass than any of the others. There is about a 90% loss from one level to the next.

28. **(B)** Adrenalin is produced by the medulla of the adrenal gland and provides quick energy for defense or flight.

29. **(B)** Tracheids are elongated cells in the wood of plants, especially gymnosperms, that consist only of cell walls when they are mature. Tracheids perform the dual functions of conduction and support.

30. **(E)** The name means "feather (or "wing") plant," perhaps referring to the feathery appearance of fern fronds.

31. **(E)** The first four are plant structures that produce eggs; the antheridium produces sperms.

32. **(A)** The central nervous system is derived from a dorsal groove in the ectoderm. The sides of the groove eventually fuse over the top to form a tube that lies beneath the outer wall. The anterior portion of that tube enlarges and develops into the brain.

33. **(D)** Presumably, all living organisms must respire to sustain life.

34. **(A)** This part of the brain is proportionally very large in humans. It does not regulate automatic body functions such as those that continue during sleep.

35. **(A)** An aneuploid organism has an irregular number of a particular chromosome (not an irregular number of whole sets). Monoploids, diploids, triploids, etc., cannot be considered aneuploid because they contain only whole sets of chromosomes. A trisomic is $2n + 1$, and a monosomic is $2n - 1$.

36. **(B)** Plants that capture and utilize animals for food have been incorrectly referred to as insectivorous. Since they capture any animal of appropriate size that chances to fall into their traps, they should be described as carnivorous or flesh-eating.

37. **(C)** Lacteals are minute lymph vessels that absorb finely emulsified fats from the intestinal cavity and transport them to the thoracic duct.

38. **(D)** While this is the major function, secondary functions might also be involved.

39. **(A)** Originally isolated from a fungal parasite of rice, gibberellins are now known from higher plants. When applied to plants, they cause a dramatic increase in size.

40. **(C)** Each fiber of skeletal muscle is a single large cell with many nuclei. This cell was formed in the embryo by the fusion of many smaller cells, called myoblasts.

41. **(E)** Races and breeds, along with strains, varieties, and forms, are subspecific groups.

42. **(E)** Because the growth region is at the base of the leaf, cropping the tips destroys only mature tissues, which are replaced from below.

43. **(D)** Proceeding from the largest (most inclusive), the scheme of taxonomic levels is kingdom, phylum (called division for plants and fungi), class, order, family, genus, species. Humans are of kingdom Animalia, phylum Chordata, class Mammalia, order Primates, genus *Homo*, species *sapiens*.

44. **(B)** Sex cells are produced by gametophytes, and the gametophytes of ferns are known as *prothallia* (sing., *prothallium*).

45. **(B)** This is an environmental problem, and ecology deals with organismal-environmental relationships.

46. **(E)** Urea, the principal nitrogenous waste molecule of vertebrate animals, includes two amino groups.

47. **(E)** Hormones secreted by the ovary are *estrogen* and *progesterone*, the former being especially important in causing the development of secondary sexual characteristics.

48. **(D)** While chromosomes are moving to the poles, the cell is in anaphase; upon reaching the poles, the cell is in telophase.

49. **(B)** Besides having no definite nuclei, monerans lack mitochondria, plastids, endoplasmic reticulum, Golgi bodies, and lysosomes.

50. **(B)** All but the trilobites (extinct arthropods with a body shape similar to the sow bug) have wings.

51. **(C)** Contractile vacuoles regularly expel excess water that diffuses into the organisms. If it were not eliminated, the organisms would burst.

52. **(B)** During the light phase of photosynthesis, water is split into hydrogen and oxygen. The hydrogen later combines with carbon dioxide and water in the synthesis of food.

53. **(B)** Deoxygenated blood is pumped by the heart through the pulmonary artery to the lungs, where it is again oxygenated.

54. **(A)** Active transport depends on something more than molecular movement, which is all that is required for passive absorption. The process requires an expenditure of energy, since molecules move from low to high concentration.

55. **(B)** Diploid cells have two sets of chromosomes, one set from each parent.

56. **(D)** In asexual reproduction there is only one parent, and the offspring has the same genes as the parent. In sexual reproduction two parents with individual differences pool their genes in producing a third individual, which will be different from either of the parents. The results may or may not be an improvement. Presumably, superior individuals can survive better.

57. **(A)** Secretory cells of the thyroid are derived from endoderm.

58. **(E)** F_1 individuals will all be Rr, or pink. See the illustration.

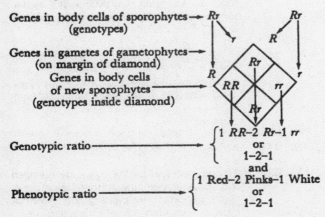

Characteristic of sporophytes→ Pink Flower × Pink Flower (phenotypes)

Genes in body cells of sporophytes → Rr Rr (genotypes)

Genes in gametes of gametophytes → (on margin of diamond)

Genes in body cells of new sporophytes → (genotypes inside diamond)

Genotypic ratio ———— { 1 RR–2 Rr–1 rr or 1–2–1

and

Phenotypic ratio ———→ { 1 Red–2 Pinks–1 White or 1–2–1

59. **(E)** Though belonging to different taxonomic groups, fishes and whales have forms that are similar, an adaptation to the same environment where they live. The resemblance is superficial, as indicated by such fundamental differences as the manner in which they breathe — gill-breathing by fish and lung-breathing by whales.

60. **(A)** A *niche* is not a location. It is a mode of life including all of its relationships. It has sometimes been likened to the profession of a person.

61. **(D)** The process is called radiocarbon dating. Carbon-14 is a radioactive isotope used to date organic items such as those mentioned. The process is reasonably accurate up to 25,000 years.

62. **(B)** The moss gives nothing to and takes nothing away from the plant to which it is attached. Such an epiphyte is maintaining a commensal relationship with the tree.

63. **(B)** By definition, *sympatric* means having the same geographic range.

64. **(A)** The nucleotide is a molecule composed of a pentose sugar to which is attached a phosphate group and a nitrogenous base (purine or pyrimidine).

65. **(A)** Since a spherical cell has a larger volume in relation to its outer boundary, it is especially suited for the storage of food.

66. **(A)** The time of flowering of many plants is keyed to the lengths of darkness and light to which they are exposed. Short-day plants bloom in the spring and fall, whereas long-day ones bloom in the summer.

67. **(A)** Although all are mammals, the monotremes are the primitive, egg-laying mammals restricted to Australia and New Guinea.

68. **(C)** Sucrose is a disaccharide sugar that is digested to the monosaccharides glucose and fructose.

69. **(D)** As cells differentiate to become skeletal muscle cells, their smooth endoplasmic reticulum takes on the proper configuration to function as sarcoplasmic reticulum. As such, this set of membranous bags controls the distribution of calcium, which is necessary for muscle contraction.

70. **(C)** The pathway is known as the hepatic portal system. The vein leaving the intestine breaks up into capillaries in the liver. The capillaries then reunite into hepatic veins that enter the inferior vena cava.

71. **(B)** The word *synapsis* is often confused with *synapse*, which is the gap over which an impulse travels between two neurons (or between neuron and muscle or other organ).

72. **(B)** The sperm enters the secondary oocyte (ordinarily called the egg), usually while it is in the Fallopian tube (oviduct). The so-called egg is not really an egg until all polar bodies form.

73. **(A)** Unspecialized limbs terminate in five digits. Any divergence from that pattern, which is present in the early embryo, is specialization. The human foot retains the five-digit pattern in the adult. The elephant's trunk is certainly a specialized adaptation of the nose, just as the human brain is an extreme development of a brain.

74. **(A)** Sea water with a salinity of 3.5% is hypertonic to body tissues, meaning that it contains less water (and more solute molecules) than the tissues. A 0.85% solution of sodium chloride or a 5% solution of glucose is approximately isotonic to human cells. Since isotonic solutions have the same concentration of osmotically active particles as the cells, there is no net movement of water into and out of them. Since sea water would have fewer water molecules than the tissues, the net movement of water would be from the tissues to the sea water in the digestive tract.

75. **(E)** A submaxillary gland is but one of several salivary glands that serve primarily to lubricate food for easy swallowing.

76. **(B)** Electrophoresis produces differential migration of molecules according to their net charges. Dialysis, ultracentrifugation, and gel exclusion chromotography all effect separations based on size and shape but not charge. Spectrophotometry can analyze molecular characteristics but is not a separation method.

77. **(E)** When a plant is abnormally hot or dry during daylight, it closes many of its stomata but continues some photosynthesis. This leads to buildup of the waste product oxygen. Excess oxygen can then begin to replace carbon dioxide in the Calvin cycle. The photorespiration reactions that follow are very inefficient since neither ATP nor carbohydrate is produced.

78. **(D)** The chromosome is composed of DNA and proteins. In shape, the chromosome is cordlike. It is not membrane-bound.

79. **(D)** The pollen grain is in reality the microgametophyte; the embryo sac, the megagametophyte. The pollen grain originates from a microspore, and the embryo sac from a megaspore.

80. **(E)** The chromatophores are specialized pigment cells that have irregular shapes and branching processes. In shape, they resemble some amoebas. There are different types containing different pigments. The stimulus to change color comes through the eyes and causes nervous and hormonal changes that regulate the chromatophores.

81. **(B)** Structural and functional defects in the fetus are sometimes produced if rubella is contracted during the first 3 months of pregnancy.

82. **(C)** Many different cancer-causing genes have been found. These oncogenes are either modified from normal genes (proto-oncogenes) or are normal genes whose product should be made only in specific parts of the life cycle (such as in embryonic stages). If such genes make an abnormal product or make a normal embryonic product in postembryonic times, the result can be a cancerous cell.

83. **(C)** Any variation from 46 produces abnormal results. At one time biologists thought the normal number was 48.

84. **(D)** The blastodisc does not develop into a hollow ball of equal cells because the egg is very asymmetrical due to the presence of a great deal of yolk. In either case, this stage immediately precedes the formation of germ layers.

85. **(B)** Homologous structures have the same embryological origin regardless of how different they appear as a result of later modification. Humans and bats are both mammals, and their arms and wings are forelimbs specialized for specific needs.

86. **(B)** While Alfred Russel Wallace was in Malaya, he sent Darwin a paper on the subject of evolution, asking him to forward the paper to Lyell, a famous geologist of that day. To the surprise of Darwin, Wallace's views were strikingly similar to his own. At first Darwin was ready to grant priority for the idea to Wallace, but another scientist arranged to have a joint presentation of their papers in which they expressed their views on the subject of natural selection.

87. **(B)** All but the lung and coronary artery are connected directly to each other and function together. The lung is a part of the respiratory system, whereas the coronary artery is a part of the circulatory system.

88. **(A)** The dendrite of a sensory neuron is connected with peripheral areas, and its axon synapses with another neuron in the spinal cord. The cell body, from which dendrite and axon extend, is located in the dorsal root ganglion.

89. **(A)** Also known as ascorbic acid.

90. **(B)** Just as with a home or an automobile radiator, heat loss is directly related to an organism's exposed surface area.

91. **(C)** A typical growth curve is sigmoid and resembles the letter S. Growth starts slowly, with few individuals. The population then enters a phase of logarithmic increase. When one or more environmental resources becomes scarce, the curve levels.

92. **(D)** In humans the death rate sharply increases in old age.

93. **(B)** When a variable characteristic in a large population is plotted, the graph is usually bell-shaped.

94. **(A)** Unlike humans, most fishes die when they are very young.

95. **(B)** Biomes are communities having large geographical dimensions where relatively uniform climatic conditions prevail. The characteristic life form of the dominant vegetation is of course related to the climate conditions: for example, deciduous forest to areas where there are distinct growing and dormant seasons, and grassland where precipitation is too low to support trees.

96. **(E)** A mutation is a single event occurring in a single cell of a single organism. Therefore, it affects that individual immediately and most profoundly.

97. **(A)** By definition, an ecosystem is a more or less self-contained community of organisms together with the environment in which it lives.

98. **(D)** A population is all of the individuals of a species or all members of the same species in a particular location. Being so closely related, they can interbreed.

99. **(D)** The first three contain a mixture of plants and animals. A population is all of one species, plant or animal.

100. **(A)** As long as the system is self-sustaining, it is an ecosystem no matter what its size.

101. **(B)** Deserts are characterized by rather evenly and widely spaced plants. The plants are similar in having adaptations to conserve water, a necessary prerequisite to survival in extremely dry environments.

102. **(D)** Because of hydrogen bonds between its molecules, water resists pressure from the legs of insects. Therefore, they can walk across its surface.

103. **(E)** As water freezes, its individual molecules spread apart. Ice therefore is less dense than liquid water and floats, allowing life to continue in ponds and streams.

104. **(B)** The sweating of humans and panting of dogs constitute a cooling mechanism that results from the fact that water takes up an unusually large amount of energy (heat) as it evaporates.

105. **(C)** Large lakes act as reservoirs of heat during summer, slowly losing it to the atmosphere in winter.

106. **(A)** The term *active site* refers to the portion of an enzyme that makes contact with a substrate. Change of this region's shape by attachment of some other material elsewhere on the enzyme will inhibit enzymatic activity.

107. **(D)** By definition, a substrate is a molecule that is changed in a reaction catalyzed by an enzyme.

108. **(B)** Some proteins are inactive until a nonprotein group is added. An example is hemoglobin, whose prosthetic groups are iron-containing heme.

109. **(E)** This is a definition of vitamins.

110. **(E)** M. Schleiden, in 1838, decided that all plants are composed of cells. T. Schwann made a similar statement about animals in the next year.

111. **(B)** The organelle is called the Golgi body or apparatus in his honor.

112. **(A)** Francis Crick shared a Nobel Prize with James Watson and Maurice Wilkins for their work on the structure of DNA. He also studied the mechanism of the translation process, whereby the message of the gene is "read" to produce a polypeptide.

113. **(C)** R. Koch's protocol for proving the bacterial basis for tuberculosis has been extended for use with any living disease-causing agent.

114. **(D)** Louis Pasteur showed that a ravaging disease in silkworms was caused by a bacterium, shortly before Koch did the same with sheep anthrax and human tuberculosis.

115. **(D)** Pasteur devised an elegant test that proved the continued sterility of a broth as long as it was sealed away from contact with airborne bacteria.

116. **(A)** Condenser lenses focus light on the object to be viewed.

117. **(C)** A light microscope's illuminator provides light; the equivalent in an electron microscope is the electron source, which sends a beam of electrons toward the object to be viewed. The advantage of using electrons is that their shorter wavelength dramatically improves resolution.

118. **(E)** Resolving power increases directly with the index of refraction of the lenses within the objective, and inversely with the wavelength of energy striking the material to be viewed. An indirect expression of the index of refraction is the numerical aperture value displayed on each objective of a microscope.

119. **(C)** A bird's gizzard contains swallowed sand, stones, and other objects that grind food before it reaches the intestinal tract.

120. **(A)** Also known as the large intestine, the colon reabsorbs much of the water added at more anterior regions of the digestive tract, a vital function for animals living on dry land.

121. **(E)** The stomach of a ruminant such as a cow secretes the milk-digesting enzyme rennin. It is an error to state that humans produce this enzyme, or to confuse it with a kidney hormone of similar name, renin.

122. **(D)** Most enzymatic breakdown of food occurs in the small intestine. Digestive enzymes may be swept into the colon and remain active there.

123. **(B)** The gallbladder, a bag on the liver's surface, collects and stores bile. Principal components of bile are bile salts that break down large globules of fat in the intestine. Bile is delivered to the intestine by a small tube, the bile duct.

124. **(E)** The point of attachment between tRNA and its matching amino acid is on the end of the tRNA that consists of three nucleotides symbolized as CCA.

125. **(A)** The only organelle in the list, endoplasmic reticulum is a membranous network to which ribosomes can attach. Translation, or protein synthesis, can occur at these ribosomes. Generally, proteins that are going to be exported from the cell via vesicles will be formed on ribosomes that are attached to the endoplasmic reticulum; other proteins for use within the cell's cytoplasm are produced on free-floating ribosomes.

126. **(D)** The word *transcription* describes the process of forming RNA under the direction of DNA.

127. **(B)** The only RNA whose structure includes a sequence of codons that specify amino acid sequence is messenger RNA.

128. **(C)** Translation is the process of building a protein or a portion of a protein. Endoplasmic reticulum, being a membranous material, contains both protein and phospholipid.

129. **(E)** Let C symbolize the allele for cleft chin, and c symbolize the allele for lack of the cleft feature. If the man is cleft-chinned, he must have the C allele. If he is homozygous, his genotype is CC. His wife, lacking the feature, must be cc. All of their children must therefore have one allele from each parent and be Cc. Since C is dominant, a Cc individual will have the cleft.

130. **(D)** Let T symbolize the allele for normal, and t symbolize the allele for Tay-Sachs disease. Each parent, being heterozygous, has the genotype Tt. For each mating, the possible outcomes are diagrammed below.

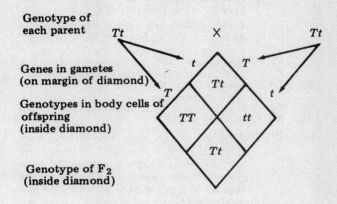

Cross between two heterozygotes for Tay-Sachs disease
Since two of every four offspring are expected to be Tt, the probability of any child being Tt (heterozygous) is 1/2, or .50.

131. **(B)** If the two genes are unlinked, this mating is the classical dihybrid cross first performed by Mendel. The analysis is as follows:

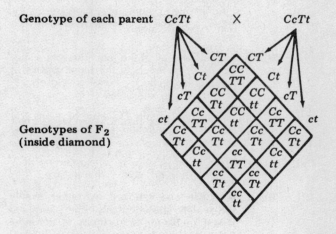

Cross between two double heterozygotes
The genotype we are seeking is ccTt. It occurs in two of the sixteen boxes, indicating a 2/16 or .125 probability at each mating. If the two genes had been linked (on the same chromosome), they would not have assorted independently and the constitution of the next generation would be unpredictable, depending on the frequency of crossing-over between the genes.

132. **(A)** Thylakoids are membranous flattened bags within chloroplasts. The "light reactions" of photosynthesis occur here.

133. **(C)** A basal body is a centriolelike object at the base of each flagellum or cilium. As with

centrioles, it is composed of microtubules in nine groups, forming a hollow cylinder.

134. **(B)** Microfilaments are composed of actin, the same protein important in muscle contraction. Although the mechanism is not yet known, these threadlike structures are associated with contraction or drawing together of cell regions, such as forming the cleavage furrow during the telophase of mitosis.

135. **(D)** Lysosomes are small bags containing digestive enzymes.

136. **(C)** A cross section of a cilium reveals an intricate pattern of microtubules, with nine pairs arranged concentrically around two individual central ones.

137. **(C)** Genetic dwarfs grow to normal size when treated with gibberellin.

138. **(E)** Photoperiodism, the response of a plant to changes in the 24-hour light-dark cycle, is mediated by a pigment called phytochrome. It changes its form when struck by light, then influences the plant's functions while in the altered state.

139. **(D)** Fruit growers use ethylene to ripen fruits that were picked while yet green.

140. **(B)** Working with auxin, cytokinin causes rapid production of new cells. Plant cells isolated in culture undergo mitosis when treated with cytokinin alone.

141. **(A)** Fritz Went, in 1926, discovered the hormonal nature of a plant's bending toward light. The class of compounds that can induce the response is auxins.

142. **(A)** While not the only auxin, IAA is the most commonly found naturally produced auxin.

143. **(A)** The clonal selection model is an alternative to the instruction model, both of which are concerned with the method by which a newly introduced antigen elicits copious production of a specifically reacting antibody. The clonal selection model states that the body contains tiny groups of cells, each capable of producing a different type of antibody. Contact with an antigen causes rapid mitosis of the appropriate cell type to form a large clone of productive cells.

144. **(C)** The image of actin filaments sliding over myosin filaments during contraction of skeletal muscle was first devised by H. E. Huxley and others in the mid-1950s.

145. **(B)** The competitive exclusion principle, also known as Gause's principle, states that, if two or more species of organism with overlapping ranges compete for some portion of the ecosystem, one will eventually gain in numbers as the other(s) declines.

146. **(D)** Lamarck and others proposed a mechanism for evolution that involves the transfer from parent to offspring of structural or functional characteristics that are acquired by the parent during its lifetime.

147. **(E)** The hypothesis involves the formation of an organism solely from nonliving materials. Biochemists believe that present earth conditions do not allow this, but that primitive earth conditions may have been conducive to this series of events.

148. **(B)** Charles Darwin culminated 20 years of study with his landmark book *On the Origin of Species* in 1859. He died in 1882.

149. **(E)** A. I. Oparin, a Russian biochemist, has written persuasively on the origins of living organisms from nonliving materials in a primitive earth setting.

150. **(B)** Darwin spent several years studying the way earthworms condition soil for optimal plant growth. With his son, he was the first to investigate the bending of plant stems toward light.

151. **(C)** Konrad Lorenz, an outstanding student of behavior, has contributed to our understanding of the type of learning shown by hatchling birds when they follow the first moving object they see.

152. **(D)** T. H. Morgan used white-eyed fruit flies as models to elucidate the inheritance of genes located on the sex chromosome.

153. **(A)** An important clue used by Watson and Crick in formulating the structure of DNA was Chargaff's data showing that the total number of DNA adenines equals the number of thymines. The same holds true for the cytosine-guanine pair.

154. **(E)** Uracil is found only within RNA.

155. **(A)** For each amino acid, there is a specific enzyme that recognizes the correct tRNA for it and catalyzes the attachment of one to the other.

156. **(B)** The specific base-pairing that occurs between the three bases of a messenger RNA's codon and the three bases of a transfer RNA's anticodon is a temporary but crucial linkage during protein synthesis.

157. **(C)** DNA polymerase catalyzes the formation of polynucleotide DNA.

158. **(E)** Transcription is the process of forming RNA. According to the rules of base-pairing, adenine can temporarily bond with thymine or uracil, but only uracil can be incorporated into RNA.

159. **(D)** Thymine, whose atoms are arranged properly to hydrogen-bond with certain atoms of adenine, is incorporated into DNA as it replicates.

160. **(B)** The mammalian cerebral cortex controls many other brain regions, taking responsibility for functions that these other regions control in nonmammalian vertebrates.

161. **(A)** Damage to the cerebellum results in loss of ability to make proper muscular responses to sensory input.

162. **(E)** The medulla is the most posterior region of the brain and merges imperceptibly with the spinal cord.

163. **(C)** The ventral outgrowth of the hypothalamus is the posterior pituitary, which produces hormones that travel the short distance to the anterior pituitary. The latter responds by releasing its own hormones, which have profound influence over several other glands of the body.

164. **(C)** It has been shown that the continents are slowly moving apart. By extrapolation, some of them seem to have once been connected. This correlates with the presence of closely related organisms on now-separated continents.

165. **(B)** Rocks formed during the Cambrian period (nearly 600 million years ago) contain many more fossils than do earlier rocks, including all of the phyla presently known.

166. **(E)** Many cell biologists believe that mitochondria and plastids were once free-living prokaryotes and that their presence in modern cells originated as a symbiotic relationship. The presence of genetic material in these organelles tends to lend credence to the theory.

167. **(A)** Adaptive radiation is evolution of two or more specialized species from a single less specialized species. Each of the resulting species is adapted to fit a particular niche. Natural selection is the most powerful means of achieving such change.

168. **(D)** Mechanisms exist which tend to ensure that more than one allele of a gene will remain represented in a population from generation to generation. This balanced polymorphism enables a population to be more likely to respond successfully to environmental changes by having some individuals whose phenotypes are a good match for new conditions.

169. **(A)** Expansion of $(p + q)^2 = 1$ gives three expressions that correspond to the three possible genotypes when a two-allele system is under scrutiny.

170. **(A)** Expansion of the equation yields $p^2 + 2pq + q^2 = 1$. If p is the frequency of the dominant allele and q is the frequency of the recessive allele, $p + q = 1$. The value for q is derived by taking the square root of q^2, which represents the frequency of the homozygous recessive individuals. Since one fourth of the population is homozygous recessive, $q^2 = 0.25$ and $q = 0.5$. The value for p must be 0.5 also, since $p = 1 - q$. The expression in the expansion which gives the expected frequency of homozygous dominant individuals is p^2. Therefore,

this value is $(0.5)^2 = 0.25$. In a total population of 400, this would be 100 individuals.

171. **(E)** Natural selection is a potent force that will upset the equilibrium and render the mathematical prediction invalid. Among other forces capable of this are genetic drift in a small population, mutation, and migration.

172. **(A)** A testcross will produce offspring whose phenotypic ratios will show whether the parent with the dominant phenotype is homozygous or heterozygous. If homozygous dominant, all offspring will have the dominant phenotype; if heterozygous, only one half of them will be of this appearance.

173. **(E)** G. H. Hardy and W. Weinberg, working independently in 1908, derived the mathematical expression for genotype frequencies in a population.

174. **(E)** Equilibrium is attainment of a genetic steady state, regardless of the nature of the forces operating within the population.

175. **(C)** The graph shows much absorbance at around 550 nm, meaning that yellow-green light enters the membrane but does not leave it. The 350–450 nm range of light does leave the membrane and is available to strike our eyes. We perceive these wavelengths as violet. The range above 650 nm, also not absorbed, is perceived as red.

176. **(C)** Another striking example is the presence of leghemoglobin, very similar in structure to vertebrate animals' hemoglobin, in certain plants. Fossils of bacteria far predate those of vertebrate animals.

177. **(A)** The chemiosmotic model of oxidative phosphorylation was proposed by P. Mitchell, who received a Nobel Prize in 1978 for this work. According to the model, the mitochondrial membrane pumps out hydrogen ions and then allows them to reenter the mitochondrion by diffusion at specific sites. The energy of their inward flow is used to produce the high-energy phosphate bond of ATP.

178. **(A)** The 280 nm peak of the graph is evidence of absorption by two aromatic amino acids —tryptophan and tyrosine—found in nearly every protein. This distinctive absorption peak is a good indicator of a protein portion in the purified purple membrane molecule.

179. **(A)** The same effect can be mimicked by voltage change imposed by other means than sodium flow.

180. **(B)** The cortical granules are already in place just under the egg membrane well before sperm contact. Under normal conditions, the sperm-egg contact initiates (indirectly) granule bursting, not forming.

181. **(B)** Evidence for this is provided by observation of both cortical granule bursting and mitosis upon treatment of an unfertilized egg with ionophores, which increase the intracellular calcium concentration.

182. **(A)** Amiloride makes the egg membrane impermeable to sodium and also blocks normal postfertilization events, including mitosis.

183. **(B)** Polyspermy leads to greater than a diploid number of chromosomes in the cell. If the zygote continues to develop, this can lead to distribution problems during cell reproduction.

184. **(B)** Although the embryology of sea urchins certainly differs in some ways from that of other animals, it continues to be a valuable model system. Because sea urchin fertilization occurs in open water rather than in the body of the female, it is currently better understood than vertebrate fertilization. Recent *in vitro* fertilization work with humans may soon change this.

185. **(B)** The article states that ionophores are drugs that mimic a component of sperm action by causing release of calcium from depots in the egg. Ionophores are not present during natural fertilization.

186. **(E)** Look, for example, at the percentage saturation of both molecules when in a 20 mm O_2 environment. Myoglobin is carrying about 60% as much O_2 as it could in a maximum-O_2 environment, and hemoglobin is carrying only about 20% as much O_2 as it could.

187. **(C)** Any population is likely to start growing slowly, then accelerate to maximum growth. If it meets some environmental limitation, such as amount of available space, its growth rate drops to zero and the population size remains constant. The population therefore describes the same S-shaped curve as the hemoglobin curve shown here.

188. **(E)** Because of the different behaviors of the proteins at low-oxygen areas (such as actively metabolizing muscles), a release-acceptance sequence will occur in the proper direction. If the two proteins were reversed in position, myoglobin would efficiently pick up O_2 at the lungs, but would fail to drop off a useful amount near the muscles. The O_2 that was released would not be picked up efficiently by hemoglobin if the latter were in muscles.

189. **(D)** Although worms are not closely related to humans, some of our cells have a similar O_2 environment to that of these worms: they both need to have O_2-accepting molecules that work in an area low in O_2.

190. **(E)** Small mammals have a high surface area-to-volume ratio, which leads to much loss of energy as heat radiation. To maintain optimal internal temperature, small mammals must run their metabolic processes at a high rate. Thus, they need hemoglobin that will release a large percentage of its O_2 at a given low-O_2 area.

191. **(E)** This is clearly stated in the paragraph.

192. **(B)** Although the offspring do not fall exactly into 1:1:1:1 ratio, they approximate this and give a reasonable clue to the inheritance pattern. If the gene is sex-linked, it may be assumed that it is located on the Z chromosome and that the cross would be:

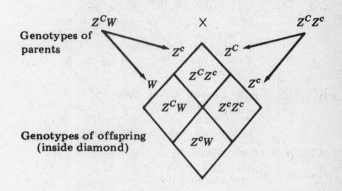

Cross involving sex-linkage
Predicted phenotypes of these offspring, in a 1:1:1:1 ratio, would be green males, cinnamon males, green females, and cinnamon females.
Here is the same cross if the gene were autosomal:

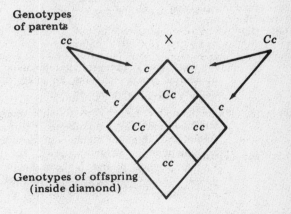

Cross involving autosomal gene
The phenotypes of these offspring would be cinnamon or green in a 1:1 ratio. Each category would include males and females in a 1:1 ratio, so the same 1:1:1:1 ratio would occur as is predicted for sex linkage.

193. **(D)** A pleiotropic gene is one that expresses itself in more than one phenotypic characteristic.

194. **(D)** A sex-linked gene is almost always carried on only one of the two different sex chromosomes. A heterozygote is an organism with two alleles of a gene in each of its cells.

Since only male canaries have two copies of the same sex chromosome, they alone could be heterozygous.

195. **(A)** If the mode of inheritance is by sex-linkage, all males of such a cross should be green. If it is an autosomal gene that is involved, one fourth of the males should be cinnamon.

If sex-linked:

If sex-linked:

Genotypes of parents

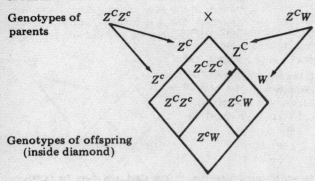

Genotypes of offspring (inside diamond)

If autosomal:

If autosomal:

Genotypes of parents

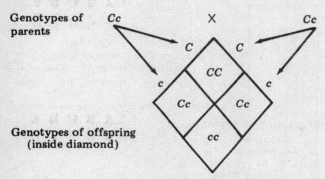

Genotypes of offspring (inside diamond)

Here, each block represents the genotype of males and females so some *cc* males (cinnamon) would be expected.

196. **(B)** Examination of Table 1 shows that regions with the same number of amino acids have significantly different numbers of those that are identical in all five species. For instance, regions *B* and *D* both have 15 amino acids, but *B* is identical at 9 of its sites while *D* is identical at only 5 of its sites.

197. **(D)** From Table 2, region *D* of tuna has no amino acids in identical positions with all five bacterial species. In each other region, at least one position has the same amino acid in all reported species.

198. **(B)** One can use either Table 1 or Table 2 to find that region *B* has 9 of its 15 positions occupied by the same amino acid in all bacteria. None of the other regions has as much as this 60% correspondence.

199. **(B)** All respiring organisms rely upon cytochromes for the essential activity of oxidative phosphorylation (production of ATP

with the aid of an electron transport system). Although some regions of cytochrome c are apparently not essential to its proper functioning, others are. These are the areas that are quite similar in most studied species regardless of their taxonomic distance.

200. **(B)** Although the bacteria are known to be attracted to oxygen, and oxygen-producing photosynthesis is most rapid in areas struck by violet and red light, one cannot rule out the possibility that the bacteria are also capable of discriminating among various types of light and moving preferentially toward some.

201. **(C)** If the alga were kept in the dark, where photosynthesis could not occur to produce an unequal distribution of oxygen, the bacteria would disperse in the uniform environment.

202. **(E)** Removal of the ability to produce oxygen by chemical poisoning of the bacteria's Photochemical System II, the portion of the photosynthesis apparatus that splits water to produce O_2, would help determine whether the bacteria are attracted by both O_2 and light.

203. **(A)** Although developmental maturation of an instinctive behavior cannot be ruled out, the gradual change of an activity as it is repeated is usually indicative of learning.

204. **(B)** The chick can recognize the mother's bill as an appropriate cue from the first day of its life, an indicator of genetically determined behavior, or instinct.

205. **(B)** Careful observation and appropriate manipulation of the environment can distinguish between instinct and learning. Behavior that at first seems to be purely instinctive often is proven to be susceptible to some modification by learning, as is the case here.

206. **(C)** The best way to test the role of vision in pecking accuracy is to alter the total time the chicks have to use their vision before they reach adulthood.

207. **(E)** A typical population growth curve is described as an S curve, and both curves *A* and *B* are of that pattern. If you had chosen either answer A or C, you would have implied that the other one was wrong.

208. **(D)** Species *A* when mixed is smaller than *A* alone, and species *B* when mixed is smaller than *B* alone.

209. **(D)** Gause's principle states that, when two species compete for the same resource, one species will eliminate the other.

210. **(D)** Population curves of the mixed cultures are the second and fourth from the top. Population *A* plus *B* is at first smaller than *A* alone; however, it is increasing at the expense of *B*. Population *B* plus *A* is almost from the beginning less than population *B* alone, and it steadily decreases until extinction.

Test in Biology

Sample Test 3

Directions for Taking Test: This sample test contains 210 questions or incomplete statements, and should be finished in 170 minutes. Each item will have five possible answers or completions. Choose the best and blacken its letter in the place provided. After finishing, you may determine your score by using the **Answer Key** at the end of this test. The Answer Key also contains comments and explanations that should clarify the concepts involved in each question.

Questions 1—90

For each of the following questions or incomplete statements there are five suggested answers or completions. Select the best choice.

1. In mature mammals, cells are very actively dividing in the
   A. muscles
   B. brain
   C. liver
   D. bone marrow
   E. kidney

   1. A B C D E

2. Which answer is the most accurate description of transpiration in plants?
   A. necessary for lifting water to leaves
   B. necessary for cooling plant
   C. mechanism for eliminating waste
   D. harmful, with no benefit
   E. potentially harmful, but unavoidable

   2. A B C D E

3. Any animal having gill slits or pouches, a notochord, and a dorsally located central nervous system will always be classified as a
   A. chordate
   B. vertebrate
   C. mammal
   D. bird
   E. fish

   3. A B C D E

4. Of the following, which is an effector?
   A. motor neuron
   B. sensory neuron
   C. brain
   D. gland
   E. reflex

   4. A B C D E

5. Crossing-over is a familiar term for
   A. hybridization
   B. migration across difficult geographical barriers
   C. interchange of sections of chromatids
   D. diffusion from one side of a membrane to the other
   E. pollination involving separate flowers, male and female

   5. A B C D E
      || || || || ||

6. Many birds claim and defend an area known as the
   A. domain
   B. field claim
   C. niche
   D. combat zone
   E. territory

   6. A B C D E
      || || || || ||

7. Water remaining in the soil after a plant has permanently wilted is
   A. groundwater
   B. hygroscopic water
   C. capillary water
   D. gravitational water
   E. field capacity

   7. A B C D E
      || || || || ||

8. Which gland serves a function other than endocrinal?
   A. thyroid
   B. pancreas
   C. parathyroid
   D. pituitary
   E. adrenal

   8. A B C D E
      || || || || ||

9. Natural systems of classification are based on
   A. body form
   B. environmental adaptations
   C. kinship
   D. community associations
   E. food relationships

   9. A B C D E
      || || || || ||

10. Tying a paper bag over the silks of an ear of corn would immediately interfere with
    A. growth of the entire plant
    B. germination
    C. pollination
    D. ovulation
    E. translocation

    10. A B C D E
        || || || || ||

11. DNA is known to be duplicated in
    A. interphase
    B. prophase
    C. metaphase
    D. anaphase
    E. telophase

    11. A B C D E
        || || || || ||

12. The pit organ of a pit viper is a
    A. thermal detector
    B. balancing organ
    C. scent gland
    D. seminal vesicle
    E. vestigial ear

    12. A B C D E
        || || || || ||

13. The heart is four-chambered in all of the following EXCEPT the
    A. kangaroo
    B. chicken
    C. dog
    D. bat
    E. frog

    13. A B C D E
        || || || || ||

14. Which cavity is found in adult insects?
    A. atrium
    B. archenteron
    C. pseudocoel
    D. hemocoel
    E. blastocoel

    14. A B C D E
        || || || || ||

15. Organisms using carbon dioxide as the only carbon source are termed
    A. autotrophic
    B. heterotrophic
    C. autoecious
    D. deliquescent
    E. haustorial

    15. A B C D E
        || || || || ||

16. The immediate source of energy for muscular contraction is
    A. ADP
    B. ATP
    C. actomyosin
    D. glycogen
    E. sucrose

    16. A B C D E
        || || || || ||

17. Generally gametes are derived by reduction division of cells that are
    A. haploid
    B. diploid
    C. triploid
    D. tetraploid
    E. pentaploid

    17. A B C D E
        || || || || ||

18. The fetus is most closely surrounded by the
    A. amnion
    B. allantois
    C. yolk sac
    D. chorion
    E. placenta

    18. A B C D E
        || || || || ||

19. Suppose that flower color is determined by a single pair of genes and that it is a case of incomplete dominance. The genotype resulting from a cross between a homozygous red *(RR)* and a homozygous white *(rr)* will be

A. red
B. white
C. *RR*
D. *Rr*
E. *rr*

19. A B C D E

20. The natural flora of Australia is particularly distinct from that of other continents because

A. most of the continent is a desert
B. it is the only continent totally within the southern hemisphere
C. it has been separated from other continental masses for a longer period of time
D. it is smaller than other continents
E. it is the youngest continent

20. A B C D E

21. The best example of secondary succession is the consecutive changes from

A. bare rock to mat of lichens and mosses
B. mat of lichens and mosses to forest
C. lake to bog
D. bog to forest
E. abandoned field to forest

21. A B C D E

22. Benthic organisms CANNOT live in the

A. littoral zone
B. bathyal zone
C. profundal zone
D. abyssal zone
E. pelagic zone

22. A B C D E

23. Haversian canals are located in the

A. inner ear
B. bones
C. brain
D. capsule of lymphoid organs
E. water-vascular system of echinoderms

23. A B C D E

24. The loss of which organ would be of LEAST consequence to humans?

A. spleen
B. liver
C. pancreas
D. pituitary
E. diaphragm

24. A B C D E

25. The zona pellucida is located

A. beneath the cerebral hemispheres
B. between seed coat and endosperm
C. around some colonies of molds growing on agar
D. at the junction of dermis and epidermis of skin
E. around a mammalian egg

25. A B C D E

26. Plant cells in the process of mitosis are found in the
  A. root cap
  B. meristem
  C. region of elongation
  D. primary phloem
  E. primary xylem

26. A B C D E
    || || || || ||

27. Mycorrhizae grow best in
  A. water
  B. soil
  C. snails
  D. bacteria
  E. fruits

27. A B C D E
    || || || || ||

28. Bacteriophages are
  A. gram-positive bacteria
  B. gram-negative bacteria
  C. viruses
  D. rickettsiae
  E. actinomycetes

28. A B C D E
    || || || || ||

29. One would look for spiracles of insects
  A. on the abdomen
  B. In the heart
  C. between the crop and stomach
  D. on the metathoracic leg
  E. in Malpighian tubes

29. A B C D E
    || || || || ||

30. Light energy used in photosynthesis is first captured by
  A. chlorophyll
  B. water
  C. carbon dioxide
  D. PGA
  E. ATP

30. A B C D E
    || || || || ||

31. Fibrinogen and prothrombin, both necessary for the clotting of blood, are located in
  A. erythrocytes
  B. granulocytes
  C. lymphocytes
  D. platelets
  E. plasma

31. A B C D E
    || || || || ||

32. Chemiosmosis occurs in both mitochondria and
  A. chloroplasts
  B. Golgi complexes
  C. microtubules
  D. nucleoli
  E. nucleosomes

32. A B C D E
    || || || || ||

33. The placenta in humans is derived from the
   A. amnion
   B. chorion
   C. chorion and uterus
   D. endometrium of uterus
   E. umbilical cord

33. A B C D E

34. Children of a color-blind mother and a normal father would be
   A. females normal; males color-blind
   B. females normal, but carriers; males color-blind
   C. females color-blind; males color-blind
   D. females color-blind; males normal
   E. females normal, but carriers; males normal

34. A B C D E

35. A climax community is recognizable because it is
   A. highly productive
   B. composed of trees
   C. uniform in composition
   D. not replaced by another community
   E. dying out

35. A B C D E

36. Organisms descending from a common ancestor by asexual propagation belong to the same
   A. cline
   B. clone
   C. placebo
   D. syndrome
   E. pride

36. A B C D E

37. Birds are unlike reptiles in having
   A. eggs covered with shells
   B. body scales
   C. nucleated red corpuscles
   D. constant body temperatures
   E. one occipital condyle

37. A B C D E

38. The clitellum of the earthworm is useful in
   A. excretion
   B. reproduction
   C. locomotion
   D. respiration
   E. circulation

38. A B C D E

39. Which of the following pigments is important in hydrogen transfer (electron transport)?
   A. phycoerythrin
   B. hemocyanin
   C. carmine
   D. safranine
   E. cytochrome

39. A B C D E

40. Which term is used in embryology for the change of position of cells as they move over the surface of a growing embryo?

    A. epiboly

    B. integration

    C. invagination

    D. evagination

    E. aggregation

40. A B C D E
  || || || || ||

41. Alternate forms of a gene at the same locus are called

    A. homologues

    B. alleles

    C. gametes

    D. difactors

    E. associates

41. A B C D E
  || || || || ||

42. Hydroponics deals with

    A. desalinating water

    B. growing plants in water

    C. controlling pollution of streams

    D. migration of aquatic animals

    E. experimenting with plankton for food

42. A B C D E
  || || || || ||

43. The approximate number of amino acids from which all proteins are constructed is

    A. 8

    B. 12

    C. 16

    D. 20

    E. 64

43. A B C D E
  || || || || ||

44. The unit most useful for measuring the diameter of a typical cell is the

    A. milliliter

    B. curie

    C. roentgen

    D. erg

    E. micrometer

44. A B C D E
  || || || || ||

45. Gymnosperms differ from angiosperms in having

    A. wind pollination

    B. seeds unenclosed in fruits

    C. needle or scalelike leaves

    D. no cotyledons

    E. embryo sacs

45. A B C D E
  || || || || ||

46. Scientists who anticipate disastrous environmental changes due to a "greenhouse effect" believe that it will occur because of
A. fluorocarbons that will destroy the ozone layer
B. increasing atmospheric dust from volcanic activity and from expanding agriculture
C. new pollutants photochemically produced in the upper atmosphere
D. burning of fossil fuels that will increase carbon dioxide concentration in the upper atmosphere
E. destruction of tropical rain forests, changing worldwide weather patterns

47. The primary function of the stomach is the
A. digestion of food
B. temporary storage of food
C. absorption of food
D. absorption of water
E. alkalization of food mixture

47. A B C D E

48. Of the following statements about bile, which is correct?
A. makes contents of small intestine acidic
B. activates lipase
C. stimulates flow of gastric juices
D. emulsifies fats
E. is enzymatic

48. A B C D E

49. Discovery of the circulation of blood in humans is credited to
A. Aristotle
B. Galen
C. Harvey
D. Malpighi
E. Oparin

49. A B C D E

50. Movement of molecules across a living membrane against a concentration gradient and requiring the expenditure of energy is known as
A. plasmolysis
B. Brownian movement
C. cyclosis
D. active transport
E. capillary action

50. A B C D E

51. During mammalian ovulation, eggs are released into the
A. ovarian tubules
B. body cavity
C. Fallopian tube
D. uterus
E. Graafian follicle

51. A B C D E

52. The gene pool is the aggregate of all of the kinds of genes in
A. a hybrid
B. a free-breeding population
C. a community of organisms
D. autosomes
E. all living organisms

52. A B C D E

53. Divergent evolution is illustrated by
    A. human and whale
    B. fish and whale
    C. cactus and succulent euphorbia
    D. bird and bat
    E. mole cricket and mole

54. Which of the following is a biome?
    A. patch of weeds
    B. bed of oysters
    C. field of corn
    D. deciduous forest
    E. balanced aquarium

55. Population explosions of small organisms in lakes result in a visual aspect called
    A. congestion
    B. bloom
    C. climax
    D. neuston
    E. dominance

56. Ontogeny means
    A. embryology
    B. evolution
    C. biogenesis
    D. comparative anatomy
    E. endocrinology

57. Which of the following is NOT part of the ribonucleic acid molecule?
    A. adenine
    B. thymine
    C. uracil
    D. guanine
    E. cytosine

58. During meiosis, synapsis of homologous chromosomes occurs in
    A. anaphase
    B. interphase
    C. metaphase
    D. prophase
    E. telophase

59. Of the following which is NOT characteristic of blue-green algae?
    A. lack of organized nuclei
    B. lack of plastids
    C. lack of sexual reproduction
    D. lack of gelatinous secretions
    E. lack of roots, stems, or leaves

60. Which of the following is NOT an osmoregulatory structure?

A. flame cell
B. Malpighian tubule
C. antennary gland
D. nephridium
E. nematocyst

60. A B C D E
|| || || || ||

61. Carbohydrate digestion begins in the

A. mouth
B. esophagus
C. stomach
D. small intestine
E. large intestine

61. A B C D E
|| || || || ||

62. The unique characteristic of a portal circulatory system is that

A. it involves the liver
B. veins branch into capillaries
C. arteries branch into capillaries
D. it empties into the lymphatic system
E. it is a vestige of an aortic arch

62. A B C D E
|| || || || ||

63. The correct term for the outer layer of the gastrula is

A. skin
B. epithelium
C. epidermis
D. ectoderm
E. gastrodermis

63. A B C D E
|| || || || ||

64. A syrinx is an organ found only in

A. birds
B. fish
C. frogs
D. mammals
E. snakes

64. A B C D E
|| || || || ||

65. The ecological niche of an organism is its

A. way of life
B. habitat
C. place of hibernation
D. foraging area
E. defended territory

65. A B C D E
|| || || || ||

66. The time required for the decomposition of 50% of the atoms in an unstable isotope is its

A. stability rate
B. activity standard
C. decay time
D. half-life
E. recovery point

66. A B C D E
|| || || || ||

67. Wind-pollinated plants differ from insect-pollinated plants in having
    A. large petals and small quantities of pollen
    B. small petals and sticky pollen
    C. small, colored petals and heavy pollen
    D. colored petals and large pollen
    E. no petals and light pollen

    67. A B C D E
    || || || || ||

68. The blooming of violets in the spring and of morning-glories in the summer is related to their response to
    A. temperature
    B. other plants with which they are associated
    C. relative length of exposure to light and darkness
    D. the size of each plant at maturity
    E. available water

    68. A B C D E
    || || || || ||

69. The difference between an herbaceous stem and a woody stem is in the relative quantity of
    A. phloem
    B. xylem
    C. cortex
    D. vascular cambium
    E. cork

    69. A B C D E
    || || || || ||

70. Bubbles of gas generated by aquatic plants are
    A. methane
    B. carbon dioxide
    C. oxygen
    D. sulfur dioxide
    E. hydrogen sulfide

    70. A B C D E
    || || || || ||

71. The skeleton is to the human what the spicules are to the
    A. sponge
    B. chiton
    C. squid
    D. coral
    E. sand dollar

    71. A B C D E
    || || || || ||

72. Which of the following is responsible for digesting fats?
    A. lactase
    B. chymotrypsin
    C. amylase
    D. lipase
    E. pepsin

    72. A B C D E
    || || || || ||

73. During digestion, disaccharides are converted to monosaccharides by the chemical addition of
    A. water
    B. carbon dioxide
    C. oxygen
    D. nitrogen
    E. hydrogen

    73. A B C D E
    || || || || ||

74. Neuron is synonymous with

    A. ganglion

    B. nerve fiber

    C. nerve cell

    D. motor nerve

    E. sensory nerve

74. A B C D E

75. Human ovulation ordinarily occurs near what day after the start of menstruation?

    A. 1st

    B. 5th

    C. 8th

    D. 14th

    E. 20th

75. A B C D E

76. Of the following structures, which are analogous?

    A. sucking and chewing mouth parts of insects

    B. swim bladder of fish and lung of human

    C. nose of human and trunk of elephant

    D. wing of insect and wing of bird

    E. fingernail of human and hoof of horse

76. A B C D E

77. In the plant system of classification, *division* is equivalent to what category in the animal system?

    A. class

    B. family

    C. genus

    D. order

    E. phylum

77. A B C D E

78. Of the following, which is derived largely from the endoderm?

    A. brain

    B. liver

    C. skeletal muscles

    D. kidney

    E. heart

78. A B C D E

79. The blastopore of a frog embryo becomes the adult

    A. anus

    B. archenteron

    C. coelom

    D. mouth

    E. spinal cord

79. A B C D E

80. Which of these is evidence of gene control in eukaryotes?

    A. An insect's giant chromosome puff patterns change during development.

    B. Human DNA inserted into a bacterial plasmid can be transcribed in the bacterium.

    C. Insect giant chromosomes have predictable striped patterns.

    D. Mitosis faithfully duplicates genetic material.

    E. The lactose operon operates under inductive control.

80. A B C D E

81. The type of light that is most efficient in initiating photosynthesis is
   A. blue
   B. green
   C. infrared
   D. ultraviolet
   E. X-ray

82. The bulk ingestion of water containing dissolved materials by a cell is called
   A. active transport
   B. exocytosis
   C. osmosis
   D. phagocytosis
   E. pinocytosis

82. A B C D E

83. A cell organelle bounded by a double membrane is
   A. a centriole
   B. a microtubule
   C. a ribosome
   D. the Golgi body
   E. the nucleus

83. A B C D E

84. The special tissue for nourishing the seedlings of many seed plants is
   A. phloem
   B. endosperm
   C. endodermis
   D. pericarp
   E. tapetum

84. A B C D E

85. A molecule acting in photoreception is
   A. actinomycin D
   B. oxytocin
   C. pheromone
   D. rhodopsin
   E. serotonin

85. A B C D E

86. Which of these is NOT a necessary factor for natural selection to occur in a population?
   A. New mutations must occur within the population during the natural selection process.
   B. Organisms must reproduce.
   C. Some of the organisms must be able to reproduce in the environment more successfully than others.
   D. Some of the organisms must be different from others.
   E. The ecosystem must have some limiting factors for the population, ensuring that some of the organisms will not survive to the age of reproduction.

86. A B C D E

87. Which of these is a method used to isolate mutant bacteria?
   A. conjugation
   B. cross-over analysis
   C. recombinant DNA techniques
   D. replica plating
   E. streaking

87. A B C D E

88. Which of these is NOT produced because of the operation of the Krebs cycle?

   A. ATP

   B. reduced FAD

   C. CO_2

   D. pyruvic acid

   E. reduced nicotinamide adenine dinucleotide

88. A B C D E

89. What is a myelin sheath?

   A. membranes of Schwann cells wrapped tightly around an axon

   B. the coating over a seed's surface

   C. the outermost fibrous layer around the brain

   D. the protective membrane that forms over a fertilized egg

   E. the tough mantle of a squid

89. A B C D E

90. After ovulation, a mammalian ovary displays a corpus luteum. This is a

   A. blood-engorged wall into which the embryo can sink to obtain nourishment

   B. fertilized egg

   C. hormone responsible for maintenance of pregnancy

   D. region where the next egg will mature

   E. yellowish region at the site of egg release, capable of releasing progesterone

90. A B C D E

The next group of questions (91–95) is based on the series of numbered sketches with lettered parts. The series depicts maturation and fertilization of the egg of the roundworm *Ascaris*. Select the best answer for each question, and mark your answer accordingly.

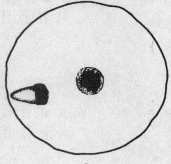

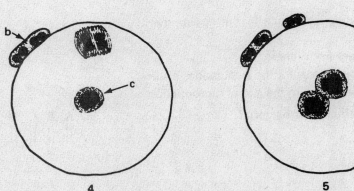

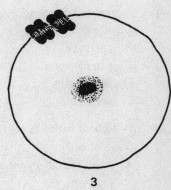

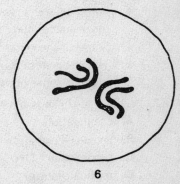

91. Which phase of division is represented in part *a*?
   A. interphase
   B. prophase
   C. metaphase
   D. anaphase
   E. telophase

91. A B C D E

92. The structure at point *b* is the
   A. centrosome
   B. first polar body
   C. second polar body
   D. egg nucleus
   E. sperm nucleus

92. A B C D E

93. What chromosome number would have resulted if fertilization had occurred in sketch *1*?
   A. 2*n*
   B. 3*n*
   C. 4*n*
   D. 5*n*
   E. 6*n*

93. A B C D E

94. When did reduction division occur in part *c*?
   A. before any of these drawings
   B. in sketch 1
   C. in sketch 2
   D. in sketch 3
   E. in sketch 6

94. A B C D E

95. What is the haploid chromosome number of *Ascaris* as revealed by the drawings?
   A. 2
   B. 4
   C. 6
   D. 8
   E. 10

95. A B C D E

The next four questions (96–99) consist of a group of lettered structures and numbered functions. For each numbered function select the appropriate lettered structure, and mark the answer accordingly. Any one of the lettered structures may be used one or more times or not at all.

   A. cilia
   B. scolex
   C. ommatidium
   D. nephron
   E. swimmeret

96. locomotion

96. A B C D E
|| || || || ||

97. excretion

97. A B C D E
|| || || || ||

98. reproduction

98. A B C D E
|| || || || ||

99. attachment

99. A B C D E
|| || || || ||

The next four questions (100–103) consist of a group of lettered structures and numbered body regions. For each numbered body region select the lettered structure that matches it and mark the answer accordingly. Any one of the lettered structures may be used one or more times or not at all.

A. pituitary
B. cochlea
C. sphincter
D. Bowman's capsule
E. adrenal

100. within the ear

100. A B C D E
|| || || || ||

101. above the kidney in humans

101. A B C D E
|| || || || ||

102. between the stomach and intestine

102. A B C D E
|| || || || ||

103. beneath the brain

103. A B C D E
|| || || || ||

The next five questions (104–108) consist of a group of lettered structures and numbered descriptions. For each numbered description select the appropriate lettered structure, and mark the answer accordingly. Any one of the lettered structures may be used one or more times or not at all.

A. parapodia
B. spiracles
C. stomata
D. tracheids
E. tracheoles

104. plant cells specialized to carry water

104. A B C D E
|| || || || ||

105. areas of insects in which gas exchange occurs

105. A B C D E
|| || || || ||

106. areas of plants in which transpiration occurs

106. A B C D E
|| || || || ||

107. gas-exchange areas of some annelids

107. A B C D E

108. structures formed by a pair of guard cells

108. A B C D E

The next six questions (109–114) consist of a group of lettered molecules and numbered descriptions. For each numbered description select the appropriate lettered molecule, and mark the answer accordingly. Any one of the lettered molecules may be used one or more times or not at all.

    A. acid phosphatase
    B. amylase
    C. hexokinase
    D. thyroxin
    E. reverse transcriptase

109. is needed by RNA viruses

109. A B C D E

110. is found in human saliva

110. A B C D E

111. is used to catalyze starch hydrolysis

111. A B C D E

112. is not an enzyme

112. A B C D E

113. catalyzes a step of glycolysis

113. A B C D E

114. is found within lysosomes

114. A B C D E

The next five questions (115–119) consist of a group of lettered places and numbered descriptions of the biological importance of the places. For each numbered description select the appropriate lettered place, and mark the answer accordingly. Any one of the lettered places may be used one or more times or not at all.

    A. England
    B. Galápagos
    C. Gondwana
    D. Tanzania
    E. Mexico

115. a destination of monarch butterflies in their annual autumn migration

115. A B C D E

116. a place where very old hominid fossils have been found

116. A B C D E

117. the place famous for Darwin's finches

117. A B C D E

118. an ancient landmass encompassing several modern continents

118. A B C D E
|| || || || ||

119. the place where industrial melanism was studied with peppered moths

119. A B C D E
|| || || || ||

The next five questions (120–124) consist of a group of lettered fields of biology and numbered activities that occur in these fields. For each numbered activity select the appropriate lettered field, and mark the answer accordingly. Any one of the lettered fields may be used one or more times or not at all.

A. biogeography
B. endocrinology
C. histology
D. immunology
E. taxonomy

120. Body symmetry is used as a clue.

120. A B C D E
|| || || || ||

121. Biomes are described.

121. A B C D E
|| || || || ||

122. Hormones are purified.

122. A B C D E
|| || || || ||

123. Vital stains are employed.

123. A B C D E
|| || || || ||

124. Antigens are classified.

124. A B C D E
|| || || || ||

The next five questions (125–129) consist of a group of lettered cell parts and numbered descriptions. For each numbered description, select the appropriate lettered cell part, and mark the answer accordingly. Any one of the lettered parts may be used one or more times or not at all.

A. cell wall
B. centriole
C. endoplasmic reticulum
D. mitochondrion
E. nucleolus

125. is continuous with outer nuclear membrane

125. A B C D E
|| || || || ||

126. contains DNA

126. A B C D E
|| || || || ||

127. is made of microtubules

127. A B C D E
|| || || || ||

128. is found in plants, but not in animals

128.A B C D E

129. is found in most animals, but is absent from many plants

129.A B C D E

The next four questions (130–133) consist of a group of lettered terms and numbered definitions. For each numbered definition select the appropriate term, and mark the answer accordingly. Any one of the lettered terms may be used one or more times or not at all.

A. biome
B. deme
C. habitat
D. niche
E. population

130. the geographical place where an organism lives

130.A B C D E

131. a stable, interbreeding group of organisms

131.A B C D E

132. a community of species dominated by a climax plant type

132.A B C D E

133. the most complex biological group or place in this list

133.A B C D E

The next five questions (134–138) consist of a group of lettered activities and numbered descriptions. For each numbered description select the appropriate lettered activity, and mark the answer accordingly. Any one of the lettered activities may be used one or more times or not at all.

A. appetitive behavior
B. circadian rhythm
C. echolocation
D. operant conditioning
E. proprioception

134. trial-and-error learning

134.A B C D E

135. a means of finding food by analysis of sound

135.A B C D E

136. awareness of body position

136.A B C D E

137. the sleep-wake cycle

137.A B C D E

138. the instinctive movements of a search for food

138.A B C D E

The next six questions (139–144) consist of a group of lettered types of organisms and numbered descriptions. For each numbered description select the appropriate lettered organism, and mark the answer accordingly. Any one of the lettered organisms may be used one or more times or not at all.

  A. decomposers
  B. primary consumers
  C. producers
  D. secondary consumers
  E. tertiary consumers

139. are likely to be least numerous in a given area

139. A B C D E
     || || || || ||

140. are exemplified by a cow

140. A B C D E
     || || || || ||

141. are exemplified by a snake when it eats a mouse

141. A B C D E
     || || || || ||

142. are exemplified by a hawk when it eats the snake described in question 141

142. A B C D E
     || || || || ||

143. could be nonphotosynthetic bacteria

143. A B C D E
     || || || || ||

144. are algae in a pond

144. A B C D E
     || || || || ||

The next five questions (145–149) consist of a group of lettered biological phenomena and numbered descriptions. For each numbered description select the appropriate phenomenon, and mark the answer accordingly. Any lettered phenomenon may be used one or more times or not at all.

  A. altruistic behavior
  B. artificial selection
  C. fitness
  D. founder effect
  E. inheritance of acquired traits

145. genetic drift caused by migration of a small group of organisms into a geographically isolated region

145. A B C D E
     || || || || ||

146. the development of new flower varieties by seed companies

146. A B C D E
     || || || || ||

147. activity that is detrimental to an individual but advantageous for the population

147. A B C D E
     || || || || ||

148. a measure of an individual's ability to send its genes to the next generation

148. A B C D E
     || || || || ||

149. Lamarckian hypothesis of evolution

149. A B C D E
     || || || || ||

The next six questions (150–155) consist of a group of lettered plant structures and numbered descriptions. For each numbered description select the appropriate lettered structure, and mark the answer accordingly. Any one of the lettered structures may be used one or more times or not at all.

A. archegonium
B. cambium
C. cone
D. flower
E. spore

0. place of egg formation in a moss

150. A B C D E

1. a structure that includes sepals

151. A B C D E

2. a structure used by angiosperms for sexual reproduction

152. A B C D E

3. the reproductive structure of most gymnosperms

153. A B C D E

4. a haploid cell that is the ancestor of a fern gametophyte

154. A B C D E

5. a structure that produces nonreproductive cells by mitosis in vascular plants

155. A B C D E

The next four questions (156–159) consist of a group of lettered cycles and numbered descriptions. For each numbered description select the appropriate cycle, and mark the answer accordingly. Any one of the lettered cycles may be used one or more times or not at all.

A. carbon cycle
B. cell cycle
C. nitrogen cycle
D. phosphorus cycle
E. water cycle

Some of the cycle involves transpiration.

156. A B C D E

Some of the cycle involves synthesis of amino acids by plants using an element obtained via the roots.

157. A B C D E

Some of the cycle involves exhalation by animals of a molecule that is produced by the Krebs cycle.

158. A B C D E

Some of the cycle involves G_1, S, and G_2 phases.

159. A B C D E

The next five questions (160–164) consist of a group of lettered genetic terms and numbered descriptions. For each numbered description select the appropriate lettered term, and mark the answer accordingly. Any one of the lettered terms may be used one or more times or not at all.

    A. Barr body
    B. episome
    C. gynandromorph
    D. lampbrush
    E. polyribosome

160. is distinctive of the cell of a human female

    160. A B C D E

161. is interpreted as a region of gene transcription

    161. A B C D E

162. is useful in studies of the genetic basis for insect behavior

    162. A B C D E

163. is a plasmid

    163. A B C D E

164. is a multicellular organism

    164. A B C D E

The next five questions (165–169) consist of a group of lettered birth control methods or devices and numbered descriptions. For each numbered description select the appropriate lettered method or device, and mark the answer accordingly. Any one of the lettered methods or devices may be used one or more times or not at all.

    A. intrauterine device
    B. oral contraceptive pill
    C. rhythm method
    D. tubal ligation
    E. vasectomy

165. It causes long-term sterility in males.

    165. A B C D E

166. It is the least effective birth control method in this list.

    166. A B C D E

167. A fertilization event occurs before the method takes effect.

    167. A B C D E

168. The female's gametes may be produced, but they are mechanically prevented from traveling to a position where fertilization would occur.

    168. A B C D E

169. Release of gametes from the ovaries is prevented.

    169. A B C D E

The remaining questions ask for analysis of experiments. For each set, read the descriptions and data carefully; then answer the questions or complete the statements by choosing among the lettered alternatives and marking your answers accordingly.

Questions 170–172

The table reproduced below shows the apparent evolutionary rate for several polypeptides. Rate values were derived by examining the degree of similarity of amino acid sequences of polypeptides obtained from a variety of organisms. The organisms were chosen to represent a range of taxonomic relatedness, which is implied from anatomy and fossil records. The evolutionary rates shown in the table are the number of amino acid substitutions per amino acid site per billion years. A high evolutionary rate value indicates a wide variance in amino acid sequences for a polypeptide from the organisms studied.

Polypeptide	Evolutionary Rate
Fibrinopeptides	9.0
Hemoglobin subunits	1.4
Animal lysozyme	1.0
Insulin	0.4
Cytochrome c	0.3
Histone type IV	0.006

70. If a protein performs a necessary function that relies heavily upon precise structure, it should be very similar in a wide variety of organisms that perform the function. Which of the listed polypeptides appears to fit this description best?

A. cytochrome c
B. fibrinopeptides
C. histone type IV
D. insulin
E. lysozyme

170. A B C D E
|| || || || ||

71. Fibrinopeptides are strings of amino acids clipped off fibrinogen as it is converted to fibrin. The excised strings appear to have no further function. Choose the statement that is LEAST likely to be true.

A. Fibrinopeptides are examples of the thesis that polypeptides which are not functionally necessary can tolerate many random changes in their structure.
B. Fibrinopeptides probably have relatively little function before they are clipped off.
C. Since a portion of proinsulin is clipped off to leave the remainder as active insulin, the clipped off portion probably has an evolutionary rate higher than 0.4.
D. The changes that have occurred in fibrinopeptides in the past have probably been a result of random mutations of their genetic material.
E. The fibrin portion of fibrinogen probably has a higher evolutionary rate value than that of fibrinopeptides.

171. A B C D E
|| || || || ||

172. Which is a correct statement?

172. A B C D E
‖ ‖ ‖ ‖ ‖

  A. Because insulin and cytochrome c have very similar evolutionary rates, they are probably similar in structure.
  B. Because the rate value for fibrinopeptides is so far above that of every other protein on the list, it should be ignored in analyses.
  C. If all of the data had been derived from organisms within a single genus, they would have been more valid indicators of evolution than if they were derived from a wider taxonomic range.
  D. The hemoglobin value in the table is of no evolutionary significance because plants do not have this protein.
  E. These data are not conclusive proof for evolution because they were derived solely from organisms alive today.

Questions 173–179

  A long-term study of an abandoned agricultural field indicated that there is a gradual change in the numbers and types of plant species. The table shows these results.

Year after Farming Ended	Total Number of Species	Number of Herbaceous Species	Number of Shrub Species	Number of Tree Species
1	30	30	0	0
5	28	26	2	0
10	33	27	4	2
20	52	32	8	12
50	75	30	20	25

  Even in the fiftieth year, only about 40% of the land was covered with plants. In the fiftieth year, the most abundant type (total number of organisms) was a herbaceous species. The second and fifth most abundant species were trees in the fiftieth year.

173. Which is the most accurate statement?

173. A B C D E
‖ ‖ ‖ ‖ ‖

  A. Since the number of herbaceous species remained nearly constant during the study, the other trends are probably invalid.
  B. The data do not support any trend in the number of species or diversity above the species level.
  C. The data show that the animal populations in the field have significantly affected the species diversity.
  D. The table shows a chronological increase in both total species and in higher taxonomic categories of organisms present.
  E. The table shows an increase in total species, but no significant trend in diversity above the species level.

174. How many years elapsed before the species were about equally divided among the three major plant types?

    A. 1
    B. 5
    C. 10
    D. 20
    E. 50

174. A B C D E

175. Which of the following is a correct statement?

    A. It is valid to predict that the total number of herbaceous plants would remain constant even to the hundredth year.

    B. Since trees are so large, the number of their species would probably stop increasing soon after the fiftieth year.

    C. The herbaceous plants are most able to populate recently tilled land.

    D. The table shows that the total number of herbaceous plants in the field was far larger than the total number of other plants in any year of the study.

    E. Year 5 was probably a drought year since the total number of species was lower than even the first year after tillage.

175. A B C D E

176. The phenomenon shown by these data is

    A. a pyramid of productivity
    B. commensalism
    C. density-dependent limitation
    D. ecological succession
    E. intraspecies competition

176. A B C D E

177. What is the prediction for animals in this field?

    A. A gradual change will occur in animal types to parallel the plant changes.

    B. Since the plants have been such successful colonizers, most animals will be unable to compete with them and will go elsewhere.

    C. Some animals will produce new mutations in response to the changes in the field.

    D. The first animals that entered the field in year 1 willl stay there, successfully defending the territory against later invaders.

    E. Animals will move into and out of the field at random, ignoring the changes occurring in the plant populations.

177. A B C D E

178. Why did some tree species become represented in large numbers even though they were among the last to enter the field?

    A. It was pure chance; some neighboring field might never be dominated by trees.

    B. They grew faster than herbaceous plants.

    C. They grew taller than other plant types and stole sunlight from them.

    D. They produced a larger number of seeds than could other plant types.

    E. Their roots strangled nearby plants.

178. A B C D E

179. In which year would you expect to find the most complex food webs?

179. A B C D E
|| || || || ||

A. first
B. fifth
C. tenth
D. twentieth
E. fiftieth

Questions 180–186

In a technique called somatic cell hybridization, mouse cells and human cells are cultured together. Some of them fuse. The resulting hybrid cells each start out containing the complete genomes of both species.

The fused cells are identified by these methods. The mouse cells were chosen because they are genetically incapable of producing an enzyme, thymidine kinase (TK), needed to produce nucleotides under certain conditions. A cell deficient in TK can normally make nucleotides but this ability is lost if the drug aminopterin is added. The human cells are capable of producing TK, and are therefore insensitive to aminopterin's effects. In the presence of aminopterin, only human cells and human-mouse fusion cells will survive. The human cells are nonproliferating leucocytes; therefore the only clones found after a while are those derived from fusion cells.

A hybrid cell begins with two complete genomes, but only that of the mouse survives intact. Human chromosomes are expelled at random. Hybrid cells usually contain from 41 to 55 chromosomes, 40 of these being the intact mouse genome. Karyotype analysis, following fluorescent staining of chromosomes with quinacrine, enables one to determine which human chromosomes remain in each clone. Since the genes of these chromosomes continue to make their products, one can also determine which genes are present by homogenizing some cells of a clone and performing enzyme assays on the homogenate. The table indicates the presence (+) or absence (−) of several human enzymes and chromosomes in selected hybrid clones.

		Clones					
		1	2	3	4	5	6
Human chromosome remaining	6	+	+	−	+	+	−
	8	+	−	+	−	−	−
	11	+	−	−	−	−	+
	15	+	−	−	+	+	−
Pepsinogen		+	+	−	+	+	−
Glutathione reductase		+	−	+	−	−	−
Pyruvate kinase		+	−	−	+	+	−
Hexosaminidase A		+	−	−	+	+	−
Hexokinase-1		−	−	−	−	−	−

Human enzyme produced

180. Which of the following is an enzyme needed to help select hybrid cells from nonfused cells?

180. A B C D E

A. aminopterin
B. pyruvate kinase
C. quinacrine
D. thymidine kinase
E. two of the above

181. Which clones are most useful in identifying the chromosomal location of the enzyme hexosaminidase A?

181.A B C D E

A. clones 1, 4, and 5
B. clones 1, 2, and 3
C. clones 2, 3, and 6
D. clones 2, 3, 4, 5, and 6
E. None of them is useful; this gene cannot be located from the data.

182. What can be said about the location of the hexokinase-1 gene?

182.A B C D E

A. It could be on any human chromosome.
B. It is NOT on chromosome 6.
C. It is NOT on chromosome 6, 8, 11, or 15.
D. It is on chromosome 6.
E. It is on chromsome 15.

183. On which chromosome is the gene for pepsinogen?

183.A B C D E

A. 6
B. 8
C. 11
D. 15
E. some other chromosome

184. Which of the following techniques also employs the fusion of cells in culture?

184.A B C D E

A. cloning of plants
B. hybridoma methods for production of monoclonal antibody
C. *in vitro* fertilization of human embryos
D. recombinant DNA technology employing plasmids
E. two of the above

185. Why are human chromosomes expelled from a hybrid cell while mouse chromosomes are not?

185.A B C D E

A. Human chromosomes are insensitive to aminopterin.
B. It was random chance; many hybrid cells would preferentially expel mouse chromosomes.
C. Karyotype analysis shows only mouse chromosomes.
D. The research cited here does not explain this.
E. The Sendai virus attacks only human chromosomes.

186. Why is the technique called *somatic cell* hybridization?

186.A B C D E

A. The cells being used are body cells other than gametes.
B. The cells being used have similar ploidies.
C. The cells being used are from different animal species.
D. The cells being used have previously been cultured outside the body.
E. The cells being used are inherently capable of fusion.

Questions 187–190

Fruit flies of two strains were crossed. The female parent was homozygous recessive for three auto-somal genes: she had echinus eyes (roughened surfaces, symbolized by *ec*), scute bristle pattern (certain thoracic bristles absent, symbolized by *sc*), and vestigial wings (symbolized by *vg*). The male was homozygous wild-type for all of these characteristics. All F_1 flies were wild-type. Virgin F_1 females were test-crossed to determine linkage; the results of this cross are summarized below.

Phenotype	Number of Individuals
sc + vg	14
+ + +	242
sc + +	12
+ + vg	232
sc ec +	240
sc ec vg	230
+ ec +	15
+ ec vg	15
total:	1000

187. Why were the F_1 females test-crossed?
A. to check for new mutations
B. to determine which alleles each of their homologous chromosomes carried
C. to determine which ones were infertile
D. to determine the F_1's phenotypes
E. to obtain an F_2 generation

187. A B C D E

188. If the three genes described above were independently assorting, what would be the expected phenotype ratios after a test-cross of F_1's?
A. 1:1:1:1:1:1:1:1
B. 1:2:4:6:4:2:1
C. the same as is shown in the actual totals of the table
D. nearly, but not exactly, the same as is shown in the actual totals
E. unpredictable since the ratio would depend upon which chromosomes carry the three genes

188. A B C D E

189. Analysis of the test-cross progeny shows that
A. all three genes are linked together
B. ec and vg are linked and sc is on a second chromosome
C. sc and ec are linked and vg is on a second chromosome
D. sc and vg are linked and ec is on a second chromosome
E. the three genes are on three separate chromosomes

189. A B C D E

190. Why were females rather than males of F_1's test-crossed?
A. It is easier to determine whether females are virgins.
B. It is traditional to use male test-crossed organisms.
C. Males could have been used with the same result; no significance should be attached to the choice of females.
D. Males of the genus *Drosophila* do not exhibit crossing-over.
E. Only females of the F_1 generation were of the proper phenotype.

190. A B C D E

Questions 191–197

The striking changes that occur all over the body of a larval frog as it progresses through metamorphosis are triggered by the hormone thyroxin (triiodothyronine, T3). This hormone is released in large quantity by the thyroid gland. A partial list of the more obvious changes includes tail resorption, breakdown of gills, development of functional lungs, shortening of the gut, appearance of eyelids, and formation of limbs. On the biochemical level, ammonia excretion is replaced by urea excretion and a host of new proteins are synthesized. These changes appear in an orderly, predictable sequence when triggered naturally. The graph shows some of the changes that occur at the subcellular level after a precocious increase of T3 provided by injection.

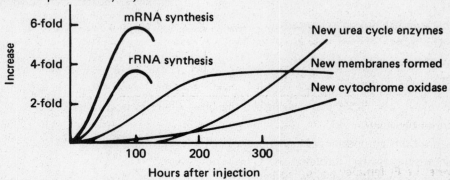

191. What is the adaptive significance of switching from an ammonia-excreting system to one that produces urea?

    191. A B C D E

  A. Ammonia is a gas; urea is a crystal.
  B. Ammonia is easily excreted across the membranes of an aquatic animal, but would dangerously accumulate in a terrestrial animal.
  C. Urea can be absorbed into the newly elongated gut of the adult, but ammonia would cause intestinal distress.
  D. Urea can be excreted across lung membranes, but ammonia cannot.
  E. Urea can carry the nitrogen derived from amino acid breakdown, but ammonia cannot.

192. What is the adaptive significance of shortening the intestinal tract at metamorphosis?

    192. A B C D E

  A. A very long gut, taking up much body space, is necessary for herbivores, but not for carnivores.
  B. Adults must process food more quickly since they cannot afford to carry an intestinal burden that would decrease their chance of escape from a predator.
  C. An adult does not eat as much as a larva, so it does not need a long tract.
  D. An adult's body length/width ratio is smaller than a tadpole's so it cannot keep a long gut.
  E. The loss of gut length reflects a loss of efficiency in food handling as adulthood approaches.

193. When was T3 injected in the organisms from which the graph was generated?

    193. A B C D E

  A. after metamorphosis had been in progress
  B. at 100 hours
  C. at the time of normal metamorphosis
  D. before the larvae would normally enter metamorphosis
  E. this information not provided

194. What does the graph show?

A. a sequential appearance of several new proteins and structures

B. a sudden, simultaneous synthesis of new proteins

C. a sudden, simultaneous synthesis of new proteins and nucleic acids

D. an appearance of new proteins and a loss of previously synthesized nucleic acids

E. the biochemical events associated with tail resorption

194. A B C D E
|| || || || ||

195. Which of these molecules increases in concentration after T3 injection?

A. ammonia

B. T3 made in the animals' thyroid

C. phospholipids

D. lysozymes

E. water

195. A B C D E
|| || || || ||

196. Why did mRNA and rRNA increase before the other changes occurred?

A. It cannot be determined.

B. They are both components of membranes, which are made later.

C. These are necessary if proteins are to be synthesized.

D. They are breakdown products of T3.

E. They are enzymes needed to produce cytochromes.

196. A B C D E
|| || || || ||

197. Which material is most closely associated with production of ATP in metamorphosing tissues?

A. cytochrome oxidase

B. membranes

C. mRNA

D. rRNA

E. urea cycle enzymes

197. A B C D E
|| || || || ||

Questions 198–200

An enzyme tends to catalyze a reaction at a characteristic rate (reaction velocity) that varies according to the initial concentration [S] of the enzyme's substrate. The graph shows such a relationship.

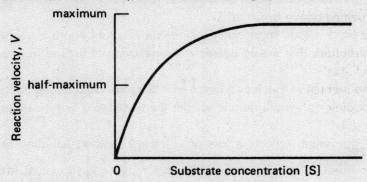

A mathematical expression of this curve is

$$V = V_{max} \frac{[S]}{[S] + K_M}$$

where V = velocity, V_{max} = theoretical maximum velocity, and K_M is a constant for each enzyme. The table below lists experimentally determined K_M values for some enzymes when operating with their substrates:

Enzyme	K_M value
Lysozyme	6×10^{-6} M
Carbonic anhydrase	8×10^{-3} M
Chymotrypsin	5×10^{-3} M
Arginine-tRNA synthetase	4×10^{-7} M

198. If all of the enzymes of the table were provided with the same concentration of their substrates and under identical environmental conditions, which enzyme would operate its reaction at the greatest velocity?

    A. arginine-tRNA synthetase

    B. carbonic anhydrase

    C. chymotrypsin

    D. lysozyme

    E. Not determinable since V_{max} may differ for each enzyme.

198. A B C D E

199. If lysozyme were provided with an analog of the substrate used for the table, it would exhibit the same V_{max}, but its K_M with the analog would become 6×10^{-8} M. What can be said about the curve generated with lysozyme and the analog when compared with the curve with lysozyme and its natural substrate?

    A. It would be identical to the original curve.

    B. It would show a higher velocity for each [S] value.

    C. It would show a higher velocity for low [S] values.

    D. It would show a lower velocity for each [S] value.

    E. It would show a lower velocity for low [S] values.

199. A B C D E

200. The equation provided above is named for

    A. Fatt and Katz

    B. Lineweaver and Burk

    C. Meselson and Stahl

    D. Michaelis and Menten

    E. Pauling and Corey

200. A B C D E

Questions 201–205

Cyclic 5'-adenosine monophosphate (cAMP) is a nucleotide produced inside brain cells after they have been stimulated by neurotransmitters. The cAMP then acts as a "second messenger" to cause complex biochemical changes in the cell. An example of this is found in cells of a brain region called the basal ganglia. A neurotransmitter, dopamine, is released by nerve cells. Upon contacting the basal ganglia cell membranes, dopamine fits into a receptor site of an enzyme, adenylate cyclase. This activates the enzyme, which then catalyzes the production of cAMP.

Two drugs have been found to react with the receptor site. Chlorpromazine attaches but does not activate the enzyme. While attached, it blocks attachment by dopamine. Apomorphine attaches to the receptor site and activates the enzyme.

Other neurons also seem to produce cAMP when stimulated. For instance, cells of the thoracic ganglia of insects respond to the neurotransmitter serotonin by producing cAMP. Another intracellular product, cyclic guanosine monophosphate (cGMP), is produced instead of cAMP in certain cells that have been stimulated by the neurotransmitter acetylcholine.

201. Parkinson's disease is caused by a lack of dopamine at the basal ganglia receptor sites. Which of these substances might be an anti-Parkinsonism agent if supplied to the basal ganglia region?

201. A B C D E
|| || || || ||

A. adenosine triphosphate
B. adenylate cyclase
C. apomorphine
D. chlorpromazine
E serotonin

202. Chlorpromazine has been used to relieve the symptoms of schizophrenia. What might be a useful hypothesis for a biochemical basis of schizophrenia?

202. A B C D E
|| || || || ||

A. People with schizophrenia can make neither cAMP nor cGMP in their brain cells.
B. Schizophrenia is caused by the presence of chlorpromazine in certain brain cells.
C. Schizophrenia is related to an overproduction of serotonin.
D. Schizophrenia is related to defective dopamine receptor cells that cannot be activated.
E. Schizophrenia is related to overactivity of dopamine-releasing cells in the brain.

203. The hallucinogenic drug lysergic acid diethylamide (LSD) is known to block serotonin receptors of certain neurons. What is the likely effect of this within the blocked cells?

203. A B C D E
|| || || || ||

A. Adenylate cyclase will be activated.
B. cAMP levels will decrease.
C. cAMP levels will increase.
D. cGMP levels will decrease.
E. Serotonin levels will decrease.

204. Nerve cells involved with the very fast transmission of messages to skeletal muscles use acetylcholine as their transmitters across the myoneural junction. In these cases, acetylcholine acts directly upon muscle fiber membranes to change their permeability. cAMP production does not occur. What is the most reasonable explanation for the fact that these nerve cells do not use cAMP?

204. A B C D E
|| || || || ||

A. Acetylcholine can easily pass through a muscle fiber membrane, going directly to the genes to affect them.
B. cAMP production and activity require a significant lapse of time between initial stimulation and final effect.
C. Muscle contraction involves calcium release, which takes over the function of cAMP.

    D. These nerve cells are at a disadvantage in not producing cAMP, but are still doing a reasonably good job.

    E. These cells produce the alternative "second messenger," cGMP.

205. Cyclic AMP has been found to be a "second messenger" in other, nonneural, portions of the body. An example is in

    A. glomeruli

    B. Haversian canals

    C. target cells for nonsteroid hormones

    D. target cells for steroid hormones

    E. the coelom

205. **A B C D E**
    || || || || ||

Questions 206–210

Terrestrial plants tend to maintain a different internal temperature from that of the surrounding air. Only some parts of a plant show this, and those parts can do so only over a certain range of external temperature. The graph shows measurements within leaves of *Citrullus colocynthis*. The plant had access at all times to water and nutrients.

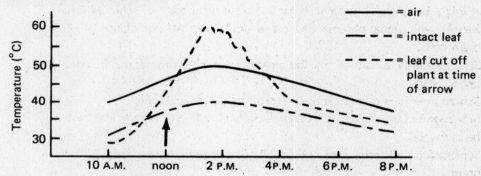

206. What is the most likely reason for the difference in temperature between an intact (attached) leaf and one that has been cut off?

    A. The intact leaf continues to perform cyclosis.

    B. The attached leaf continues to perform photosynthesis.

    C. The attached leaf continues to perform transpiration.

    D. The detached leaf cannot be shaded by other leaves of the plant.

    E. The detached leaf cannot move to avoid direct sunlight.

206. **A B C D E**
    || || || || ||

207. What is the most likely condition of the intact leaf at 2 P.M.?

    A. Cell walls have thickened.

    B. Petioles are twisted helically.

    C. Stomata are open.

    D. The leaf has wilted.

    E. Xylem tubes are closed.

207. **A B C D E**
    || || || || ||

208. A plant undergoes heat injury at 46° and above. Did this happen to the intact leaf?

    A. No, because the air never became warmer than 55°.

    B. No, because the leaf's interior never was exposed to direct sunlight.

    C. No, because the leaf's interior never became warmer than 40°.

    D. Yes, because the leaf's internal temperature reached 60° at times.

    E. Yes, because the leaf surface was probably hotter than its interior.

208. **A B C D E**
    || || || || ||

209. What is a good explanation for a higher temperature inside a severed leaf than in the surrounding air?

A. The leaf was dark, absorbing heat more readily than air.

B. The leaf was decomposing, an activity that generates heat.

C. The leaf was still metabolizing, an activity that generates heat.

D. The temperature readings were incorrect, since no inanimate object can be warmer than its surroundings.

E. The severed leaf lost access to fresh nutrients and began to burn its stored nutrients.

210. What animal activity is similar to the graphed activity of an intact leaf at mid-day?

A. excreting nitrogenous waste in a very concentrated urine

B. hiding underground at mid-day

C. using water of metabolism rather than drinking

D. shedding excess fur in summer

E. panting

Answer Key
for Sample Test 3
(with Comments and Explanations)

1. **(D)** The cells of many tissues cease most reproduction when they reach maturity. Some, like those in connective tissue and the lower layer of the epidermis, continue to divide throughout life. Bone marrow is one type of connective tissue with cells that continuously divide. They generate most types of blood cells.

2. **(E)** Transpiration is potentially harmful in that water is wasted by evaporation; it is unavoidable because the structure of the plant is such that the necessary exchange of gases must occur through exposed surfaces from which water can also evaporate.

3. **(A)** Most chordates are vertebrates that have among other things a segmented spinal (vertebral) column. The chordate characteristics given in the question are found at some stage of development but may not all be present in adults.

4. **(D)** Effectors are responding structures, the most common of which are glands that secrete and muscles that contract.

5. **(C)** Crossing-over occurs during the synapsis and separation of homologous chromosomes in meiosis.

6. **(E)** Birds defend the territory most vigorously against their keenest competitors, which are members of their own species. Many other animals, especially mammals, also claim and defend territories.

7. **(B)** Hygroscopic water is closely bound to soil particles and is not free to diffuse into the roots. After a plant dies for lack of water, the presence of hygroscopic water can be demonstrated. The soil is first weighed, then put into an oven hot enough to "drive off" the bound water, and finally weighed again to determine the loss.

8. **(B)** In addition to producing the hormones *insulin* and *glucagon*, the pancreas secretes the digestive enzymes *amylase, lipase, trypsin, chymotrypsin*, and *carboxypeptidase*.

9. **(C)** What this really means is that the system is based on the consideration of evolutionary relationships through common ancestry to the extent that they are understood. Body form may not show true kinship — as in the case of a whale and a fish, which have similar body forms but belong to different vertebrate classes.

10. **(C)** The silks of corn are styles and stigmas of pistils. Covering them with a bag would shield them from incoming pollen, which is produced in the staminate flowers located in the tassel.

11. **(A)** DNA duplicates itself during 'interphase. This can be determined by radioactive assay. The radioactive isotope hydrogen-3 (tritium) may be substituted in the thymidine and then incorporated in the DNA nucleotide containing thymine. The relative quantity of it can be measured at different times during interphase by extracting the DNA from the cell and measuring its radioactivity with an instrument called a liquid scintillation counter.

12. **(A)** Copperheads, cottonmouths, and rattlesnakes are pit vipers. The special pit organ is on the side of the face between the eyes and nostrils. It is useful in helping the snakes detect warm-bodied (endothermic) animals such as rodents and birds, which are their major items of food.

13. **(E)** The frog has two atria and one ventricle.

14. **(D)** Insects have open circulatory systems, that is, blood is not confined to vessels. Through most of its circulation it flows around internal organs in space designated the *hemocoel*. There is only one major vessel, the heart, which is located dorsally. Blood enters it through paired valves and is pumped forward into the hemocoel.

15. **(A)** Carbon dioxide is used in the process of photosynthesis. Plants that manufacture their own food by photosynthesis or chemosynthesis are autotrophic (independent).

16. **(B)** Known as the *storehouse of energy*, ATP is the ready source of energy for cell work. The energy is stored in each molecule in a high-energy phosphate bond. When the bond is broken and the energy released, the remaining molecule is ADP.

17. **(B)** A diploid cell in the ovary or testis undergoes meiosis, or reduction division, to produce haploid gametes, or germ cells — sperm or egg. When the nuclei of gametes fuse in fertilization, the resulting cell, with both maternal and paternal chromosomes, is diploid.

18. **(A)** The amnion encloses the embryo except at the navel. It is the *water sac* that insulates the embryo (fetus) during development. The amnion is immediately inside the chorion.

19. **(D)** First of all, *red* and *white* are phenotypes, not genotypes. Crossing *RR* with *rr* produces offspring with *Rr* only.

20. **(C)** During the long interval of time, evolution proceeded in isolation with what ancestral genetic material was available. Elsewhere there was less isolation and more opportunities for gene flow.

21. **(E)** Secondary succession begins when an ongoing community is disrupted by such things as lumbering, clearing, cultivation,

grazing, pollution, fire, floods, storms, or strip mining.

22. **(E)** Benthic organisms are bottom-dwellers, and the pelagic zone is the open sea.

23. **(B)** Each canal contains an artery, a vein, and a nerve supply and is surrounded by several encircling zones of cells.

24. **(A)** Although the spleen is useful, it is often removed when damaged without causing grievous effects. The other organs listed perform vital functions.

25. **(E)** The zona pellucida is a translucent, noncellular layer surrounding eggs.

26. **(B)** Meristem is embryonic plant tissue. Its cells are unspecialized and capable of dividing.

27. **(B)** A mycorrhiza is not a single organism but two organisms symbiotically associated. Since the association consists of fungal mycelia and roots of plants, the habitat is soil.

28. **(C)** Bacteriophages are viruses that parasitize bacteria. Often they are simply called phages.

29. **(A)** Spiracles occur as paired pores in the abdominal segments. They are also present on other parts of the body but are not always as easy to locate. They are the openings to tracheae.

30. **(A)** Another way of expressing the same idea is to say that the chlorophyll is activated.

31. **(E)** Fibrinogen is the plasma protein that is converted from a sol to a gel state (fibrin) during the clotting process. Prothrombin is a globulin protein of the plasma. It must be converted to thrombin, which in turn converts fibrinogen to fibrin.

32. **(A)** Both mitochondria and chloroplasts are specialized to transfer the energy of electrons to the chemical bonds of ATP. This process, chemiosmosis, occurs in and on certain internal membranes of these organelles.

33. **(C)** The maternal portion is from the uterus, and the embryonic portion is from the chorion, the outer extraembryonic membrane derived from the trophoblast of the blastodermic vesicle.

34. **(B)** See the following illustration:

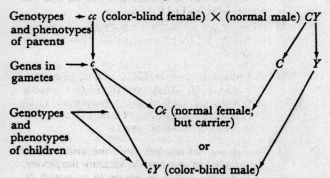

Genotypes and phenotypes of parents → *cc* (color-blind female) × (normal male) *CY*

Genes in gametes → *c*   *C*   *Y*

Genotypes and phenotypes of children → *Cc* (normal female, but carrier)

or

cY (color-blind male)

35. **(D)** This means that a climax community can survive indefinitely, whereas a successional community is replaced by one of another type.

36. **(B)** The term *clone* is often used to describe a clump of plants that spread by runners or other vegetative means. Since all descendants come from a single parent and have the same genetic composition, they are highly uniform.

37. **(D)** Birds and mammals maintain a constant body temperature, but other animals have temperatures that fluctuate with the environment. The former are called endothermic; the latter, ectothermic.

38. **(B)** The clitellum is the conspicuous glandular swelling of segments thirty-two to thirty-seven. Specialized setae on the ventral side of the clitellum clasp the copulating portions together. The glandular cells secrete a slime tube around each of the worms during copulation to aid in directing sperm to the seminal vesicles of the partner and later to form cocoons to hold the eggs. They also secrete albumin into the cocoons to nourish the embryos.

39. **(E)** Cytochromes are iron-containing cellular pigments that act as acceptors during hydrogen transfer.

40. **(A)** Another way of expressing the same idea is to say that epiboly means differential growth of the cells of one embryonic part over and around another.

41. **(B)** What this means is that the genes, though different, affect the same characteristic, e.g., blue and brown eye color. *Allele* is shortened from the word *allelomorph*.

42. **(B)** The practice is more fascinating than practical. There are many problems with substituting water for soil.

43. **(D)** With about 20 amino acids, the possible combinations are considerable, easily accounting for the many differences among living organisms.

44. **(E)** This is a unit of distance on the metric scale — one millionth of a meter or one thousandth of a millimeter.

45. **(B)** Gymnosperms are described as naked-seeded, meaning that the seeds are produced on the outer surface of the megasporophyll (scale of pine cone) instead of enclosed by it as in the angiosperms. The megasporophylls that enclose the seeds of angiosperms are known as carpels. A single carpel may fuse along its margin, or several carpels may fuse together to form one or more compartments in which the seeds are located. The structure that is composed of one or more carpels is the pistil, and the basal part of it (ovary) contains the seeds.

46. **(D)** Much of the energy driving the industrial enterprises of the world comes from fossil fuels, including coal and oil. In addition, better living standards depend on transportation and electrical uses closely linked to the same energy sources. Energy is released from fossil fuels by combustion which produces carbon dioxide. Some of the light energy reaching the earth is changed into heat energy of a longer wavelength, which cannot be reradiated into space. It is known that a high concentration of carbon dioxide in the upper atmosphere, like glass in a greenhouse, allows light to come in but blocks the reradiation of heat.

47. **(B)** Some preparation and digestion occur in the stomach, but most digestion and absorption occur in the intestine. The stomach holds food up to 3 or 4 hours and discharges some of it intermittently into the small intestine.

48. **(D)** Bile does not digest fats to fatty acids and glycerol but does break them into tiny droplets, thereby greatly increasing the surface area upon which enzymes can act.

49. **(C)** Before Harvey's day people believed that blood left the heart and returned to it in the same vessels, much like the flowing and ebbing of the tides. Harvey knew that the heart is the pumping organ and proved that blood flows from it in arteries and returns to it in veins. Not having the benefit of a microscope, he did not know that the two are connected by capillaries.

50. **(D)** This means that cells can accumulate substances in larger quantities than occur in the surroundings. If diffusion were passive, movement would be in proportion to the number of molecules and the speed of their motion. In such a case the net movement would be from places of higher concentration to places of lower concentration.

51. **(B)** Because the egg is released in such close proximity to the funnel-like opening of the Fallopian tube and cilia within the oviduct create a current, the egg is usually quickly drawn into and moved down the tube to the uterus. Of course, cases are known in which the egg was fertilized in the abdominal cavity, where it became implanted and started development in an inappropriate place.

52. **(B)** The "gene pool" is all of the genes available to a species for making genetic combinations; that is, all of the genes in an interbreeding natural group.

53. **(A)** Both are mammals, related but dissimilar in their adaptations to different environments.

54. **(D)** A biome is a large natural community of organisms characterized by a dominant life form that is adapted to the prevailing climatic conditions.

55. **(B)** Most of the time it is the population explosion of a single species that produces a conspicuous aspect such as a green or red color.

56. **(A)** The word *ontogeny* is most often heard in the statement "*Ontogeny recapitulates phylogeny,*" which means embryology repeats evolution.

57. **(B)** Both ribonucleic acid (RNA) and deoxyribonucleic acid (DNA) have adenine, guanine, and cytosine in their molecules. In addition, ribonucleic acid has uracil, and deoxyribonucleic acid has thymine.

58. **(D)** Subsequently, the synaptic maternal and paternal chromosomes separate and go individually to the poles. Sometimes parts of the two chromosomes become entangled and exchanged during synapsis. The exchange is known as crossing-over.

59. **(D)** Like many of the bacteria, blue-green algae often secrete gelatinous sheaths. This and other resemblances lead many authorities to classify blue-green algae as cyanobacteria.

60. **(E)** The nematocyst is a stinger found in cnidaria like the jellyfish and Portuguese man-of-war.

61. **(A)** Saliva contains amylase and maltase. The former acts upon starch, and the latter upon maltose (malt sugar).

62. **(B)** Portal systems are of two types, renal and hepatic; thus they serve the kidneys and liver. A portal system consists of a vein that branches into capillaries as it permeates an organ. The blood is then recollected and channeled into a major systematic vessel. Humans have only the hepatic portal system.

63. **(D)** In the gastrula stage of development there is an external and an internal layer of cells. The external one is ectoderm; the internal one, endoderm. Most animals produce a third layer, the mesoderm, between the ectoderm and endoderm. These are the germ layers from which mature tissues and organs later develop.

64. **(A)** The syrinx is an organ for voice production found in birds. It is at the junction of the trachea and bronchi. The larynx of mammals, a similar structure, is located at the anterior end of the trachea.

65. **(A)** *Way of life* includes such things as requirements for living and relationship to other organisms.

66. **(D)** Examples: carbon-14 (5730 years), phosphorus-32 (14.5 days), cobalt-60 (5.2 years), calcium-45 (160 days), nitrogen-16 (7.35 seconds), sodium-24 (14.8 hours), and thorium-232 (10 billion years).

67. **(E)** Petals are not needed since the vision of insects is not involved in locating the flower, and light pollen is easier to transport by

wind. Most structural features of organisms are logical adaptations.

68. **(C)** The blooming of plants after proper exposure to light and darkness is photoperiodism. Violets are known as short-day plants; morning-glories, as long-day plants. The phenomenon of photoperiodism was discovered by Garner and Allard in 1920.

69. **(B)** Xylem is wood. Woody stems have a relatively large amount of wood in proportion to soft tissues; herbaceous stems have a relatively large amount of soft tissues in proportion to wood. Herbaceous plants are much more nutritious as food because they contain more protoplasm in proportion to cellulose and lignin, which are generally indigestible by humans.

70. **(C)** The plants are photosynthesizing and releasing oxygen. Since light is required for photosynthesis, the bubbles are generated during the day.

71. **(A)** Spicules are needlelike skeletal parts of sponges.

72. **(D)** In humans, lipase is produced by the stomach, pancreas, and intestine.

73. **(A)** A single disaccharide molecule combines with a single water molecule and breaks into two monosaccharide molecules.

74. **(C)** Neurons, or nerve cells, have protoplasmic processes that synapse with other neuronic processes. Nerves are bundles of neuronic processes bound together with connective tissue.

75. **(D)** Ovulation occurs near the middle of the period, but cannot be depended upon for regularity.

76. **(D)** Both serve the same use but have different embryological origins.

77. **(E)** Plant and animal taxonomists usually meet separately and make their own rules of classification. Although these rules are similar, botanists prefer *division* for a group of closely related classes, while zoologists use the term *phylum*.

78. **(B)** The liver originates as a diverticulum (blind outpocket) from the ventral wall of the foregut.

79. **(A)** A frog, like all vertebrates, is a deuterostome animal. This means that the mouth forms after the anus. The first-formed opening of the gut to the exterior is the blastopore, which remains as the anus.

80. **(A)** The giant chromosomes of some insects have regions of unfolding to produce greatly enlarged "puffs." The exact areas of each chromosome that are like this will change in a predictable fashion as the insect moves from one developmental stage to another. Predictable changes in puff patterns can be induced by introduction of certain hormones. The puffs are believed to represent DNA that is spreading to enable transcription.

81. **(A)** Blue light is heavily absorbed by chlorophyll and efficiently starts the light reactions of photosynthesis. Ultraviolet light and X-rays can also cause chlorophyll oxidation, but are so energetic that they also damage molecules necessary for normal operation.

82. **(E)** Pinocytosis is a mechanism similar to phagocytosis, but on a smaller scale. Phagocytosis is the ingestion of particulate matter such as detritus and cells, and pinocytosis is the ingestion of water with dissolved materials.

83. **(E)** The nuclear envelope is actually a pair of membranes in close proximity. The outermost membrane extends at points into the cytoplasm, becoming endoplasmic reticulum.

84. **(B)** The endosperm is parenchymatous tissue derived from polar (endosperm) nuclei fertilized by one of the two sperms produced by a pollen grain. It is located in some seeds; and if present, nourishes the developing seedling. If endosperm is absent, food is stored in the cotyledons of embryos.

85. **(D)** In the retina of vertebrates, rhodopsin changes its shape in reponse to light. This, in some way, changes the membrane of a rod cell to stimulate a nearby neuron.

86. **(A)** If significant variation is present, no new genetic instructions need be added. The variations are significant if they cause nonrandom reproduction.

87. **(D)** The Lederbergs demonstrated that bacterial mutants can be easily found. They devised a method to transfer bacterial colonies from plate to plate without disturbing their spatial relations. Examination of patterns before and after transfer of colonies to a hostile environment indicates those that survive because of mutant ability.

88. **(D)** Pyruvic acid is converted to a 2-carbon molecule that is the starting material for the Krebs cycle, but it is not synthesized in the cycle.

89. **(A)** Schwann cells wrap tightly around a developing motor neuron's elongated axon. By repeatedly twisting around the axon's axis, each Schwann cell becomes modified into a concentric set of membrane layers. These act as insulators and speed neural transmission.

90. **(E)** The corpus luteum, translated from Latin as "yellow body," is the tissue from which an egg has been released. It produces progesterone and estrogen, which help the uterus to prepare for accepting an embryo by increasing its wall thickness.

91. **(C)** The four chromosomes are aligned at the equator of the spindle in metaphase. Homologous chromosomes are paired at this point.

92. **(B)** The first polar body has been discharged, and the remaining cell is the secondary oocyte. Sometimes first polar bodies (vestigial secondary oocytes) divide into second polar bodies (vestigial ootids — eggs).

93. **(B)** The sperm has the *n* number of chromosomes, and the nucleus of the large cells, the primary oocyte, has the 2*n* number. Together the number is 3*n*.

94. **(A)** Part c is the sperm nucleus. The dividing nucleus at the periphery is in the process of throwing off the second polar body and becoming the egg nucleus.

95. **(A)** The diploid number — 4 — is revealed in sketch 2, where there are four chromosomes consisting of two chromatids each, and in sketch 6, where the four chromosomes are clearly visible in the plate view (equatorial section in metaphase). The haploid number then is 2.

96. **(A)** Cilia (sing., cilium) are hairlike organelles found on the surfaces of many types of cells. An entire class of Protozoa (class Ciliata) uses these devices for locomotion. In humans, cells that line several tracts (such as the respiratory tract) use cilia to move objects through the lumens.

97. **(D)** The vertebrate kidney's functional units are nephrons. These are tiny tubules closed at one end and opening at the other end into collecting ducts that fuse to become paired ureters carrying urine to the urinary bladder.

98. **(E)** Swimmerets (pleopods) are appendages located on the abdomen of many aquatic crustaceans. In the crayfish and lobster there are five pairs. They function as organs of respiration and reproduction. In males, the first two pairs are modified as copulatory organs; in females, they carry the eggs and young.

99. **(B)** The scolex is the head of a tapeworm, by which it attaches itself to the wall of the intestine and from which body segments are budded. To aid in anchorage, the scolex of the pork tapeworm has a circle of hooks and four suckers.

100. **(B)** The cochlea is a spiral canal in the inner ear, so named because it resembles the coiled shell of a snail. It contains the sensory endings of the auditory nerve.

101. **(E)** In humans, adrenal glands are located above the kidney. Among the secretions of this tissue are the hormones cortisone and epinephrin (adrenalin).

102. **(C)** A sphincter is a valve consisting of a circular band of muscles located in the wall of the digestive tract and some other tubular organs. The one between the stomach and intestine, the pyloric sphincter, regulates the discharge of food into the intestine.

103. **(A)** The pituitary is actually attached to the brain by a slender stalk. It produces so many important hormones that it is called the "master gland." Embryologically it is derived from parts of the brain and mouth cavity.

104. **(D)** Certain cells of some vascular plants become elongated and hollow. These tracheids, aligned longitudinally, form the xylem.

105. **(E)** Tracheae are paired tubes leading into an insect's body. They branch and rebranch to tiny dead-end tubules called tracheoles. No cell is very far from an air-filled tracheole. Gas exchange occurs at the liquid-filled tips of tracheoles.

106. **(C)** Transpiration, the evaporation of water from leaves, would not be possible if there were not holes scattered over the leaf surfaces. These stomata open and close by a homeostatic mechanism based on the amount of water in nearby cells.

107. **(A)** The paired appendages of polychaete worms (phylum Annelida, class Polychaeta) are vascularized areas capable of gas exchange with the environment.

108. **(C)** Paired guard cells, whose shapes change as their turgor condition changes, form the boundaries of stomata on leaf surfaces (see answer 106, above).

109. **(E)** An RNA virus is one whose genetic material is ribonucleic acid, rather than the usual deoxyribonucleic acid. Transcription by such a virus begins with the production of a single-stranded DNA under the direction of the enzyme reverse transcriptase. This DNA then transcribes messenger RNA in the familiar fashion of other organisms.

110. **(B)** Salivary amylase is one of the first enzymes encountered by the food that humans eat. It acts specifically upon starches, hydrolyzing them.

111. **(B)** See answer 110, above.

112. **(D)** Thyroxin is an amino acid that acts as a hormone. It is manufactured in the thyroid, incorporated into a protein called thyroglobulin, and transported in that form to target cells via the bloodstream.

113. **(C)** Hexokinase is the enzyme catalyzing the first step of glycolysis, the addition of a phosphate group to glucose.

114. **(A)** Lysosomes are membranous vesicles within a cell, containing digestive enzymes. The principal enzyme is acid phosphatase, whose presence is diagnostic of lysosomes.

115. **(E)** Millions of monarch butterflies (*Danaus plexippus*) hatched in North America in late summer migrate southward to escape winter's cold. Many of them have been found to congregate in a rather small area of

mountainous central Mexico, where they literally cover the landscape.

116. **(D)** Parts of Tanzania (in East Africa) have yielded skulls of *Australopithecus africanus*, estimated to be 2.5 to 3 million years old.

117. **(B)** Thirteen species of finches are found on the Galápagos Islands, a volcanic group west of Ecuador. Darwin, visiting the area in 1835, studied these birds and later cited their anatomical differences as examples of adaptive radiaton.

118. **(C)** According to the theory of continental drift, certain large landmasses now separated by water were once attached. The area given the name Gondwana included the present Africa, South America, India, and Antarctica.

119. **(A)** Industrial melanism is the phenomenon whereby darkening of the landscape by industrial soot leads to selection for dark-colored individuals within animal populations. The peppered moths *(Biston betularia)* of England provide a classic example of evolution triggered by this environmental change.

120. **(E)** Taxonomy is the study of how organisms should be classified. Although adult anatomy, including type of symmetry, is an important clue to relatedness, the entire life cycle of an organism should be examined, and molecular structure may also provide important information.

121. **(A)** Biogeography is the study of the relationship between populations and their geographical distributions. To understand why particular organisms succeed in each region, one must examine the nature of the biome. A biome is a large community dominated by a characteristic life form, often a plant type.

122. **(B)** Endocrine glands are tissues or organs that secrete hormones into the bloodstream.

123. **(C)** A histologist studies the microscopic anatomy of organisms. An important tool in this field is the enhancement of visual contrast among cell organelles by the use of stains that preferentially attach to certain molecules. A vital stain is one that is not toxic to a living cell.

124. **(D)** The immune system involves recognition by the body of materials that are foreign. These antigens are then attacked by various methods, including antibody attachment and lymphocyte engulfment.

125. **(C)** The outermost membrane that composes the nuclear boundary sends outgrowths into the cytoplasm as rounded or flattened tubules. This network, the endoplasmic reticulum, provides a large surface to which ribosomes may attach and may act as transportation conduits.

126. **(D)** A mitochondrion not only contains DNA, but also uses this material to direct synthesis of its own proteins independently of the rest of the cell.

127. **(B)** Microtubules, proteinaceous hollow rods, build a number of structures, including the centrioles of animal cells.

128. **(A)** A fundamental difference between kingdom Plantae and kingdom Animalia is that cells of the former produce tough cell walls composed largely of polysaccharides. Bacteria (kingdom Monera), some Protista (such as the algae), and the Fungi also produce cell walls.

129. **(B)** The centrioles of animal cells seem to be necessary for normal spindle fiber production. However, many plants produce this mitotic and meiotic apparatus without centrioles.

130. **(C)** A habitat includes the geographical location in which an organism lives.

131. **(E)** A deme is a relatively temporary interbreeding group; a population is a larger and therefore more permanent group.

132. **(A)** See answer 121, above.

133. **(A)** Biomes can be relatively large communities, sometimes covering millions of square miles. They include all of the organisms within these geographical bounds.

134. **(D)** Operant conditioning is the sort of learning in which an animal does something, after which it remembers that it was either rewarded or hurt. If rewarded, the animal will try the same activity upon the next opportunity. If hurt, the animal learns to avoid the same action when the opportunity arises again.

135. **(C)** Bats find flying insects in darkness by sending out high-frequency sound and analyzing its return pattern as it reflects from objects.

136. **(E)** Muscles have specialized regions called proprioceptors that respond to being stretched by the contraction of nearby fibers. Proprioceptors that are stretched initiate nerve messages to the central nervous system. The brain collects and analyzes all of these messages from the body and constructs an image of body position.

137. **(B)** A circadian rhythm is a pattern of activity that cycles approximately every 24 hours.

138. **(A)** Appetitive behavior is the first activity or set of activities that an animal performs to satisfy a drive such as hunger. If appetitive behavior leads to the possibility of satisfying the drive (e.g., the animal finds food), the next set of activities is the one called the "consummatory act" (e.g., eating the food).

139. **(E)** As energy flows from organism to organism in an ecosystem, some is lost in the form of heat. A tertiary consumer (an animal that

eats animals that eat animals that eat plants) obtains a very small percentage of the energy that was first stored in the plants. Therefore, the plants can support only a small number of tertiary consumers, more secondary consumers, and even more primary consumers.

140. **(B)** Any herbivore is a primary consumer.

141. **(D)** Since mice are primary consumers (herbivores), any animal that eats a mouse is a secondary consumer.

142. **(E)** See answer 139, above, for the definition of a tertiary consumer.

143. **(A)** Decomposers are bacteria or fungi that convert the complex macromolecules of dead organisms to much simpler molecules which can be released for use by living organisms.

144. **(C)** Any photosynthetic organism is a producer, as demonstrated by its ability to manufacture and store organic molecules holding energy in their bonds.

145. **(D)** A small population reproductively separated from the rest of the species may have a gene pool significantly different in its gene frequencies from the species as a whole. Even though the few "founders" of a newly inhabited area mate randomly among themselves, they may be closely related and therefore perpetuate their genetic differences from the rest of the species.

146. **(B)** When humans purposefully provide the selection pressure, as in breeding programs, the evolution that occurs is said to be caused by artificial selection.

147. **(A)** Biologists who study animal societies believe that some animals sometimes sacrifice their own reproductive potential in deference to the welfare of the population. In a societal population of similar genomes, this serves to enhance the chance of an individual's genes reaching the next generation even if "by proxy," that is, by another, similar individual doing the actual reproduction.

148. **(C)** A fitness value of 1.0 is assigned to an organism that has a phenotype allowing it to reproduce more successfully (placing more copies of its genes into the next generation) than any other organism of the population. Less successful organisms are assigned values below 1.0, with a value of zero going to those that die before reproducing or are sterile.

149. **(E)** Jean Baptiste de Lamarck (1744–1829) was the first scientist to develop an hypothesis of speciation. He believed that phenotypic changes newly acquired in a lifetime can be transmitted to the next generation. This evolutionary method has been disproved for many characteristics.

150. **(A)** An archegonium is the female sex organ of the moss gametophyte. The archegonium produces an egg that will be fertilized by a sperm from another gametophytic structure, the antheridium.

151. **(D)** Sepals are the modified leaves, usually green in color, forming the base of a flower.

152. **(D)** By definition, any plant using a flower as its reproductive portion is an angiosperm.

153. **(C)** Most gymnosperms are plants that produce seed-bearing cones. Well-known examples are the pines.

154. **(E)** The sporophytic form of a fern sends some of its diploid cells into meiosis to become haploid spores. Upon release, a spore can become the progenitor of a multicellular haploid organism, the gametophyte.

155. **(B)** Cambium is meristematic tissue of stems and roots, capable of reproducing asexually to provide cells that will mature into new xylem and phloem.

156. **(E)** A major route by which water reenters the atmosphere is evaporation from leaf surfaces. This water was drawn from the soil by plants.

157. **(C)** Plants obtain nitrogen from soil and use it to produce amino acids (one nitrogen atom per molecule). Herbivorous animals send the nitrogen further in the cycle when they eat plants.

158. **(A)** Animals (and plants) produce carbon dioxide as an end product of the Krebs cycle. Exhalation is the final act of removing this material from the body, releasing it to the atmosphere. Water is also exhaled; it is not produced by the Krebs cycle, but is made during oxidative phosphorylation, which follows the Krebs cycle.

159. **(B)** A cell of an actively reproducing tissue goes through G_1, S, and G_2 portions of interphase as it prepares for mitosis. G symbolizes "gap," and S symbolizes "synthesis" of new DNA.

160. **(A)** A Barr body is a visually detectable object in the nucleus of each cell of a female. It has been identified as one of a female's two X chromosomes.

161. **(D)** Lampbrush configurations, so named because they resemble the feathery appearance of cleaning brushes for nineteenth century kerosene lamps, are uncoiled regions of chromosomes that are producing RNA (transcribing). This activity is demonstrated by finding isotopically labeled uracil at these areas.

162. **(C)** A gynandromorphic fruit fly (Drosophila) is one that has XX (female) cells in some regions of its body and XY (male) cells in oth-

144 | *PART II SAMPLE TESTS*

ers. Genes for instinctive behavior, if located on the sex chromosome, can be studied through use of this bizarre organism. Seymour Benzer is a pioneer in such work.

163. **(B)** Episomes, including the plasmids that have become so valuable in recombinant DNA work, are pieces of DNA that can exist either as part of a chromosome or free.

164. **(C)** See answer 162, above.

165. **(E)** Vasectomy is surgical removal of a section of each vas deferens, the tube that carries sperm from a testis. As long as this structure's continuity is interrupted, the male cannot externally release sperm cells. It is possible to reconnect the vas in some cases.

166. **(C)** The rhythm method involves sexual abstinence during the days when an egg is in the portion of the reproductive tract where it can be fertilized. Since its success involves accurate detection of this period and exercise of willpower, it can be ineffective.

167. **(A)** An intrauterine device (IUD) interferes with implantation of an early embryo in the uterine wall. Since fertilization takes place in the upper Fallopian tube, the embryo may consist of 100 or more cells before it reaches the uterus. If not implanted, it dies for lack of nutrition.

168. **(D)** The female counterpart of vasectomy, tubal ligation is surgical interruption of the Fallopian tubes, which carry eggs from the region of the ovaries toward the uterus. This is also the route by which sperm cells reach a released egg.

169. **(B)** The most commonly used birth control pills contain analogs of estrogen and progesterone, the ovarian hormones. The artificially high concentration of these materials in the blood prevents the pituitary from releasing luteinizing hormone (LH), which normally induces ovulation (release of an egg).

170. **(C)** The value for histone, 0.006, is far below any other in the table, indicating very little variation in amino acid sequence among the organisms studied.

171. **(E)** The fibrin portion of fibrinogen plays a vital role in blood clotting in a wide range of animals. Since this is the functional portion, one would expect that its amino acid sequence would be vital to its function and would therefore be conserved.

172. **(E)** Only living organisms could provide intact proteins for this study. Since significant evolution requires much time, the materials are not available for a self-reliant proof of such evolution. These data are pieces of evidence that, when added to others, point toward evolution as a useful theory of organismal diversity.

173. **(D)** After 1 year, the field contained 30 species of herbs, but no other types of plant. After 50 years, all three plant categories were represented among the 75 species.

174. **(E)** Only in the fiftieth year did the shrubs and trees show approximately the same species abundance as herbs.

175. **(C)** The first colonizers of the field (year 1) were all herbs. One may assume that the seeds of all three plant types were available, so the herbs must have been best adapted for this environment.

176. **(D)** Succession is a predictable, gradual change in the types of organisms that inhabit a region.

177. **(A)** Many animal species are dependent upon the specific plants of their habitat; therefore, a succession will also occur among animals.

178. **(C)** In temperate regions where rainfall is sufficiently high to support trees, it is predictable that trees will eventually dominate, since their canopies cast shadows over low-growing herbs and shrubs. Their success in competition for sun is reflected by their presence in large numbers.

179. **(E)** The number of herbivorous species will increase as the number of plant species rises. Also rising will be the number of animal species dependent upon these herbivores for food. A mature plant community is characterized by complex webs of interdependence.

180. **(D)** Aminopterin is a drug used with thymidine kinase to eliminate unfused mouse cells, but aminopterin is not an enzyme.

181. **(D)** Clone 1 does not help eliminate any chromosome from consideration since it contains four chromosomes. The chromosome pattern of clones 2, 3, 4, 5, and 6 perfectly matches the appearance of hexosaminidase A in these clones. The gene is on chromosome 15, since only clones that include this chromosome also produce the enzyme.

182. **(C)** Chromosomes 6, 8, 11, and 15, for which representative clones exist, can be eliminated since those clones do not produce hexokinase-1. Any of the other 19 human chromosomes not mentioned in the table could be correct. (Hexokinase-1 is known to be controlled by a gene on chromosome 10.)

183. **(A)** All clones positive for pepsinogen production also contain chromosome 6. Clone 2 is especially useful, since it contains only this human chromosome and produces the enzyme.

184. **(E)** Hybridomas are fusion cells combining malignant cells and antibody-producing plasma cells. Each clone derived from such a fusion produces a single type of antibody in large quantity. The egg-sperm interaction

of fertilization is a naturally occurring fusion of cells of the same species.

185. **(D)** The reason for preferential expulsion of human chromosomes is neither mentioned here nor understood.

186. **(A)** The word *somatic* comes from the Greek *soma*, meaning "body." It refers to any cell of a multicellular organism that is not a gamete (sex cell).

187. **(B)** Linkage (two or more genes on the same chromosome) is analyzed by looking for evidence of gene recombination via crossing-over. Crossing-over is determined by finding which alleles of linked genes are together on the same chromosome. A testcross (mating to a homozygous recessive individual) shows, by the phenotypes of its progeny, which alleles are linked on each chromosome.

188. **(A)** The F_1's would be triply heterozygous *(sc/+ ec/+ vg/+)*. Mating them in a test-cross with a triply homozygous recessive individual *(sc/sc ec/ec vg/vg)* would yield eight phenotypes in equal numbers. Look, for instance, at the *sc* gene. A heterozygote for this gene, when mated with a homozygous recessive, produces two phenotypes in equal numbers: scute and wild-type, that is, the probability of each of these is 1/2. If none of the three genes is linked to another, various combinations of the alleles occur by random assortment. Since the chance of any single phenotypic character is 1/2, the chance of any single combination of three characters is $(1/2)^3 = 1/8$.

189. **(C)** As explained in answer 188, above, all phenotypes would occur in nearly equal numbers if there were no linkage. If all three genes were linked, there would be only two large groups of phenotypes, resulting from the two noncrossover chromosome types (remember, crossing-over is a relatively rare event, so nonrecombinant test-cross progeny would be most prevalent). These would be *sc ec vg* individuals and + + + individuals. The actual results include four large groups, the two just mentioned plus *sc ec* + and + + *vg*. This indicates that one of the three genes is not linked to the others. But which of the three is independent? Look at the test-cross progeny, *ignoring* the wing characteristic (*vg* or +). Only two large groups appear, *sc ec* (240 + 230 = 470) and + + (242 + 232 = 474). They are in nearly equal numbers, as expected if they are from nonrecombinant F_1's with the *sc* and *ec* genes linked. If, on the other hand, we look at the categories of *ec* and *vg*, ignoring *sc*, we find four large categories in nearly equal numbers: + *vg* (232 + 14), *ec vg* (230 + 15), + + (242 + 12), and *ec* + (240 + 15). This 1:1:1:1

ratio is what would be expected if *ec* and *sc* were linked and the pair were assorting independently of *vg*. Our conclusion is that this is the case.

190. **(D)** Although the phenomenon is not understood, males of the species do not show genetic signs of crossing-over. Since crossing-over analysis is vital in determining linkage, only females of the F_1 generation would be appropriate.

191. **(B)** Many terrestrial animals, including humans, excrete their nitrogenous wastes in the form of urea, which can be tolerated in higher concentration than ammonia. Terrestrial animals conserve water by using urea.

192. **(A)** The intestine of an herbivore (plant eater) needs extra time to digest the tough cell walls of plants. This time is provided by a longer intestinal tract.

193. **(D)** The introductory paragraph states that a *precocious* increase of T3 was artificially induced. The word means "before the normal time" — here meaning before a natural increase that occurs just prior to metamorphic change.

194. **(A)** There is an orderly progression of change after injection of T3, just as occurs in natural metamorphosis.

195. **(C)** The graph shows synthesis of new membranes. Phospholipid is a major component of membranes.

196. **(C)** Messenger RNA carries codes for building proteins, such as cytochrome oxidase, urea cycle enzymes, and enzymes that catalyze membrane synthesis. Ribosomal RNA forms a portion of ribosomes, the sites of protein synthesis. The nucleus must produce and release these nucleic acids before the other events shown on the graph can occur. Treatment of T3-injected animals with the drug actinomycin D (a transcription inhibitor) causes a halt in metamorphic events.

197. **(A)** Cytochrome oxidase is an enzyme that accepts electrons from the cytochromes of the electron transport system and passes them to oxygen. During their passage through the system, electrons transfer their energy to ATP, a newly synthesized material.

198. **(E)** Each enzyme shows a characteristic maximum reaction velocity. Although difficult to determine experimentally (since a very large substrate concentration would be required), the theoretical V_{max} can be determined through the use of a Lineweaver-Burk plot. This is a double-reciprocal plot of the same data, where the x-axis is $1/V$ and the y-axis is $1/[S]$. The point at which the plotted curve strikes the x-axis is $1/V_{max}$.

199. **(C)** Decreasing the value of K_M in the equation decreases the denominator, which increases the value for V. The question states

that V_{max} (at high substrate concentration) remains constant, so the decrease of V must occur only at the lower range of substrate concentrations.

200. **(D)** Leonor Michaelis and Maud Menten derived the equation in 1913. The hyperbolic curve is sometimes said to describe "Michaelis-Menten kinetics," and K_M is the Michaelis constant.

201. **(C)** The passage cited evidence that apomorphine can mimic dopamine by activating the dopamine receptor site, therefore causing cAMP production. It could replace the dopamine that is not produced by a victim of Parkinson's disease.

202. **(E)** Chlorpromazine blocks and inactivates dopamine receptors, making it less likely that dopamine will activate them. Therefore, it is possible that schizophrenia involves overstimulation of these receptors by an inappropriately large release of dopamine.

203. **(B)** Any agent that blocks a neurotransmitter receptor site causes inactivation of its enzymatic activity. Serotonin receptor sites, if activated, catalyze production of cAMP, so the intracellular level of this substance will drop after LSD blocks further production.

204. **(B)** Since skeletal muscles must react quickly to stimuli if they are to be useful, it would be intolerable for them to depend upon the relatively slow process of adenylate cyclase activation, cAMP production, and biochemical changes induced by cAMP. It is quicker to have a direct-stimulation method whereby acetylcholine itself causes the critical membrane permeability changes that stimulate a muscle fiber.

205. **(C)** Nonlipid hormones have great difficulty entering target cells through the lipid-containing cytoplasmic membrane. Many examples are known in which they act in much the same way described here for neurotransmitters. They stimulate the membrane to begin enzymatic activity leading to cAMP production within the cell. The first known example of this was the action of adrenalin upon liver cells. Lipid hormones, such as the steroid sex hormones, can easily pass through cytoplasmic membranes and have a direct effect upon the interiors of their target cells.

206. **(C)** Transpiration is the loss of water at a leaf surface by evaporation. Because of the high heat of vaporization of water, this process leads to a large heat transfer to the air. A detached leaf has lost its connection with a water supply that is necessary if it is to continue transpiration.

207. **(C)** Stomata are the openings on a leaf surface that are widest when transpiration is most active.

208. **(C)** The graph shows that the maximum internal temperature of an intact leaf was about 40°, well below the danger level.

209. **(A)** Any dark object absorbs heat. Since tissue contains a large quantity of water, and since water has the property of holding heat a long time, and since the severed leaf has lost the benefit of transpiration, it tends to become warmer than the surrounding air.

210. **(E)** Panting by dogs is an activity that allows maximum evaporation of water from the tongue surface. Heat is transferred from the body core to this surface by blood flow.

Test in Biology

Sample Test 4

Directions for Taking Test: This sample test contains 210 questions or incomplete statements, and should be finished in 170 minutes. Each item will have five possible answers or completions. Choose the best and blacken its letter in the place provided. After finishing, you may determine your score by using the **Answer Key** at the end of this test. The Answer Key also contains comments and explanations that should clarify the concepts involved in each question.

Questions 1–98

For each of the following questions or incomplete statements there are five suggested answers or completions. Select the best choice.

1. The organelle active in the synthesis of proteins is the
   A. nucleus
   B. plastid
   C. mitochondrion
   D. ribosome
   E. lysosome

   1.A B C D E

2. In the Krebs cycle, a receptor that picks up hydrogen is
   A. NAD
   B. ADP
   C. acetyl-coenzyme A
   D. ACTH
   E. DNA polymerase

   2.A B C D E

3. In a 25-year-old oak stem the
   A. pith would be 25 years old
   B. secondary xylem would be limited to the outer growth ring
   C. phloem would be next to the primary xylem
   D. outer protective covering would be epidermis
   E. primary phloem would be in a band outside the vascular cambium

   3.A B C D E

4. Guttation is greatest when
   A. the stomates are open
   B. the temperature is low
   C. transpiration is high
   D. the temperature is high
   E. leaves are injured

   4.A B C D E

5. Contractile vacuoles in protozoa
   A. store food
   B. eliminate excess water
   C. circulate cytoplasm
   D. propel the organisms
   E. digest ingested microorganisms

   5.A B C D E
   || || || || ||

6. The sea squirt is classified with other animals that have
   A. notochords, gill slits, and dorsally located central nervous systems
   B. radial symmetry, tentacles, and mesoglea
   C. unsegmented bodies, mantles, and muscular feet variously modified
   D. spiracles, jointed appendages, and compound eyes
   E. water vascular systems, skin gills, and spines

   6.A B C D E
   || || || || ||

7. Marsupials are most abundant in
   A. Africa
   B. Australia
   C. southeastern United States
   D. Central America
   E. East Indies

   7.A B C D E
   || || || || ||

8. If cancer originates in the large intestine, it will probably spread first to the
   A. spleen
   B. stomach
   C. kidney
   D. bladder
   E. liver

   8.A B C D E
   || || || || ||

9. Which substances cannot normally cross the placenta?
   A. red blood cell antigens
   B. viruses
   C. carbon dioxide
   D. drugs
   E. hormones

   9.A B C D E
   || || || || ||

10. If the sequence of nucleotides in a gene is T–T–A–C–G–A–G, the sequence of nucleotides in mRNA synthesized by it is
    A. T–T–A–C–G–A–G
    B. A–A–U–G–C–U–C
    C. A–A–T–G–C–T–C
    D. A–A–T–G–C–T–G
    E. T–T–U–G–C–U–G

    10.A B C D E
    || || || || ||

11. Magnolias and alligators occur naturally in widely separated areas of the southeastern United States and China. This fact is best explained by
    A. convergent evolution
    B. continental drift
    C. survival of the fittest
    D. Pleistocene glaciation
    E. adaptive radiation

    11.A B C D E
    || || || || ||

12. Biologists use several kinds of microscopes for different purposes. Which of the following statements about them is correct?

   A. The phase contrast microscope is useless for viewing living microorganisms because the image appears too transparent.
   B. The image in a dissecting microscope is reversed.
   C. The electron microscope achieves a higher magnification than other microscopes because its fluorescent screen is larger than glass lenses.
   D. The stereoscopic microscope is essentially two microscopes that focus on the object from different angles.
   E. The field of view can be enlarged in the compound microscope by changing to an objective with a higher magnification.

   12. A B C D E
   || || || || ||

13. In cold climates a large mammal has a decided advantage over a small one because

   A. it can retain body heat better
   B. it can defend itself better from its enemies
   C. it can store more food in its body
   D. its territory is larger
   E. it does not get entrapped by deep snow

   13. A B C D E
   || || || || ||

14. Which of the following are equivalents?

   A. monosaccharide; sucrose
   B. disaccharide; maltose
   C. trisaccharide; lactose
   D. oligosaccharide; fructose
   E. polysaccharide; raffinose

   14. A B C D E
   || || || || ||

15. Salt marshes are functionally most like

   A. mangrove forests
   B. prairies
   C. savannas
   D. steppes
   E. tundras

   15. A B C D E
   || || || || ||

16. Which statement about viruses is INCORRECT?

   A. They do not have protoplasm.
   B. They do not take in food.
   C. They do not mutate.
   D. They do not reproduce outside cells.
   E. They do not respire.

   16. A B C D E
   || || || || ||

17. The arrangement of microtubules in cilia is

   A. 9 + 2
   B. 4 + 4
   C. 2 + 2
   D. 8 + 2
   E. 7 + 3

   17. A B C D E
   || || || || ||

18. Which sensory organ is correctly related to its function?
    A. lateral line of fish — chemical perception
    B. statocysts of jellyfish — balance
    C. pit organs of pit vipers — pressure perception
    D. cochlea of humans — kinesthetic perception
    E. antennule of crayfish — olfactory perception

18.**A B C D E**

19. In the human brain sight is perceived by the
    A. olfactory lobe
    B. cerebrum
    C. medulla
    D. cerebellum
    E. pons

19.**A B C D E**

20. The greater risk in childbirth by an Rh-negative mother and an Rh-positive father is caused by
    A. antibodies produced by an Rh-positive fetus
    B. the production of antigens by an Rh-positive fetus that are toxic to the Rh-negative mother
    C. Rh-negative antigens produced by the mother
    D. the combined toxic effect of antigens produced by an Rh-negative fetus and an Rh-negative mother
    E. lack of vigor of all Rh-neutral fetuses

20.**A B C D E**

21. The sites of particular genes on a chromosome can be determined by
    A. using radioactive tracers
    B. crossing-over of chromosomes
    C. making a back-cross
    D. segregation
    E. base pairing

21.**A B C D E**

22. Down's syndrome is an example of
    A. monosomy
    B. disomy
    C. trisomy
    D. triploidy
    E. polyploidy

22.**A B C D E**

23. One key point in Darwin's theory of evolution is the recognition that
    A. change occurs by big steps called mutations
    B. characteristics acquired during the lifetime of an individual modify genes
    C. individuals of every generation vary in their ability to survive under prevailing conditions
    D. hybridization between existing species accounts for the origin of new species
    E. the direction of evolution is always from simple to complex

23.**A B C D E**

24. Slopes of tall mountains are often covered by several zones of vegetation. Which statement about zones is INCORRECT?

24. A B C D E
|| || || || ||

    A. The zone at the top of the mountain is above timber line.

    B. The zone at the bottom of the mountain is probably the climax vegetation of the region where the mountain is located.

    C. The sequence of zones found at increasing altitudes is similar to the sequence found at increasing latitudes.

    D. Altitude alone cannot account for the size and composition of the zones.

    E. A zone may vary considerably in altitudinal location and floristic composition between the north- and south-facing slopes.

25. An example of a fat is

25. A B C D E
|| || || || ||

    A. cellulose

    B. chitin

    C. agar

    D. hemoglobin

    E. stearin

26. Which one of the following discovered bacteria?

26. A B C D E
|| || || || ||

    A. Koch

    B. Pasteur

    C. van Leeuwenhoek

    D. Spallanzani

    E. Lister

27. Grass growing better near the trunk of a tree than several feet away from it means that

27. A B C D E
|| || || || ||

    A. the tree was recently planted

    B. more fertilizer was applied under the tree

    C. the roots next to the trunk do not absorb water and solutes

    D. grass grows better in the shade

    E. the tap root is damaged

28. It is believed that whales evolved from terrestrial mammals because whales

28. A B C D E
|| || || || ||

    A. are vertebrate animals

    B. are viviparous

    C. lack scales on their exterior

    D. protect their young

    E. use lungs for gas exchange

29. The immediate ancestors of birds were

29. A B C D E
|| || || || ||

    A. bats

    B. insects

    C. amphibians

    D. reptiles

    E. fishes

30. The exchange of chromosomal parts between nonhomologous pairs of chromosomes is

    A. inversion

    B. translocation

    C. deletion

    D. duplication

    E. crossing-over

30. A B C D E

31. The production of which of these is largely under the control of genes NOT carried on nuclear chromosomes?

    A. cytoplasmic enzymes

    B. hormones

    C. mitochondria

    D. nuclear membranes

    E. ribosomes

31. A B C D E

32. The evolution of a new species is dependent upon isolating mechanisms that prevent mating between individuals of two populations. Which of the following was probably most significant in the evolution of Darwin's finches?

    A. geographical isolation

    B. seasonal isolation

    C. gametic isolation

    D. behavioral isolation

    E. mechanical isolation

32. A B C D E

33. In free-living protozoans like amoebae, food is digested

    A. by enzymes they secrete into the water

    B. in vacuoles

    C. in the cytoplasm

    D. by bacteria within the cell

    E. by bacteria outside the cell

33. A B C D E

34. Most endothermic animals have

    A. nucleated red blood cells

    B. hair or feathers

    C. placentae

    D. mammary glands

    E. cloacas

34. A B C D E

35. Ciliated epithelium lines the

    A. digestive tract of mammals

    B. oviduct (Fallopian tube) of humans

    C. sperm duct of humans

    D. lung of birds

    E. bladder of mammals

35. A B C D E

36. Color blindness is more likely to occur in males than females because
   A. males have a tendency to deposit cholesterol in small blood vessels, thereby reducing the oxygen and food supply to the retina
   B. genes for the characteristic are located on the X chromosome
   C. the trait is dominant in males and recessive in females
   D. males require more vitamin A to achieve the same sensitivity in the rods and cones of the retina
   E. some males have difficulty absorbing vitamin A, a necessary prerequisite to the synthesis of visual purple (rhodopsin)

36. A B C D E

37. Of the following habitats, which covers the largest portion of the earth?
   A. saline water
   B. deserts
   C. grasslands
   D. forests
   E. fresh water

37. A B C D E

38. The presence of three number 21 chromosomes in humans causes a condition known as
   A. cleft palate
   B. Down's syndrome
   C. hydrocephaly
   D. clubfoot
   E. sickle-cell anemia

38. A B C D E

39. A major evolutionary advancement of seed plants over any other plants is the
   A. acquisition of vascular tissue
   B. acquisition of pollen tubes
   C. acquisition of fruits
   D. acquisition of perennial life spans
   E. loss of the gametophytic stage

39. A B C D E

40. Which pyrimidine is found in both DNA and RNA?
   A. adenine
   B. guanine
   C. cytosine
   D. thymine
   E. uracil

40. A B C D E

41. Which type of cell in a plant stem is capable of cell division?
   A. pith
   B. wood
   C. cork
   D. cambium
   E. fiber

41. A B C D E

42. The pitcher plant is a carnivorous plant that captures and digests insects between its two leaves clamped tightly together. If the openings of the leaves are plugged with cotton,
    A. the plant will soon starve for lack of food
    B. the plant will manufacture its own food
    C. the leaves will wither and rot
    D. digestive enzymes will quickly dissolve the cotton
    E. the leaves will turn yellow for lack of oxygen

42. A B C D E
    ‖ ‖ ‖ ‖ ‖

43. What kind of organism is NOT found in plankton?
    A. dinoflagellates
    B. green algae
    C. diatoms
    D. radiolaria
    E. sporozoans

43. A B C D E
    ‖ ‖ ‖ ‖ ‖

44. The brain of a vertebrate animal develops from
    A. dorsal ectoderm
    B. ganglia
    C. mesenchyme
    D. notochord
    E. the archenteron roof

44. A B C D E
    ‖ ‖ ‖ ‖ ‖

45. After ceasing physical exertion, a person continues to breathe heavily until
    A. accumulated carbon dioxide is removed from the muscles
    B. lactic acid is consumed or converted to something else
    C. the body cools
    D. glycolysis begins
    E. the food that was stored in the muscles is replaced

45. A B C D E
    ‖ ‖ ‖ ‖ ‖

46. One contractile protein in muscles is
    A. histidine
    B. fibrinogen
    C. cytosine
    D. oxytocin
    E. myosin

46. A B C D E
    ‖ ‖ ‖ ‖ ‖

47. ATP is used in a cell to
    A. accept energy
    B. become part of the nuclear membranes
    C. regulate membrane permeability
    D. store energy
    E. digest polysaccharides

47. A B C D E
    ‖ ‖ ‖ ‖ ‖

48. Which sequence best describes the plant life cycle?
    A. zygote → sporophyte
    B. spore → sporophyte
    C. ovary → seed
    D. cotyledon→ endosperm
    E. integument → pericarp

48. A B C D E
    ‖ ‖ ‖ ‖ ‖

49. Which statement about photosynthesis is INCORRECT? 49. A B C D E
   A. During the light phase, water is broken down to hydrogen and oxygen.
   B. During the dark phase, carbon dioxide is broken down to carbon and oxygen.
   C. An end product is fructose diphosphate.
   D. Chlorophyll molecules are not used up in the process.
   E. NADP combines with free hydrogen.

50. If the flower of a Winesap apple is pollinated by pollen from a Delicious 50. A B C D E
   apple, the apple produced by the Winesap flower will be a
   A. Winesap
   B. Delicious
   C. mosaic
   D. new strain
   E. hybrid

51. In which of the following groups are the individuals most closely related? 51. A B C D E
   A. tick, louse, leech
   B. snake, lizard, salamander
   C. elephant, whale, alligator
   D. clam, snail, slug
   E. starfish, sea lily, sea squirt

52. Which of the following organisms has both intracellular and extracellular 52. A B C D E
   digestion?
   A. sponge
   B. hydra
   C. earthworm
   D. insect
   E. man

53. In humans, the extraembryonic membrane in contact with the uterus is the 53. A B C D E
   A. allantois
   B. yolk sac
   C. amnion
   D. chorion
   E. endometrium

54. Which of the following is an enzyme that performs an important function in 54. A B C D E
   the nervous system?
   A. catalase
   B. DNA polymerase
   C. cholinesterase
   D. lysozyme
   E. peptidase

55. The one gene — one enzyme hypothesis came from the work of 55. A B C D E
   A. Beadle and Tatum
   B. Morgan
   C. Conway
   D. Kormondy
   E. Stokes and Kramer

56. Of the following traits, which is evolutionarily most advanced?
    A. foot of man
    B. foot of horse
    C. open circulatory system
    D. pronephric kidney
    E. body supported by two pairs of limbs

56. A B C D E

57. The Secchi disk is used to
    A. connect vertebrae
    B. filter air
    C. filter water
    D. measure turbidity of water
    E. polarize light

57. A B C D E

58. The transfer of genetic material from one bacterial cell to another by a virus is called
    A. transduction
    B. transference
    C. transformation
    D. transfusion
    E. translocation

58. A B C D E

59. The deliberate setting of fire to pine forests is practiced by foresters for several reasons. The most important one is to
    A. quickly recycle the elements bound in the litter of the forest floor
    B. kill the undergrowth which is competitive with the pines
    C. kill the pines to make way for hardwoods
    D. open the forest for easier passage and visibility for hunters, thus making multiple usage of it possible
    E. stimulate root growth

59. A B C D E

60. The following groups of organisms represent different trophic levels. Which of the five has the greatest biomass?
    A. herbivores
    B. carnivores
    C. autotrophs
    D. scavengers
    E. decomposers

60. A B C D E

61. The Golgi complex performs the following function:
    A. secretion
    B. reproduction
    C. regeneration
    D. protein synthesis
    E. sensory perception

61. A B C D E

62. Organic compounds always contain the element
    A. nitrogen
    B. carbon
    C. sulfur
    D. phosphorus
    E. oxygen

62. A B C D E

63. For mosses to grow as large as most ferns, they would need

    A. less competition from larger plants

    B. stomates in their leaves

    C. better waterproofing of external surfaces

    D. auxins

    E. vascular tissue

63. A B C D E
  || || || || ||

64. Of the light that falls on a green plant, approximately what percent is used in photosynthesis?

    A. 1%

    B. 10%

    C. 25%

    D. 50%

    E. 95%

64. A B C D E
  || || || || ||

65. Which statement about different animals is INCORRECT?

    A. Sponges have no muscles.

    B. Cnidaria have no brains.

    C. Tapeworms have no hearts.

    D. Sharks have no bones.

    E. Fishes have no livers.

65. A B C D E
  || || || || ||

66. When a protein is broken down to its component amino acids, the type of reaction doing this is

    A. a condensation reaction

    B. a deamination reaction

    C. a hydrolysis reaction

    D. a peptide reaction

    E. an anabolic reaction

66. A B C D E
  || || || || ||

67. The amnion in mammals is most useful in

    A. cushioning shock

    B. keeping the fetus clean

    C. regulating temperature

    D. transporting oxygen from the placenta

    E. storing food for the fetus

67. A B C D E
  || || || || ||

68. Motor neuron impulses are transmitted to skeletal muscle by

    A. acetylcholine

    B. ATP

    C. secretin

    D. electron transport

    E. sodium ions

68. A B C D E
  || || || || ||

69. Which statement about mitosis is INCORRECT?

    A. Prophase takes longer than metaphase or anaphase.

    B. When chromosomes move to the poles, the centromeres lead the way.

    C. During the interphase stage, all metabolic activity ceases.

    D. Chromosomes are fully formed during prophase.

    E. Mitosis is in telophase when chromosomes reach the poles.

69. A B C D E
  || || || || ||

70. The DNA nucleotide is composed of
  A. phosphate, deoxyribose, and nitrogenous base
  B. purine and pyrimidine
  C. thymine, guanine, cytosine, and adenine
  D. ribose, uracil, and phosphate
  E. polypeptide, purine, and pyrimidine

70.A B C D E
|| || || || ||

71. The sex-influenced gene governing the presence of horns in sheep exhibits dominance in males but acts recessively in females. When individuals of the Dorset breed (both sexes horned) with genotype *hh* is crossed with those of the Suffolk breed (both sexes hornless) with genotype *h'h'*, what proportion of the F₁ males will be hornless?
  A. none
  B. all
  C. 25%
  D. 50%
  E. 75%

71.A B C D E
|| || || || ||

72. The wings of a bat are homologous to the
  A. two long tentacles of a squid
  B. wings of a butterfly
  C. arms of a human
  D. jumping legs of a grasshopper
  E. chelipeds of a lobster

72.A B C D E
|| || || || ||

73. The most successful parasite is the one that
  A. has a life cycle involving a sequence of hosts
  B. is permanently attached to the host
  C. is highly specialized
  D. originated first
  E. makes minimal demands on the host

73.A B C D E
|| || || || ||

74. An ecological niche is occupied by
  A. a population
  B. a small community
  C. a host and its parasites
  D. a balanced mixture of autotrophic and heterotrophic organisms.
  E. competing species

74.A B C D E
|| || || || ||

75. The function most closely associated with the thylakoid membranes of chloroplasts is
  A. gene replication
  B. glycolysis
  C. oxidative phosphorylation
  D. photophosphorylation
  E. protein synthesis

75.A B C D E
|| || || || ||

76. When a slime mold cell moves toward a source of cyclic AMP, this phenomenon is termed
    A. chemotaxis
    B. cyclosis
    C. cytokinesis
    D. pinocytosis
    E. plasmolysis

77. All of the following statements about gametophytes are generally true EX- 77. **A B C D E**
    CEPT:
    A. Gametophytes have no true roots, stems, or leaves.
    B. The chromosome number of gametophytes is haploid.
    C. Gametophytes are seedless.
    D. Gametophytes grow from spores and produce gametes.
    E. Gametophytes are smaller than sporophytes and parasitic upon them.

78. In which pair of structures, do the two structures NOT have the same em- 78. **A B C D E**
    bryological origin?
    A. gill pouch and Eustachian tube
    B. penis and clitoris
    C. liver and spleen
    D. lung and pancreas
    E. brain and fingernail

79. Which color of light is LEAST used in photosynthesis? 79. **A B C D E**
    A. red
    B. green
    C. yellow
    D. blue
    E. orange

80. At the time food passes through the pyloric sphincter of the alimentary canal, 80. **A B C D E**
    A. bile secreted by the liver has emulsified the fats
    B. proteins have been digested to amino acids
    C. the mixture is acid
    D. rennin has not yet been activated
    E. pancreatic enzymes are already actively digesting the food

81. During the interphase of mitosis, 81. **A B C D E**
    A. chromatin replicates
    B. chromosomes break up into chromatin
    C. nucleoli disappear
    D. chromosomes are distinctly double
    E. homologous chromosomes are paired

82. Leaves are generally well adapted to the environmental conditions where they live. Which statement concerning their relation to habitat is FALSE?
   A. Leaves on aquatic plants often have large air spaces.
   B. Vertical leaves do not have palisade mesophyll.
   C. Shade leaves tend to be large and thin.
   D. Multiple layers of epidermis are characteristic of leaves submerged in water.
   E. Leaves that are round in cross section conserve water.

82. A B C D E
   || || || || ||

83. *Neurospora* ranks as one of the leading subjects for genetic studies. As an experimental organism, *Neurospora* exhibits all of the following characteristics EXCEPT:
   A. It is easily cultured in the laboratory.
   B. It has a short life cycle of about 10 days.
   C. It is normally haploid, which means that recessive genes are not masked by dominant ones.
   D. Its meiospores (ascospores) are arranged in ordered tetrads.
   E. Its spores are unaffected by radiation.

83. A B C D E
   || || || || ||

84. When a lethal characteristic like albinism occurs in green plants, the
   A. lethal gene is always dominant
   B. characteristic can occur only because of a new mutation
   C. gene expresses itself in alternate generations
   D. characteristic is carried by green plants into the next generation
   E. cause is viral rather than genetic

84. A B C D E
   || || || || ||

85. A green plant with vestigial stomates would be expected to live
   A. on deserts
   B. in water
   C. as a parasite
   D. in the tundra -
   E. on salt flats

85. A B C D E
   || || || || ||

86. A community is obviously at the climax stage of development when
   A. hardwoods predominate
   B. pines predominate
   C. the number of species is relatively low
   D. the plants are reproducing themselves
   E. the plants are similar

86. A B C D E
   || || || || ||

87. Laterization is a process that results in
   A. nitrogen fixation
   B. soil formation
   C. self-sterility
   D. purification of water
   E. deadening of pain

87. A B C D E
   || || || || ||

88. Sex attractants secreted by the female silkworm moth belong to a group of substances known as
   A. flavones
   B. estrogens
   C. auxins
   D. pheromones
   E. secretins

89. A dominant sex-limited gene is known to cause premature baldness in men but has no effect in women. What proportion of the male offspring from heterozygous parents will be bald?
   A. 1/4
   B. 3/8
   C. 1/2
   D. 5/8
   E. 3/4

90. This type of chromosomal configuration results from

   A. inversion
   B. translocation
   C. deletion
   D. duplication
   E. crossing-over

91. Which of the following chromosomal aberrations produces a configuration as illustrated?

   A. inversion
   B. translocation
   C. deletion
   D. duplication
   E. crossing-over

92. Turgid cells are
   A. dehydrated
   B. swollen
   C. wilted
   D. coagulated
   E. plasmolyzed

92. A B C D E
   || || || || ||

93. In plants, cellular respiration occurs in
   A. all cells
   B. all living cells
   C. growing tissues only
   D. all living cells except where photosynthesis is in progress
   E. all living cells except at night

93. A B C D E
   || || || || ||

94. Stomates are opened by
   A. auxins
   B. starch accumulation in guard cells
   C. sugar deficiency
   D. photonastic movement
   E. water swelling the guard cells

94. A B C D E
   || || || || ||

95. Lichen growing on the bark of a tree would best be characterized as a(n)
   A. parasite
   B. saprophyte
   C. epiphyte
   D. commensal
   E. bryophyte

95. A B C D E
   || || || || ||

96. Of the following, which is totally unrelated to the others?
   A. nephridia
   B. alveoli
   C. Malpighian tubules
   D. kidney
   E. antennary gland

96. A B C D E
   || || || || ||

97. In a family that has three girls and one boy, what is the probability that a fifth child will be a boy?
   A. 25%
   B. 50%
   C. 75%
   D. 100%
   E. 0%

97. A B C D E
   || || || || ||

98. If the probability of having Aa is one in two births, bb one in four births, and CC one in four births, what is the chance of having $AabbCC$?
   A. 1:2
   B. 1:4
   C. 1:8
   D. 1:16
   E. 1:32

98. A B C D E
   || || || || ||

The next five questions (99–103) are based on the pedigree of a family afflicted with hemophilia. The characteristic is recessive and sex-linked. Study the relationships carefully, and answer the questions accordingly.

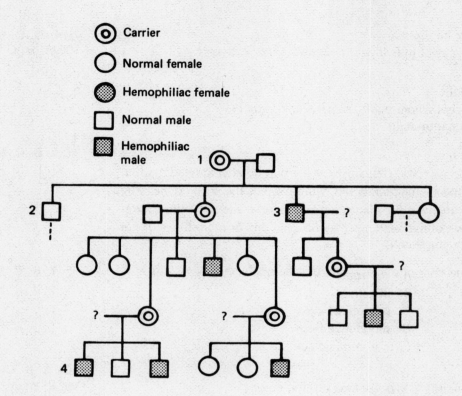

99. The genotype of individual 1 is
  A. unknown
  B. probably heterozygous
  C. definitely heterozygous
  D. definitely homozygous recessive
  E. probably homozygous recessive

99. A B C D E
|| || || || ||

100. If individual 3 marries a normal woman and fathers several children, all
  A. children will be normal
  B. children will be hemophiliac
  C. males will be normal
  D. males will be carriers
  E. females will be normal

100. A B C D E
|| || || || ||

101. Judging from the information available, individual 2
  A. could have a carrier mother
  B. must have had a normal father
  C. must have had two normal parents
  D. could father a hemophiliac daughter
  E. could father a carrier son

101. A B C D E
|| || || || ||

102. If individual 4 marries a normal woman, what is the chance that their child will be hemophiliac?

    A. 0
    B. 25%
    C. 50%
    D. 74%
    E. 100%

102. A B C D E
    || || || || ||

103. What are the genotypes of individuals 1, 2, and 3, respectively?

    A. *Hh, hO, HO*
    B. unknown, *hO, HO*
    C. *Hh, HO, hO*
    D. unknown, *hO,* unknown
    E. *Hh, HH, hh*

103. A B C D E
    || || || || ||

The next four questions (104–107) consist of a group of lettered headings and numbered biomes. For each numbered biome select the lettered heading which characterizes many of the plants that live therein, and mark the answer accordingly. Any one of the headings may be used one or more times or not at all.

    A. stilt roots
    B. drip tips
    C. succulents
    D. diminutive trees
    E. autumn leaf coloration

104. deciduous forest

104. A B C D E
    || || || || ||

105. mangrove forest

105. A B C D E
    || || || || ||

106. tropical rainforest

106. A B C D E
    || || || || ||

107. desert

107. A B C D E
    || || || || ||

The next four questions (108–111) are based on the trophic pyramid illustrated on p. 165. The trophic levels in the pyramid are labeled with letters. For each question select the lettered trophic level that corresponds to it, and mark the answer accordingly. Any one of the lettered levels may be used one or more times or not at all.

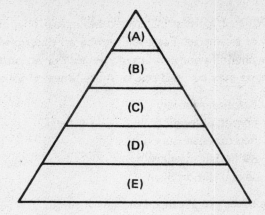

108. primary consumers

108. A B C D E
|| || || || ||

109. secondary consumers

109. A B C D E
|| || || || ||

110. tertiary consumers

110. A B C D E
|| || || || ||

111. producers

111. A B C D E
|| || || || ||

The next six questions (112–117) consist of lettered structures and numbered descriptions. For each numbered description select the appropriate lettered structure, and mark the answer accordingly. Any of the lettered structures may be used one or more times or not at all.

A. zygote
B. erythrocyte
C. pollen
D. Schwann cell
E. sperm

112. usually consists of more than one cell

112. A B C D E
|| || || || ||

113. is a single haploid cell

113. A B C D E
|| || || || ||

114. in humans, lacks chromatin when fully differentiated

114. A B C D E
|| || || || ||

115. is a highly differentiated cell associated with rapid nerve transmission

115. A B C D E
|| || || || ||

116. the immediate result of fertilization

116. A B C D E
|| || || || ||

117. is the only cell type in the list capable of prolonged life away from a watery environment

117. A B C D E
|| || || || ||

The next five questions (118–122) consist of lettered biological phenomena and numbered descriptions or examples. For each numbered description select the appropriate lettered phenomenon, and mark the answer accordingly. Any of the lettered phenomena may be used one or more times or not at all.

    A. Batesian mimicry
    B. cryptic coloration
    C. heterozygote superiority
    D. Müllerian mimicry
    E. sexual dimorphism

118. A species of fly looks and sounds like a wasp, but cannot sting.

118. A B C D E
    || || || || ||

119. A bee and a wasp both have yellow and black stripes.

119. A B C D E
    || || || || ||

120. Carriers of the sickle-cell hemoglobin allele have selective advantage over other individuals in certain environments.

120. A B C D E
    || || || || ||

121. The fish known as a flounder can match with its skin pigments the pattern of the background environment.

121. A B C D E
    || || || || ||

122. This phenomenon leads to recognition between potential mates.

122. A B C D E
    || || || || ||

The next five questions (123–127) consist of lettered animals and numbered descriptions of nervous systems. For each numbered description select the appropriate lettered animal, and mark the answer accordingly. Any of the lettered animals may be used one or more times or not at all.

    A. cat
    B. hydra
    C. planaria
    D. shark
    E. sponge

123. It has no central nervous system but possesses neurons.

123. A B C D E
    || || || || ||

124. Its cerebrum dominates other brain regions.

124. A B C D E
    || || || || ||

125. Its brain is a collection of neurons without any regions corresponding to those of a human brain.

125. A B C D E
    || || || || ||

126. It is characterized by a brain that has a relatively large olfactory region.

126. A B C D E
    || || || || ||

127. It has no neurons.

127. A B C D E
    || || || || ||

The next six questions (128–133) consist of lettered groups within kingdom Animalia and numbered descriptions. For each numbered description select the appropriate lettered group, and mark the answer accordingly. Any of the lettered groups may be used one or more times or not at all.

A. Annelida
B. Arthropoda
C. Chordata
D. Insecta
E. Porifera

128. the phylum that includes colonial, benthic animals

128. A B C D E
|| || || || ||

129. the group that includes the earthworms

129. A B C D E
|| || || || ||

130. the class that includes externally segmented animals with exoskeletons

130. A B C D E
|| || || || ||

131. the phylum whose members have an open circulatory system

131. A B C D E
|| ||, || || ||

132. the group in this list with the largest number of living species

132. A B C D E
|| || || || ||

133. the phylum to which you belong

133. A B C D E
|| || || || ||

The next five questions (134–138) consist of lettered regions of a bacterial chromosome's inducible gene system (see diagram below) and numbered questions about the regions. For each numbered question select the appropriate lettered region, and mark the answer accordingly. Any of the lettered regions may be used one or more times or not at all.

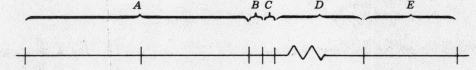

134. Since area A is a pair of structural genes containing codes for building enzymes, which area is the operator?

134. A B C D E
|| || || || ||

135. Which is the region that carries the code for building a functional repressor protein?

135. A B C D E
|| || || || ||

136. Which is the region to which a functional repressor protein can attach, leading to repression?

136. A B C D E
|| || || || ||

137. Which area manufactures a product only when an inducer molecule is in the cell?

137. A B C D E
|| || || || ||

138. Which region is the first to be touched by RNA polymerase if the system is to operate?

138. A B C D E
|| || || || ||

The next five questions (139–143) consist of lettered substances and numbered descriptions. For each numbered description select the appropriate lettered substance, and mark the answer accordingly. Any lettered substance may be used one or more times or not at all.

A. calcium
B. collagen
C. epinephrine
D. indoleacetic acid
E. pyruvic acid

139. a substance made in animals and plants

139. A B C D E
|| || || || ||

140. a substance that is not a molecule

140. A B C D E
|| || || || ||

141. a plant hormone

141. A B C D E
|| || || || ||

142. an animal hormone

142. A B C D E
|| || || || ||

143. a protein

143. A B C D E
|| || || || ||

The next four questions (144–147) consist of lettered cell structures and numbered descriptions of muscle. For each numbered description select the appropriate lettered structure, and mark the answer accordingly. Any of the lettered structures may be used one or more times or not at all.

A. endoplasmic reticulum
B. myoneuronal junction
C. sarcomere
D. sarcoplasmic reticulum
E. transverse tubule

144. the portion of skeletal muscle that contracts

144. A B C D E
|| || || || ||

145. a membrane system that carries an action potential deep inside a muscle fiber

145. A B C D E
|| || || || ||

146. a membrane system that can operate an active transport pump which keeps calcium ions from a muscle fiber's contractile proteins

146. A B C D E
|| || || || ||

147. the synapse that links the nervous system to a muscle fiber

147. A B C D E
|| || || || ||

The next five questions (148–152) consist of lettered ecologically important concepts and numbered descriptions. For each numbered description select the appropriate lettered concept, and mark the answer accordingly. Any of the lettered concepts may be used one or more times or not at all.

A. carrying capacity
B. chemosynthesis
C. food web
D. greenhouse effect
E. symbiosis

148. an increase of atmospheric temperature caused by carbon dioxide's absorption of infrared rays

148. A B C D E
|| || || || ||

149. a complex interaction among producers and consumers

149. A B C D E
|| || || || ||

150. ability of an organism to gain energy from a nonliving source other than the sun

150. A B C D E
|| || || || ||

151. the maximum size of a population in a particular ecosystem

151. A B C D E
|| || || || ||

152. long-term interaction between species

152. A B C D E
|| || || || ||

The next five questions (153–157) consist of lettered vertebrate hormones and numbered descriptions. For each numbered description select the appropriate lettered hormone, and mark the answer accordingly. Any of the lettered hormones may be used one or more times or not at all.

A. follicle-stimulating hormone
B. insulin
C. parathyroid hormone
D. progesterone
E. testosterone

153. is a pituitary hormone influencing reproduction

153. A B C D E
|| || || || ||

154. helps prepare the uterus wall for nurture of an embryo

154. A B C D E
|| || || || ||

155. is produced by the pancreas

155. A B C D E
|| || || || ||

156. controls calcium levels in the body

156. A B C D E
|| || || || ||

157. stimulates the growth of facial hair

157. A B C D E
|| || || || ||

The next four questions (158–161) consist of lettered plant structures and numbered descriptions. For each numbered description select the appropriate lettered structure, and mark the answer accordingly. Any of the lettered structures may be used one or more times or not at all.

A. adventitious roots
B. haustorial roots
C. fibrous roots
D. prop roots
E. taproots

158. roots of dodder, a parasitic plant

158.**A B C D E**
|| || || || ||

159. roots of dandelions

159.**A B C D E**
|| || || || ||

160. roots of carrots

160.**A B C D E**
|| || || || ||

161. roots of grass

161.**A B C D E**
|| || || || ||

The next five questions (162–166) consist of lettered organisms and numbered descriptions. For each numbered description select the appropriate lettered organism, and mark the answer accordingly. Any of the lettered organisms may be used one or more times or not at all.

A. bacterium
B. fruit fly *(Drosophila)*
C. human
D. *Neurospora*
E. virus

162. Some of these use RNA as their chromosomal material.

162.**A B C D E**
|| || || || ||

163. This organism was the first in which sex linkage of genes was shown.

163.**A B C D E**
|| || || || ||

164. These organisms can transfer genes by conjugation.

164.**A B C D E**
|| || || || ||

165. Crossing-over analysis of regions within a single gene was first performed with this organism.

165.**A B C D E**
|| || || || ||

166. Avery, MacLeod, and McCarty used this organism to demonstrate for the first time that DNA can be the carrier of genetic information.

166.**A B C D E**
|| || || || ||

The remaining questions ask for analysis of experiments. For each set, read the descriptions and data carefully; then answer the questions or complete the statements by choosing among the lettered alternatives and marking your answers accordingly.

Questions 167–170

A number of species of moths living in industrial areas of Britain have two color forms, light and dark. A dark form was first observed in 1850 and has since become common. Both forms of moths settle on trunks of trees when at rest. In some places soot from homes and factories have destroyed bark lichens and blackened the bark with deposits. Light-colored moths are conspicuous on dark bark and inconspicuous on light bark, whereas dark-colored moths are conspicuous on light bark and inconspicuous on dark bark. Doubtless, the ability to blend with the background is a protection from birds that are known to feed on moths. The development of melanin in insects in general is known to be achieved by both dominant and recessive genes. However, in the case of the dark moths all known genetic information confirms that melanism is spread by a dominant gene.

167. The evolution of dark moths from light ones can be attributed to
    A. gene mutations caused by soot
    B. gene mutations induced by need
    C. gene mutations occurring accidentally
    D. absence of recessive genes for dark forms
    E. light moths being more susceptible to gene mutations than dark ones

167. A B C D E

168. Evidence is sufficient for one to conclude that
    A. gene mutations for melanism did not originate before 1850
    B. a change in the environment accelerated favorable mutations
    C. birds feed mostly on light-colored moths
    D. colored forms reproduce faster than light forms
    E. similar mutations can occur in different organisms

168. A B C D E

169. If melanism is inherited as a simple dominant characteristic, what would be expected from crossing a heterozygous dark moth with a homozygous light moth?
    A. All offspring would be dark.
    B. All offspring would be light.
    C. All offspring would be intermediate between dark and light.
    D. Half of the offspring would be dark and half light.
    E. Three fourths of the offspring would be dark and one fourth light.

169. A B C D E

170. If the environment could suddenly revert to its original condition before industrialization came, the effect on moths would be that
    A. genes for melanism would mutate back to the original condition
    B. dark-colored moths, being less concealed, would be eliminated by birds faster than light-colored ones
    C. light-colored moths would reproduce faster than dark-colored ones
    D. light-colored moths would breed primarily with light-colored mates
    E. the proportion of white individuals would increase as a result of white forms mating with dark forms

170. A B C D E

Questions 171–173
    The next three questions are based on the information given in the sketches of five quadrats that follow. The numbers contained within them stand for five species of organisms. Each number represents an individual.

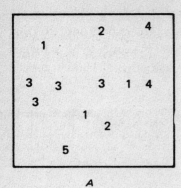

A

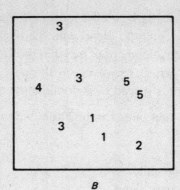

B

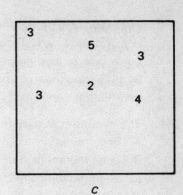

C

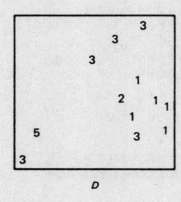

D

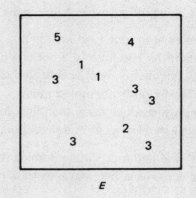

E

171. It is obvious from the information given that
   A. species 1 has a density of 12
   B. species 2 has a density of 6/5 or 1.2
   C. species 3 has a density of 60
   D. species 4 has a density of 40
   E. species 5 has a density of 100%

171. A B C D E
     || || || || ||

172. The correct frequency for
   A. species 1 is 80%
   B. species 2 is 6
   C. species 3 is 4
   D. species 4 is 1
   E. species 5 is 120%

172. A B C D E
     || || || || ||

173. Which statement is correct about the relative importance of the five species?
   A. The data given are insufficient to determine the *importance value* of each species.
   B. It is obvious from the sketches that species 3 is the most important species present.
   C. Species 3 is more important than species 1 because it is found in all of the quadrats.
   D. Species 1 is more important than species 2 because it is twice as abundant.
   E. Species 2 and species 5 are equally important because they occur in equal numbers.

173. A B C D E
     || || || || ||

Questions 174–177

A survivorship curve is a graphic representation of the relation between the life span of individuals in a population and the maximum life span for the species. The graph below is a composite of the survivorship curves for four species of animal.

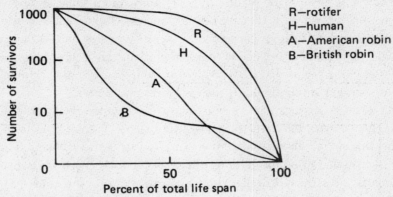

R—rotifer
H—human
A—American robin
B—British robin

174. Which species has the longest life span?

A. American robin
B. British robin
C. human
D. rotifer
E. impossible to determine from the curves

174. A B C D E
‖ ‖ ‖ ‖ ‖

175. Which species has the greatest mortality in the first portion of its maximum life span?

A. American robin
B. British robin
C. human
D. rotifer
E. impossible to determine from the curves

175. A B C D E
‖ ‖ ‖ ‖ ‖

176. Which of these figures is closest to the percentage of American robins remaining from a population of 1000 when 50% of the maximum life time was reached?

A. 0.05%
B. 0.5%
C. 5%
D. 50%
E. 75%

176. A B C D E
‖ ‖ ‖ ‖ ‖

177. Which one of these would be the explanation LEAST biologically plausible for the difference in survival curves between the American robin and the British robin?

A. The British robin does not have as efficient a set of instincts for parental care.
B. The British robin has a different set of predators which are more efficient in capturing very young birds.
C. The American robin is more successful in obtaining food early in life.
D. The American robin population has a greater proportion of females, which live longer than males.
E. The American robin has a less conspicuous color.

177. A B C D E
‖ ‖ ‖ ‖ ‖

Questions 178–184

Lectins are proteins capable of binding to certain sugars on the surfaces of cells. They are also called agglutinins because each has multiple binding sites and can therefore act as a bridge between two cells, causing them to clump (agglutinate). In this way, lectins are like antibodies such as the blood group antibodies. Lectins occur in many plants. They are normal molecular components of the organisms that produce them, synthesized in predictable regions and developmental stages.

Lectins differ considerably from each other, especially in size and in the sugar group that is bound. Among specific sugars bound by lectins of different plants are each of the human ABO blood saccharides. The blood group lectins have been useful since they also bind with the A, B, or O antigens that are sometimes secreted into body fluids such as saliva and urine.

It was discovered by chance that certain lectins bind preferentially to (and agglutinate) malignant human cells. This fact was the basis for a powerful diagnostic tool, but it also led workers to focus for the first time upon the plasma membrane as a fundamentally changed portion of a malignantly transformed cell. Some important theories of cancer are now based upon plasma membrane changes. Other workers have discovered similar changes in cells during the course of normal animal development. For instance, a lectin from the jack bean agglutinates cells obtained from the retina of an 8-day chick embryo, but will not bind cells from the retina of a chick near hatching age. It was at first believed that such changes involve changes in the number of lectin-binding sugar molecules on a cell's surface. However, when radioactively labeled lectins were added to normal and to cancerous cells (the former failing to agglutinate, the latter agglutinating), it was found that both types had bound the same number of lectin molecules per cell. Fluorescently labeled lectin molecules were then used to see whether the two cell types had their binding sugars distributed differently. Views of the cell under the ultraviolet microscope showed that normal cells have random distribution of binding sites, but malignant cells have theirs clustered in one or a few small areas.

The biological function of lectins within the organisms that produce them has been hard to determine. Wheat-germ agglutinin may inhibit growth of certain fungi that attack the seed. Other plants may be producing specific lectins as protective agents against their own pathogens.

178. How are lectins different from antibodies?

178. A B C D E

A. Antibodies act as catalysts.

B. Antibodies are specific in their choice of antigens; lectins attach to any sugar group.

C. Antibodies cannot bind to sugar groups.

D. Lectins are proteins.

E. Lectins are routinely present in certain plants, not arising only in response to new introduction of antigen.

179. Why is human blood type O-specific lectin especially useful?

179. A B C D E

A. Human anti-O antibody is hard to purify.

B. It also binds specifically to cancer cells.

C. It is larger than any other antibody.

D. No human manufactures antibody against type O blood cell antigen, since all humans produce this antigen.

E. People with type O blood are somewhat more susceptible to heart disease than are other people.

180. What is the most plausible explanation for the presence in a plant of a protein that binds to animal blood cells?

   A. Both animals and plants have common pathogenic organisms to combat.
   B. Some saccharides of identical form are widely distributed among organisms; therefore, a valuable lectin for a plant may cross-react with animal cells that carry the same binding site.
   C. The animal eats plant material and incorporates intact some of the plant's molecules into its own cells.
   D. The plant or its ancestors must have been previously exposed to the animal cells.
   E. The two cross-reacting organisms are much more closely related than previously suspected.

181. What significant thing does the preferential binding of certain lectins to malignant cells say about cancer?

   A. An important distinguishing feature about cancerous cells is their surface membrane structure.
   B. Cells gain many more lectin-binding sites as they become cancerous.
   C. Embryonic cells also bind lectins.
   D. There is a hitherto unsuspected link between cancer and pathogenic fungi.
   E. Cancers might be successfully treated with extracts of plants.

182. From the cited research with lectins, what is a logical conclusion concerning animal embryos?

   A. Their blood groups change in a predictable manner.
   B. Their cell surfaces undergo programmed molecular changes as the cells differentiate.
   C. They can be invaded by pathogenic bacteria or fungi.
   D. They change lectins as they differentiate.
   E. They have cancerous cells.

183. What is the best explanation for the fact that malignant cells are clumped by a particular agglutinin, but normal cells are not?

   A. A malignant cell concentrates its binding sites in a few places, leading to the possibility of a strong bridge forming between cells.
   B. A malignant cell has the ability to change the shape of a lectin to match its surface saccharides.
   C. A malignant cell spreads its binding sites evenly over the cell surface, so that two cells can be bound by lectin like opposite shores of a river bound by a bridge.
   D. A malignant cell turns on genes to manufacture lectin-specific sugars that were not produced before.
   E. Malignant cells can make their own lectins.

184. What technique showed that the distribution of lectin binding sites on a cell can change during the cell's lifetime?

184. A B C D E

    A. fluorescent-antibody labeling

    B. fluorescent-lectin labeling

    C. observation of agglutination at one time and nonagglutination at another time

    D. radioactive tagging of binding-site sugars

    E. radioactive tagging of lectin

Questions 185–189

The kangaroo rat is adapted for life in the desert. It saves water by concentrating its urinary urea to 1.6 times the value for a laboratory rat. It also conserves water when it avoids loss for thermoregulation by spending daylight hours in a cool, humid burrow.

Furthermore, it saves much of the water that would usually be lost in exhalation. The kangaroo rat's nose is set up anatomically to operate as a countercurrent exchange system. Inhaled air, cooler than the body core, flows through tiny passageways, progressively becoming warmed by surrounding blood-filled tissue. A gradient of warmth is set up along the passageways, which become warmer as they approach the lungs. The farther inhaled air moves, the warmer it gets by transfer of heat from nearby tissues; the farther exhalation air moves, the cooler it gets by transfer of heat to passageway walls. The outermost end of the nasal passage is actually cooler than incoming dry air because of evaporation of water from its surface into the incoming air. Thus, exhalation air, just before it leaves the animal, passes walls cooler than the outside world, and this air is cooled to nearly that extent. This cooling conserves water. Air entering the nose from the lungs is saturated with water. Dropping the air's temperature causes it to lose some of this water via condensation on the walls of the exhalation passage.

A camel has another device for saving even more water, by providing a hygroscopic surface to catch water vapor in exhalation air. When inhaling extremely dry air, the camel undergoes drying of the nasal passage walls. Dry mucus and debris act like filter paper, absorbing water from exhalation air. This surface is alternately dried and wetted with each inhalation and exhalation, changing the state of the water but losing very little to the outside.

185. Considering the method by which the nasal system works, it appears that the kangaroo rat's MAJOR need is to

185. A B C D E

    A. provide a hygroscopic surface

    B. remove excess heat

    C. remove excess water

    D. save water

    E. warm incoming air before it reaches the lungs

186. Which of these activities is NOT done to any great extent by a kangaroo rat?

186. A B C D E

    A. avoiding high ambient temperatures

    B. cooling exhalation air by relying on a countercurrent heat exchange system

    C. cooling exhalation air by relying on condensation of water from it

    D. cooling the body by relying on evaporation of water from surfaces

    E. conserving water by urine concentration

187. What is a hygroscopic surface?
A. one that cools nearby air
B. one that has a countercurrent exchange capacity
C. one that is always covered with moist mucus
D. one that is dry and porous, capable of absorbing water
E. one with a large surface area

188. Which of the following is the best description of a kangaroo rat's nasal area?
A. It alternates between having dry walls and moist walls.
B. It consists of narrow, long passages having intimate contact with blood-filled tissues.
C. It features an area of contact at the outside end with vessels carrying very cold blood.
D. It is a very wide cavern, rather than a narrow tube.
E. There are separate inhalation and exhalation passageways, running parallel and close to each other.

189. Countercurrent exchange systems have been found in other physiological systems. One of these is the
A. flow of blood through a mammalian heart
B. loop of Henle in the nephron
C. retina pattern
D. sliding filament system of skeletal muscle
E. synapse between a neuron and a muscle

Questions 190–196

The single-celled flagellate, *Gonyaulax*, contains chlorophyll but has the additional feature of producing light. It produces both luciferin and luciferase of the same light-producing system as that of a firefly. Light flashes can be elicited by shaking a culture of the organisms. When a photomultiplier tube is used to measure the amount of light emitted, it is found that the quantity per shake is dependent upon the time of day. A great deal of luminescence occurs after only slight shaking at night, but a much lower quantity of light results from even violent shaking at mid-day. At any time, the light intensity varies directly with the intensity of agitation.

This cyclic change in response, regulated by an internal 24-hour "clock," is shown in Graph 1. When a culture is artificially subjected to constant darkness, the luminescent response pattern occurs as shown in Graph 2. The change illustrated in Graph 2 can be reversed by short periods of illumination. The wavelengths that will reverse the change are those that are most active in initiating photosynthesis. A culture places in continuous illumination produces luminescence in a pattern similar to that of Graph 2.

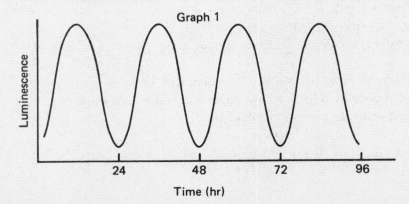

Graph 1

Time (hr)

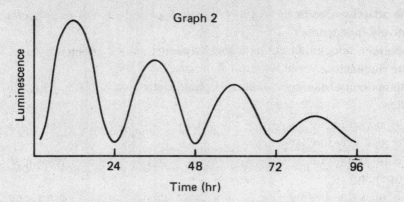

Graph 2

The cycling of luminescence. is not very dependent upon temperature. From 16° to 27° the pattern persists, although the frequency decreases a small amount as temperature rises.

The phase of a rhythm is the time of day at which a particular activity occurs. The phasing of the luminescence cycle of *Gonyaulax* under natural lighting conditions has already been described. To change a culture's phase, one subjects it to light sometime while it is doing what it normally does in darkness. The type of light used in an attempted phase change is critical. The most useful light is of 254 nm, 475 nm, or 650 nm. None of these is light that is useful in initiating photosynthesis in chlorophyll *a*. The phase-changing light spectra of other organisms are not the same as for *Gonyaulax*. The phasing of luminescence can also be reset by large temperature changes over several hours, but not by small changes or changes that last for a short time. If two cultures working in different 24-hour phases are mixed together, both groups continue in their own patterns, neither one influencing the other to change its phase

190. From the information in the article, which of the following is the most accurate statement about *Gonyaulax*?

190. A B C D E

    || || || || ||

A. *Gonyaulax* probably uses a different phase-change receptor molecule than do some other species.

B. Movement of the organism from one location to another is necessary for phase-changing.

C. Phase-changing cannot be initiated by ultraviolet light.

D. The phase-changing molecule is probably chlorophyll *a*.

E. The phase-changing molecule is probably luciferase.

191. Which of the following proves the presence of a 24-hour periodicity based on an internal "clock" mechanism in *Gonyaulax* cells?

191. A B C D E

    || || || || ||

A. continuance of the periodicity when cultures are in constant darkness

B. elicitation of luminescence by shaking

C. gradual loss of luminescence intensity as cultures remain in constant darkness

D. presence of luciferin and luciferase in the cells

E. simple observation of the periodicity during normal days and nights

192. What is the adaptive significance of this "clock's" periodicity (24-hour cycle) being relatively independent of temperature?

192. A B C D E

    A. An important "clock" would be hopelessly inaccurate if affected by temperature fluctuations.

    B. High temperature damages molecules that might be responsible for the periodicity.

    C. There is no value in this, since the watery environment of *Gonyaulax* remains relatively unchanged.

    D. There is no value in this, since the phasing is much more important than the periodicity.

    E. There is no value in this, since temperature changes always correspond with changes in light availability.

193. If the "clock" were dependent on temperature, and if it depended on biochemical reaction, what would be the expected trend as temperature rises?

193. A B C D E

    A. "Clock" speeds up, doubling its rate for every rise of 10°

    B. "Clock" slows down, halving its rate for every rise of 10°

    C. "Clock" remains unaffected.

    D. "Clock" speeds up, 1 minute per degree of rise.

    E. "Clock" slows down, 1 minute per degree of rise.

194. In obtaining the results used to make Graphs 1 and 2, a worker would have to be careful to

194. A B C D E

    A. avoid shaking the culture while light intensity was being measured

    B. obtain each data point on the same day of the week

    C. obtain each data point at the same time of day

    D. shake the culture more violently in the "clock's" day period than in its night period

    E. shake the culture with the same degree of violence each time

195. The periodicity display by *Gonyaulax* is

195. A B C D E

    A. annual

    B. circadian

    C. hourly

    D. lunar

    E. tidal

196. What is the relation between photosynthesis and the ability to luminesce?

196. A B C D E

    A. If photosynthesis is stopped, the organism continues a luminescent cycle, but the intensity drops after each succeeding cycle.

    B. There is no relation, since phase-changing is accomplished by wavelengths not used in photosynthesis.

    C. Photosynthesis produces luciferin.

    D. The ability to detect the period of time between luminescence activities is totally dependent upon photosynthesis.

    E. Luminescence, a production of light, allows a significant amount of photosynthesis to occur at night.

Questions 197–202

A mouse tumor was transplanted to the body wall of a 2-day chick embryo. Nearby nerve fibers enlarged and grew into the tumor mass. Although both sensory and motor neurons were in the region, only the sensory neurons responded and connected to the tumor. When the same type of tumor was placed on a chick chorioallantoic membrane (in contact with the chick's bloodstream but not near its body mass), all of the sympathetic and sensory ganglia increased in size.

A chemical agent of the tumor was sought. Called nerve growth factor (NGF), it was isolated and characterized as a protein. This material was also found in the submaxillary glands of adult mice. NGF caused the same stimulation of chick embryo ganglia as the tumor did. It caused growth of ganglia cultures *in vitro.*

Antibodies to NGF caused several changes when injected into normal embryos. Sympathetic and sensory neurons were destroyed all over the body. Significant but less severe damage to sympathetic, but not sensory, neurons occurred after injection of anti-NGF into adult animals. Embryos or adults treated with anti-NGF were able to continue normal life activities despite the radical loss of sympathetic ganglia.

Radioactively labeled NGF was injected into chick embryos. Autoradiography showed that this material attached to the membranes of neurons at their terminal ends, and then traveled up the axons to the cell bodies in the dorsal root ganglia. If this flow was blocked by chemical destruction of axonal microtubules, the neurons died.

When an NGF-impregnated block was placed in a culture vessel also containing a sensory ganglion, axons grew toward the block in a nonrandom fashion.

197. Which of the following showed that a nerve-stimulating chemical exists and is released by certain tissues?
A. injecting an embryo with anti-NGF
B. placing a mouse tumor in the body of a chick embryo
C. placing a mouse tumor on a chick's chorioallantoic membrane
D. watching motor neurons connect only to muscles
E. watching neurons grow toward their target tissue

197. A B C D E
|| || || || ||

198. Which of the following is a correct statement?
A. Absence of NGF leads to death or severe neural symptoms.
B. At least some dependence of neurons upon NGF occurs in mature adults.
C. Both sensory and sympathetic neurons are adversely affected if an animal is deprived of NGF by treatment after reaching adulthood.
D. If NGF is placed on a chick's chorioallantoic membrane, sympathetic neurons will grow out to innervate that membrane.
E. Radioactively labeled NGF damages ganglia.

198. A B C D E
|| || || || ||

199. Which experiment showed that NGF must be supplied specifically to a neuron's cell body in order to keep the neuron alive?
A. autoradiographical analysis of NGF's travel route in the body
B. depriving a cultured ganglion of NGF
C. destruction of the cell's microtubules
D. injecting an embryo with anti-NGF
E. placing a mouse tumor on a chick's chorioallantoic membrane

199. A B C D E
|| || || || ||

200. What is nerve growth factor?
A. a protein capable of promoting growth only of sympathetic neurons
B. a protein capable of promoting growth of both sympathetic and sensory neurons
C. a nonprotein chemical promoting growth of neurons into mouse submaxillary glands
D. a protein capable of promoting growth of some neurons but unable to specify the direction of that growth
E. a protein of the class called antibodies

201. Autoradiography was an important tool in one of the experiments cited. To perform autoradiography one must have
A. a centrifuge
B. a Geiger counter
C. a scintillation counter
D. heavy lead shielding
E. some photographic emulsion

202. Which of the following experiments shows that NGF is responsible for specific connections being made, such as a motor neuron attaching to a muscle rather than to epidermis?
A. not shown by cited experiments
B. purification of nerve growth factor
C. transplanting a mouse tumor to a chick embryo's body
D. transplanting a mouse tumor to a chick's chorioallantoic membrane
E. treating a chick embryo with antibody to nerve growth factor

Questions 203–206

Beggiatoa, a large sulfur bacterium, was tested for its ability to allow various molecules to cross its plasma membrane. Graph 1 relates the permeabilities of these molecules to their relative sizes. Permeability was measured by determining for each molecule the environmental concentration that caused lysis of cells.

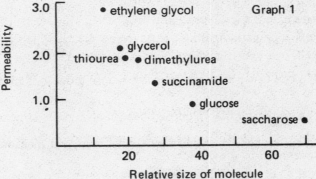

The partition coefficient of a molecule is the ratio of its solubility in lipid to its solubility in water. Graph 2 shows the relationship between the partition coefficients of certain molecules and their permeability through *Beggiattoa* membranes.

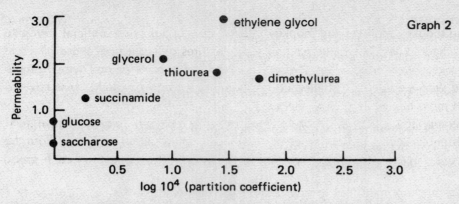

Graph 2

203. What is the relationship between the "permeability" of a molecule and the environmental concentration of the molecule capable of causing lysis of a cell?

    A. The greater the permeability, the greater the environmental concentration needed to lyse.

    B. The greater the permeability, the lower the environmental concentration needed to lyse.

    C. The greater the permeability, the larger the partition coefficient.

    D. The greater the permeability, the larger the size of the molecule.

    E. There is no obvious relationship between these two properties.

203. **A B C D E**
    || || || || ||

204. Which molecule has a significantly lower ability to enter a cell than its solubility in lipid would indicate?

    A. dimethylurea

    B. ethylene glycol

    C. glucose

    D. glycerol

    E. succinamide

204. **A B C D E**
    || || || || ||

205. Which of the following is a correct statement?

    A. Although not very soluble in lipids, saccharose is able to enter a cell easily because of its size.

    B. Dimethylurea is less soluble in lipids than is thiourea.

    C. Ethylene glycol enters a cell very easily because it is both small and very soluble in lipids.

    D. Glucose enters a cell faster than saccharose because glucose is more soluble in lipids.

    E. Glycerol enters a cell faster than glucose because glycerol is larger.

205. **A B C D E**
    || || || || ||

206. Why was the partition coefficient of these molecules a logical measurement to take?

    A. A cell's plasma membrane is largely lipid.

    B. Most of a cell's membrane is water.

    C. The plasma membrane is a partition.

    D. The partition coefficient is directly indicative of a molecule's size.

    E. The partition coefficient is the easiest measurement to take.

206. **A B C D E**
    || || || || ||

Questions 207–210

The relationship between monkey mothers and monkey infants was studied using artificial surrogate "mothers." Each "mother" had some lifelike features and some features different from those of a real mother. Two types of surrogate were used. One, "wire," consisted of a bare welded wire cylinder topped by a block of wood with a crude face painted on it. The other surrogate, "cloth," was covered with fuzzy cloth and had a more lifelike face. Both included a bottle of milk.

One group of infants was supplied with both surrogate types, but only the cloth "mothers" gave milk. A second group, also with equal access to both types of "mothers," could obtain milk only from the wire "mothers." Both groups thrived physiologically. The graph shows how much time each group spent with the surrogates.

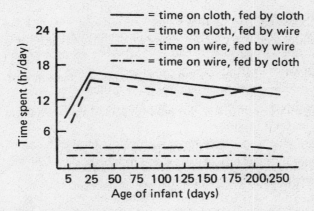

A second phase of the research involved observing an infant as it encountered a stressful situation. When an infant was placed in a room containing only inanimate objects, it showed signs of fear. The table below shows an attempt to attach quantitative values to displays of stress. A high emotionality score indicates great stress.

Group	Emotionality Score with No "Mother" Present	Emotionality Score with Cloth "Mother" Present	Emotionality Score with Wire "Mother" Present
Reared with equal access to both "mothers"	3.1	1.3	—
Reared with cloth "mother"	2.8	1.5	—
Reared with wire "mother"	4.9	—	5.0
Reared with no mother	2.8	3.9	—

07. What physical difference between the two types of surrogates proved to be more important than any other in attracting infants?

A. the color of the "body"
B. the "face"
C. the size of the "body"
D. the texture of the "body"
E. not determinable from the data

207. A B C D E
|| || || || ||

208. Which statement is supported by the data from this research project?

    A. Affection toward a mother is learned or derived solely from the reduction of hunger that is associated with it.

    B. Infants spent more time clinging to a suitable "mother" figure than was needed for gaining milk.

    C. Mother-infant contact during nursing provides no psychological benefit.

    D. The position of the milk-providing apparatus helps determine whether an infant will accept a surrogate "mother."

    E. Surrogate "mothers" that did not supply any milk were nevertheless accepted by the infants.

208. A B C D E

209. The data of the table indicate that

    A. emotional dependence on a mother may be a result of imprinting

    B. infants that have had contact with any "mother," whether wire or cloth, quickly learn to accept comfort from a cloth "mother"

    C. infants that have had no previous experience with a mother, real or surrogate, show significantly less anxiety when left alone than do those who have come to depend upon a mother

    D. the amount of time an infant spends with a surrogate "mother" before being placed in a stressful environment helps determine the level of anxiety that will occur when left alone

    E. the infant behavior shown by this experiment is completely instinctive

209. A B C D E

210. What would be the best way to test endurance of the preference for a cloth "mother"?

    A. Mate two "cloth-preference" infants when they reach maturity, and observe the preference of their offspring.

    B. Continuously keep infants in rooms that have both wire and cloth surrogates.

    C. Erect a nearly insurmountable barrier between an infant and a cloth "mother," but place no such obstacle in front of a wire "mother."

    D. Provide an infant with several wire "mothers" per cloth "mother."

    E. Remove the cloth surrogates from the presence of infants raised with them, and then return them after a period of time.

210. A B C D E

Answer Key
for Sample Test 4
(with Comments and Explanations)

1. **(D)** Ribosomes are tiny cytoplasmic granules, free in the cytoplasm or attached to the endoplasmic reticulum. In composition, they are rich in RNA and proteins.

2. **(A)** NAD is nicotinamide adenine dinucleotide. A second hydrogen transport molecule active in the Krebs cycle is FAD, flavin adenine dinucleotide. Both molecules carry hydrogen and associated energy to ATP-manufacturing sites within mitochondria.

3. **(A)** Pith is a primary tissue. Primary tissues are produced by growing tips. Secondary tissues are added outside the pith and primary xylem, both of which persist indefinitely, barring the absence of decay.

4. **(B)** Guttation is the elimination of excess water in liquid form. Water accumulates in drops, particularly at the tips or along the margins of leaves. The water is usually given off from special structures called hydathodes. Conditions favoring guttation are abundance of soil water and cool temperatures.

5. **(B)** As water continues to diffuse into the cell, the excess is periodically expelled to the outside, keeping the cell from bursting.

6. **(A)** The three characteristics given are those of phylum Chordata. Adult sea squirts do not possess all of the characteristics, but all are present in the larval stage. Before Kowalevsky studied the embryology of sea squirts, the true relationship of these strange animals was unknown.

7. **(B)** Australian marsupials fill many ecological niches normally filled by placental mammals elsewhere. They vary in size from large kangaroos all the way down to small-mice-sized animals. Marsupials are not found on other continents except the Americas, which are the home of the opossum and a few small ratlike or shrewlike types (confined to the Andes of South America).

8. **(E)** The circulatory pathway from the intestine is directly to the liver by way of the hepatic portal system. The portal vein enters the liver and breaks up into a network of capillaries, which then reunite into larger vessels leading back to the heart. All of the circumstances are ideal for filtering out dislodged cancer cells.

9. **(A)** Antigens A and B, found in types A, B, and AB blood, and antigen Rh, found in Rh-positive blood, are carried by red blood cells and therefore are not diffusible.

10. **(B)** Messenger RNA is written as mRNA, and nitrogenous bases in the nucleotides are symbolized by letters. Strands of mRNA are synthesized beside strands of DNA with the bases pairing A to T, U to A, C to G, and G to C. There is no thymine (T) in RNA, but uracil (U) takes its place. The mRNA strand formed beside the DNA pattern is as follows (the phosphate group and sugars are not symbolized):

DNA strand	mRNA strand
T	A
T	A
A	U
C	G
G	C
A	U
G	C

11. **(D)** Preceding the Pleistocene, Asia and North America were connected across the Bering Sea. The climate was uniformly mild, and plants and animals migrated freely. The advancing ice moved southward like a wedge and isolated organisms in the two widely separated areas, where the descendants of several relic species still survive.

12. **(D)** Stereoscopic microscopes give the image three dimensions: height, width, and depth. Other microscopes give only height and width. The dimension of depth is obtained by viewing an object from two different directions simultaneously. Humans naturally perceive depth because the eyes focus from different directions. The stereoscopic microscope is simply an optical extension of that ability.

13. **(A)** The larger the body, the less surface area it will have in contact with the environment, compared to its volume. Obviously, a small surface area will result in a correspondingly small loss of heat.

14. **(B)** Maltose is malt sugar, a disaccharide. Upon digestion, it is hydrolyzed to two molecules of glucose.

15. **(A)** Although salt marshes look more like grassland, they grow in places more like the mangrove forest. Both are in saline environments that are flooded by ocean tides. In a sense they are buffer zones between the ocean and the continent. Both are important nurseries for many types of marine organisms.

16. **(C)** An example of a mutant virus was the one that caused the virulent Asian flu in 1959. Besides mutating, viruses are also lifelike in being able to reproduce themselves. On the other hand, they do not have proto-

plasm or cellular organization. Neither do they take in food or respire.

17. **(A)** Each cilium (or flagellum) is characterized by 9 pairs of microtubules surrounding 2 single microtubules located in the center of the organelle. Microtubules are composed of tubulin plus other proteins.

18. **(B)** Statocysts are balancing organs located among the bases of tentacles on the margin of the medusa. They are hollow spheres containing tiny calcareous granules within the cavity. The granules stimulate different nerve endings on the inner surface of the cavity depending on the way the medusa is tilted. The statocysts provide the animal with whatever information is necessary to evoke responses that keep it in an upright position.

19. **(B)** Loss of the cerebral cortices in humans results in total blindness and extensive paralysis. The cerebrum has many functions including intellectual activities.

20. **(B)** Antigens are carried by red blood cells. Although the cells do not normally cross the placenta, they may do so if some seepage occurs, as it sometimes does late in pregnancy. The antigens introduced into the bloodstream of the Rh-negative mother cause her to produce counteracting antibodies. In her next pregnancy, antibodies might leak into the fetus's bloodstream. If the fetus is Rh-positive, fetal red cells clump together and serious medical consequences can result.

21. **(B)** If genes are located on separate chromosomes, a dihybrid cross will produce a phenotypic ratio of 9:3:3:1 in the F_2. If genes are unalterably linked together on the same chromosome, the ratio will be 3:1 (see example).

Genotype and → *BbSs* (black, short) × (black, short) *BbSs*
phenotype of parents like individuals of F_1

Gene combinations in gametes on margin of diamond

Genotypes and phenotypes of F_2 generation inside diamond

bs ← → *BS*

BbSs Black Short

BS — *bs*

BBSS Black Short — *bbss* Brown Long

BbSs Black Short

Phenotypic ratio → { 3 black, short–1 brown, long or 3:1 ratio }

Note that *BS* and *bs* go to separate gametes because they are on the same chromosome (also refer to A in next column). Sometimes a few gametes are produced with *Bs* and *bS*.

This is explainable by the crossing-over of sections of chromatids that become entangled during synapsis. Study the following series of illustrations.

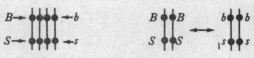

A. Two chromosomes pairing (synapsis). Each chromosome composed of two chromatids

B. Normal separation of chromosomes

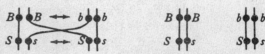

C. Chromosome mates separating but two chromatids tangled

D. Chromosomes separated after crossing-over

E. New chromosomes (composed of single chromatids) separated after aligning themselves at equator in division following synapsis. One goes to each of four gametes

Behavior of chromosomes during and after synapsis. The middle chromatids in sketch C are stretched out of proportion to give room to show what is happening.

A. Easier to cross between genes here

B. Harder to cross between genes here

Spacing of genes on chromatids as related to opportunities for crossing-over.

Crossing-over indicates the distance between genes as well as their linear sequence. The closer together, the less chance the chromatids have to cross; the farther away, the greater the chance. Should the sequence of hypothetical genes *A, B,* and *C* be desired, the percentage of crossing-over between *A* and *B, B* and *C,* and *A* and *C* is tested. If, after many crosses, the percentage should be six between *A* and *B*, four between *A* and *C*, and two between *B* and *C*, the linear arrangement would have to be *ACB*.

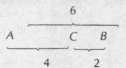

22. **(C)** Down's syndrome is caused by the presence of an extra 21st chromosome, meaning that the chromosome number is 47 ($2n + 1$). Trisomy is the abnormal chromosomal variation of $2n + 1$.

23. **(C)** Darwin recognized individual variations and said that some of them would be more advantageous than others wherever an organism lived. He supposed that the fittest individuals would have a better chance of surviving in natural competition.

24. **(A)** The position of a timberline, if present, depends on the location of the mountain and its altitude. The zone at the top of most mountains in the eastern part of the United States is forested (below timberline).

25. **(E)** Stearin is a fat common to many animals and plants. It is used to make soap and candles and also to size textile products.

26. **(C)** Van Leeuwenhoek (1632–1723) was a skillful lens maker who used tiny glass beads as magnifying lenses. With them he was able to discover protozoa, rotifers, bacteria, blood cells, sperm, and the fertilization of frog eggs.

27. **(C)** The root system of an established tree usually extends beyond the edge of its crown. The root hairs are at the extremities of the roots, not on the large trunk roots. Old roots, like old stems, are covered with cork and therefore cannot absorb water and solutes. In other words, the root system of the tree is competing with grass several feet away from its trunk.

28. **(E)** Like land mammals, whales breathe with lungs. Aquatic animals, mammals excepted, perform gas exchange via gills or the body surface. Whales also have other mammalian features, such as hair and milk glands.

29. **(D)** Birds and reptiles have so many characteristics in common that their close kinship is obvious. From fossil records and comparative studies, it is evident that reptiles came earlier and gave rise to the birds.

30. **(B)** When reciprocal translocation between different chromosomes occurs, the synaptic configuration is like the illustration in answer 21, above. The translocation may be simply the transfer of a broken piece of a chromosome to the end of another chromosome, as illustrated in *A*, or the shift of a piece of one chromosome into the break of another chromosome, as illustrated in *B*.

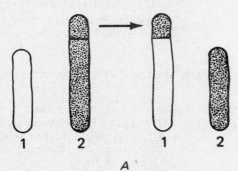

1 2 1 2

A

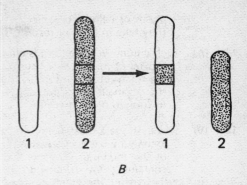

1 2 1 2

B

31. **(C)** Like chloroplasts, mitochondria are self-reproducing organelles. Both contain their own circular DNA, which carries sufficient genetic information to make most of their materials.

32. **(A)** The probable first cause of isolation was geographical. The Galápagos Islands, where the finches are found, consist of volcanic islands isolated from the mainland of South America, and the birds do not readily traverse the stretches of water separating them.

33. **(B)** Food particles are engulfed by cytoplasmic extensions. The food does not actually become a part of the cytoplasm but is enclosed in a vacuole, known as a food vacuole. The cytoplasm secretes enzymes into the vacuole, where the food is digested. The digested foods can then diffuse through the vacuolar membrane into the cytoplasm surrounding it. A food vacuole functions like a miniature stomach or intestine.

34. **(B)** Endothermic animals are sometimes known as homeothermic or warm-blooded. They keep an even body temeprature regardless of the temperature of the surroundings. Most endothermic animals are mammals or birds.

35. **(B)** The mucosal lining of the Fallopian tubes consists of columnar epithelium, some cells of which are ciliated. The cilia beat toward the uterus, creating currents that usually pick up the discharged ovum and transport it into the tube. Movement down the Fallopian tube to the uterus is aided by peristaltic muscular contractions of the tube wall.

36. **(B)** Study the examples below and on p. 188.

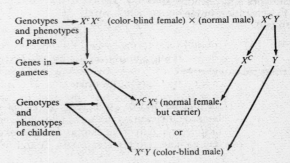

Genotypes and phenotypes of parents → X^cX^c (color-blind female) × (normal male) X^CY

Genes in gametes → X^c X^C Y

Genotypes and phenotypes of children → X^CX^c (normal female, but carrier)

or

X^cY (color-blind male)

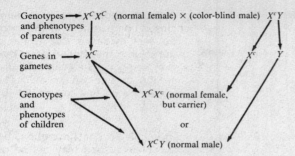

Genotypes and phenotypes of parents → $X^C X^C$ (normal female) × (color-blind male) $X^c Y$

Genes in gametes → X^C X^c Y

Genotypes and phenotypes of children → $X^C X^c$ (normal female, but carrier)

or

$X^C Y$ (normal male)

Sex linkage. Crosses between color-blind female and normal male and between normal female and color-blind male.

37. **(A)** Salt water covers about 70% of the earth's surface. As for quantity, the ratio of the volume of water held in the oceanic basin to the volume of land above sea level is 19:1.

38. **(B)** See answer 22.

39. **(B)** All plants except those that produce seeds can reproduce only when water is available for fertilization. Seed plants do not need water because their sperm are transferred through pollen tubes to the eggs. This permits them to reproduce in the driest of weather.

40. **(C)** The nitrogenous bases that are common to both DNA and RNA are adenine, guanine, and cytosine. The first two are purines; the latter is a pyrimidine. Thymine is also a pyrimidine but is found only in DNA. Uracil is a pyrimidine. Pyrimidines have a single ring structure.

41. **(D)** Cambium is a meristematic tissue, undifferentiated and capable of dividing. The others are mature tissues, mostly dead.

42. **(B)** The pitcher plant is a green plant capable of manufacturing its own food. It also captures and digests insects. Just how it utilizes animal food is not completely understood, but the nitrogen in proteins may be a useful supplement since these plants usually live in nitrogen-impoverished soils.

43. **(E)** Sporozoans are all parasitic protozoa, not free-living aquatic forms.

44. **(A)** A neural tube forms by an infolding of ectoderm along a mid-dorsal line. At first, a groove forms; then, by closing, it becomes a tube beneath the body surface. The anterior portion of this tube enlarges to form the brain. The archenteron roof participates in these events by releasing an inductive chemical that initiates the tube formation in the overlying ectoderm.

45. **(B)** Anaerobic glycolysis and fermentation help supply energy for the body when aerobic respiration is shut down due to lack of oxygen. The product of fermentation is lactic acid, some of which accumulates in the muscles and some is carried to the liver. Continued breathing after exertion ceases provides oxygen to use some of the lactic acid for energy and to convert the remainder to glycogen for storage.

46. **(E)** Two major components of the contractile part of muscles are the two proteins *actin* and *myosin*. Separately they do not contract but together they do. They occur naturally in a loose complex called *actomyosin*. This protein complex will contract in the presence of ATP and calcium.

47. **(D)** ATP (adenosine triphosphate) is known as the *storehouse of energy*. The compound contains three phosphate groups, but the energy for cell work comes from the high-energy bond of the third group. Upon the breaking of that bond and the separation of the phosphate group, a simpler molecule remains, namely, ADP (adenosine diphosphate).

48. **(A)** In plant life cycles the zygote grows into an embryonic sporophytic plant.

49. **(B)** Carbon dioxide is fixed into foods, not broken down into its constituent elements. Water, on the other hand, is broken into hydrogen and oxygen.

50. **(A)** Pollination and subsequent fertilization have nothing to do with the genetics of the tree that produces the apple. The consequences of such a cross would be incorporated in the genetic composition of embryonic plants produced in the seeds. The edible part of the apple is the enlarged hypanthium of the flower of the Winesap tree.

51. **(D)** All are in phylum Mollusca.

52. **(B)** The gastrodermis of hydra contains glandular cells that secrete digestive enzymes into the gastrovascular cavity, where foods are digested and then absorbed. Other cells, called epitheliomuscular cells, extend pseudopodia that engulf food particles in the same way that amoebas do. The particles are contained in food vacuoles where digestion takes place. Sponges also have intracellular, but no extracellular, digestion.

53. **(D)** The chorion lies between the amnion and the uterus. It originates from the trophoblast of the blastodermic vesicle (in mammals).

54. **(C)** Cholinesterase is an enzyme that destroys the neurotransmitter acetylcholine at the synapse. Were it not for its action, separate impulses would blend together.

55. **(A)** George W. Beadle and Edward L. Tatum proposed the one gene-one enzyme hypothesis while they were working with the mold *Neurospora*. According to the hypothesis, the production of each cellular enzyme is controlled by a single gene. The enzymes control chemical reactions that in turn determine phenotypic characteristics. This hypothesis has been modified to become the one gene-one polypeptide hypothesis. This accounts for the observation that some enzymes are composed of two or more subunits, each controlled by a separate gene.

56. **(B)** The foot of a horse evolved from the primitive limb pattern which terminated in five toes. The modern horse walks on the tip of the surviving middle toe. The result is the lengthening of its stride, an adaptation favorable to fleeing. The hoof is a highly specialized structure homologous to nails or claws.

57. **(D)** Turbidity is cloudiness of water due to suspended particles. A way to measure it is to determine how far light can penetrate water and be reflected back to the eye. The Secchi disk is a circular object, usually painted white or black and white, that is lowered into the body of water by a cord or chain until it disappears from sight. The depth at which it disappeared can then be compared to similar measurements made in other bodies of water containing more or less suspended materials. This is an important tool in studying the ecology of ponds, lakes, and similar bodies of water.

58. **(A)** The vehicle of transport by the virus is transduction. In the process, portions of bacterial chromosome are incorporated into the virus and carried into another bacterium by the invading virus. Transformation is another way a bacterium can receive "foreign" genetic material. In this case, fragments of DNA from lysed bacteria are absorbed directly, not transported by a virus.

59. **(B)** Although controlled burning may have several advantages, it is used most often to reduce underbrush. The scrub growth is not only competitive with the trees but also contributes to an accumulation of litter that can cause destructive high-intensity fires.

60. **(C)** Autotrophs are the original source of all foods; therefore, they support all of the other levels. About 90% of the energy (biomass) is lost between them and the herbivores that comprise the next higher level. Likewise, the loss is approximately the same between each of the succeeding levels and the next higher one.

61. **(A)** The Golgi complex (apparatus) is a membrane-enclosed compartment in the cytoplasm. The best evidence that it has a secretory function comes from the fact that it contains proteins that are eventually discharged to the outside of the cell. The Golgi complex was first described by Camillo Golgi in 1898.

62. **(B)** Organic compounds all contain carbon, but some that contain carbon may not be organic (e.g., earthlike substances like calcium carbonate). Organic compounds are called organic because of the original belief that they came from living organisms. Today thousands of organic compounds not found in nature are being synthesized in laboratories. Carbon is unique in being able to combine with itself and other substances to form molecular chains and rings, most of which are large and complex.

63. **(E)** Without specialized vascular tissues, conduction is a slow cell-to-cell movement by diffusion. All nonvascular terrestrial plants are small.

64. **(A)** In calculating the percentage of light used in photosynthesis, consideration must be given to many variables such as quantity, quality, reflection, and penetration of light as well as vigor of the plant and availability of the raw materials carbon dioxide and water. An often cited figure is the one calculated by Transeau, who found that 1.6% of the radiant energy falling on a cornfield was used by the plants. Of the amount falling on the plant, it is estimated that only about 4% is absorbed by chlorophyll. Of the amount absorbed by chlorophyll, about 90% is converted into chemical energy.

65. **(E)** Everybody has heard about cod-liver oil.

66. **(C)** When a peptide bond between two amino acids is broken, as in digestion, a water molecule is also split (*hydro* = water, *lysis* = split). The H portion of the water becomes bonded to the amino end of one amino acid, and the OH portion of the water becomes bonded to the carboxyl end of the second amino acid.

67. **(A)** Known as the water sac, the amnion contains the fetus in its fluid. This permits the fetus to move freely and diffuses bumps or blows that might otherwise damage it.

68. **(A)** Acetylcholine is one of the neurotransmitters secreted by neurons at the synapse. It is the medium by which a new action potential is initiated at the "receiving" portion of a synapse, at the junction between a motor neuron and a muscle fiber.

69. **(C)** Interphase was once called the resting stage because nothing visible was happening in the cell. We now know that the cell is metabolically active during this stage. Furthermore, one of the most important mitotic processes is taking place, namely, the duplication of DNA.

70. **(A)** The nucleotide is the building block of DNA composed of a phosphate group, a pentose sugar (deoxyribose), and a nitrogenous base (either a purine or pyrimidine).

71. **(A)** See the following example:

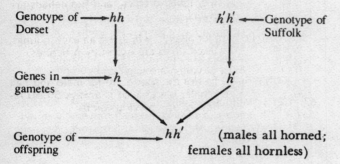

72. **(C)** The wings of a bat and the arms of a human are mammalian forelimbs. The big point of difference is that the bat limb has very long, webbed digits, a highly specialized adaptation for flight.

73. **(E)** A parasite has maximum security if its host is strong. If it weakens the host, it jeopardizes its own existence; if it kills the host, it assures its own death.

74. **(A)** A niche is a mode of life, and closely related organisms have the same mode.

75. **(D)** The thylakoid membranes are sites of proton pumping (chemiosmosis), which leads to ATP production during the light reactions of photosynthesis. Another source of ATP is oxidative phosphorylation, which also involves chemiosmosis. However, that process occurs at the cristae of mitochondria.

76. **(A)** A taxis is a reflex movement of an organism to orient itself with respect to an external stimulus. In chemotaxis, the stimulus is a diffusing chemical. Individual slime mold cells move toward an "aggregation center" of high cAMP concentration. When many converge, they interact to form a multicellular reproductive body.

77. **(E)** In lower plants the gametophytes are usually larger or more conspicuous than the sporophytes. In mosses, for example, the gametophytes are usually most conspicuous, and the sporophytes are parasitic upon them.

78. **(C)** The liver is derived from endoderm, whereas the spleen comes from mesoderm.

79. **(B)** Plants look green because the green wavelengths of light are reflected instead of being absorbed.

80. **(C)** Hydrochloric acid is secreted by cells in the wall of the stomach. It helps macerate foods, curdles milk, and activates the enzyme pepsin. The stomach contents are very acid — usually pH 1.5–2.5.

81. **(A)** The replication of chromatin can be confirmed by substituting ^{3}H (tritium) in thymidine and then incorporating it in nucleotides containing thymidine. The relative quantity of it is measurable by exposing the cells to photographic film, which records the radiation from ^{3}H incorporated in the thymine portion of the molecule.

82. **(D)** Epidermal cells are normally protective, especially against the loss of water. Some plants living in arid environments even have multiple layers. Submerged leaves do not need to conserve water and are not so adapted. In some aquatic plants like elodea, the mesoderm is absent, and the leaf consists of only two layers of epidermis. Their cells are filled with chloroplasts.

83. **(E)** Any living cell can be affected by radiation. Beadle and Tatum, who did so much work with *Neurospora*, produced mutations by irradiating its spores with X-rays.

84. **(D)** The lethal gene is recessive and carried by heterozygous green plants. When two heterozygous parents cross, approximately 25% of the offspring will be homozygous recessive and lethal.

85. **(B)** A green plant normally needs stomates through which to exchange gases with the atmosphere. It also needs guard cells to help regulate the loss of water by transpiration. The leaf of a typical submerged aquatic plant is uncutinized and thin, adapted to exchange substances directly with the water. Aquatic plants derived from terrestrial ancestors may adapt to their new mode of life but still retain vestiges of structures that were previously functional.

86. **(D)** When organisms in a community are reproducing themselves, the community is self-perpetuating as long as the same climatic conditions prevail.

87. **(B)** Laterization occurs in humid tropical and subtropical regions. Acids produced by decay cause the leaching of alkaline materials and silica from the surface zone, leaving a soil rich in iron and aluminum compounds. Lateritic soils are red in color.

88. **(D)** Pheromones are external secretions that influence the physiology or behavior of other organisms in the same species.

89. **(E)** See the following example:

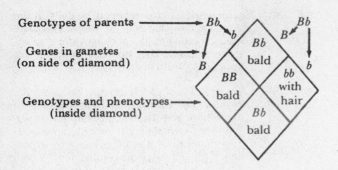

Genotypes of parents ⟶ *Bb*   *Bb*

Genes in gametes (on side of diamond) ⟶

Genotypes and phenotypes (inside diamond) ⟶

90. **(A)** An inversion is the reversal of a segment of a chromosome so that the order of the genes contained therein is backward.

gene sequence in normal homologue   A·B·C·D·E·F·G·H·I·J·K·L·M·N

gene sequence in homologue with inversion   A·B·E·K·J·I·H·G·F·E·D·C·M·N

When the homologues synapse, the lower chromosome forms a loop like the one illustrated in the question. The looping brings corresponding genes together.

91. **(B)** The configuration illustrates a reciprocal translocation between two different (non-homologous) chromosomes. The difference in shading in the following illustration shows how the chromosomes were originally linked:

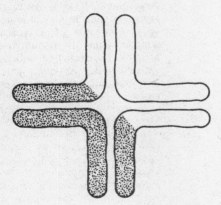

92. **(B)** All cells swell when placed in pure water because they contain a lower percentage of water. While water diffuses through membranes in both directions, the net movement is into the cells.

93. **(B)** One of the attributes of life is obtaining energy by respiration.

94. **(E)** Guard cells have walls that are not uniform in thickness throughout. When they absorb water, they swell asymmetrically so that they stand apart, making an opening (stomate) between them. When they lose water, the process is reversed. Although there are many unanswered questions about the chemical conversion that occurs within the guard cells, most people believe that an increase in the amount of sugar within the guard cells accounts for the absorption of water and consequent swelling.

95. **(C)** An epiphyte is a nonparasitic plant that lives attached to another plant. Many lichens, mosses, ferns, orchids, and bromeliads are epiphytic.

96. **(B)** Except for alveoli, which are air sacs in lungs, the listed items are excretory structures.

97. **(B)** Since half of the sperm are for male and half for female, the chance is always 50:50 regardless of any previous births.

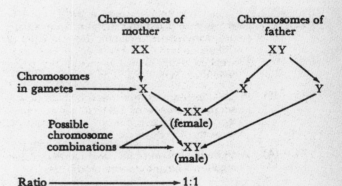

Sex determination in most animals.

98. **(E)** To obtain the probability of getting several gene combinations at the same time, determine the probability of getting each pair separately and then multiply the two values together:
$$1/2 \times 1/4 \times 1/4 = 1/32 \text{ or } 3.12\%$$

99. **(C)** In such a cross as this, a single gene determines the male phenotype and two genes the female phenotype. Therefore, the male with be *hO* (hemophiliac) or *HO* (normal); the female will be *HH* (normal), *Hh* (carrier), or *hh* (hemophiliac). Since her husband is normal *(HO)* and since their son (number 3) is a hemophiliac *(hO),* she will have to be a carrier *(Hh).* (The letter O could represent the Y chromosome of a male, as well as signifying the absence of the hemophilia gene.)

100. **(C)** See the following example:

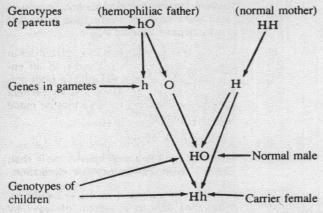

Genotypes of parents   (hemophiliac father) hO   (normal mother) HH

Genes in gametes ⟶ h   O   H

HO ⟵ Normal male

Genotypes of children ⟶ Hh ⟵ Carrier female

101. **(A)** The man has the genotype HO. He received the O from his father and the H from his mother. His father could have been hO or HO.

102. **(A)** For the cross between a hemophiliac father (hO) and a normal mother (HH), see answer 100, above.

103. **(C)** Individual 1 is a carrier female (Hh), individual 2 is a normal male (HO), and individual 3 is a hemophiliac male (hO).

104. **(E)** The deciduous condition in plants is caused either by aridity or by cold weather. In the latter case, the abscission of leaves is normally preceded by the loss of chlorophyll and the changing of color to yellow, orange, red, or brown.

105. **(A)** The mangrove forest is located in the intertidal zone of the tropics wherever the substratum is suitable. Although the trees belong in different taxonomic groups, they are similar in having stiltlike roots through which the tides freely flow.

106. **(B)** The characteristic trees of the tropical rainforest have broad, evergreen leaves. Many of the leaves have prolonged tips, from which they shed water as from a spout.

107. **(C)** Many desert plants are water-storing succulents. The larger and more picturesque ones belong in the cactus and euphorbia families.

108. **(D)** Level D is composed of primary consumers (herbivores) that feed on green plants of level E.

109. **(C)** Level C is composed of carnivores that feed on herbivores of level D.

110. **(B)** Level B is composed of carnivores that feed on other carnivores of level C.

111. **(E)** Level E is composed of green plants, the producers.

112. **(C)** A pollen grain is usually three haploid cells, two of them sperm cells and one a cell that will begin to form the pollen tube.

113. **(E)** A sperm cell is the product of male meiosis, and is therefore haploid (1n).

114. **(B)** Mammalian erythrocytes (red blood cells or corpuscles) form in the bone marrow. When fully differentiated, they lack a nucleus or chromosomes. Chromatin is the deeply staining portion of each chromosome.

115. **(D)** Schwann cells wrap tightly around the axons of certain neurons of vertebrates, forming the myelin sheath.

116. **(A)** Upon fusion of the egg and sperm nuclei, a diploid (2n) zygote exists. It is the ancestor of all of the embryonic and adult cells, which form by mitosis.

117. **(C)** A pollen grain is equipped with a tough wall that protects it from desiccation. This is necessary since pollen is usually carried from place to place by wind or on the exterior surface of terrestrial animals.

118. **(A)** Named for H. W. Bates, this phenomenon is an organism's avoidance of predators by looking and/or acting like a noxious or dangerous organism even though the mimic is neither unpalatable nor dangerous. The advantage of doing this is obvious.

119. **(D)** Müllerian mimicry, named for F. Müller, involves two or more species that have a common protective characteristic and use the same type of warning signal to would-be predators, indicating to them that they are either noxious or dangerous. Use of identical signals tends to reinforce and hasten the learning process of a potential predator.

120. **(C)** The example provided here can be explained by the observation that the erythrocytes of heterozygotes are hostile environments to the protozoan that causes malaria. Human populations in malaria-infested areas derive greater benefit from some of their members being heterozygous than harm from some of their members dying of sickle-cell anemia expressed by homozygous recessive erythrocytes.

121. **(B)** Cryptic coloration is also called hiding coloration. Some animals retain a lifelong color and pattern, relying on finding a matching background. Others, like the flounder and chameleon, can change their color over some range to match the environment in which they find themselves.

122. **(E)** The word dimorphism means "the existence of two forms" and refers here to the widespread phenomenon of males and females of a species being strikingly different in size, shape, color, voice, behavior, etc.

123. **(B)** The hydra and other Cnidaria use a network of neurons to provide coordinated body movements, but there is no central processing area such as a ganglion or brain. These

animals also differ from animals with more advanced nervous systems by demonstrating two-way transmission at synapses.

124. **(A)** Cerebral dominance is a characteristic of all mammals.

125. **(C)** Planaria, or *Dugesia*, has a pair of cerebral ganglia in the anterior region of the body. However, this "brain" is not homologous to that of a vertebrate.

126. **(D)** A shark relies a great deal upon the sensing of chemicals in its environment ("smelling"). This is reflected in its greatly enlarged olfactory lobes at the anterior end of the brain.

127. **(E)** A sponge (phylum Porifera) has no discernible neurons. It is capable of only localized responses to environmental change.

128. **(E)** Sponges reproduce sexually but also produce buds which become attached adults of a colony. They are bottom dwellers (benthic).

129. **(A)** The earthworm (such as *Lumbricus terrestris*) is a member of phylum Annelida. This group is segmented both externally (by grooves) and internally (by septa).

130. **(D)** Insecta is the only group in the list that is a class rather than a phylum.

131. **(B)** An open circulatory system includes large caverns as well as arteries and veins. This relatively inefficient pattern is found in arthropods.

132. **(B)** With more than one million classified species within one of its classes (Insecta), phylum Arthropoda is by far the largest.

133. **(C)** Humans belong to phylum Chordata (subphylum Vertebrata), class Mammalia, order Primates, genus *Homo*, and species *sapiens*.

134. **(B)** The operator region is adjacent to the structural genes over which it has control.

135. **(E)** The regulator gene is usually quite far down the chromosome from the rest of the inducible gene system. Its function is to produce a messenger RNA which carries the code for building a repressor protein. In an inducible system, the repressor is produced in the correct shape to attach to the operator.

136. **(B)** See answer 135, above. The repression occurs because of the repressor's physical hindrance to the attachment of RNA polymerase at the promoter region (labeled C).

137. **(A)** Transcription of structural genes occurs only if RNA polymerase can reach them to catalyze the reaction. An inducer molecule must combine with the repressor, making it unable to attach to the operator, before RNA polymerase can come to the proper position.

138. **(C)** When the operator region is free of a repressor, RNA polymerase can first attach to the promoter region (labeled C) and then successfully move to the nearest end of the first structural gene (labeled A).

139. **(E)** Pyruvic acid is an end product of glycolysis in any organism that uses glucose as an energy source. Calcium is found in both animals and plants; but since it is an element rather than a molecule, it cannot be *made* by any organism.

140. **(A)** See answer 139, above.

141. **(D)** Indoleacetic acid is a well-known auxin that, like any auxin, can induce cell elongation.

142. **(C)** Secreted by the adrenal medulla, epinephrine (adrenalin) acts in a variety of ways to stimulate the metabolic rate of cells.

143. **(B)** Collagen is a fibrous protein of connective tissue such as tendons.

144. **(C)** A sarcomere is the area between two Z lines along a myofibril. Within a sarcomere actin fibers are capable of sliding over myosin fibers as the sarcomere contracts.

145. **(E)** The transverse tubule (T-tubule) system is a complex set of tubes which are extensions of the muscle fiber's outer plasma membrane. An action potential moves along the outside of the fiber and then travels down the tubules to reach the responsive areas.

146. **(D)** The critical material needed to initiate myosin movements is calcium in its ionic form. When such movement is inappropriate, a system of connected membranous bags of the sarcoplasmic reticulum sequesters these ions. An action potential reaching the membranes via nearby transverse tubules causes a momentary breakdown of this pumping system, allowing calcium ions to flow by diffusion throughout the sarcomere.

147. **(B)** The word *myoneural* is a compound of *myo-* (muscle) and *-neural* (nervous), describing the location of this modified synapse.

148. **(D)** Light rays in the visible range easily penetrate the atmosphere from the sun. Some of their energy is radiated back from terrestrial objects as infrared rays. Energy in this form can be absorbed by atmospheric carbon dioxide and thus is trapped as heat. Some workers feel that industrialization will increase the temperature of the earth's surface by adding atmospheric carbon dioxide from combustion, especially of fossil fuels.

149. **(C)** Food webs are diagrams showing which organisms use others as food. They are called webs because they show complex interactions in most ecosystems.

150. **(B)** Certain bacteria can gain energy in total darkness by processing hydrogen sulfide. Recently discovered deep sea sources of hy-

drogen sulfide (produced with help from the heat of the earth's interior) provide energy not only for chemosynthetic bacteria but also for large animals that use the bacteria as producers.

151. **(A)** Carrying capacity is the number of individuals that can be indefinitely supported by the resources of an ecosystem.

152. **(E)** Types of symbiosis are parasitism (one species benefits, the other is harmed), commensalism (one benefits, the other is neutral), and mutualism (both benefit). To qualify as symbiosis, the interaction must occur at close quarters.

153. **(A)** Follicle-stimulating hormone (FSH) is made in the anterior pituitary. Its target organ is the ovary, where it stimulates the maturation of an egg and its surrounding follicle cells.

154. **(D)** Progesterone, made by the corpus luteum of an ovary, causes maturation of uterine wall glands. The corpus luteum is a yellowish mass of cells in the region that has just released an egg.

155. **(B)** The pancreas, in addition to producing digestive enzymes for the intestinal tract, makes and releases to the blood two hormones needed all over the body for carbohydrate metabolism. One is insulin, whose primary action is to change the permeability of cell membranes to allow more glucose to enter from blood plasma. The second hormone, glucagon, does the opposite: it causes release of glucose from the polysaccharide glycogen, thus increasing the blood glucose concentration.

156. **(C)** The parathyroids are four small organs embedded near the surface of the thyroid gland. Their hormone causes elevation of blood calcium concentration and decrease of blood phosphate concentration.

157. **(E)** Testosterone, made in the testes of males, stimulates the development of masculine secondary sexual characteristics.

158. **(B)** Some plants, like dodder, are parasitic upon other plants by growing their roots into the host plants. Such roots are called haustoria.

159. **(E)** The taproot of a dandelion is capable of regenerating one or more entire plants if it remains in the ground after the rest of the plant is cut off.

160. **(E)** Carrots and dandelions are examples of plants with a single large primary root.

161. **(C)** Grasses produce fibrous networks of roots, all of about the same size.

162. **(E)** RNA viruses (or retroviruses) store information in RNA. They then produce a single-stranded DNA from it, finally making messenger RNA from the single-stranded DNA.

163. **(B)** In the early 1900s, Thomas Hunt Morgan discovered and studied the X-linked gene that produces white eyes in the fruit fly.

164. **(A)** Conjugation between bacteria is analogous to sexual mating in eukaryotes, since it involves new combinations of genes being placed in an organism. In conjugation, one bacterium builds a hollow tube connecting it to another; then some DNA is passed to the second cell.

165. **(E)** Genetic fine-mapping was first performed by Seymour Benzer, using T-series bacteriophages (viruses that inhabit bacteria). He coined the word *cistron* to describe some of his map results.

166. **(A)** In 1944 Avery et al. used pneumococci as a source of DNA which could be taken up by live bacteria and which would change the phenotypes of these recipients.

167. **(C)** Mutations are of a random nature. If they produce characteristics that better fit the organism for a particular environment, the organism has an advantage over others of its kind in that environment and is more likely to survive and reproduce. If the mutation does not result in the organism's being better adapted to its environment, the organism and its descendants are at a disadvantage and will probably not survive.

168. **(E)** As stated, the development of melanin is dominant in some insects and recessive in others. The characteristic is by no means limited to the moths mentioned.

169. **(D)** For example:

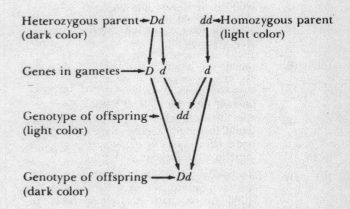

Heterozygous parent → *Dd* (dark color)   *dd* → Homozygous parent (light color)

Genes in gametes → *D d   d*

Genotype of offspring → *dd* (light color)

Genotype of offspring → *Dd* (dark color)

170. **(B)** If color is the only difference, birds will eat the moths that they can see.

171. **(B)** Density is the average number of individuals found in the quadrats sampled. In the five quadrats, there were six specimens of species 2; therefore, the density is 1.2.

172. **(A)** Frequency is the percentage of quadrats in which a species is found. Species 1 is found in four out of five quadrats, which is 80%.

173. **(A)** Importance value is the sum of relative density, relative frequency, and relative dominance (basal area). The last of these cannot be calculated from the information given here.

174. **(E)** Since each of the species has a radically different life span (in years) than most of the others, the graph was constructed to show only percentage of the maximum life span.

175. **(B)** The British robin population (curve *B*) loses most of its members before half of the maximum life span has passed.

176. **(C)** The vertical axis of the graph is logarithmic. At 50% of total life span, curve *A* shows only about 50 of the original 1000 birds surviving.

177. **(D)** There is no reason to expect a significant deviation from a 1:1 male-female ratio in either population. In addition a female bird expends a great deal of energy in producing eggs; this tends to weaken her and make her more likely to die young.

178. **(E)** An antibody is not detectable in an animal's blood until after an antigen has been introduced. Lectins, however, are built under an invariant developmental program and are normal constituents of their organisms.

179. **(D)** No matter what our final blood type, we all produce a substance called H. This sugar remains unmodified in type O people and is the material to which O-specific lectins attach. Type A, B, or AB people modify the H substance to become either A substance or B substance. However, they do not recognize the H sugar as an antigen if type O blood is transfused into them because H is always present in their bone marrow cells that are being differentiated into mature erythrocytes.

180. **(B)** A saccharide group is not nearly as complex as, say, proteins or nucleic acids. Therefore, the same sugars are made and incorporated into the cells of many organisms. For instance, chitin is a polysaccharide found in fungi, insects, and molluscs. Its basic structural unit is *N*-acetyl glucosamine in all of these organisms.

181. **(A)** The changing distribution of binding sites as a cell is transformed indicates that the cell surface is changing. This, coupled with the observations that malignant cells have less binding ability with each other than do cells of normal tissues and that malignant cells change in their ability to move materials through the cell membrane, has led to a number of important theories on how cancer operates.

182. **(B)** The cited work on chick eye development shows that the retinal cell surface changes during embryogenesis.

183. **(A)** The radioactive tagging study, combined with the fluorescent tagging study, shows that the number of lectin-binding sites remains unchanged as a cell is transformed but that the sites become redistributed into concentrated clumps. This makes possible the formation of many lectin bridges between two malignant cells in a compact configuration.

184. **(B)** Lectin was tagged with a fluorescent compound and then added to cells. Under an ultraviolet microscope the pattern of glowing lectins bound to their specific sites could be seen.

185. **(D)** By having a countercurrent system of heat exchange, the kangaroo rat conserves water when it exhales cooler air that holds less of it. Answer (B) cannot be correct because lost heat is absorbed by the inhaled air, thereby increasing the body temperature.

186. **(D)** The article mentions that the kangaroo rat does not use water for thermoregulation. Many animals do, for example, human sweating and dog's panting.

187. **(D)** The camel's nasal passage is hygroscopic only when it is dry. The passage likens this to a filter paper that can absorb water.

188. **(B)** Some countercurrent systems involve flow of two materials past each other in long, parallel tubes. However, the nasal passage accomplishes the same function by forcing air alternately back and forth through the same set of long, narrow tubes. The walls of the tubes, holding varying amounts of heat, serve to replace opposite-flow tubes.

189. **(B)** The loop of Henle is doubled over on itself so that liquid flows down the loop and then back up. The two halves are parallel to each other and in intimate contact. Active transport of sodium ions from the distal end of the tube leads to the return of some, but not all, of these ions to the fluid in the nearby proximal tube portion. The net result is a constantly maintained gradient of sodium ions in nearby tissue, with the highest concentration at the bend of the loop. This tissue condition leads to water removal by diffusion from urine in nearby collecting tubules, which are also parallel to the loop of Henle.

190. **(A)** Other luminescent organisms respond to different wavelengths for phase-changing, indicating that they use different mechanisms.

191. **(A)** An internal "clock" is indicated by the ability of an inherent mechanism to continue a cycling phenomenon when normal environmental clues are absent.

192. **(A)** If the "clock" responded markedly to temperature fluctuations, it would order periodicity changes with the seasonal temperature changes. The luminescence pattern would no longer match the 24-hour day length.

193. **(A)** Biochemical reactions normally follow the "Q_{10} law"; as temperature increases by

"Q_{10} law"; as temperature increases by 10°, the reaction rate approximately doubles. The "clock" mechanism in *Gonyaulax* is apparently independent of this, since it actually slows a bit as temperature rises.

194. **(E)** Luminescence is elicited by agitation of the culture, but intensity of luminescence varies directly with the intensity of agitation.

195. **(B)** The word *circadian* comes from two Latin words meaning "around the day." A synonymous word is *diurnal*.

196. **(A)** This is shown by Graph 2.

197. **(C)** Seeing an effect when two tissues are connected only by blood flow is good evidence for a diffusible chemical's action.

198. **(B)** If anti-NGF, capable of rendering NGF inactive, is injected into a previously untreated adult, the animal's sympathetic ganglia shrink.

199. **(C)** Microtubules of an axon form transportation routes for proteins. Autoradiography showed that NGF travels through the axon toward the cell body. Chemical destruction of microtubules leads to interruption of this travel and also to death of the cell.

200. **(B)** Although NGF is not responsible for maintenance of adult sensory neurons, it does promote growth of both embryonic sympathetic and sensory neurons.

201. **(E)** Autoradiography is a much used means of locating radioactively tagged substances in tissues or cells. After the substances have been given time to reach a destination, the tissue is sectioned and prepared as for microscopic examination. Photographic emulsion is spread over the slide in darkness, and the slide is stored for some time. Emissions from the radioactive tag cause the same chemical changes in the emulsion as would occur if light hit it. The slide is then developed as if it were a normal photographic film. Microscopic examination of the tissue reveals dark specks wherever the radioactivity was.

202. **(A)** None of these experiments bears directly upon the question of how a growing fiber "recognizes" which nearby tissue is the proper sort for making synapses. This question has not yet been adequately answered.

203. **(B)** Generally, the rate of influx of a type of molecule will be greater if the concentration gradient of that molecule (between the inside and outside of the cell) is larger.

204. **(A)** Graph 2 shows that dimethylurea and ethyleneglycol have nearly the same partition coefficient (a measure of solubility in lipid), but dimethylurea has less than half the ability to enter the cell (permeability). Each of the other molecules in this list shows a direct relationship between partition coefficient and permeability.

205. **(C)** Ethyleneglycol is the smallest of the tested molecules (Graph 1) and has a partition coefficient smaller than only one of the tested molecules (Graph 2). These are both features that ease passage of a molecule through a porous, lipid-containing membrane.

206. **(A)** The partition coefficient is a value showing how easily a molecule enters a region of lipids. This is very important in considering the ability of a molecule to pass through a cell membrane, since a major portion of the membrane is phospholipids.

207. **(E)** The two surrogates differed in both facial features and body texture, so these experiments did not determine whether one of these features is the most important clue that an infant uses in identifying a mother.

208. **(B)** This is shown by the observation that infants who spent little time on "mothers" that were wire and supplied milk were as healthy as those who spent much more time on cloth "mothers."

209. **(A)** Imprinting is a type of learning that occurs early in life. The infants reared without a mother did not derive any security from a surrogate cloth "mother." Actually, they were *more* frightened with the surrogate present than with it absent.

210. **(E)** Endurance of a preference (not to be confused with "strength") is measured by the length of time over which it remains observable. This should involve a period of deprivation, to distinguish preference from insignificant habit. If one marked answer A, one would be expressing the unproved belief that the preference is heritable and that Lamarckian evolution (inheritance of acquired traits) occurs.

Part Three Review Aids

Index of Review Aids

Topics Worth Reviewing

Check off each topic when you feel confident that you know it.

_____ Branches of biology
_____ Nature and role of carbohydrates, fats, proteins, enzymes, nucleic acids
_____ Meaning of pH and buffering
_____ Radioactive isotopes: uses and meaning of half-life
_____ Cell parts: their structures and functions
_____ Fluid mosaic model of membranes
_____ The cytoskeleton
_____ Mechanism of transport across cellular membranes (active and passive)
_____ Plant tissues
_____ Animal tissues
_____ Mitosis
_____ Meiosis
_____ Photosynthesis
_____ Respiration: aerobic and anaerobic
_____ Krebs cycle in respiration

_____ Hydrogen transfer, chemiosmotic model, electron transport

_____ Role of NAD and NADP in hydrogen transfer

_____ ADP and ATP: their nature and relationship

_____ Role of ADP and ATP in energy relations

_____ Route and mechanism of conduction in plants

_____ Circulation of blood in higher animals

_____ Neurotransmitters

_____ Eye: its structure and function

_____ Ear: its structure and functions

_____ Plant hormones and hormonelike substances

_____ Animal hormones: where produced and effects produced

_____ Theory of muscular contraction

_____ Contractile proteins in muscles

_____ Nephron: its structure and action

_____ Homeostasis

_____ Cleavage stages of zygote and early embryo

_____ Origin of germ layers

_____ Derivatives of germ layers

_____ Embryogenesis: molecular and genetic bases

_____ Embryonic organizers, induction

_____ Carcinogenesis: oncogenes

_____ Insect metamorphosis

_____ Nature of genes, the genetic code

_____ DNA: its location, characteristics, and function

_____ RNA: its location, characteristics, and function

_____ Protein synthesis

_____ Gene control

_____ Meaning of allele, dominance, recessiveness, homozygote, and heterozygote

_____ Monohybrid and dihybrid crosses

_____ Linkage (including sex-linkage)

_____ Crossing-over

_____ Phenotypic and genotypic ratios

_____ Autopolyploidy, allopolyploidy, euploidy, autotetraploidy, amphidiploidy, and aneuploidy

_____ Transformation, transduction, conjugation of bacteria

_____ Artificial gene recombination (recombinant DNA technology)

_____ Chi-square test

_____ Mutations and DNA repair mechanisms

_____ Clotting of blood

_____ Antigen-antibody reaction

_____ Humoral and cellular immune systems

_____ Antibody synthesis mechanisms

_____ Digestive organs of higher animals

_____ Digestive enzymes

_____ Breakdown of foods in digestion

_____ Vitamins

_____ Parts of brain

_____ Reflex arc

_____ Meaning of neuron, synapse, nerve, and ganglion
_____ Autonomic nervous system
_____ Mechanism of action potential
_____ Tree growth
_____ Plant structures and classification
_____ Life cycles of mosses, ferns, gymnosperms, and angiosperms
_____ Flower parts
_____ Nature of pollen and embryo sacs
_____ Origin of seeds and fruits
_____ Nitrogen fixation, nitrification, and denitrification
_____ Tropisms
_____ Viruses
_____ Monera
_____ Classification of Protista: overview
_____ Classification of plants: overview
_____ Characteristics of major groups of plants
_____ Classification of animals: overview
_____ Characteristics of major groups of animals
_____ Theories of evolution
_____ Homology and analogy
_____ Convergence and divergence
_____ Evolution of humans
_____ Molecular evolution
_____ Hardy-Weinberg law
_____ Highlights of Geologic Time Scale and fossil record, especially origins, extinctions, and coexisting groups
_____ Energy relations: food web and trophic pyramid
_____ Meaning of population, community, biome, and ecosystem
_____ Meaning of niche, succession, and climax
_____ Meaning of xerophytes, mesophytes, and hydrophytes
_____ Lake and oceanic zones
_____ Cause of turnover in lakes
_____ Biogeographic realms
_____ Uses of chromatography, electrophoresis, dialysis, centrifugation, immunology, recombinant DNA technology
_____ Importance of pheromones
_____ Animal behavior
_____ Animal societies

Laws of Thermodynamics

1. The total energy of the universe is always constant (law of the conservation of energy).
2. All processes (physical, chemical, and biological) proceed in such a way that there is a net increase in entropy (measure of degree of disorder or randomness).
3. At the temperature of absolute zero, the entropy of a pure, solid substance tends to zero.

Spectrum of Organizational Complexity
(in order of increasing complexity)

Elementary particles — the small units of which matter is made; of three types: protons, neutrons, and electrons

Atom — the smallest unit of an element; two to many elementary particles bound together

Molecules — two to many atoms chemically bound together

Cell — the structural and functional unit of which living organisms are made

Tissue — a group of similar cells that function as a unit, e.g., nervous, epithelial, vascular

Organ — a group of tissues that function as a unit, e.g., heart, brain, lung

System — a group of organs that function as a unit, e.g., circulatory, digestive, skeletal

Individual (organism) — a discrete living entity; a body, consisting of a single cell or many cells

Population — a group of similar interbreeding individuals; all individuals of a species or all members of a species living in a specific location

Community — a group of different kinds of interacting organisms living together in the same place. The largest type of community is the *biome,* which occupies a climatic region and is characterized by organisms that have a specific life form, e.g., deciduous forest, tundra, desert

Ecosystem — a more or less self-contained community of organisms together with the environment in which it lives

Chemical Elements Important in Living Organisms

Element	Symbol	Some Uses in Living Organisms
Boron	B	Affects plant growth
Calcium	Ca	Component of bone and teeth; important in clotting of blood; in plants, a component of the middle lamella in the form of calcium pectate; in plants, calcium oxalate and calcium carbonate deposited crystals, probably excretory; in all cells, regulating metabolic processes
Carbon	C	Constituent of organic compounds
Chlorine	Cl	Component of NaCl, one of the most important salts related to life; an important ion in body fluids
Cobalt	Co	In vitamin B_{12}
Copper	Cu	Part of hemocyanin, a transporter of oxygen in some animals; in some enzymes
Fluorine	F	In teeth and bone
Hydrogen	H	Constituent of organic compounds and water; carrier of energy in metabolic processes
Iodine	I	Part of thyroxin, the thyroid hormone
Iron	Fe	Part of hemoglobin and many enzymes; essential for synthesis of chlorophyll (not a part of chlorophyll molecule)
Magnesium	Mg	Component of chlorophyll; necessary in some enzyme activities
Manganese	Mn	Necessary in some enzyme activities
Molybdenum	Mo	Necessary in some enzyme activities; used in nitrogen metabolism
Nitrogen	N	Constituent of proteins and nucleic acids

(Continued)

Chemical Elements Important in Living Organisms (cont'd)

Element	Symbol	Some Uses in Living Organisms
Oxygen	O	Constituent of organic compounds and water; final electron acceptor in aerobic respiration
Phosphorus	P	Constituent of many proteins; in ADP, ATP, and nucleic acids; in calcium phosphate, a major constituent of bone
Potassium	K	Necessary for action of some enzymes and for nerve and muscle function
Silicon	Si	Deposited in walls of some plant cells
Sodium	Na	Component of the salt NaCl; component of bile salts; in sodium bicarbonate, which serves as a buffer, and neutralizes lactic acid; in sodium bicarbonate, which provides an alkaline environment for action of pancreatic enzymes; necessary for nerve and muscle function
Sulfur	S	Component of many proteins
Zinc	Zn	Used in synthesis of indoleacetic acid, a plant hormone; component of some enzymes

Isotopes Commonly Used as Tracers

Isotope	Half-Life	Emissions
Hydrogen-2 (^{2}H)		None
Hydrogen-3 (^{3}H)	12.4 years	Beta
Carbon-13 (^{13}C)		None
Carbon-14 (^{14}C)	5730 years	Beta
Nitrogen-15 (^{15}N)		None
Oxygen-18 (^{18}O)		None
Sodium-22 (^{22}Na)	2.6 years	Beta and gamma
Sodium-24 (^{24}Na)	15 hours	Beta and gamma
Magnesium-27 (^{27}Mg)	9 minutes	Beta and gamma
Phosphorus-32 (^{32}P)	14.5 days	Beta
Sulfur-35 (^{35}S)	87 days	Beta
Chlorine-36 (^{36}Cl)	4×10^5 years	Beta
Potassium-40 (^{40}K)	1.2×10^9 years	Beta and gamma
Potassium-42 (^{42}K)	12.4 hours	Beta and gamma
Calcium-45 (^{45}Ca)	160 days	Beta
Manganese-54 (^{54}Mn)	300 days	Beta and gamma
Iron-59 (^{59}Fe)	45 days	Beta and gamma
Cobalt-60 (^{60}Co)	5.2 years	Beta and gamma
Copper-64 (^{64}Cu)	12.8 hours	Beta and gamma
Zinc-65 (^{65}Zn)	250 days	Beta and gamma
Iodine-131 (^{131}I)	8.05 days	Beta and gamma

Functional Groups of Organic Molecules

Although organic molecules exist in a huge variety of forms, certain configurations appear repeatedly. The diagrams below represent these groups of atoms, which often have great influence on their molecules' biological activities.

Functional Group	Name	Typical Use
$-OH$	hydroxyl	In any alcohol; acts as a base
$-C{\displaystyle{\atop\diagup}}^{O}_{OH}$	carboxyl	In any amino acid; acts as an acid
$-\overset{\overset{O}{\|\|}}{C}-H$	aldehyde	In some sugars (when ring broken)
$-NH_2$	amino	In any amino acid
$-\overset{\overset{O}{\|\|}}{C}-O-C-$	ester	In any fat
$-\overset{\overset{O}{\|\|}}{C}-$	ketone	In some sugars (when ring broken)
$-CH_3$	methyl	Side group in many complex molecules
$-O-\overset{\overset{O^-}{\|}}{\underset{\underset{O}{\|}}{P}}-O^-$	phosphate	In phospholipids, nucleotides
$-SH$	sulfhydryl	In one amino acid (cysteine)
$-S-S-$	disulfide	Stabilizes conformation of many proteins

Some Organic Compounds of Biological Importance

Classification	Name	Constituent Simpler Substances	Other Information
Carbohydrates $(C_nH_{2n}O_n)$			Primary energy source
Monosaccharides			Composed of one molecule
Triose sugar $(C_3H_6O_3)$			With three carbon atoms
	Glyceraldehyde		One of two possible triose sugars
Tetrose sugar $(C_4H_8O_4)$	Erythrose		Used in photosynthesis
Pentose sugar $(C_5H_{10}O_5)$			With five carbon atoms
	Ribose		In RNA
	Deoxyribose		In DNA
	Ribulose		In ribulose bisphosphate (photosynthesis intermediate)
	Xylose		Obtained from xylan
	Arabinose		Obtained from gum arabic
Hexose sugar $(C_6H_{12}O_6)$			With six carbon atoms
	Glucose		Grape sugar, common in plants and animals
	Fructose		Fruit sugar
	Galactose		From milk sugar and some gums
	Mannose		In ivory nut
Heptose sugar $(C_7H_{14}O_7)$	Sedoheptulose		An intermediate in photosynthesis
Disaccharides			Composed of two hexose sugar molecules
	Sucrose	Glucose and fructose	Common "table sugar"
	Maltose	Two glucoses	Produced when starch is enzymatically broken down

(Continued)

Some Organic Compounds of Biological Importance (cont'd)

Classification	Name	Constituent Simpler Substances	Other Information
Trisaccharides ($C_{18}H_{32}O_{16}$)	Lactose	Glucose and galactose	Found in mammalian milk
			Composed of three hexose sugar molecules
	Raffinose	Glucose, fructose, and galactose	In cotton seeds and sugar beets
Polysaccharides ($C_6H_{10}O_5)_n$			Composed of six or more hexose sugar molecules
	Starch	Glucose	Common food stored in plants
	Glycogen	Glucose	Animal starch, common in liver and muscle
	Inulin	Fructose	Especially abundant in tubers of plants
	Cellulosans	Pentose sugars	More soluble than cellulose; one constituent of hemicelluloses
	Cellulose	Glucose	Structural material, primarily in cell walls of plants
	Xylans	Xylose	In cell walls of plants
	Gums	Galactose in some	Exudates of plants
	Agar	Galactose	Extract of seaweeds used for culturing bacteria and for many industrial purposes
	Pectic substances	Pentoses and/or hexoses	Hydrophilic and amorphous; one constituent of hemicelluloses
	Dextrins	Glucose	Soluble and gummy, formed by the incomplete decomposition of starch
	Chitin	Nitrogenous hexoses	Part of exoskeleton of arthropod animals
Lipids			Most concentrated source of energy
Fatty acids	Stearic, oleic, etc.		Either free or in combination with other substances
Fats	Triglycerides (neutral fats)	Fatty acids and alcohol (usually glycerol)	Solids; stored food; component of cellular membranes and myelin sheaths
Oils	Olive, cotton seed, etc.	Triglycerides; often fatty acids and alcohol (usually glycerol)	Liquids; a group of very different substances, often mixtures
Waxes	Beewax	Wax and other substances	Secreted by bees
	Cutin	Wax and other substances	Produced by epidermal cells of plants
Steroids	Cholesterol		In animal cells, bile, gallstones, and egg yolk
	Sex hormones		
	Testosterone		A male hormone
	Progesterone		A female hormone
	Estrogen		A female hormone
	Cortisone		Hormone produced by adrenal cortex
	Vitamin D		Prevents rickets
Phospholipids	Lecithins, cephalins, etc.	Phosphate group, fatty acids, usually a glyceride, usually a nitrogenous base	Important constituent of cellular membranes
Proteins			Major organic constituent of protoplasm
Simple			Composed of amino acids only

(Continued)

Some Organic Compounds of Biological Importance (cont'd)

Classification	Name	Constituent Simpler Substances	Other Information
Globular			Soluble in aqueous media
	Albumin	Amino acids	In blood serum, muscle, milk, egg, and vegetable tissues
	Gamma globulins	Amino acids	Immunizing function
	Some **hormones**	Amino acids	Examples: insulin, somatotropin, gastrin
	Enzymes	Amino acids	Examples: pepsin, trypsin
Fibrous			Water-insoluble
	Collagen	Amino acids	In connective tissue
	Elastin	Amino acids	In elastic connective tissue
	Fibrin	Amino acids	In fibers of blood clot
	Keratin	Amino acids	In hair, horn, nails, and feathers
	Fibroin	Amino acids	In silk
	Actin and **myosin**	Amino acids	In contractile fibers of muscles
Conjugated			Proteins combined with another substance
	Nucleoproteins	Nucleic acids and proteins	Chromosomes, chromatin
	Glycoproteins	Carbohydrates and proteins	Many enzymes
	Chromoproteins	Pigment groups and proteins	
	Hemoglobin		Blood pigment—carries O_2 via heme (Fe)
	Cytochromes		Respiratory pigments in cells—transfer electrons
	Myoglobin		Muscle pigment—carries O_2 via heme (Fe)
	Hemocyanin		In blood of many mollusks and crustaceans—carries O_2 via Cu
	Phosphoproteins	Phosphorus-containing groups and proteins	Casein of milk and vitellin of egg yolks
	Lipoproteins	Lipids and proteins	In cell membranes, milk, blood, and egg yolks
Nucleosides			Composed of a pentose sugar and a nitrogenous base (purine or pyrimidine); purines are adenine and guanine; pyrimidines are cytosine, thymine, and uracil
	Adenosine	Sugar and purine (adenine)	In ADP and ATP
Nucleotides			Composed of a pentose sugar, a nitrogenous base, and 1–3 phosphate groups
	cAMP (cyclic AMP)		Adenosine plus one phosphate group; second messenger for some hormones
	ADP		Adenosine plus two phosphate groups; becomes ATP by addition of a third phosphate group bound by a high-energy bond
	ATP		A cellular storehouse of energy; upon hydrolysis yields energy for cell work, reverts to ADP
Nucleic acids (polynucleotides)			Composed of a polynucleotide macromolecule
	DNA	Deoxyribonucleotides	Deoxyribonucleic acid, the genetic material of nearly all organisms
	RNA	Ribonucleotides	Ribonucleic acid, involved in protein synthesis, and the genetic material of some viruses

Amino Acids Found in Proteins

Name	Abbreviation
Alanine	Ala
Arginine	Arg
Asparagine	Asn
Aspartic acid	Asp
Cysteine	CysH or CySH
Glutamic acid	Glu
Glutamine	Gln
Glycine	Gly
Histidine	His
Isoleucine	Ile
Leucine	Leu
Lysine	Lys
Methionine	Met
Phenylalanine	Phe
Proline	Pro
Serine	Ser
Threonine	Thr
Tryptophan	Try
Tryosine	Tyr
Valine	Val

Common Organic Compounds Better Known by Their Abbreviations

Abbreviation	Name	Comments
ADP*	Adenosine diphosphate	Converted to ATP by the addition of a third phosphate group bound by a high-energy bond
AMP*	Adenosine monophosphate	Converted to ADP by the addition of a second phosphate group
ATP*	Adenosine triphosphate	Known as *storehouse of energy* because energy for cell work comes from high-energy phosphate bond when ATP is converted to ADP
DNA	Deoxyribonucleic acid	A nucleic acid that comprises the genes
DPN	Diphosphopyridine nucleotide	Used in hydrogen transfer; now known as NAD
FAD	Flavin adenine dinucleotide	Used in hydrogen transfer
FMN	Flavin mononucleotide	Used in hydrogen transfer
NAD	Nicotinamide adenine dinucleotide	Used in hydrogen transfer; formerly called DPN or coenzyme 1
NADP	Nicotinamide adenine dinucleotide phosphate	Used in hydrogen transfer; formerly called TPN or coenzyme 2
PGA	Phosphoglyceric acid	A 3-carbon compound regarded as the first organic compound synthesized from carbon dioxide and water during photosynthesis
PGAL	Phosphoglyceraldehyde	A 3-carbon food regarded as the end product of photosynthesis
RUBP	Ribulose bisphosphate	In photosynthesis, combines with carbon dioxide and water to form PGA
RNA†	Ribonucleic acid	A nucleic acid important in the synthesis of proteins
TPN	Triphosphopyridine nucleotide	Used in hydrogen transfer; now known as NADP

*These compounds contain the nitrogenous base adenine; other similar compounds contain, instead, cytosine, guanine, thymine, and uracil, making such compounds as CMP, GDP, TTP, and UDP. If any of these abbreviations is preceded by the small letter d, as in dADP, the d indicates that the sugar is deoxyribose rather than ribose.
†tRNA stands for transfer-RNA, mRNA stands for messenger-RNA, and rRNA stands for ribosomal-RNA.

DNA: Structure and Replication

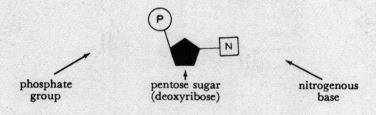

1. Nucleotide molecule of DNA.

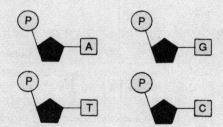

2. Nucleotide molecule symbolized.

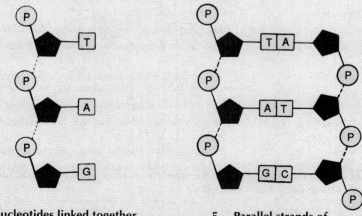

3. Four nucleotides differing in their nitrogenous bases: adenine, thymine, guanine, and cytosine.

4. Nucleotides linked together in a chain as in DNA.

5. Parallel strands of nucleotides.

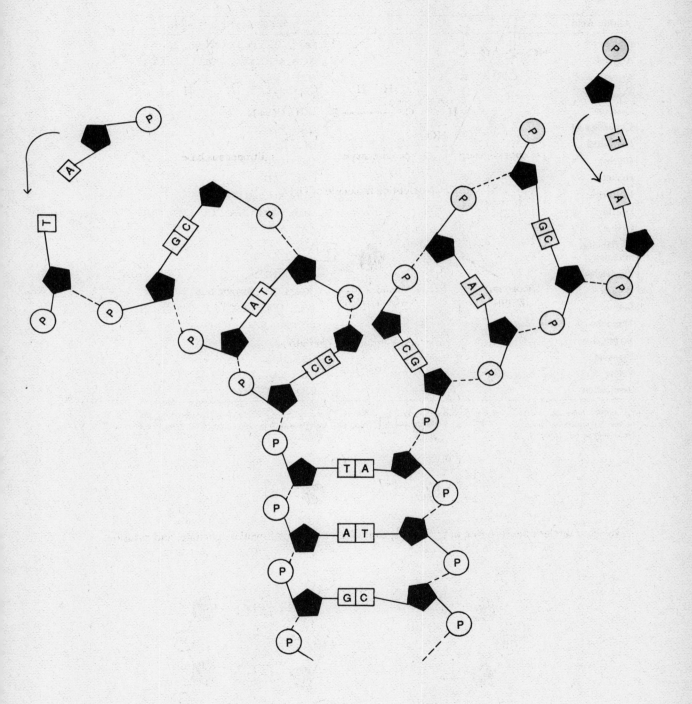

6. **Reduplication of new strands of DNA from free nucleotide molecules. Note that adenine and thymine always pair, as do also guanine and cytosine.**

Messenger RNA* Codons and Their Meanings

Although knowledge of specific codons is not required for the GRE Biology Test, this table is useful since it reveals how the coding scheme operates, especially its degenerate nature (synonyms present) and its inclusion of "punctuation" (initiator and terminator codons).

Amino Acid	Codon(s) Signifying It
Alanine	GCA, GCC, GCG, GCU
Arginine	AGA, AGG, CGA, CGC, CGG, CGU
Aspartic acid	GAC, GAU
Asparagine	AAC, AAU
Cysteine	UGC, UGU
Glutamic acid	GAA, GAG
Glutamine	CAA, CAG
Glycine	GGA, GGC, GGG, GGU
Histidine	CAC, CAU
Isoleucine	AUA, AUC, AUU
Leucine	UUA, UUG, CUA, CUC, CUG, CUU
Lysine	AAA, AAG
Methionine, initiation	AUG
Phenylalanine	UUC, UUU
Proline	CCA, CCC, CCG, CCU
Serine	AGC, AGU, UCA, UCC, UCG, UCU
Threonine	ACA, ACC, ACG, ACU
Tryptophan	UGG
Tyrosine	UAC, UAU
Valine	GUA, GUC, GUG, GUU
termination	UAA, UAG, UGA

*A similar table can be compiled for the three-base sets on DNA that produce these RNA codons, by observing the following conversion rules: $C \rightarrow G$, $G \rightarrow C$, $U \rightarrow A$, $A \rightarrow T$. Thus, CGU of RNA was produced because there was a GCA segment of DNA.

Cellular Organization and Functions of Parts

Protoplasmic	**Nucleus**	**Nuclear membranes**	Boundary through which materials enter and leave the nucleus
		Nuclear sap (karyoplasm)	Nuclear soluble material
		Chromosomes / chromatin	Contain DNA, the determiner of hereditary characteristics; recognizable in certain phases of cell cycle
		Nucleolus	Important in ribosomal RNA synthesis
	Cytoplasm	**Cell membrane** (plasma membrane)	Living boundary of cell; regulates passage of materials in and out of cell
		Protoplasmic projections:	
		Cilia	Circulation and locomotion
		Flagella	Circulation and locomotion
		Pseudopods	Locomotion and engulfment of food
		Microvilli	Absorption and secretion
		Stereocilia	Secretion
		Sensory hairs	Perception of stimuli
		Pinocytic vesicles	Engulfment
		Endoplasmic reticulum	Intracellular transfer; attachment for ribosomes
		Ribosomes	Synthesis of proteins
		Mitochondria	Centers of respiration
		Centrioles	Become mitotic poles
		Vacuolar membrane	Boundary of vacuole; regulates movement of materials in and out of vacuole
		Microfilaments	Contractile fibers, proteinaceous
		Microtubules	Hollow proteinaceous tubes, forming spindle fibers, centrioles; motile portions of flagella and cilia
		Intermediate filaments	Tough proteinaceous fibers of cytoskeleton
		Plastids:	
		Chloroplasts	Synthesis of PGAL (photosynthesis)
		Chromoplasts	Locations of some pigments that give color to flowers, fruits, and vegetative parts; chemical activities not clear
		Leucoplasts	Forerunner of chloroplasts; storage of starch
		Golgi complex	Storage, modification, and packaging of secretory product
		Lysosomes	Contain hydrolytic enzymes
		Fibrils:	
		Myofibrils	Contraction of muscles
		Neurofibrils	Function uncertain
		Tonofibrils	Probably give stability to some epithelial cells
Nonprotoplasmic		**Wall**	Nonliving boundary; protection and support
		Crystals	Probably waste products
		Grains	Stored food and pigments
		Droplets	Stored food
		Vacuole	Contains wastes, foods, and some plant pigments; determines osmotic conditions of cell; contractile vacuoles regulate water content of cell; food vacuoles contain food in the process of digestion

Cell Division (Mitosis and Cytokinesis)

1. **Phases in a plant cell preceding and during division.**

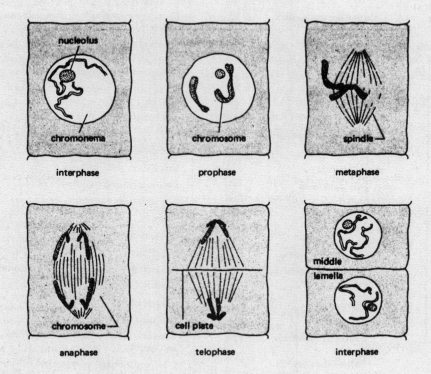

2. **Summary of highlights in cellular phases preceding and during division.**

INTERPHASE (before mitosis and cytokinesis begins)
    Chromosomes not condensed (in form of extended chromatin), therefore not easily visible under microscope.
    Nuclear membranes present.
    Nucleoli may be present.
    In preparation for cell division, the DNA of each chromosome is replicated.

PROPHASE
    Chromosomes condensing.
    Spindle or amphiaster forming.
    Nuclear membrane disappearing.
    Nucleoli disappearing.

METAPHASE
    Chromosomes arranged in equatorial plane of spindle.

ANAPHASE
    New chromosomes moving toward poles of spindle.

TELOPHASE
    Chromosomes at poles and in process of transforming to the interphase chromatin pattern.
    Nuclear membrane reforming.
    Nucleoli reforming.
    Cytoplasm dividing across equator of cell.

Plant Tissues

Name	Characteristics	Primary Uses	Some Locations
Immature (meristems)			
Apical meristem	Undifferentiated, cells dividing	Growth, produces primary tissues	Tips of roots and stems
Vascular cambium	Undifferentiated, cells dividing	Produces secondary phloem and xylem	Between phloem and xylem
Cork cambium (phellogen)	Undifferentiated, cells dividing	Produces cork and often parenchyma	Bark
Mature (simple tissues)			
Epidermis	Outside covering, usually one layer thick; outer surface usually covered with cutin; cells alive	Protection	External layer of leaves, fruits, young roots, and young stems
Cork	Replaces epidermis in older stems and roots; cell walls impregnated with suberin; cells dead	Protection	Outside part of older roots and stems
Parenchyma	Cells alive, with thin walls of cellulose	Storage of food or water	Flesh of fruits; some of cortex; some pith
Chlorenchyma	A variety of parenchyma distinguished by containing chlorophyll	Site of photosynthesis	Mesophyll of leaves and beneath epidermis of young stems and fruits
Collenchyma	Cells alive, walls unevenly thickened	Support	Especially herbaceous structures like young leaves and stems; often a distinct zone just beneath the epidermis
Sclerenchyma	Cells dead, walls thickened with secondary deposits; in form of stone cells, fibers; tracheids, or tracheae (vessels)	Support, conduction, and protection	Especially wood and shells of nuts; often present in phloem or cortex in form of fibers
Mature (complex tissues)			
Phloem	Composed of several types of cells such as sieve tubes, companion cells, parenchyma, and fibers	Conduction of food from leaves to places of use and storage	Vascular bundles (steles)
Xylem	Composed of several types of cells such as tracheids, tracheae, fibers, and parenchyma	Conduction of water and solutes from roots to place of use, particularly leaves	Vascular bundles (steles)

Parts of a Flowering Plant (Sporophytic Generation)
(examples or explanations in parentheses)

I. Leaves
  A. Arrangement
    1. Alternate (oak)
    2. Opposite (maple)
    3. Whorled (buttonbush)
    4. Rosette (plantain)
  B. Types
    1. Regular
      a. Simple (grass)
      b. Compound

      (1) Pinnate (vetch)

      (2) Bipinnate (mimosa)

      (3) Palmate (buckeye)

      (4) Decompound (carrot)

  2. Modified

    a. Succulent (cabbage)

    b. Carnivorous (pitcher plant)

    c. Microphyll (pineweed)

    d. Sclerophyll (evergreen oaks)

    e. Scales (bud scales of tree)

    f. Tendril (leaflet of vetch)

    g. Spines (stipules of black locust)

    h. Phyllode *(Lilaeopsis)* — A flat, expanded petiole replacing the blade of a leaf.

    i. Floral

      (1) Bract ("petal" of dogwood)

      (2) Sepal (bud scale of rose)

      (3) Petal (rose)

      (4) Stamen (lily) — See sporophyll.

      (5) Carpel (lily) — See sporophyll.

    j. Sporophyll (bearing spores)

      (1) Microsporophyll (stamen: composed of anther and filament) — Produces microspores.

      (2) Megasporophyll (carpel) — Produces megaspores.

        (a) Simple pistil (derived from one carpel: composed of stigma, style, and ovary)

        (b) Compound pistil (derived from more than one carpel: composed of stigma, style, and ovary)

C. External structures

  1. Gross structures

    a. Blade

    b. Petiole

    c. Stipules

  2. Minute structures

    Epidermis

    (1) Regular epidermal cells

    (2) Cuticle

    (3) Trichomes

    (4) Stomates

    (5) Guard cells

D. Internal structures

  1. Mesophyll

    a. Palisade mesophyll

    b. Spongy mesophyll

  2. Veins

    a. Xylem

    b. Phloem

    c. Sclerenchyma (sheath)

E. Functions
   1. Photosynthesis (all green leaves)
   2. Respiration (all living leaves)
   3. Transpiration (all normal leaves)
   4. Guttation (grass)
   5. Storage of food (cabbage)
   6. Reproduction (African violet)
   7. Support (tendril-bearing plants)
   8. Capture and digestion (carnivorous plants)
   9. Protection (bud scales)

II. Stems
   A. Form
      1. Columnar (coconut) — Unbranched.
      2. Excurrent (tulip poplar) ⎤
      3. Deliquescent (apple)   ⎦ Branched.
   B. Method of growth
      1. Sympodial (sumac) — From a lateral bud.
      2. Monopodial (hickory) — From terminal bud.
   C. Size and toughness
      1. Herbaceous (bean) — Little xylem.
      2. Woody (maple) — Much xylem.
   D. Modified types
      1. Succulent (asparagus)
      2. Phylloclade (cactus) — A stem modified as a leaf.
      3. Cladophyll or cladode (asparagus) — A type of phylloclade resembling a leaf and arising from the axil of a reduced leaf.
      4. Rhizome (iris)
      5. Tuber (Irish potato)
      6. Bulb (onion)
      7. Corm (crocus)
      8. Tendril (Virginia creeper)
      9. Thorn (hawthorn)
      10. Twining (vines)
      11. Stolon (strawberry)
   E. Structure
      1. External
         a. Nodes
         b. Internodes
         c. Lenticels
         d. Epidermis (on young stems)
         e. Cork (on older stems)
         f. Scars, leaf and bud scales
         g. Buds
            (1) According to location
               (a) Terminal
               (b) Lateral
                   Axillary
                   Adventitious
               (c) Accessory

(2) According to content

    (a) Floral

    (b) Vegetative

    (c) Mixed

(3) According to degree of protection

    (a) Naked

    (b) Protected (winter)

(4) According to degree of activity

    (a) Active

    (b) Dormant

2. Internal

a. Bark
- epidermis or cork
- cortex
- endodermis (if present)

- pericycle (if present)
- phloem
- cambium

b. Wood
- xylem
- pith (if present)

vascular bundle (stele)

F. Functions

1. Conduction

2. Support and display of leaves

3. Reproduction (runners, cuttings, bulbs, etc.)

4. Storage (Irish potato)

5. Photosynthesis, respiration, transpiration (cactus and asparagus)

III. Roots

A. Types

1. Primary (from tip of hypocotyl)

2. Secondary (from primary root or other places but not from tip of hypocotyl)

3. Tap (dandelion) — A primary root that becomes the main root.

4. Fibrous (grass) — One of many fine roots.

5. Adventitious (on cuttings) — From stems or junction of stems and roots.

6. Fleshy (sweet potato) — Tuberous.

7. Fascicled (dahlia) — Clustered, fleshy.

8. Prop (corn)

9. Aerial (orchid)

10. Parasitic (dodder)

11. Climbing (ivy)

B. Structure

1. External

a. Root cap

b. Growth region

c. Root hair region (absorption zone)

d. Waterproof region (cork covered)

e. Branch roots

2. Internal

a. Bark {
  epidermis or cork
  cortex
  endodermis (if present)
  pericycle (if present)
  phloem
  cambium

  vascular bundle
  (stele)
}

b. Wood xylem

C. Function
  1. Absorption
  2. Anchorage
  3. Storage
  4. Reproduction
  5. Climbing

Classification of Animal Tissues

I. REPRODUCTIVE TISSUES — precursors of gametes.

II. EMBRYONIC TISSUES — temporary, capable of developing into mature tissues.

III. MATURE TISSUES — serving specialized functions.

A. **Epithelial tissues** — limiting membranes and glands; protective, secretory, or excretory.

1. Simple — single layer of cells above a basement membrane.

a. Squamous — cells are flattened with irregular outline in surface view, enlarged where nucleus located; nuclei eccentrically located. Examples: Bowman's capsule of kidney, respiratory epithelium, endothelium (wall of capillaries and lining of large blood vessels), mesothelium (lining of coelomic cavities), inner layer of endocardium (lining of heart).

b. Cuboidal — cells tend to be hexagonal; nuclei near center of cells. Examples: liver, pancreas, thyroid, salivary glands, sebaceous glands, walls of many small tubes (as in kidney).

c. Columnar — cells are elongated and perpendicular to the basement membrane; nuclei near bases of cells. Example: lining of most of alimentary tract.

d. Pseudostratified — all cells are attached to basement membrane but vary in height; nuclei are at different levels, the basal ones being smaller and darker; cells sometimes ciliated at surface. Examples: lining of nasal cavity, trachea, bronchi, part of urethra.

2. Stratified — more than one layer of cells; cells next to basement membrane are small cuboidal or small columnar.

a. Stratified squamous — cells several layers thick; cells larger toward middle and flattened toward surface. Examples: lining of mouth cavity, nasal cavity, and esophagus; epidermis of skin.

b. Stratified cuboidal — cells larger toward surface. Examples: tubules of testis, ducts of sweat glands.

c. Stratified columnar — basal cells cuboidal, surface cells columnar. Examples: lining in part of pharynx, part of larynx, part of urethra.

d. Transitional — surface cells large, basal cells rounded, other cells pear-shaped. Example: inner surface of urinary bladder.

B. **Connective and supporting tissues** — cells more or less scattered in an intercellular substance containing fibers.

    1.   Connective — cells usually branched and flattened.

        a. Mucous — cells in a gelatinous matrix. Example: vitreous humor of eye.

        b. Reticular — network of stellate cells in a viscous fluid containing fine fibers. Examples: lymph nodes, spleen, bone marrow, beneath epithelium of digestive tract.

        c. Areolar — components loosely arranged; white fibers more abundant than elastic fibers. Examples: submucosa of digestive tract, in mesenteries, connecting various tissues of organs.

        d. Dense fibrous — cells (fibroblasts) flattened among close fibers; white fibers predominate. Examples: ligaments, tendons, organ capsules, periosteum, perichondrium, epimysium.

        e. Elastic fibrous — elastic fibers predominate. Examples: vocal cords, in walls of large blood vessels.

        f. Adipose — nuclei of cells pushed to side by large, central oil droplets; cytoplasm reduced to a film; cells embedded in reticular or areolar tissue. Examples: beneath skin, around various other organs.

    2.   Supporting — cells tend to be spherical, separated by a firm groundmass.

        a. Cartilage (gristle) — matrix of organic materials; cells in spaces called lacunae.

            (1) Hyaline — glassy in appearance; fibers show only when especially prepared. Examples: joint surfaces, end of ribs, end of nose, rings of trachea.

            (2) Fibrous — matrix very fibrous. Examples: pubic symphysis, intervertebral discs.

            (3) Elastic — begins as hyaline cartilage but elastic fibers added. Examples: epiglottis, external ear.

        b. Bone — matrix of inorganic salts; cells in spaces called lacunae.

            (1) Cancellous — spongy in appearance. Examples: epiphyses of long bones, inside flat bones.

            (2) Compact — solid appearance; containing Haversian canal, lacunae, canaliculi, and lamellae. Example: outer part of bones.

C. **Vascular tissues** — fluid consistency, medium of transport.

    1.   Blood—composed of cells in a fluid matrix. Cellular constituents as follows:

        a. Erythrocytes—red blood cells.

        b. Leucocytes—white blood cells.

            (1) Lymphocytes—with large spherical nuclei; produced in lymphatic tissue.

            (2) Monocytes—large cells with nuclei frequently kidney-shaped; produced in bone marrow.

            (3) Granulocytes — cytoplasm granular; nuclei shrunk, of many shapes.

                (a) Neutrophils — small granules stain reddish with Wright's stain.

(b) Eosinophils — large granules stain reddish with Wright's stain.

(c) Basophils — large granules stain blue or purple with Wright's stain.

(d) Platelets—fragments of cells called megakaryocytes.

2. Lymph — a fluid similar to blood plasma and containing some leucocytes.

D. **Muscular tissue** — specialized for contraction; cells elongated.

1. Smooth — not striated; in longitudinal view cells like spindles; individual cells difficult to recognize, nucleus elongate and centrally located; in cross sections cells are round and of various diameters depending on where they are cut, larger cross sections through middle of cells contain nuclei; involuntary. Examples: part of digestive tract wall, in visceral pleura.

2. Skeletal—multinucleated, striated, voluntary; nuclei on periphery of fibers. Examples: muscles attached to skeleton.

3. Cardiac — striated and involuntary; fibers anastomose and partitioned by intercalary discs; nuclei centrally located. Example: heart.

E. **Nervous tissue** — composed of neurons that transmit impulses. Component neurons may be classified as follows:

1. According to function.
   a. Sensory — receiving stimuli.
   b. Motor — leading to a responsive tissue.
   c. Association — connecting other neurons.
2. According to the number of their processes.
   a. Unipolar — one process that divides shortly after leaving cell body; sensory neurons of spinal nerves.
   b. Bipolar — two processes; rods and cones of retina.
   c. Multipolar — several processes; spinal and brain neurons.

Best-Known Hormones in Mammals

Produced by	Name of Hormone	Abbreviation	Primary Target	Principal Action
Pituitary, anterior (adenohypophysis)	Adrenocorticotropic hormone (corticotropic)	ACTH	Adrenal cortex	Increases activity of adrenal cortex
	Gonadotropic hormones: Follicle-stimulating hormone	FSH	Ovary and testis	In females, stimulates growth of ovarian follicle; in males, stimulates germinal epithelium of seminiferous tubules
	Luteinizing hormone (interstitial-cell-stimulating hormone)	LH (ICSH)	Ovary and testis	Stimulates development and action of corpus luteum; stimulates development of seminiferous tubules and action of interstitial cells
	Prolactin		Mammary gland and ovary	Stimulates the secretion of milk; stimulates the corpus luteum
	Growth hormone (somatotropic hormone)	GH	Body	Regulates body growth
	Thyrotropic hormone (thyroid-stimulating hormone)	TH	Thyroid	Regulates action of thyroid

(Continued)

Best-Known Hormones in Mammals (cont'd)

Produced by	Name of Hormone	Abbreviation	Primary Target	Principal Action
Pituitary, posterior (neurohypophysis)	**Oxytocin**		Uterus and mammary glands	Causes contraction of muscles of uterus as well as those that express milk from follicles and ducts of mammary gland
	Antidiuretic hormone (vasopressin)	ADH	Arterioles, kidneys	Stimulates contraction of muscles in arterioles, thus causing an increase in blood pressure; water retention in kidneys
Thyroid	**Thyroxin**		Body tissues	Regulates rate of metabolism, thus influencing growth and development
Parathyroid	**Parathormone**		Body tissues, especially bone and blood	Regulates calcium and phosphorus metabolism
Stomach	**Gastrin**		Stomach	Together with the nervous system, causes the secretion of gastric juice
Duodenal mucosa	**Secretin**		Pancreas	Stimulates secretion of pancreatic juice, especially increasing its water content
	Pancreozymin		Pancreas	Stimulates secretion of enzymatic content of pancreatic juice
	Enterogastrone		Stomach	Inhibits gastric secretion and contraction
	Cholecystokinin		Gallbladder	Causes contraction and discharge of bile
Pancreas	**Insulin**		Body tissues	Facilitates cellular uptake of glucose, causes conversion of glucose to glycogen in liver
	Glucagon (hyperglycemic factor)	HGF	Liver	Converts glycogen to glucose, thus increasing blood sugar
Adrenal cortex	Corticoids:			
	Aldosterone		Body tissues	Regulates sodium and potassium metabolism
	Androgens (such as adrenosterone)		Body tissues, especially in sexual organs	Causes masculine characteristics
	Cortisone		Body tissues	Inhibits inflammatory processes
	Desoxycorticosterone	DOCA	Body tissues	Regulates salt and water metabolism
	Hydrocortisone		Body tissues	Stimulates conversion of proteins to carbohydrates
Adrenal medulla	**Epinephrine**		Body tissues and circulatory system	Increases cellular respiration; causes vasoconstriction and increases heartbeat, thus increasing blood pressure
	Norepinephrine		Body tissues and circulatory system	Increases cellular respiration; causes vasoconstriction and increases heartbeat, thus increasing blood pressure
Kidney	**Angiotensin**		Circulatory system	Increases blood pressure
	Renin		Blood	Causes formation of angiotensin
Ovary (follicle)	**Estrogens** (such as estradiol)		Entire body, especially sexual organs	Causes femininity; responsible for the proliferative stage of the uterus in the menstrual cycle
Ovary (corpus luteum)	**Progesterone**		Uterus and breast	Responsible for the secretory stage of the uterus in the menstrual cycle; causes breast development during pregnancy

(Continued)

Best-Known Hormones in Mammals (cont'd)

Produced by	Name of Hormone	Abbreviation	Primary Target	Principal Action
Placenta	**Estrogens** (such as estradiol)		Same as in ovary	Same as in ovary
	Gonadotropin		Corpus luteum	Stimulates continued production of progesterone
	Progesterone		Same as in ovary	Same as in ovary
Testis	**Androgens** (such as testosterone)		Entire body, especially sexual organs	Causes masculinity
Neuron endings	**Acetylcholine**		Dendrites of parasympathetic neurons and tissues innervated by the parasympathetic system	Transmits nerve impulses across synapses and from terminal axons to tissues
	Adrenalin		Dendrites of sympathetic nervous system and tissues innervated by sympathetic system	Transmits nerve impulses across synapses and from terminal axons to tissues
	Noradrenalin		Same as adrenalin	Same as adrenalin

Best-Known Hormones in Plants

Name of Hormone	Abbreviation	Principal Actions
Indole-3-acetic acid (an auxin)	IAA	Stimulates cell elongation in coleoptile and roots; suppresses cell enlargement in lower branches; works with cytokinins to stimulate cell division
Gibberellic acid (a gibberellin)	GA_3	Increases size and number of cells in stems; triggers flowering of some plants
Kinetin (a cytokinin)		Works with auxins to stimulate rate of cell division; inhibits leaf senescence
Abscisic acid		Prepares buds and seeds for dormancy; inhibits water loss in drought; promotes senescence; triggers leaf loss by abscission
Ethylene		Hastens fruit ripening
Florigen (hypothetical)		Induces flowering (not yet isolated)

Photosynthesis

1. **Light Reactions, to Produce ATP and Energize the Dark Reactions**

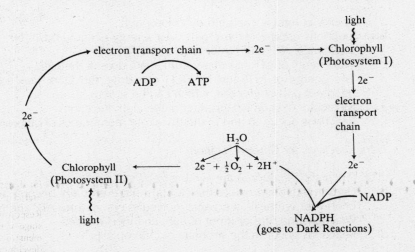

2. Dark Reactions, to Synthesize Organic Molecules

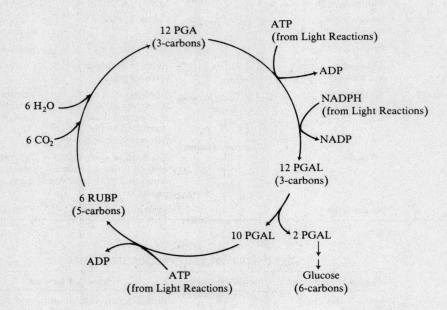

3. Summary of Photosynthesis

Light Reactions

a. Energy of light is captured by chlorophyll.
b. Electrons escape chlorophyll; their energy is captured in two newly synthesized molecules, ATP and NADPH.
c. The energy of ATP has many immediate uses in the cell.
d. The energy of ATP and NADPH can drive the Dark Reactions, and eventually becomes part of glucose, which can be stored.
e. Molecular oxygen is a product of the Light Reactions.
f. Reactions occur on and in the thylakoid membranes of chloroplasts.

Dark Reactions (or Carbon Fixation)

a. Precursors of glucose are synthesized.
b. Carbon dioxide provides the carbons that eventually become part of glucose.
c. Energy for synthesis of organic molecules comes from ATP and NADPH of the Light Reactions; no further input of light energy is needed.
d. Reactions occur in the stromata of chloroplasts.

Some Major Steps in Glycolysis and the Citric Acid Cycle

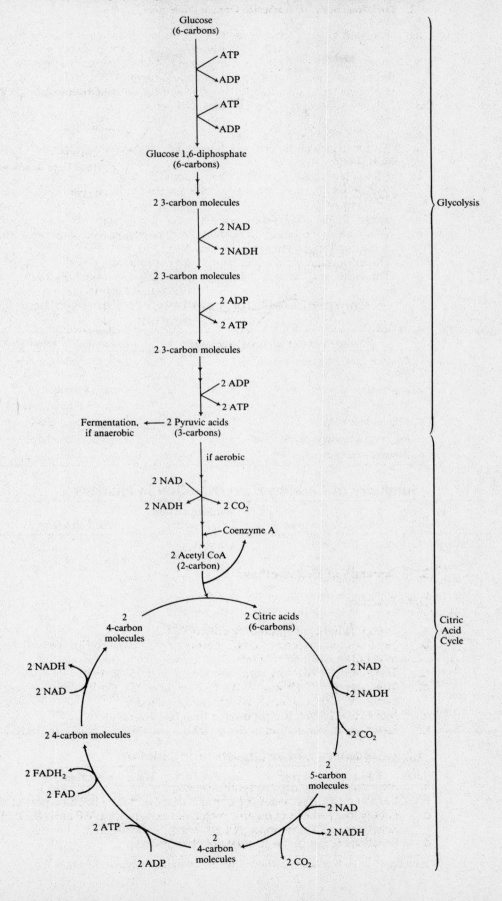

Summary of glycolysis and the citric acid cycle.

Glycolsis
a.   For each glucose, two molecules of extant ATP are used to provide starting energy. Four molecules of ATP are then newly formed; thus the net gain is 2 ATP.
b.   Two molecules of NADH carry energy from glucose, and can later provide this energy to chemiosmosis to produce additional ATP (under aerobic conditions).
c.   Glycolysis can operate under either aerobic or anaerobic conditions.
d.   Glycolysis occurs in the cytoplasm of cells.

Citric Acid (Krebs) Cycle
a.   All 6 carbons of the original glucose become separated from each other and from their hydrogens.
b.   For each glucose, 6 NADH's are produced.
c.   Two $FADH_2$'s are produced; each can provide its energy to chemiosmosis to produce ATP.
d.   Two ATP are produced as a direct result of the cycle, not via chemiosmosis.
e.   When all ATP production resulting from both glycolysis and the citric acid cycle is accounted for, the net gain per glucose is 36 ATP.
f.   The citric acid cycle occurs only under aerobic conditions.
g.   The citric acid cycle and chemiosmosis occur in mitochondria.

Conspicuous Differences between Photosynthesis and Respiration

Photosynthesis	Respiration
1. Converts light energy into a chemical form	Releases chemical energy into a usable form
2. Increases biomass	Decreases biomass
3. Requires light	Occurs in light or darkness
4. Requires chlorophyll	Occurs without chlorophyll
5. Requires carbon dioxide and water	Requires food molecules and oxygen
6. Releases water and oxygen	Releases carbon dioxide and water

Summary of Carbohydrate Digestion in Humans

Place	Food	Enzyme	Intermediate Product	End Product	Where Absorbed
Oral cavity	Polysaccharides	Amylase	Dextrin and disaccharides		
	Disaccharide (maltose)	Disaccharidase (maltase)		Glucose	Small intestine
Stomach	Continuation of digestion started in mouth				
Small intestine	Polysaccharides	Amylase (intestinal and pancreatic)	Dextrin and disaccharides		
	Disaccharide (maltose)	Disaccharidase (maltase)		Glucose	Small intestine
	Disaccharide (sucrose)	Disaccharidase (sucrase)		Glucose and fructose	Small intestine
	Disaccharide (lactose)	Disaccharidase (lactase)		Glucose and galactose	Small intestine
Large intestine	Continuation of digestion already underway			Glucose, fructose, and galactose	Large intestine

Summary of Fat Digestion in Humans

Place	Food	Enzyme	End Product	Where Absorbed
Stomach	Fats	Lipase (gastric)	Fatty acids and glycerol	Small intestine
Small intestine	Fats*	Lipase (intestinal and pancreatic)	Fatty acids and glycerol	Small intestine

*Fats emulsified by bile; some colloidal particles absorbed without digestion.

Summary of Protein Digestion in Humans

Place	Food	Enzyme	Intermediate Product	End Product	Where Absorbed
Stomach					
	{ Proteins { Casein	Pepsin	{ Proteoses { Peptones { Peptides	Amino acids	Small intestine
Small intestine	Proteins	{ Trypsin (pancreatic) Chymotrypsin (pancreatic)	{ Proteoses { Peptones { Polypeptides		
	{ Proteoses { Peptones { Polypeptides	{ Aminopeptidase (intestinal) Carboxypeptidase (pancreatic)	Dipeptides		
	Dipeptides	Dipeptidase		Amino acids	Small intestine
Large intestine	Continuation of digestion underway, plus some bacterial action				

Some Common Vitamins

Name	Solubility	Sources	Function	Deficiency Effect
Vitamin A	Fat	Green vegetables Yellow foods Liver	Maintenance of epithelial cells of eyes, skin, digestive and respiratory tracts Chemistry of vision Bone formation	Weakened resistance of epithelial tissue to disease Night blindness Abnormal growth
Vitamin B₁ (thiamine)	Water	Whole grain, especially the germ Vegetables Nuts Yeast Liver Pork meat	Carbohydrate metabolism	Mild deficiency: loss of appetite, fatigue, etc. Extreme deficiency: beriberi
Vitamin B₂ (riboflavin)	Water	Milk and its products Yeast Liver Wheat germ Meat Eggs	Coenzyme used in metabolism of glucose and amino acids and in some oxidative processes	Retarded growth Inflammation of eyes Dermatitis Cracking of corner of mouth
Pantothenic acid	Water	Liver Meat Eggs Peanuts Sweet potato	Maintenance of skin, nerve, and cardiovascular system	Degenerative changes in skin, nerves, and cardiovascular system
Vitamin B₆ (pyridoxine)	Water	Whole grain products	Amino acid and fatty acid metabolism	Dermatitis, nerve disorders
Niacin (nicotinamide)	Water	Yeast Vegetables Meat Liver	Important in formation of NAD and NADP (hydrogen acceptors)	Pellagra
Biotin	Water	Liver Egg yolk Meats Vegetables	Protein metabolism	Dermatitis Weakness
Folic acid	Water	Vegetables Liver Yeast Bacterial synthesis in intestine	Nucleic acid synthesis; red and white blood cell formation	Anemia Leucopenia
Vitamin B₁₂ (cyanocobalamin)	Water	Liver Meat Milk and its products	Nucleic acid synthesis	Anemia

(Continued)

Some Common Vitamins (cont'd)

Name	Solubility	Sources	Function	Deficiency Effect
Vitamin C (ascorbic acid)	Water	Citrus fruits Vegetables	Maintenance of connective tissues Metabolism of some amino acids	Scurvy
Vitamin D (calciferol)	Fat	Liver oils Milk products Eggs Manufactured by body	Calcium and phosphorus absorption and metabolism; bone and tooth formation	Rickets
Vitamin E (tocopherol)	Fat	Wheat germ Vegetable oils Most other foods	Antioxidant; maintains red blood cells	Fragility of red blood cells
Vitamin K	Fat	Most foods, especially vegetables Bacterial synthesis in intestines	In prothrombin synthesis	Hemorrhaging

Strategies Used by Vertebrate Animals to Maintain Salt and Water Balance and to Excrete Nitrogenous Wastes

Animal	Problem Faced	Water Solution	Salt Solution	Waste Solution
Marine cartilagenous fish	Isotonic to environment (by retention of urea)	None needed	Active transport outward at kidneys and at rectal gland	Ammonia, urea excreted
Marine bony fish	Hypotonic to environment	Concentrated urine; drinking seawater	Active transport outward at gills	Ammonia excreted
Freshwater fish	Hypertonic to environment	Dilute, copious urine	Active transport inward at gills	Ammonia excreted
Amphibian	Hypertonic to environment	Dilute, copious urine	Active transport inward at skin	Ammonia, urea excreted
Terrestrial reptile, bird	Hypertonic to environment	Nearly solid nitrogenous waste, drinking fresh water	Active transport inward at kidneys	Uric acid excreted
Marine reptile, bird	Hypotonic to drinking water	Drinking seawater	Salt excretion at salt glands	Uric acid excreted (bird), urea and ammonia excreted (reptile)
Terrestrial mammal	Hypertonic to environment	Controlling water loss at kidneys; drinking fresh water	Salt retention at kidneys	Urea excreted
Marine mammal	Hypotonic to environment	Making some metabolic water; drinking seawater	Salt excretion at kidneys (?)	Urea excreted

Generalized Embryonic Development Illustrating Embryonic Membranes

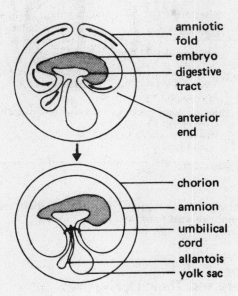

Extraembryonic Membranes of Mammals, Birds, and Reptiles

Membrane	Location	Mammals		Birds and Reptiles		Germ Layer Lining Cavity
		Origin	Function	Origin	Function	
Chorion	Outer enveloping membrane (surrounds amnion)	Essentially serosal somatopleure and allantoic Splanchnopleure	Organ of exchange between embryo (fetus) and mother	Serosa	Protection, probably respiration, and possibly some excretion	Mesoderm
Amnion	Inner enveloping membrane (surrounds embryo)	Somatopleure	Protection against shock and adhesions	Somatopleure	Protection against shocks and adhesions	Ectoderm
Yolk sac	Ventral wall of midgut	Splanchnopleure	Essentially vestigial	Splanchnopleure	Contains food reserve	Endoderm
Allantois	Outpocket of ventral wall of hindgut	Splanchnopleure	Unites with serosa to become part of the chorion, an organ of exchange between the embryo (fetus) and the mother	Splanchnopleure	Respiration and excretion	Endoderm

Early Development of the Human

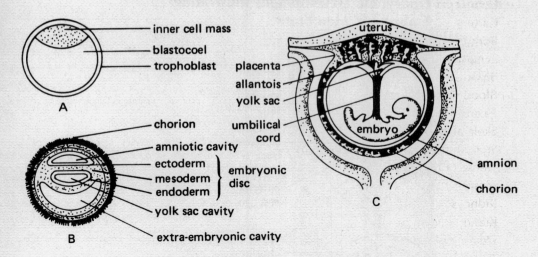

Three stages of development. A, blastodermic vesicle (blastula); B, differentiation of germ layers; C, uterus, placenta, embryo and membranes.

Germ Layers and Their Derivatives

ECTODERM

Epidermis and associated parts such as hair and nails

Lens and retina of eye

Enamel of teeth

Nerve cells (individually or as part of nerve, ganglion, spinal cord, or brain)

Medulla of adrenal gland

Inner ear

Epithelium of nasal and buccal cavities

Epithelium of anal canal

Part of mammary, sebaceous, sweat, and pituitary glands

ENDODERM

Inner lining of —

    Alimentary canal

    Middle ear and Eustachian tube

    Gallbladder

    Lung tubes

    Lungs

    Urethra

    Urinary bladder

Bulk of —

    Thyroid

    Parathyroids

    Thymus

    Pancreas

    Liver

    Prostate gland

MESODERM
- Dermis of skin
- Connective tissue
- Cartilage
- Bone
- Lymphoid tissue
- Blood
- Blood vessels
- Heart
- Skeletal muscles
- Smooth muscles of internal organs
- Lining of body cavities
- Mesenteries
- Kidneys
- Kidney ducts
- Dentine of teeth
- Testes
- Ovaries
- Oviducts, uterus, and vagina
- Cortex of adrenal gland

Generalized Life Cycle of Plants

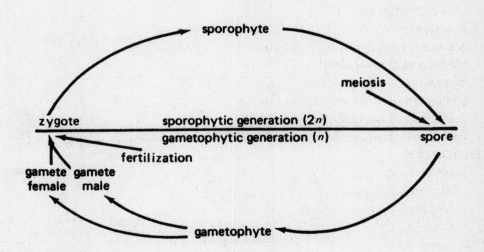

Moss Life Cycle

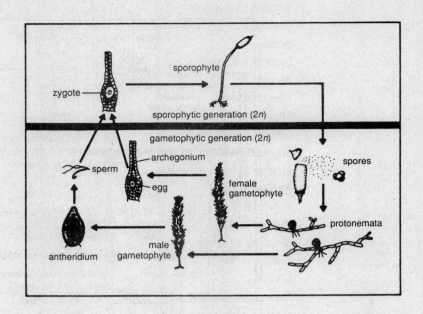

Fern Life Cycle

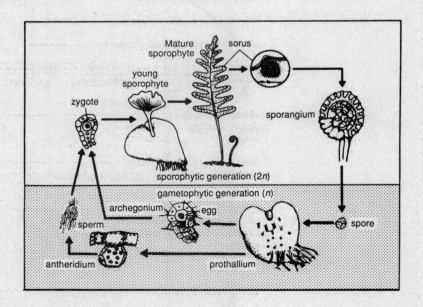

Life Cycle of Flowering Seed Plant

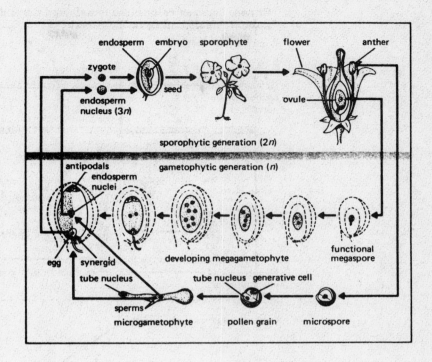

Monohybrid Cross

Simple cross of pea plants involving dominance and recessiveness.

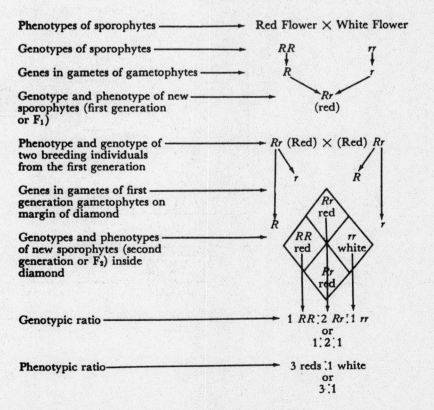

Phenotypes of sporophytes ⟶ Red Flower × White Flower

Genotypes of sporophytes ⟶ *RR*   *rr*

Genes in gametes of gametophytes ⟶ *R*   *r*

Genotype and phenotype of new sporophytes (first generation or F₁) ⟶ *Rr* (red)

Phenotype and genotype of two breeding individuals from the first generation ⟶ *Rr* (Red) × (Red) *Rr*

Genes in gametes of first generation gametophytes on margin of diamond

Genotypes and phenotypes of new sporophytes (second generation or F₂) inside diamond ⟶ *Rr* red / *RR* red / *rr* white / *Rr* red

Genotypic ratio ⟶ 1 *RR* : 2 *Rr* : 1 *rr* or 1 : 2 : 1

Phenotypic ratio ⟶ 3 reds : 1 white or 3 : 1

Sex-Linkage

Crosses between color-blind female and normal male and between normal female and color-blind male.

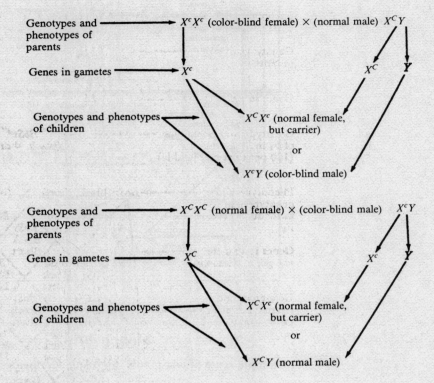

Genotypes and phenotypes of parents → $X^c X^c$ (color-blind female) × (normal male) $X^C Y$

Genes in gametes → X^c X^C Y

Genotypes and phenotypes of children → $X^C X^c$ (normal female, but carrier)

or

$X^c Y$ (color-blind male)

Genotypes and phenotypes of parents → $X^C X^C$ (normal female) × (color-blind male) $X^c Y$

Genes in gametes → X^C X^c Y

Genotypes and phenotypes of children → $X^C X^c$ (normal female, but carrier)

or

$X^C Y$ (normal male)

Dihybrid Cross

Cross between a black, short-haired guinea pig and a brown, long-haired guinea pig. Black and short hair are dominant. Taken to F_2 generation.

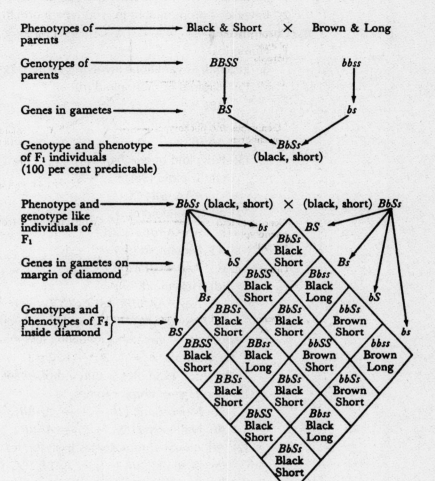

Phenotypes of parents ⟶ Black & Short × Brown & Long

Genotypes of parents ⟶ *BBSS*   *bbss*

Genes in gametes ⟶ *BS*   *bs*

Genotype and phenotype of F_1 individuals (100 per cent predictable) ⟶ *BbSs* (black, short)

Phenotype and genotype like individuals of F_1 ⟶ *BbSs* (black, short) × (black, short) *BbSs*

Genes in gametes on margin of diamond ⟶ *bs*   *BS*   *bS*   *Bs*   *Bs*   *bS*

Genotypes and phenotypes of F_2 inside diamond ⟶ *BS*   *bs*

	BbSs Black Short		
	BbSS Black Short	*Bbss* Black Long	
	BBSs Black Short	*BbSs* Black Short	*bbSs* Brown Short
BBSS Black Short	*BBss* Black Long	*bbSS* Brown Short	*bbss* Brown Long
	BBSs Black Short	*BbSs* Black Short	*bbSs* Brown Short
	BbSS Black Short	*Bbss* Black Long	
	BbSs Black Short		

Sources of Genetic Variations

I. Mutations
  A. Genic (point)
    1. Forward — from wild type (normal) to mutant
    2. Reverse — from mutant to wild type (normal)
  B. Chromosomal
    1. Numerical
      a. Euploid — variations involving entire sets of chromosomes
        (1) Haploid or monoploid *(n)*
          ABC
        (2) Diploid (2*n*)
          AABBCC
        (3) Polyploid (more than 2*n*)
          (a) Triploid (3*n*)
            AAABBBCCC
          (b) Tetraploid (4*n*)
            AAAABBBBCCCC
          (c) Pentaploid (5*n*)
            AAAAABBBBBCCCCC
          (d) Hexaploid (6*n*)
            AAAAAABBBBBBCCCCCC
          (e) Septaploid (7*n*), octoploid (8*n*), etc.
      b. Aneuploid — variations involving less than a set of chromosomes:
        for example, *n* + 1, 2*n* − 1, 2*n* + 1, and 3*n* + 1.
        Common examples within a diploid set (2*n* or disomic) follow:
        (1) Shortage of chromosomes
          (a) Monosomic (2*n* − 1) — AABBC
          (b) Nullosomic (2*n* − 2) — AABB
        (2) Additional chromosomes (polysomic)
          (a) Trisomic (2*n* + 1) − AABBCCC
          (b) Double trisomic (2*n* + 1 + 1) − AABBBCCC
          (c) Tetrasomic (2*n* + 2) − AABBCCCC
          (d) Pentasomic (2*n* + 3), etc.
    2. Structural
      a. Additions or deletions of chromosomal material
        (1) Deficiencies—the loss of a segment of genetic material from a
          chromosome

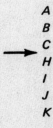

(2) Duplications — the addition of a segment of genetic material

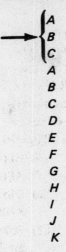

b. Rearrangement of chromosomal material

    (1) Inversions — rearrangement of the gene sequence in one of a homologous pair of chromosomes

        (a) Paracentric — rearrangement of the gene sequence in a part of the chromosome where the centromere is not located

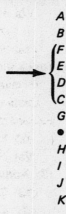

        (b) Pericentric — rearrangement of the gene sequence in a part of the chromosome where the centromere is located

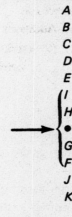

(2) Translocations

  (a) Simple — involves a single break; the broken piece attaches to the end of another chromosome

```
A                        (A
B  ───────────────────►  {B
C◄──── break             (C
D        S        D       S
E        T        E       T
F        U        F       U
G        V        G       V
H        W        H       W
I        X        I       X
J        Y        J       Y
K        Z        K       Z
```

  (b) Shift — involves three breaks; a two-break section in the break of another chromosome

```
A                              S
B                              T
C◄─break 1                     U
D        S        A            V
E        T        B           (D
F◄─break 2 U     C────────►   {E
G  break 3►V     G            (F
H        W        H            W
I        X        I            X
J        Y        J            Y
K        Z        K            Z
```

  (c) Reciprocal (interchange) — involves a single break in two non-homologous chromosomes; two broken parts are exchanged

```
A                        (S
B                        {T
C           ───────────► {U
D◄─break 1  S            (V
E           T       E    (A
F           U       F    {B
G break 2►  V       G    {C
H           W       H    (D
I           X       I     W
J           Y       J     X
K           Z       K     Y
                          Z
```

II. Recombinations

  A. Heterozygosity — with alleles originating from two kinds of homozygous parents

  B. Random assortment — the random distribution of one of each pair of chromosomes to the gametes.

  C. Crossing-over — genetic exchange between nonsister chromatids of homologous chromosomes

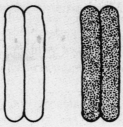

III. Introduced genes
  A. Transformation — the incorporation by an organism of foreign fragments of genetic material from the surrounding medium, where they were liberated from other organisms
  B. Transduction — the transfer of genetic material from one host cell to another by a virus

Hardy-Weinberg Equilibrium: Necessary Conditions

The prediction (based on probability) is that a population of organisms will *not* undergo change in the frequency of its genes (alleles) as it goes from one generation to the next, if the following conditions prevail.

1. There is *normal Mendelian segregation* of the alleles.
2. There is only *random mating* within the population (all individuals equally likely to mate).
3. There is *no intergenerational mating* (nonoverlapping generations).
4. There is *no selection* for or against organisms, concerning any genetically determined characteristics.
5. There are *no migrations* into or out of the population.
6. There are *no mutations* of genes carried within the population.
7. The population is *sufficiently large* to avoid gene frequency changes by genetic drift (many agree on the cutoff being 1000 individuals).

Isolating Mechanisms Important in Evolution

I. Spatial isolation — allopatric; geographical barriers separate different populations

II. Genetic isolation — allopatric or sympatric; genetic barriers separate populations or interfere with their maximum reproductive potential

  A. Barriers to mating

    1. Habitat — potential mates do not interbreed because they do not live in the same kind of places

    2. Temporal — potential mates do not mate because their breeding periods are at different times of the day or year

    3. Behavioral — potential mates do not interbreed because they are not attracted to each other

    4. Morphological — potential mates do not interbreed because their reproductive structures do not match

  B. Barriers to successful reproduction and survival after mating

    1. Gametic incompatibility — sperm will not fertilize eggs

    2. Zygotic mortality — fertilization occurs but the zygote will not develop

    3. Hybrid inviability — offspring are weak

    4. Hybrid sterility — the hybrid offspring cannot reproduce themselves

    5. Hybrid breakdown — the first-generation hybrids thrive but later generations lose their vigor or become sterile

The Geologic Sequence (Timetable)

Era	Period	Epoch	Time*	Physical Events	Life
CENOZOIC "age of mammals, birds, and angiosperms"	Neogene	Pleistocene	1	Glaciation and recession of ice	Rise and dominance of human species, last of great mammals, relative increase of herbaceous plants over woody plants
		Pliocene	10 (11)	Cool climate, coast ranges rising, deserts of Southwest develop	Increase in herbaceous plants
		Miocene	15 (26)	Cool climate, coast ranges rising, extensive lava flows	Modern birds and trees, first grasses
	Paleogene	Oligocene	10 (36)	Mild climate	First elephants
		Eocene	20 (56)	Mild climate	First apes
		Paleocene	5 (61)	Warm, humid climate	Hardwood forests predominate, first placental animals
Laramide Revolution					
MESOZOIC "age of reptiles"	Cretaceous		65 (126)	Warm climate, Rocky Mts. formed, inland submergence	Early angiosperms and decline of gymnosperms, last of dinosaurs
	Jurassic		30 (156)	Arid climate	First frogs, birds, and mammals; reptiles diversified, abundant gymnosperms
	Triassic		40 (196)	Desert climate, volcanic activity	First dinosaurs, abundant gymnosperms
Appalachian Revolution					
PALEOZOIC	Permian		45 (241)	Appalachians elevated, widespread glaciation and aridity	First conifers, last of trilobites
	Pennsylvanian (Carboniferous) "coal age"		35 (276)	Warm, moist climate; coal-forming swamps	First reptiles, swamp floras of giant ferns and seed ferns
	Mississippian (Carboniferous) "coal age"		25 (301)	Warm, moist climate; considerable submergence	First insects, abundance of sharks, dominant plants lycopods and horsetails
	Devonian "age of fishes"		50 (361)	Aridity, emergence	Many fishes, first amphibians, first forests
	Silurian		30 (390)	Extensive submergence	First land plants and animals, first freshwater fishes
	Ordovician		70 (461)	Mild climate, extensive submergence	First vertebrates (fishes)
	Cambrian "age of invertebrates and thallophytes"		100 (561)	Mild climate	All life marine, trilobites and brachiopods dominant
Killarney Revolution					
PROTEROZOIC			1000 (1561)	Extensive igneous activity, first evidence of glaciation	Marine algae, marine sponges, marine worms
Laurentian Revolution					
ARCHEOZOIC			2000 (2561)	Extensive igneous activity	First plant life (bacteria and algae)

*Time in millions of years. First number is duration; number in parentheses is time before the present.

Major Terrestrial Biomes of the World

1. Forest biomes
    A. Tropical (low-latitude) forests
        a. Rain forest (including jungle, galeria, and mangrove)
        b. Semideciduous forest (monsoon)
        c. Scrub forest
    B. Nontropical (middle- and high-latitude) forests
        a. Mediterranean scrub forest
        b. Broadleaf (and broadleaf-coniferous) forest
        c. Coniferous forest
2. Grassland biomes
    A. Tropical grassland (savanna)
    B. Middle-latitude grassland (steppe and prairie)
3. Desert biomes
    A. Desert (dry desert)
    B. Tundra (frozen desert)

Zones of Vegetation in and around Lakes*
(from deep water to climax vegetation)

1. **Floating plants** (e.g., duckweed, wolffia) — may be over all depths of water and are the only vegetation possible where light cannot penetrate to the bottom
2. **Rooted plants completely submerged** (e.g., elodea, chara, nitella) — enough light penetrates to carry on photosynthesis but water is too deep for plants to reach the surface
3. **Rooted plants with floating leaves** (e.g., water-lily, water-shield)
4. **Emergent plants** (e.g., cattail, iris) — often in standing water but projecting above it
5. **Marginal vegetation,** a meadow (e.g., grasses, sedges) or shrub (e.g., alders, willows) fringe
6. **Bottomland trees** (e.g., willows, poplars, ash, box elder, water oak)
7. **Climax vegetation of area** (e.g., deciduous forest, coniferous forest, grass)

*All zones may not be present.

Major Oceanic Environments (Depths not Proportional)

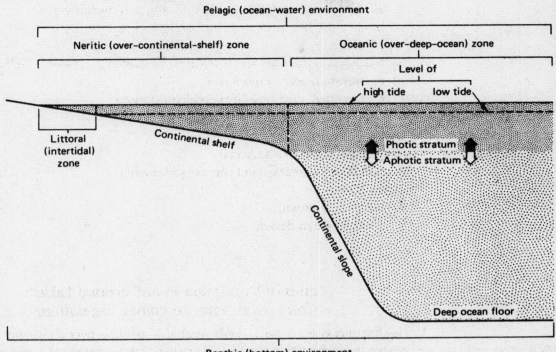

S and J Population Growth Curves

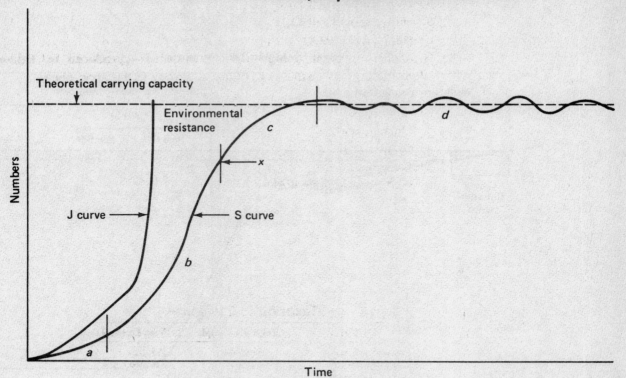

The J curve represents the theoretical population increase due to the biotic potential of a species. The S curve represents the actual increase; this is less than the theoretical increase because of environmental resistance. Segment *a* is the positive acceleration phase; segment *b*, the logarithmic phase; segment *c*, the negative acceleration phase; segment *d*, the plateau phase. Point *x* marks the time when the rate of population increase markedly slows because of environmental resistance. The broke line (plateau) represents the theoretical carrying capacity; the actual population, marked by the wavy line, fluctuates near this level.

Common Classes of Atmospheric Pollutants*

I. Particulate matter — aggregates of molecules smaller than 0.5 mm in diameter; called *aerosols* if less than 0.1 mm in diameter
   A. Pollen
   B. Dust
      1. Natural (volcanic, storm, plowing, earth moving, transportation, etc.)
      2. Industrial (processing, refuse, and fly ash)
   C. Smoke
   D. Vapors (droplets)
   E. Metals
II. Nonparticulate matter
   A. Primary pollutants
      1. Carbon monoxide (CO)
      2. Carbon dioxide (CO_2) — may cause weather changes

*Some items may fit more than one category; they may also be characterized as poisons, irritants, odors, corroders, cloggers, etc.

    3. Chlorine (Cl)

    4. Hydrocarbons (HC)

    5. Nitrogen oxides (NO_x)

    6. Sulfur oxides (SO_x)

B. Secondary pollutants (photochemical oxidants) — produced by light-influenced chemical changes of pollutants already in the atmosphere

    1. Ozone (O_3)

    2. Aldehydes

    3. Organic acids

    4. Sulfuric acid

    5. Peroxides

    6. Peroxyacetylnitrate (PAN)

Taxonomic Categories

Level	Animal Example	Plant Example
Kingdom	Animalia	Plantae
Phylum (Division*)	Chordata	Tracheophyta
Class	Mammalia	Angiospermae
Order	Primates	Commelinales
Family	Hominidae	Poaceae
Genus	*Homo*	*Zea*
Species	*sapiens*	*mays*
(Common name)	(human)	(corn)

Botanists use the word "division" in the same way that zoologists use "phylum."

Classification of Living Organisms

No universally acceptable scheme of classification is available. Classification is ever changing to accommodate new ideas and findings. The somewhat abbreviated scheme given on pages 244–249 divides organisms into five kingdoms, as proposed by R. H. Whittaker. Kingdom Monera includes all prokaryotic organisms. Kingdom Protista comprises primarily unicellular eukaryotic organisms, whether autotrophic or heterotrophic. Kingdom Fungi encompasses the heterotrophs which surround their cells with walls. Kingdom Plantae includes multicellular autotrophs, and Kingdom Animalia consists of the multicellular heterotrophs whose cells do not produce walls. Viruses, since they are not cellular, fit into none of these kingdoms.

Prokaryotes and Eukaryotes Contrasted

Prokaryotes (bacteria)	Eukaryotes (organisms except bacteria)
Protoplasm relatively rigid; relatively resistant to desiccation, osmotic shock, and thermal alteration.	Protoplasm relatively more fluid; more sensitive to desiccation, osmotic shock, and thermal alteration.
Cells generally small.	Cells generally large.
Nuclear membrane absent.	Nuclear membrane present.
Chromosomes composed of DNA only, fibril-like, sometimes circular.	Chromosomes cordlike, several to many; usually composed of DNA and proteins.
Endoplasmic reticulum absent.	Endoplasmic reticulum usually present.
Mitochondria absent.	Mitochondria present.
Plastids absent.	Plastids present in autotrophic species.
Golgi complex absent.	Golgi complex present.
Microtubules absent.	Microtubules present.
Vacuoles absent.	Vacuoles present or absent.
Lysosomes absent.	Lysosomes present or absent.
Centrioles absent.	Centrioles present or absent.
Flagella, when present, generally a simple fibril; not with a 9 + 2 pattern of microtubules.	Cilia or flagella, when present, compound; usually with a 9 + 2 pattern of microtubules.
Cell division amitotic.	Cell division usually mitotic.
Many species can use atmospheric nitrogen.	Cannot use atmospheric nitrogen.
Sexual reproduction seldom present.	Sexual reproduction often present.
Cell walls, when present, contain muramic acid and amino sugars but no cellulose.	Cell walls, when present, do not contain muramic acid and amino sugars but do contain cellulose.
Cells not connected by protoplasmic processes.	Cells often connected by protoplasmic processes.
No cyclosis or amoeboid movement.	Sometimes with cyclosis or amoeboid movement.

Classification of Kingdom Monera

Prokaryotic organisms lacking nuclear membranes, mitochondria, plastids, and a number of other cellular organelles. Most prokaryotes are unicellular and asexual. Flagella, when present, consist of a single fibril, unlike the 9 + 2 pattern characteristic of eukaryotes.

Division Schizomycetes (Bacteria, rickettsias, and spirochetes). Unicellular heterotrophs that usually reproduce asexually by fission.

Division Cyanobacteria (Blue-green algae). Usually autotrophic but chlorophyll not contained in plastids; cell walls usually covered by a gelatinous coating; reproduction by fission.

Division Chloroxybacteria (Prochlorophyta). Autotrophic, free-living or symbiotic with marine animals; resemble chloroplasts.

Division Archaebacteria. Methane-producers (methanogens), sulfur-dependent (sulfobales), and those living in high-salt environments (halobacteria). May comprise a separate kingdom.

Classification of Kingdom Protista*

Primitive eukaryotes that are unicellular or multicellular (with little or no differentiation into tissues). Included are organisms with animal-like or plantlike characteristics.

Division Euglenophyta (Euglenoids). Unicellular, usually with an apical flagellum; reproduction by longitudinal division.

Division Chrysophyta (Golden brown algae and diatoms). Unicellular, colonial, filamentous organisms or algae whose walls, if present, consist mainly of pectic compounds, sometimes heavily silicified; food stored as leucosin or oil.

Class Chrysophyceae (Golden algae).

Class Bacillariophyceae (Diatoms). Unicellular or colonial, each protoplast enclosed in a silicious box consisting of two sculptured valves that fit together like the bottom and top of a pillbox.

Division Pyrrophyta (Fire algae).

Class Dinophyceae (Dinoflagellates). Unicellular algae with two dissimilar flagella inserted in transverse or spiral grooves.

Division Myxomycota (True slime molds). Heterotrophic organisms with animal-like and plantlike stages in their life cycles. The animal-like stage (plasmodium) is coenocytic; the plantlike stage is sporangial.

Division Oomycota (Egg fungi). With motile cells at some stage of development; heterogamous; commonly with cellulose in walls.

Division Acrasiomycota (cellular slime molds).

Division Rhodophyta (Red algae). Mostly multicellular forms; contain phycobilin pigments in addition to chlorophylls; food stored as floridean starch and floridoside; mostly marine, especially abundant in warmer water; produce gelatinous materials such as agar and carageenin.

Division Phaeophyta (Brown algae). Multicellular; filamentous or sheetlike forms; contain fucoxanthin pigment in addition to chlorophylls; food stored as laminarin; mostly marine, especially abundant in colder water; produce a category of gelatinous products called algin.

Division Chlorophyta (Green algae). Diverse forms and sizes; bright green with chlorophylls a and b; food stored as starch; cellulose usually present in cell walls.

Phylum Sarcomastigophora (amoeboid or flagellated, unicellular).

Subphylum Mastigophora. Locomotion by flagella.

Class Phytomastigophora. Photosynthetic.

Class Zoomastigophora. Not photosynthetic.

Subphylum Opalinata. Parasitic in amphibians.

Subphylum Sarcodina. Locomotion by pseudopodia.

Phylum Apicomplexa (anterior penetration organelles, usually lacking locomotion devices, parasitic).

Class Perkinsea. Parasitic in oysters.

Class Sporozoa. Parasitic, most form spores.

Phylum Microspora (intracellular parasites, lacking mitochondria).

Phylum Ciliophora (locomotion by cilia).

Some smaller groups are omitted.

Classification of Kingdom Fungi

Heterotrophic; mostly composed of filaments (distinct or fused); coenocytic or septate; walls usually chitinous. A fungal filament is called a hypha; a mass of vegetative hyphae comprising a fungus is called a mycelium.

Division Zygomycota (Conjugation fungi). Terrestrial; coenocytic; isogamous.

Division Ascomycota (Sac fungi). Hyphae (when present) septate, uninucleate or dikaryotic; meiospores produced in saclike cells called asci, often eight in each ascus. Lichens are often included here because many of their fungal components are ascomycetes.

Division Basidiomycota (Club fungi). Hyphae septate, uninucleate or dikaryotic; meiospores produced by clublike cells called basidia, often four in each basidium.

Classification of Kingdom Plantae*

Most species autotrophic and with substantial tissue differentiation; gametes are produced by meiosis; well developed; gametangia multicellular; sporophytic generation parasitic on the gametophytic generation, at least in the beginning.

Division Bryophyta (Moss plants and their related liverworts and hornworts). Sperm cells biflagellated; gametophytic generation independent and usually more conspicuous; sporophytic generation parasitic on the gametophytic and usually ephemeral; vascular tissue absent or poorly developed.

Division Psilophyta (Whisk ferns). Sporophytes with dichotomously branched stems, and rootless.

Division Lycophyta (Club mosses and their relatives). Small plants with microphylls; spores commonly produced in cones.

Division Sphenophyta (Horsetails). Siliceous plants with jointed stems and whorled, scalelike leaves; spores produced in cones of the macrophyllous type.

Division Pterophyta (Ferns). Leaves usually compounded; spores commonly produced in sporangia that are usually borne in clusters called sori; gametophytes are small and thallose.

Division Coniferophyta (Conifers). Naked-seeded plants (seeds produced on outer surface of cone scales, not within a fruit); leaves simple, usually needle- or scale-shaped; cambium present; sperm cells nonmotile, produced by pollen grains that are male gametophytes.

Division Cycadophyta (Cycads). Fernlike gymnosperms with fronds clustered in an apical crown at apex of unbranched stems; sperm are motile though produced by pollen grains.

Division Ginkgophyta (Maiden-hair or duck's-foot tree). Broad-leaved deciduous gymnosperm; seeds with fleshy coating; sperm cells motile though produced by pollen grains; leaves with dichotomous venation.

*Some smaller groups are omitted.

Division Gnetophyta (Gnetophytes). Gymnosperms with some angiosperm features; include vessels.

Division Anthophyta (Flowering plants or angiosperms). Seeds produced inside fruits, dry or fleshy; vessels in the xylem; gametophytes small; males are pollen grains and females are embryo sacs; leaves are usually macrophylls.

Class Dicotyledons (Dicots). Embryos with two cotyledons; flower parts usually in sets of four or five; leaf venation usually branched; primary vascular bundles arranged in a ring; vascular cambium usually present, producing secondary growth.

Class Monocotyledons (Monocots). Embryos with one cotyledon; flower parts usually in sets of three; leaf venation usually parallel; primary vascular bundles scattered; cambium usually absent.

Classification of Kingdom Animalia*

Eukaryotic, heterotrophic, multicellular organisms whose cells generally lack walls; reproduction primarily sexual, with gametes produced by meiosis; usually dioecious.

Phylum Mesozoa (Mesozoans). Simplest animals; 20 or 30 cells surrounding a long, slender reproductive cell; parasitic within molluscs.

Phylum Porifera (Sponges). Aquatic; lacking organs, with poorly defined tissues; no muscle or nerve cells; body with many pores leading to an internal chamber; filter feeders; mineral or proteinaceous skeletal elements.

Phylum Cnidaria. Aquatic; radially symmetrical; some alternate between polyp and medusa body forms; gastrovascular cavity with mouth only; some diploblastic, some triploblastic; nerve net present, but lacking a central nervous system; asexual budding and sexual reproduction.

Class Hydrozoa (Hydrozoans). Digestive cavity without partitions; medusae with velums, e.g., *Hydra, Obelia.*

Class Scyphozoa (True jellyfishes). Polyp stage reduced or absent; medusae without velums.

Class Anthozoa (Sea anemones). No medusae; digestive cavity partitioned.

Phylum Ctenophora (Comb jellies). Marine; biradial symmetry; mesoglea with some cells and muscle fibers, therefore triploblastic.

Phylum Platyhelminthes (Flatworms). Aquatic or parasitic; bilaterally symmetrical; triploblastic; body flattened dorsoventrally; no coelom; nervous system including anterior ganglia; most forms monoecious; digestive tract (if present) with mouth only.

Class Turbellaria (Turbellarians). Usually free-living; ciliated epidermis; e.g., *Dugesia* (planaria).

Class Trematoda (Flukes). Parasitic; body covered with cuticle; suckers around mouth.

Class Cestoda (Tapeworms). Parasitic; scolex for attachment of host's intestine; no digestive tract; body covered with cuticle; body divided into proglottids containing gametes and embryos.

*Some smaller groups are omitted.

Phylum Nemertea (Rhynchocoela). Ribbon worms or nemertine worms. Marine; complete digestive tract; blood vascular system; dioecious.

Phylum Rotifera (Rotifers). Usually free-living; wheel-like arrangement of cilia at anterior; pseudocoelom.

Phylum Nematoda (Roundworms). "Tube-within-a-tube" body form; complete digestive tract; usually parasitic; pseudocoelom.

Phylum Mollusca (Molluscs). Aquatic or terrestrial; true coelomates; protostome; body unsegmented and often covered by shell secreted by underlying mantle; monoecious or dioecious.

Class Polyplacophora (Chitons). Shell composed of eight dorsal plates, or absent; foot large and flat.

Class Scaphopoda (Tooth shells). Shell tubular, shaped like a tusk.

Class Gastropoda (Gastropods). Body usually asymmetrical, often within a coiled shell; e.g., snail, slug.

Class Bivalvia (or Pelecypoda). Shell consisting of two lateral portions, hinged; e.g., clam, scallop, shipworm.

Class Cephalopoda (Cephalopods). Well-developed head with brain and large eyes; foot modified into tentacles or arms; e.g., octopus, squid, nautilus.

Phylum Annelida (Segmented worms). Aquatic or dwelling in moist soil; body metamerically segmented; closed circulatory system; protostome; monoecious or dioecious.

Class Oligochaeta (Earthworms). Most inhabit moist soil; setae few and small; clitellum present; monoecious.

Class Hirudinea (Leeches). Aquatic; usually ectoparasitic; no setae, clitellum present; monoecious.

Class Polychaeta (Polychaetes). Mostly marine; many setae; parapodia; usually dioecious; e.g., clamworm, tube worms.

Phylum Onychophora (Peripatus). Inhabit moist land; not externally segmented, but with paired appendages that are unjointed and with claws; share features of annelids and arthropods.

Phylum Arthropoda (Arthropods). Inhabit all environments; body segmented and covered with chitinous exoskeleton; paired jointed appendages; protostome; open circulation; nearly always dioecious; parthenogenesis in some species.

Class Merostomata (Horseshoe crabs). Marine; unsegmented large carapace; long tailpiece; book gills; mandibles absent.

Class Arachnida (Arachnids). Terrestrial; six pairs of appendages, four pairs being walking legs; mandibles absent; no antennae; eyes simple; e.g., spiders, scorpions, ticks, mites.

Class Crustacea (Crustaceans). Usually aquatic; numerous appendages, including mandibles and two pairs of antennae; eyes compound; e.g., crayfish, lobster, shrimp, sow bug.

Class Chilopoda (Centipedes). Terrestrial; typically one pair of appendages per segment, including mandibles and one pair of antennae; carnivorous.

Class Diplopoda (Millipedes). Terrestrial; two pairs of appendages per segment, including mandibles and one pair of antennae; usually herbivorous.

Class Insecta (Insects). Inhabit all environments, but generally terrestrial; comprise 80% of all named animal species; body consists of head, thorax, and abdomen; mandibles and one pair of antennae; often two pairs of wings;

eyes both simple and compound; e.g., fly, bee, louse, dragonfly, mayfly, stonefly, grasshopper, cockroach, termite, earwig, bug, cicada, butterfly, beetle, flea.

Phylum Echinodermata (Echinoderms). Marine; radially symmetrical as adult; deuterostome; endoskeleton with dermal ossicles or projecting spines; water vascular system; nervous, blood circulatory, and excretory systems reduced or absent; usually dioecious.

Class Asteroidea (Sea stars). Arms not sharply distinct from central disc; tube feet in ambulacral grooves.

Class Ophiuroidea (Brittle stars). Arms slender and distinct from central disc; no ambulacral groove.

Class Echinoidea (Sea urchins and sand dollars). Hemispherical to cookie-shaped; armless; movable spines; endoskeletal plates united into a solid shell.

Class Holothuroidea (Sea cucumbers). Body elongated; arms and spines absent.

Class Crinoidea (Sea lilies and feather stars). Flower-shaped body attached to a long stalk (sea lily) or without stalk as adult (feather star).

Phylum Hemichordata (Acorn worms). Marine; gill slits and primitive dorsal nerve cord; not a true notochord; no digestive system; closed circulation; deuterostome; dioecious.

Phylum Chordata (Chordates). Inhabit all environments; dorsal hollow nerve cord; pharyngeal gill slits, notochord, and postanal tail at some stage of life; closed circulation; cartilagenous or bony endoskeleton in most; deuterostome; generally dioecious.

Subphylum Urochordata (Tunicates). Marine; notochord and nerve cord usually present only in larval stage; e.g., sea squirts.

Subphylum Cephalochordata (Lancelets). Marine; all diagnostic features of phylum Chordata present throughout life; e.g., amphioxus.

Subphylum Vertebrata (Vertebrates). Inhabit all environments; segmented spinal column (vertebrae present); protective braincase (cranium).

Class Agnatha (Cyclostomes). Jawless fishes; scaleless; skeleton of cartilage; e.g., hagfish, lamprey.

Class Chondrichthyes (Cartilaginous fishes). Skeleton of cartilage; mouth ventral; tail fin usually asymmetrical; usually with placoid scales; gill slits open directly to outside; no air bladder; e.g., shark, ray.

Class Osteichthyes (Bony fishes). Skeletons chiefly of bone; body covered with flattened overlapping scales; mouth usually terminal; gills covered with an operculum; tail fin usually symmetrical; air bladder usually present; e.g., bass, carp, trout, flounder.

Class Amphibia (Amphibians). Usually pass through an aquatic larval stage; adults usually terrestrial; skin soft, scaleless; e.g., frog, toad, salamander.

Class Reptilia (Reptiles). Body covered with scales or scutes; lung-breathers; reproduce on land; e.g., snake, lizard, turtle, alligator.

Class Aves (Birds). Homeothermic, covered with feathers and scales; front limbs modified into wings; e.g., ostrich, turkey, hawk, finch.

Class Mammalia (Mammals). Homeothermic; with mammary glands to nourish young; hair on body (sometimes scant); e.g., dog, deer, rat, human.

Adjectives and Specific Body Parts to Which They Pertain

Abdominal—abdomen
Alimentary—digestive tract
Anal—anus
Arterial—artery
Auditory—ear
Auricular—ear; auricle of heart
Axillary—armpit

Brachial—arm
Branchial—gill
Bronchial—bronchi or their branches, lung tubes below the trachea
Buccal—cavity of mouth

Cardiac—heart
Caudal—cauda, tail
Cecal—cecum, blind beginning of the large intestine
Celiac—cavity of abdomen
Cephalic—head
Cerebral—cerebrum, part of brain concerned with conscious mental processes
Cervical—neck; cervix
Chondral—cartilage
Coccygeal—coccyx, end of vertebral column
Coelomic—coelom, a body cavity lined by mesothelium
Corneal—cornea, transparent covering of the front of the eyeball
Cortical—cortex (of organs)
Costal—costa (*pl.* costae), a rib
Cranial—cranium, part of skull enclosing the brain
Cutaneous—skin
Cystic—bladder (gall or urinary)

Dental—teeth
Dermal—skin
Duodenal—duodenum, first part of the small intestine

Endoneural—endoneurium, connective tissue surrounding individual nerve fibers
Endothelial—epithelium of mesodermal origin lining heart, blood vessels, and lymph vessels
Enteric—enteron, alimentary canal or intestine
Epineural—epineurium, external sheath of a nerve
Epiphyseal—epiphysis, a process on a bone
Epithelial—epithelium
Erythrocytic—erythrocyte, red blood cell
Esophageal—esophagus, gullet

Femoral—femur or thigh
Follicular—follicle, a small cavity with or without an opening
Frontal—forehead or frontal bone

Gastric—stomach
Genital—genitals, sexual organs
Gingival—gingiva (*pl.* gingivae), gum of mouth
Glossal—tongue
Glottal—glottis, opening from pharynx to larynx

Hematopoietic—blood-forming tissue
Hepatic—liver
Humeral—humerus, bone between shoulder and elbow
Hypophyseal—hypophysis, pituitary body

Inguinal—groin
Intestinal—intestine

Jejunal—middle division of small intestine
Jugular—throat or neck

Labial—lips
Laryngeal—larynx, organ of voice
Leucocytic—leucocyte, white blood cell
Lingual—tongue
Lumbar—loin
Lymphatic— lymph
Lymphoid—lymph

Mammary—mamma (*pl.* mammae), milk gland
Mandibular—mandible, lower jaw
Maxillary—maxilla, upper jaw
Mediastinal—mediastinum, space between plural sacs of lungs and containing all organs in the chest except lungs
Medullary—medulla (of organs)
Meningeal—meninges (*sing.* meninx)
Mesenteric—mesentery, supporting membrane of abdominal organs
Mesothelial—mesothelium, epithelium of mesodermal origin lining coelomic cavities
Muscular—muscle
Myocardial—myocardium, muscular part of heart

Nasal—nose
Nervous—nerve
Neural—nerve

Occipital—occiput, back part of skull
Olfactory—organ of smell
Optic—eye
Oral—mouth
Osseous—bone
Osteal—bone
Otic—ear
Ovarian—ovary

Palatine—palate, roof of the mouth
Palmar—palm of hand
Pancreatic—pancreas
Parietal—paries (*pl.* parietes), wall of a hollow organ
Parotid—parotid gland, salivary gland located near the ear
Parotoid—resembling a parotid gland
Pectoral—chest
Pedal—foot
Pelvic—pelvis
Penial—penis
Pericardial—pericardium, membrane covering and enclosing the heart
Perichondrial—perichondrium, sheath of connective tissue around cartilage
Perimysial—perimysium, sheath of connective tissue around a muscle
Perineal—perineum, region including the outlets of the pelvis
Periosteal—periosteum, sheath of connective tissue around bone
Peritoneal—peritoneum, serous membrane covering and enclosing abdominal organs
Phalangeal—phalanges (*sing.* phalanx), digital bones
Pharyngeal—pharynx, that part of the alimentary canal between the mouth cavity and the esophagus
Phrenic—diaphragm
Pineal—pineal body, an appendage on the roof of the brain
Pituitary—pituitary body
Placental—placenta, organ of maternal and embryonic origin through which exchanges occur between the embryo (or fetus) and the mother
Plantar—sole of foot
Pleural—pleura (*pl.* plurae), a serous membrane covering and enclosing the lung
Portal—vein branching into capillaries
Prostatic—prostate gland, located at base of the urethra in males
Pubic—pubis, ventral bone of the pelvis

Pulmonary—lungs
Pyloric—pylorus, part of the stomach

Radial—radius, a bone of the forearm
Rectal—rectum
Renal—kidney
Retinal—retina

Sacral—sacrum, that part of the vertebral column forming part of the pelvis
Salivary—saliva or salivary gland
Sciatic—hip
Sclerotic—outer layer of eye
Scrotal—scrotum, sac containing the testes
Sebaceous—sebum, a fatty secretion of skin glands
Skeletal—skeleton
Spinal—spine
Splenic—spleen
Sternal—sternum, breastbone

Testicular—testis
Thoracic—thorax, chest
Thymic—thymus, a gland of chest and neck
Thyroid—thyroid gland
Tibial—tibia, shank
Tracheal—trachea, windpipe

Umbilical—umbilicus, navel
Urethral—urethra, tube from urinary bladder to the outside of the body
Uterine—uterus, womb

Vaginal—vagina
Vascular—blood vessels
Venous—veins
Ventricular—ventricle, a heart chamber
Vertebral—vertebra (*pl.* vertebrae), a bone of the spinal column
Visceral—viscera (*sing.* viscus), organs contained in cavities of the trunk

Zygomatic—zygoma, cheekbone

Derivation of Words

Understanding word derivation is a skill that any student in biology will find useful. Commonly used words roots, prefixes, and suffixes are in the list that follows. Examples are given in parentheses.

Colors

alb(i): white (albino)
chlor(o): green (chloroplast)
chrom(o): color (chromoplast)
cyan(o): blue (cyanophyta)
erythr(o): red (erythrocyte)
leuc(o): white (leucoplast)
xanth(o): yellow (xanthophyll)

Size

is(o): equal (isogamete)
ium: small (basidium)
macr(o): large (macronucleus)
meg(a): large (megaspore)
micr(o): small (microbe)
ule: little (venule)

Quantity

amph(i): double (amphiaster)
cent(i): one hundred (centipede)
di: two (dicotyledon)
dipl(o): double (diplococcus)
hemi: one-half (hemiptera)
hex(a): six (hexapod)
hyper: excessive (hyperthyroidism)
hypo: less than normal (hypoactive)
mill(i): one thousand (millipede)
mon(o): one (monocotyledon)
oct(o): eight (octopus)
pent(a): five (pentamerous)
poly: many (polysaccharide)
quadr(i): four (quadriped)
sept: seven (septuplets)
tetr(a): four (tetraspore)
tri: three (triploid)
un(i): one (unisexual)

Organisms

arbor: tree (arborescent)
entom(o): insect (entomology)
helmin(th): worm (Platyhelminthes)
herpet(o): reptile (herpetology)
ichthy(o): fish (ichthyology)
myc(o): fungus (mycology)
orni(tho): bird (ornithology)
phyt(o): plant (phytogeography)
zo(o): animal (zoology)

Parts of Organisms

brachi(o): arm (brachiopod)
branch(io): gill (branchiopod)
carp: fruit (pericarp)
caud(i): tail (caudiform)
card(io): heart (electrocardiogram)
cephal(o): head (cephalopod)
cervi(c): neck (cervicitis)
chondr(o): cartilage (chondrocranium)
corp: body (corpuscle)
cost(o): rib (costoscapular)
cyst(o): bladder (cystocarp)
cyt(o): cell (cytoplasm)
dent(i): tooth (dentiform)
derm: skin (epidermis)
encephal: brain (encephalitis)
enter(o): intestine (Enterobios)
gast(r): stomach (gastrula)
hem(o): blood (hemoglobin)
hepat: liver (hepatitis)
hist: tissue (histamine)
hymen: membrane (hymenium)
my(o): muscle (myofibril)
oss: bone (ossicle)
phyll: leaf (sporophyll)
pod: foot (pelecypod)
pter(o): wing (pterodactyl)
pulmo(n): lung (pulmonary)
ren(i): kidney (reniform)
sperm: seed (gymnosperm)
stom(o): mouth (stomodaeum)
vas(o): vessel (vasoconstrictor)

Positions

ab: away from (aboral)
ana: up (anaphase)
anti: against (antipodal)
co: with (coenzyme)
ect(o): outside (ectoderm)
end(o): inner (endoplasm)
ent(o): inner (entoderm)
ep(i): upon (epiphyte)
exo: outside (exoskeleton)
hyper: above (hyperbranchial)
hypo: below (hypogynous)
infra: below (infraspinous)
inter: between (interstitial)
intra: within (intracutaneous)

mes(o): middle (mesothorax)
met(a): after (metathorax)
ob: reversed (oblanceolate)
para: beside (parathyroid)
peri: around (peristome)
pleur(i): side (pleurisy)
post: behind (postcava)
pre: before (precava)
pro: in front (prothorax)
prot(o): first (protozoa)
sub: under (submaxillary)
super: over (superciliary)
supra: over (supraorbital)
sy(n): together (synapsis)

Miscellaneous

a: without (asexual)
amyl(o): starch (amyloplast)
andr: male (androecium)
anti: counter (antitoxin)
arch: beginning (archenteron)
arium: depository (herbarium)
ary: place for keeping (aviary)
asc(o): bag (ascocarp)
aster: star (amphiaster)

bio: life (biogenèsis)
coel: hollow (coelenteron)
copr(o): excrement (coprophagous)
cotyl: cavity (hypocotyl)
crypt(o): hidden (cryptogam)
eu: true (eumycophyta)
genous: hidden (hypogenous)
gyn: female (gynoecium)
heter(o): different (heterogametes)
hom(o): alike (homosporous)
hydr(o): water (hydrophyte)
ite: fossil (ammonite)
itis: inflammation (peritonitis)
mal: bad (malaria)
oid: form (ovoid)
ov(i): egg (ovipositor)
osis: disease (mycosis)
pach(y): thick (pachyderm)
phot(o): light (phototropism)
plast: formed (chloroplast)
plat(y): flat (Platyhelminthes)
pseud(o): false (pseudopodium)
scler: hard (sclerenchyma)
schiz(o); split (Schizomycetes)
tel(o): end (telophase)
xer(o): dry (xerophyte)

Prefixes Generally Used to Denote Multiples or Fractions of Units of Measurement and the Most Common Quantities Used in Biology

Prefix	Quantity	Length*	Weight*	Volume*	Energy*	Quantity of Radioactive Substance*
giga	$1,000,000,000\ (10^9)$					
mega	$1,000,000\ (10^6)$					
myria	$10,000\ (10^4)$					
kilo	$1,000\ (10^3)$	kilometer (km)	kilogram (kg)		kilocalorie (kcal)	
hecto	$100\ (10^2)$					
deca	10					
(no prefix)	1	meter (m)	gram (g)	liter (l)	calorie (cal)	curie (Ci)
deci	0.1					
centi	$0.01\ (10^{-2})$	centimeter (cm)	centigram (cg)			
milli	$0.001\ (10^{-3})$	millimeter (mm)	milligram (mg)	milliliter (ml)		
micro	$0.000001\ (10^{-6})$	micrometer (μm)	microgram (μg)	microliter (μl)		microcurie (μCi)
nano	$0.000000001\ (10^{-9})$					
	$0.0000000001\ (10^{-10})$	Angstrom (A or Å)				
pico	$0.000000000001\ (10^{-12})$					

All abbreviations in column are both singular and plural.

Miscellaneous Biological Abbreviations

ABA	Abscisic acid	**ATP**	Adenosine triphosphate
ACTH	Adrenocorticotropic hormone	**atm**	Atmosphere
ADH	Antidiuretic hormone	**A-V**	Atrioventricular
ADP	Adenosine diphosphate		

BMR	Basal metabolism rate	**IR-8**	Strain of rice (International Rice-8)
BOD	Biological oxygen demand		
bp	Boiling point	**iu**	International unit
BTS	Biological treatment systems	**iv**	Intravenous
		I.V.	Importance value
C₃	Type of plant whose photosynthetic process makes a 3-carbon compound (PGA)	**kcal**	Kilocalorie
C₄	Type of plant whose photosynthetic process makes 4-carbon compounds (malic and aspartic acids)	**LD**	Lethal dose
		LGH	Lactogenic hormone
		LH	Luteinizing hormone
		LTH	Luteotropic hormone
ca	About, around		
cal	Calorie	**M**	Molar
CAM	Type of photosynthesis (crassulacean acid metabolism)	**mcal**	Megacalorie
		mp	Melting point
cAMP	Cyclic adenosine monophosphate	**MS**	Multiple sclerosis
		MSH	Melanocyte-stimulating hormone
CNS	Central nervous system	**m.t.**	Metric ton
CoA	Coenzyme A		
CSF	Cerebrospinal fluid	**n**	Haploid (chromosome set)
cv	Cultivar (*cultivarietas*)	**NA**	Noradrenalin
		NAD	Nicotinamide adenine dinucleotide
DDT	Dichlorodiphenyltrichloroethane		
det.	Identified by	**NADP**	Nicotinamide adenine dinucleotide phosphate
DNA	Deoxyribonucleic acid		
		NH₃	Ammonia
ECG	Electrocardiogram	**NH₄⁺**	Ammonium
E. coli	The bacterium *Escherichia coli*	**NO₂⁻**	Nitrite
EEG	Electroencephalogram	**NO₃⁻**	Nitrate
e.g.	*exempli gratia* (for example)		
ER	Endoplasmic reticulum	**OH⁻**	Hydroxyl ion
ERG	Electroretinogram	**org.**	Organic
		pH	Negative log of the hydrogen-ion concentration
f.	Offspring, son (*filius*); form (*forma*)		
		p.m.	Postmortem
F₁	First generation	**PCO₂**	Carbon dioxide pressure
F₂	Second generation	**PO₂**	Oxygen pressure
FAA	Formalin-acetic acid-alcohol mixture	**ppb**	Parts per billion
		pphm	Parts per hundred million
FSH	Follicle-stimulating hormone	**ppm**	Parts per million
		P/R	Photosynthesis-respiration ratio
G	Gravity	**PTH**	Parathormone
GA	Gibberellic acid		
GI	Gastrointestinal	**RBC**	Red blood cells
		R-E	Reticuloendothelial
H⁺	Hydrogen ion	**rem**	Roentgen equivalent for human
hab.	Habitat	**Rh**	Rhesus factor in blood
Hb	Hemoglobin	**RH**	Relative humidity
HC	Hydrocarbon	**RNA**	Ribonucleic acid
HCG	Human chorionic gonadotropin	**RQ**	Respiratory quotient
HCGP	Human chorionic growth hormone prolactin		$\left(\dfrac{\text{volume of } CO_2 \text{ expired}}{\text{volume of } O_2 \text{ inspired}}\right)$
herb.	Herbarium		
hort.	Horticultural, horticulture		
		S-A	Sinoatrial
IAA	Indoleacetic acid	**sc**	Subcutaneous
ICSH	Interstitial-cell-stimulating hormone	**SI**	International System of Measurement (*Système Internationale*)
i.e.	*id est* (that is)	**sp.**	Species (singular)
im	Intramuscular	**sp.gr.**	Specific gravity
ip	Intraperitoneal	**sp. nov.**	*Species nova* (new species)

spp.	Species (plural)
ssp.	Subspecies
STH	Somatotropic hormone
TTH	Thyrotropic hormone
U/B	Ratio of some substance in urine and blood
U/P	Ratio of urinary osmotic pressure to plasma osmotic pressure

U.S.P.	United States Pharmacopeia
vac.	Vacuum
V.F.	Visual field
WBC	White blood cells
wd.	Wood

Symbols Used in Biology

♂	Male	≮	Is not less than
□	Male in pedigree charts	>	Is more than
♀	Female	≯	Is not more than
○	Female in pedigree charts	~	Approximately
⊕	Sporophyte	#	Number
=	Equals; is equal to	×	Times; multiplied by; crossed with
≠ or ╪	Is not equal to		
≈	Is approximately equal to	Σ	Sum
<	Is less than	∞	Infinity

Some Equipment Used by Biologists

Anemometer—Measures velocity of wind.

Aspirator—Removes fluids by suction (a suction pump).

Atmometer—Measures rate of evaporation of water in atmosphere.

Autoclave—Sterilizes with steam under pressure; used especially in bacteriological work.

Balances, analytical—Used for accurate weighing of small quantities.

  Ultramicro—Ranges down to 0.1 microgram.

  Micro—Ranges down to 0.001 milligram.

  Semimicro—Ranges down to 0.01 milligram.

Barometer—Measures atmospheric pressure.

Burette—Used for measuring liquids or gases delivered or received; a graduated glass tube, usually with a stopcock and a small opening.

Centrifuges—Separates substances having different densities.

  Clinical—Maximum speeds produce force of about 2,000 × G; used in such work as blood separation.

  High-speed—Maximum speeds produce force of about 50,000 × G; used to separate cell fractions such as microsomes and mitochondria.

  Ultra—Maximum speeds produce force of about 150,000 × G; used in separating substances composed of large molecules and in identifying them by determining their sedimentation rates.

Chromatograph—Used for analyzing mixtures of similar substances by separating their components.

Colorimeter—Used for routine chemical analyses of solutions; a photometer that uses colored filters in producing light to be absorbed by solutions whose concentrations are being analyzed.

Computer—Analyzes large numbers of data and makes complicated calculations at a high rate of speed.

Conibear trap—A trap for humanely catching mammals (kills instantly).

Densitometer—Quantifies materials separated on electrophoresis and thin-layer chromatography surfaces.

Desiccator—Used to dry substances.

Dialyzer—Separates particles of different sizes with a differentially permeable membrane.

Distilling apparatus—Purifies liquids.

Dredge—Used for collecting bottom-dwelling organisms, especially shellfish; a bag net attached to an iron frame and dragged on the bottom.

Earth augers—Used for taking soil samples.

Electrophoresis apparatus—Separates electrically charged molecules.

Environmental control chamber—Provides an area in which such entities as temperature, light, and humidity can be closely controlled.

Fraction collector—Automatically separates liquid coming off a chromatography apparatus, placing aliquots into a series of test tubes for further analysis.

Gas chromatograph—Separates samples of volatile substances into components that can be detected in trace amounts; allows for both qualitative and quantitative analyses.

G-M (Geiger-Muller) tube—An electronic instrument for quantitative determination of radioactivity.

Hemocytometer—Used in counting blood corpuscles (also yeast cells).

Hemoglobinometer—Determines quantity of hemoglobin.

Herbarium cases—Used for storage of plants preserved by drying.

High-performance liquid chromatograph (HPLC)—Performs liquid chromatography at very high pressures, giving good separations very quickly.

Homogenizer—Breaks down cells preparatory to separation of their parts; prepares cell-free extracts; prepares emulsions.

Hydrometer—Used for determining specific gravity of liquids.

Hygrograph—Continuously records variations in relative humidity of the atmosphere.

Hygrometer—Measures relative humidity of the atmosphere.

Hygrothermograph—Continuously records variations in relative humidity and temperature of the atmosphere.

Increment borer—Used for removing a core of wood from the trunk of a tree to determine age of tree.

Incubators—Chambers where temperatures can be regulated to provide ideal conditions for growth, as for hatching eggs or growing bacteria.

Kymograph—Records magnitude of muscular contractions and other physiological activities.

Laser—Provides coherent light source for varied uses, including spectrophotometry and knifeless surgery.

Lyophilizer (freeze-dryer)—Removes water from samples by sublimation in a vacuum.

Manometer—Measures pressure of gases and vapors.

Mass spectrometer—Separates electrified particles into a spectrum according to their masses.

Maximum-minimum thermometer—Records highest and lowest temperature during a specific period of time.

Metabolic apparatus—Measures metabolic rate based on speed of oxygen consumption.

Microscopes:
Electron—Reveals structures too small to reflect light, e.g., ultrastructure of a cell.
Fluorescence—Reveals location of objects on slide that include fluorescent materials.
Light—Uses visible light wavelengths, often relies upon staining to show details of biological objects.
Phase contrast—Makes visible or improves visibility of structures in living cells.
Polarizing—Makes visible fine structures of some biological materials.

Microtomes:
Cryostat—Used for sectioning frozen tissues.
Rotary—Used for making thin sections of soft tissues embedded in paraffin.
Sliding—Used for sectioning hard or large structures.

Nets—Used for capturing insects, fishes, etc.

Oscilloscope—Used to amplify electrical changes in tissues and project these changes by means of an electron beam onto a fluorescent screen.

Paraffin oven—Keeps paraffin melted while embedding tissues.

Petri dishes—Used for culturing bacteria and fungi.

pH meter—An electronic device for measuring acidity and alkalinity.

Photometer—Measures intensity of light.

Physiograph—A recording system comprising several transducers, amplifiers, and chart recorders useful in measuring several physiological phenomena simultaneously.

Press—Used for extracting by compression.

Rain gauge—Measures precipitation.

Refrigerator, walk-in—A place for working with unstable cellular components or for reducing metabolic processes in living organisms.

Scintillation counter—Detects presence and measures quantity of radiation by responding with flashes of light.

Secchi disc—Measures turbidity of water.

Sling psychrometer—Measures relative humidity of the atmosphere.

Soil sieves—Used for classifying soils according to texture.

Sonicator—Provides ultrasonic vibrations for disruption of cells.

Spectrophotometer—Used to identify compounds by determining the wavelength of light absorbed by their molecules; also used in studying enzyme kinetics.

Sphygmomanometer—Measures blood pressure.

Spirometer—Measures vital capacity of the lungs.

Thermistors—Electrically measure temperatures in difficult places.

Thermocouple—An electronic device for measuring temperature.

Thermograph—Continuously records changes in temperature.

Tissuematon—Automatically processes tissues in preparation for sectioning and mounting.

Titrator—Determines strength of a solution or concentration of a substance in solution.

Trawl—A bag net dragged on the bottom for catching fish and other aquatic organisms.

Ultraviolet lamp—Induces mutations; detects fluorescent compounds.

Vasculum—A metal container for the temporary storage of plants as they are collected.

Warburg apparatus—Used in studies of cell and tissue metabolism.

Waring blender—Macerates plant and animal materials.

Water bath—Maintains a uniform temperature around a container in which some process is occurring.

X-ray machine—Induces mutations; photographs internal body structures.

Glossary

A

abscission layer. A layer along which a leaf or fruit naturally separates from the stem.

acellular. Not composed of cells with distinct boundaries.

acetylcholine. A neurotransmitter acting as a transmitter substance in the synapses of many neurons of the central and peripheral nervous systems and of the parasympathetic portion of the autonomic nervous system.

acid. A substance that gives up hydrogen ions when dissolved; the opposite of a base.

action potential. The rapid change of electrical potential across the plasma membrane, which moves along the membrane like a wave, e.g., a nerve impulse.

action spectrum. That portion of electromagnetic energy that can be absorbed to trigger a chemical process; the wavelengths of light used in photosynthesis.

activation energy. The amount of energy needed to cause molecules to react chemically; lowered by catalysts, such as enzymes.

active site. The portion of an enzyme with proper shape and chemical groups to interact with a substrate.

active transport. An energy-consuming movement of molecules or ions across a membrane in the direction opposite that expected by diffusion, i.e., against a concentration gradient.

adaptive radiation. An evolutionary process whereby populations of one species move into other environments and adapt to them.

adenine. A nitrogenous base of the purine type that is a constituent of some nucleotides.

ADP, adenosine diphosphate. Adenosine with two phosphate groups; converted to ATP by the addition of another phosphate group bound by a high-energy bond.

adventitious root. Any new root growing from a nonroot portion of a plant.

aerobic. Requiring molecular oxygen.

aerobic respiration. Respiration in which gaseous oxygen is used as a hydrogen acceptor.

aggregate fruit. A fruit derived from several pistils of a single flower, e.g., the strawberry.

alga. A photosynthetic eukaryote without the multicellular sex organs or vascular tissues found in higher plants.

allantois. A sac extending from the rear part of the primitive digestive tract of an embryo; in reptiles and birds, large and highly functional as a respiratory and excretory organ.

allele. One of two or more contrasting forms of a gene.

allelopathy. The influence that plants exert on other plants by their metabolic products; the inhibition of competitors by toxic metabolic products.

Allen's rule. Animals normally living in cold habitats tend to have shorter appendages than those in warmer habitats, thus reducing heat loss by convection.

allopatric. An ecological term describing similar populations that live in separate and widely differing geographical areas and are reproductively incompatible.

allosteric change. Modification of an enzyme's shape by interaction with another molecule; can lead to either activation or inhibition of the enzyme.

alveolus. An air pocket of the lung through whose wall gases are exchanged.

amino acid. An organic compound containing an amino group (NH_2) and, together with other similar compounds, comprising proteins.

amnion. The sac immediately surrounding an embryo (or fetus).

amphiaster. A structure arising from the cell center during cell division in animals and some lower plants. It consists of two asters occupying polar positions between which the radiations (fibers) form a spindle.

amylase. A starch-digesting enzyme.

amyloplast. A plastid containing stored starch.

anabolism. Chemical reactions leading to molecules being built from smaller precursors; the opposite of catabolism.

anaerobic. Not requiring molecular oxygen.

analogous. Having different embryological origins but similar use.

anaphase. That phase of mitosis when chromosomes are moving toward the poles of the spindle.

androgens. Male hormones.

aneuploidy. Genetic condition in which one or more chromosomes are either missing or in above-normal numbers in a cell.

angiosperm. A flowering plant; a plant that produces seeds enclosed within a fruit.

anther. The distal part of a stamen that produces pollen.

antheridium. A male gametangium in many kinds of plants.

antibody. A specific protein produced by an animal in response to the presence of a foreign substance (antigen) with which it can react.

anticodon. A sequence of three nucleotides of transfer RNA that pairs with a codon of messenger RNA.

antigen. A foreign substance entering a body that causes the formation of an antibody that reacts with it; usually a protein, saccharide, or nucleic acid.

anus. The exit of a digestive system.

aorta. The large artery leaving the heart and supplying aerated blood to all parts of the body.

apical meristem. Actively growing tissue at tips of roots and stems.

archegonium. An egg-producing organ in many plants; consisting of a base, venter, and neck.

archenteron. The cavity of the gastrular stage of an embryo.

arteriole. A small artery.

artery. A vessel (tube) through which blood travels away from the heart.

ascus. A saclike container of spores in ascomycetes.

asexual. Sexless.

assimilation. Process by which nonliving substances become part of protoplasm.

association neuron. A nerve cell between two other nerve cells.

ATP, adenosine triphosphate. Adenosine with three phosphate groups; converted to ADP by the loss of one phosphate group; known as "storehouse of energy" because energy released from the high-energy phosphate bond during ATP's conversion to ADP is used for cell work.

atrium. A compartment of the heart receiving blood from the body.

autoimmunity. Abnormal condition in which the organism produces antibodies against its own cells or molecules.

autonomic nervous system. That part of the nervous system regulating involuntary reactions of many organs of the body, especially the viscera.

autosome. Any chromosome other than those that determine sex.

autotroph. An organism that produces its own food; opposite of heterotroph.

auxins. Plant hormones produced by actively growing tissues.

axon. A portion of a neuron conducting impulses away from the body of the neuron.

B

bacillus. A rod-shaped bacterium.

backcross. Crossing a dominant phenotype with a homozygous (pure) recessive to determine whether the phenotype is homozygous or heterozygous.

bacteriophage. A virus that parasitizes bacteria; also called *phage*.

bacterium. A prokaryote; nearly all organisms of kingdom Monera are bacteria.

bark. All tissues outside the vascular cambium of roots and stems.

base. A substance that forms hydroxyl (— OH) ions when in water; the opposite of an acid. Also, the basic portion of a nucleotide; either a purine or a pyrimidine.

basidium. A club-shaped spore-producing structure in basidiomycetes.

B cell. One of two major types (with T cells) in an immune system; produces antibody.

benthos. Bottom-dwelling plants and animals of the sea.

biofeedback. Self-regulation of a biological process whereby the process is accelerated by hypoactivity or slowed by hyperactivity; conscious control of processes that normally are self-regulating.

bioluminescence. Light produced by living organisms from chemical energy.

biomass. The quantity of organisms in a specific location, usually expressed as live or dry weight.

biome. A large biotic community of wide geographical extent characterized by a dominating life form; e.g., grass or deciduous trees.

blastodisc. A disc of cells developing on one side of the yolk of a chicken's egg and corresponding to the blastular stage.

blastomere. Any cell of a blastula.

blastopore. An opening to the archenteron in the gastrular stage of the embryo; becomes either mouth (in protostome animals) or anus (in deuterostome animals).

blastula. An early stage of the embryo consisting of a hollow ball of cells.

Bohr effect. An increase in oxygen-binding by hemoglobin as environmental pH rises, and a fall as pH falls.

book lungs or gills. Respiratory organs constructed of thin folds of tissue stacked together like the pages in a book; found in spiders and horseshoe crabs.

boreal forest. A high-latitude coniferous forest.

Bowman's capsule. The bulbous upper part of a renal tubule surrounding the glomerulus.

bronchiole. A small air passage in the lung.

bronchus. An air passageway leading from the trachea into the lung.

Brownian movement. Movement of small particles due to differential bombardment by surrounding molecules.

budding. An asexual reproductive process in which a fragment is separated from the body and grows into a new organism; a form of grafting in which a bud is used as the scion.

buffer. A substance releasing hydrogen atoms when environmental hydrogen concentration is low, and capturing hydrogen atoms when environmental hydrogen concentration is high.

C

calorie. A unit of heat; the kilogram-calorie is the amount of heat required to raise the temperature of one liter of water one degree centigrade.

cambium. A meristematic tissue occurring in layers in roots and stems and producing secondary tissues.

cAMP. Cyclic adenosine monophosphate; a molecule that acts as a "second messenger" within the target cells of many hormones.

capillary. A small blood vessel consisting of only one layer of endothelium and usually connecting arteries and veins.

capillary water. Water that can move on surfaces against the pull of gravity.

carbohydrate. An organic molecule composed of carbon, hydrogen, and oxygen in which hydrogen and oxygen occur in the same proportion as in water.

carbon fixation. The second phase of photosynthesis in which CO_2 molecules are joined to form complex organic molecules; also called dark reactions and Calvin cycle.

carnivore. A flesh-eating (predatory) organism.

carotene. A class of yellow pigments in plants.

carpel. A megasporophyll; pistils of flowers are composed of one or more carpels.

carrying capacity. The largest population that can be sustained in the population's environment; determined by the resources available.

catabolism. Chemical reactions in which molecules are broken down; opposite of anabolism.

catalyst. A molecule that speeds up a reaction without itself being used up; in organisms, usually an enzyme.

cell wall. A relatively firm, nonliving envelope forming the outer boundary of certain cells, such as those of plants, fungi, and bacteria.

cellular immunity. Attack upon antigenic cells or substances by the immune system's T cells.

cellulose. A polysaccharide making up the framework of the walls of plant cells.

centriole. A cellular organelle containing microtubule subunits (tubulin) that acts as a center for building spindle fibers during mitosis or meiosis.

centromere. The point on a chromosome where a spindle fiber is attached.

cephalothorax. The fused head and thorax of animals like crustaceans.

cerebellum. The part of the hindbrain that coordinates muscular activity.

cerebrum. The part of the forebrain that acts as the chief coordinating center of the brain.

cervix. The neck-shaped part of the outer end of the uterus; a constricted portion of an organ or structure.

chalones. A class of chemicals that inhibit mitosis.

chaparral. A shrubby type of vegetation in semitropical areas where the rainy season is in the winter.

chemiosmosis. A model for cellular energy capture, in which protons are pumped across mitochondrial and chloroplast membranes and the energy of their return movement is placed in a bond as ATP is produced from ADP and inorganic phosphate.

chemosynthesis. In some simple autotrophs, a process used to synthesize simple carbohydrates from carbon dioxide and water, in which chemicals rather than light are the source of energy.

chemotaxis. Movement of an organism or cell toward or away from a source of a particular chemical.

chitin. The horny skeletal material of arthropods; a nitrogen-containing polysaccharide.

chlorenchyma. A plant tissue composed of thin-walled cells that contain chlorophyll.

chlorophyll *a*. The most common type of green pigment in most plants.

chloroplast. A plastid containing chlorophyll and other pigments.

cholinesterase. An enzyme that quickly destroys the neurotransmitter acetylcholine.

chorion. The outer membrane surrounding a mammalian embryo (or fetus).

chromatid. The longitudinal half of a chromosome, after DNA replication.

chromatin. Stained nucleoproteins seen in the interphase stage of a cell.

chromonemata. Fine nuclear threads; chromosomes in an early stage of development during mitosis.

chromosome. Tightly coiled DNA; the site of genes.

chymotrypsin. A pancreatic enzyme that digests proteins.

cilia. Small protoplasmic projections from eukaryotic cells, used to circulate materials over the surface of stationary cells or to propel some small organisms.

citric acid cycle. Krebs cycle of respiration, a cyclic phase during which carbon dioxide and hydrogen are released.

cleavage. The early division of an embryo during which there is no increase in the volume of protoplasm beyond what was present in the zygote.

climax community. A mixture of organisms living together, and maintained by a rather stable environment.

clitellum. A swollen glandular region of an

earthworm that secretes slime for binding copulating worms together and for constructing the egg case.

clone. A genetically uniform group of cells or organisms originating asexually from a single ancestor.

coccus. A spherical bacterium.

codon. A sequence of three nucleotides that codes for a single amino acid.

coelom. A body cavity lined with cells of mesodermal origin.

coenzyme. A compound, often a vitamin or vitamin derivative, necessary for an enzyme to function.

cofactor. A nonprotein component that binds temporarily to an enzyme, helping the enzyme to function; often a metal ion or a coenzyme.

coleoptile. A sheath covering the epicotyl of the embryo of a grass plant.

collenchyma. A simple plant tissue composed of cells with some thickening of the walls, especially in the corners.

colloid. A dispersion system in which dispersed particles are either large individual molecules or clumps of molecules that do not respond to gravity.

commensalism. A close relationship between two organisms where one member benefits and the other is unaffected.

community. A group of organisms living together.

companion cells. Small phloem cells adjacent to sieve tubes.

competitive exclusion. The principle that two species cannot occupy the same niche at the same time and place.

complete flower. A flower with all kinds of floral parts.

compound pistil. A pistil composed of two or more carpels.

conjugation. In bacteria or some protozoans, the exchange of genetic material between two cells mediated by a temporary cytoplasmic bridge.

consumers. Organisms that get their energy by eating plants or other animals.

contractile vacuole. A vacuole in freshwater protozoa that periodically expels excess water to the outside.

convergence. The evolving of organisms in dissimilar groups so that they are similarly adapted to similar environments.

corm. A modified stem similar in general appearance to a bulb but solid like a potato.

corpus luteum. In the ovary, yellow cells filling the follicular space after ovulation and producing progesterone.

cortex. The outer part of some organs; in plant stems and roots, the zone between the vascular tissues and the outer protective layer.

cortisone. A complex of hormones produced by the cortex of the adrenal gland.

cotyledon. The leaf on an embryonic seed plant; the seed leaf.

countercurrent exchange. An efficient mechanism for exchange of materials (gases, heat, etc.); two fluids move in opposite directions past each other, separated by a permeable interface, and a material flows across the interface.

crossing-over. An exchange of genes on homologous chromosomes during synapsis in prophase I of meiosis.

cutin. A waterproofing material associated with the epidermis of plants.

cyclic photophosphorylation. A light-driven process in photosynthesis, producing ATP.

cyclosis. Circulation of cytoplasm within a cell.

cytochrome. A cellular pigment, a hydrogen acceptor during hydrogen transfer.

cytokinesis. Cytoplasmic division accompanying mitosis.

cytoplasm. Semifluid substance of a cell, outside the nucleus.

cytosine. A nitrogenous base of the pyrimidine type that is a constituent of nucleotides.

cytoskeleton. A latticework of microfilaments, microtubules, and filaments within a cell; organelles are suspended within it; provides framework for cell cytoplasm.

D

dark reactions. The processes of photosynthesis that do not require light energy; carbon dioxide is reduced to form PGAL, which can then be used to make glucose.

deciduous. Denoting plants that shed their leaves after the growing season.

decomposers. Organisms that gain energy by tearing down the organic materials left from other organisms.

deme. A recognizable, interbreeding local population.

dendrite. A portion of a neuron conducting impulses toward the body of the neuron.

deuterostome. An animal whose embryonic blastopore becomes an anus, and whose mouth is formed later.

deoxyribose. A pentose sugar in DNA.

diastase. A natural enzyme in sprouting seeds that converts starch to sugar.

dicot (dicotyledon). A seed plant that is in part distinguished by embryos that have two cotyledons.

differentiation. Specialization of cells to perform a specific function.

diffusion. The scattering of molecules due to molecular action; net movement is from higher to lower concentration.

digestion. The breaking of large food molecules into smaller molecules.

dihybrid. A genetic cross involving two characteristics.

dioecious. Having the sexes in separate bodies.

diploid. Containing two sets of chromosomes as in zygotes or body cells.

disaccharide. A compound sugar; each molecule can be broken into two monosaccharide molecules.

disc flowers. The radially symmetrical flowers in a composite head, frequently surrounded by ray flowers that look like petals.

divergence. The evolving of closely related individuals so that they become dissimilar when they adapt to different environments.

DNA, deoxyribonucleic acid. A polynucleotide, usually double-stranded and helical, whose 5-carbon sugar is deoxyribose; the most commonly employed molecule for storage of genetic information.

dominant. Expressed; used to describe a gene whose characteristic hides the characteristic of a recessive allele.

dorsal root. The upper branch of a spinal nerve connecting with the spinal cord; the pathway of sensory neurons entering the spinal cord.

double fertilization. A nearly simultaneous process found in angiosperms where one of the two sperms from a single pollen grain fertilizes an egg, forming a zygote, and the other fertilizes polar nuclei, forming a food-storage tissue called endosperm.

duodenum. The first part of the small intestine, the part into which the liver and pancreas discharge their secretions.

E

ecology. The branch of biology dealing with the relationships between organisms and their environments.

ecosystem. A more or less self-contained community of organisms together with the environment in which it lives.

ecotone. The zone of overlap between adjacent communities.

ectoderm. The outer germ layer of an early stage of the embryo.

ectothermic. The condition of animals whose body temperatures are primarily determined by heat absorbed from the environment.

effector. The part of a body responding to a stimulus.

electron transport chain. The portion of cellular respiration in which hydrogens are reduced and their electrons are passed along a chain of membrane proteins, with accompanying transfer of energy to form ATP's from ADP and inorganic phosphate.

embryo. As applied to humans, an early period of development when the organism is taking human shape, up to about 8 weeks of age.

embryo sac. The megagametophyte of flowering plants.

emulsification. The action of bile in breaking fats into small droplets.

endocarp. The inner layer of a fruit wall (pericarp).

endocrine gland. A gland that secretes hormones, into the bloodstream.

endoderm. The inner germ layer of an early stage of the embryo.

endometrium. The vascular inner layer of the uterine wall.

endoplasmic reticulum. A system of cytoplasmic membranes involved in lipid biosynthesis (SER) or protein biosynthesis (RER); may be associated with outer nuclear membrane.

endorphins. A class of naturally produced neuroactive compounds whose effect is as an opiate in the brain.

endosperm. A food-storage tissue in seeds, located adjacent to the embryo.

endosperm nuclei. Two nuclei in the center of the embryo sac that fuse with a sperm to develop into a food-storage tissue called the endosperm.

endothermic. A term referring to the condition of birds, mammals, and a few other animals in which their body temperatures are primarily obtained and regulated by their own metabolic processes.

enzyme. A protein (usually) that catalyzes biological reactions.

epicotyl. The bud of an embryonic seed plant, located above the cotyledon(s).

epinephrine (adrenalin). A hormone secreted by the medulla of the adrenal gland.

epiphyte. A nonparasitic plant that lives attached to another plant.

erythrocyte. A red blood cell.

estrogen. A hormone produced by the ovarian follicle and responsible for feminine characteristics.

ethology. The study of animal behavior.

ethylene. A plant growth substance that influences the ripening of fruits.

eukaryotes. Organisms whose DNA is enclosed within a membrane-bound nucleus; contain many other membrane-bound organelles, such as mitochondria and lysosomes.

eutrophic. Refers to a lake whose conditions promote a great deal of biological activity; opposite of oligotrophic.

evolution. Change in the genetic composition (gene pool) of a population.

excretion. The discharge of metabolic waste.

exocarp. The outside layer of a fruit wall (pericarp).

exocrine gland. A gland whose product is exported via a duct (tube).

exon. In eukaryotes, a sequence of nucleotides in a gene that appears in mRNA and that codes for a polypeptide.

exponential growth curve. The graphical description of a population's growth when it is unchecked; population size repeatedly doubles.

extracellular digestion. Digestion of foods outside cells.

F

facultative anaerobe. An anaerobic organism that is also capable of using gaseous oxygen in respiration.

Fallopian tube. An oviduct in the human female.

fat. A class of lipids; each molecule is composed of glycerol and attached fatty acids.

fermentation. Partial decomposition of organic compounds in the absence of atmospheric oxygen.

fertilization. The fusion of gametes.

fetus. As applied to humans, the developing organism from about 8 weeks until birth, having a definite human form.

fission. Asexual reproduction of unicellular organisms whereby the cell is divided into two cells of approximately equal size.

flagella. Hairlike projections used for locomotion by some motile cells and for circulation as in flame cells. Flagella are longer than cilia. Composed of microtubules in 9 + 2 arrangement in eukaryotes.

food chain. A sequence of food relationships —from plant to herbivore to carnivore.

fraternal twins. Twins derived from separate zygotes.

frond. A pinnately compound leaf as in ferns.

fructose. A six-carbon monosaccharide sugar.

G

gametangium. A plant organ producing gametes.

gamete. A sexual cell—sperm or egg.

gametophyte. A gamete-producing plant, usually hapoid.

ganglion. A clump of neuronic bodies.

gap junction. A specialized region of the plasma membrane connecting adjacent cells in animals; serves to pass ions and molecules.

gastrin. A gastric hormone that activates cells to produce gastric juice.

gastrovascular cavity. A pouchlike cavity in cnidaria that is used for digestion and circulation.

gastrula. An early stage of the embryo consisting of two germ layers.

gastrulation. The infolding of one side of the blastula stage of an embryo to form the gastrula.

gene. A portion of a nucleic acid encoding information on how to build a polypeptide or an RNA molecule; the basic unit of hereditary information.

gene pool. All of the genes in a free-breeding population.

generative cell. A cell in a pollen grain that divides into two male gametes.

genetic drift. Changes in gene frequency in small populations that are due entirely to chance and not to mutations, selection, or migration.

genome. The complete set of genes possessed by an organism; sometimes synonymous with genotype.

genotype. The genetic composition of an individual.

genotypic ratio. The proportion of genotypes resulting from a specific cross.

genus. A group of closely related species; the first part of the scientific name of an organism.

germ cells. Sexual cells or the cells from which they originate.

germination. The sprouting of a seed or spore.

germ layer. An early layer of the embryo from which certain tissues arise; the layers are ectoderm, mesoderm, and endoderm.

gestation. The prebirth period.

gibberellins. A group of substances that stimulates growth in plants.

gill. A specialized gas-exchange region of many aquatic animals.

gland. An organ or group of cells producing a secretion.

glomerulus. A bundle of capillaries from which many substances leave the circulatory system and enter the renal tubule.

glottis. The opening between the pharynx and larynx.

glucagon. A hormone produced by the pancreas and influencing the change of liver glycogen to sugar.

glucose. A six-carbon monosaccharide sugar, with five carbons in its ring.

glycogen. A polysaccharide of animals, used to store glucose.

glycolysis. The first phase of respiration, during which glucose is converted to pyruvic acid.

Golgi complex (apparatus). Membranous cellular organelle that concentrates and chemically modifies secretory proteins.

gonad. A sex organ—testis or ovary.

grana. Concentrations of "stacked" membranes in chloroplasts; chlorophyll is concentrated in them.

granulocytes. Types of white corpuscles with distinctive cytoplasmic granules, produced in bone marrow.

guanine. A nitrogenous base of the purine type that is a constituent of nucleotides.

gymnosperm. A seed plant whose seeds are naked (not produced in a fruit).

H

habitat. The place where an individual or group of individuals lives.

haploid. Containing one set of chromosomes as in gametes.

Hardy-Weinberg Law. Mathematical predictions concerning the likelihood of a population's gene pool changing as generations pass, and describing the conditions that must be considered.

Haversian canal. A small canal of bone tissue, containing a small artery and vein as well as a nerve supply and surrounded by several zones of bone cells.

hemoglobin. The iron-containing blood pigment that transports oxygen.

herbivore. A plant-eating animal.

hermaphroditic. Producing both male and female reproductive cells in the same body; monoecious.

heterocyst. An enlarged cell found in filaments of some blue-green algae, a focal point for fragmentation.

heterotroph. An organism that must obtain its food from the environment, not capable of manufacturing food; opposite of autotroph.

heterozygous. Having two different alleles at corresponding loci of homologous chromosomes.

homeostasis. The ability of an organism to maintain a relatively constant and optimal internal environment despite changes in the external environment.

homologous. Of similar embryological origin.

homozygous. Having identical alleles at corresponding loci of homologous chromosomes.

hormone. A secretion of some cells that produces profound stimulating effects, usually elsewhere in the organism.

humoral immunity. The protective immunity provided by antibodies that are produced by B cells.

hybrid. The offspring of parents that differ in varying degrees; often the offspring that results from the crossing of parents belonging to different species.

hydrogen acceptor. Chemicals that combine with hydrogen during respiration (hydrogen transfer) and photosynthesis; NAD, FAD, etc.

hydrogen bond. A weak electrostatic attraction between two atoms with small but opposite charges; the positive atom is hydrogen.

hypertonic solution. A solution whose concentration of solute is greater than that of another solution being compared to it.

hypha. The filament of a fungal plant.

hypocotyl. The stem of an embryonic plant, located below the cotyledon(s).

hypotonic solution. A solution whose concentration of solute is less than that of another solution being compared to it.

I

ileum. The last and longest part of the small intestine.

immunity. The state of being protected from the effects of a foreign material by the action of the humoral and/or cellular immune systems.

imperfect flower. A flower lacking either kind of essential parts, staminate or pistillate.

imprinting. A type of learning, generally irreversible, that occurs at specific times in early life.

inbreeding. Breeding to close kin.

inclusion. A nonliving grain, crystal, or droplet contained in cytoplasm.

incomplete flower. A flower with one or more kinds of floral parts missing.

induced fit. A shape change of an enzyme's active site, initiated by interaction with the appropriate substrate; increases the binding between enzyme and substrate.

inferior ovary. In plants, an ovary partially or completely embedded in the receptacle.

inflorescence. The flowering part of a plant; the arrangement of flowers on a plant.

instinct. Relatively invariant behavior in response to a specific stimulus; genetically determined.

insulin. A hormone produced by the pancreas, involved in carbohydrate metabolism.

interneuron. An association neuron.

interphase. The state of a cell when not dividing.

interstitial cells. Cells located among seminiferous tubules of the testis and secreting testosterone.

intracellular digestion. Digestion within a cell.

intron. In eukaryotic cells, a sequence of nucleotides in a gene that is cleaved out of mRNA; it does not code for a polypeptide and is excised before translation begins.

ion. An atom or group of atoms having lost or gained one or more electrons, thus electrically charged.

irregular flower. A flower with bilateral symmetry.

isogametes. Gametes that are visibly alike but sexually different.

isotonic solution. A solution whose concentration of solute is equal to that of another solution being compared to it.

isotope. A variant of an element differing from the more common form in having a different number of neutrons in the nucleus.

J

jejunum. The second part of the small intestine.

K

karyotype. Chromosomes arranged as pairs according to size and centromere location.

Krebs cycle. Citric acid cycle of respiration, a cyclic phase during which carbon dioxide and hydrogen are released.

K-selected species. Those whose members use the reproductive strategy of producing offspring late in life, with the offspring being small in number and well prepared to compete for resources.

L

lactase. The lactose-digesting enzyme.

lactic acid. A product of anaerobic respiration. Its accumulation in muscles causes fatigue.

lactose. Milk sugar, a disaccharide.

lacuna. A cavity in which a bone or cartilage cell is located.

larynx. The organ of voice in mammals, the modified upper part of the trachea.

learning. The modification of behavior due to memory of past experiences.

lentic. Of lakes.

lenticel. A patch of loosely arranged cells through which gaseous exchange can occur, in the corky layer of stems.

leucocyte. A white blood cell.

leucoplast. A colorless plastid.

light reactions. The portion of photosynthetic reactions in which light is required and in which ATP, NADPH, and molecular oxygen are produced.

lignin. A complex organic constituent of the walls of sclerenchyma.

linkage. The association of genes in the same chromosome.

lipase. A fat-digesting enzyme.

lipids. Class of organic molecules that are insoluble in water, including substances such as fats, waxes, steroids, and oils.

littoral zone. A shallow zone around the margin of lakes where rooted plants grow; in oceans, between high and low tides.

loop of Henle. The U-shaped portion of a nephron that makes possible the production of hypertonic urine.

lotic. Of streams.

lymph. Constituents of blood that seep through capillary walls into tissue spaces, eventually returned to veins by way of the lymphatic system.

lymphatic system. A system of tubes that collects lymph and returns it to veins.

lymphocyte. A type of white blood cell produced in lymph tissue; active in immunity.

lysosome. A spherical membranous bag within a cell, containing digestive enzymes.

M

macronucleus. A large nucleus in *Paramecium*, concerned with metabolic activities.

major histocompatibility genes. A group of genes that code for proteins that are particularly likely to mark transplanted tissue as foreign, enabling the body to mount an immune response against it.

malignancy. Cancerous condition of a cell in which the rate of cell division outpaces cell death, leading to uncontrolled growth of tissue.

Malpighian tubules. Excretory tubules in insects.

maltase. The maltose-digesting enzyme.

maltose. Malt sugar, a disaccharide.

mammary gland. A milk-secreting gland.

mantle. A fold of tissue that secretes the shell of a mollusc.

marsupials. Nonplacental mammals that give birth to offspring in a partially developed condition and place them in an abdominal pouch, where they attach themselves to nipples and continue their development.

medulla. The inner part of some organs; the posterior part of the brain connected to the spinal cord.

medusa. A free-swimming form of a cnidarian; the jellyfish stage.

megagametophyte. The egg-producing phase of a plant life cycle.

megaspore. A large spore that grows into a female gametophytic plant.

meiosis. Reduction division; the production of haploid reproductive cells from diploid cells.

meiospore. A spore produced by meiosis.

melanin. A pigment located in the skin, hair, and retina of mammals; also present in many other animals.

meninges. Membranes around the brain and spinal cord.

meristem. A plant tissue consisting of unspecialized cells that are capable of active cell division.

mesocarp. The middle layer of a fruit wall (pericarp).

mesoderm. The middle germ layer of an early embryo.

mesoglea. A jellylike layer between the two cellular layers of cnidaria; the jelly of a jellyfish.

mesophyll. A tissue in leaves located between the two epidermal layers.

mesophyte. A plant living in intermediate situations with respect to available water supply.

messenger RNA. RNA that carries the encoded messages for polypeptides from DNA to the ribosomes.

metabolism. The chemical changes in cells commonly classified as energy-releasing processes.

metamorphosis. Abrupt transformation from one stage to another in developing animals.

metaphase. That stage of mitosis when chromosomes are aligned at the equator of the spindle.

metastasis. Propensity for cancer cells to break away from a tumor and move to other parts of the body, producing secondary tumors.

metazoa. Multicellular animals.

microfilament. A threadlike fiber of actin, part of the cytoskeleton of a cell.

microgametophyte. The sperm-producing phase of a plant life cycle.

micronucleus. A small nucleus in *Paramecium*, concerned with genetic activity.

micropyle. A pore in the ovule through which the pollen tube grows.

microspore. A small spore that grows into a male gametophytic plant.

microtubule. A hollow proteinaceous tube; part of the cytoskeleton, cilia and flagella, centrioles, and mitotic spindle.

middle lamella. The first layer of a cell wall deposited by the two daughter cells during cell division.

mitochondrion. A cellular organelle, the center of respiratory activity.

mitosis. Division of a cell to produce two new cells identical genetically to the parent cell.

monocot (monocotyledon). A seed plant that is in part distinguished by embryos that have only one cotyledon.

monoecious. Having both sexes in the same body.

monohybrid A genetic cross involving one characteristic.

monosaccharide. The simplest kind of sugar, e.g., glucose or fructose.

monotremes. Mammals whose females lay eggs.

morphogenesis. The shaping of the body during development.

morula. An early stage of the embryo consisting of a berry-shaped mass of cells.

motor neuron. A neuron leading to a responsive organ (effector).

mutagen. Any agent that causes a mutation.

mutation. A sudden genetic change that may involve a single nucleotide, or larger chromosomal regions, and which may be transmitted to future generations if occurring in a sex cell.

mutualism. A symbiotic relationship between two organisms whereby both members are benefited.

mycelium. The vegetative hyphae of a fungus.

mycorrhiza. The symbiotic association of fungal hyphae with plant roots.

myelin sheath. An insulative layer of living cells encompassing the axons of certain neurons; enhances rate of nerve impulse propagation.

myofibril. A subunit of a muscle fiber consisting of many sarcomeres in tandem.

myoneural junction. The region of synaptic connection between a motor neuron and a muscle fiber.

N

NAD, nicotinamide adenine dinucleotide. An acceptor of hydrogen.

NADP, nicotinamide adenine dinucleotide phosphate. An acceptor of hydrogen.

natural selection. The process by which the environment eliminates organisms having unsuitable characteristics for survival and sustains those having suitable characteristics.

negative feedback. A self-regulating system in which the high concentration of a product inhibits the reactions that produce more of the product.

nephridium. A tubular excreting structure as in earthworms.

nephron. An excreting unit of the kidney, consisting of a renal corpuscle and tubule.

nerve. A cord containing processes of neurons bound together with connective tissue.

neuron. A nerve cell.

neurotransmitters. Molecules such as adrenalin, noradrenalin, and acetylcholine that are secreted by ends of neurons and transmit stimuli across the synapses.

niche. The position or status of an organism with respect to other organisms with which it is associated; the total way of life for a species.

nitrogen fixation. The combining of atmospheric nitrogen with other elements into forms that can be used by plants.

nitrogenous base. Nitrogen-containing purine or pyrimidine molecules that have basic chemical properties; part of nucleotide.

nondisjunction. Failure of homologous chromosomes to separate during meiosis.

notochord. The dorsally located, gristlelike supporting rod of chordates.

nucleic acids. DNA and RNA, composed of units called nucleotides and arranged in strands.

nucleolus. A spherical body seen in the nucleus during interphase. It is the site for manufacture of ribosomal RNA.

nucleoprotein. A complex composed of proteins in combinations with nucleic acids.

nucleotide. A unit of nucleic acids composed of a phosphate group, a pentose sugar, and a nitrogenous base.

nucleus. A membrane-bounded portion of the eukaryotic cell containing the genetic material (chromatin).

nymph. An intermediate developmental stage of some insects, resembling the adult but having disproportionate body parts.

O

obligate anaerobe. An anaerobic organism that cannot use gaseous oxygen in respiration.

oligotrophic. Refers to a lake whose conditions are not conducive to promoting much biological activity; opposite of eutrophic.

omnivore. An organism that eats both plants and animals.

oncogene. A gene capable (immediately or after modification) of causing transformation of a cell to malignancy.

ontogeny. The course of development of individual organisms.

oogonium. A unicellular female gametangium; in animals, an ovarian cell capable of developing into the primary oocyte.

ootid. A cell resulting from the division of a secondary oocyte and maturing into a functional egg.

operon. A set of bacterial genes that is controlled by a single ON-OFF switching mechanism, plus the DNA which constitutes the switch; a set of structural genes plus a promoter and an operator.

organ. A group of several tissues arranged to perform one or more functions efficiently.

organelle. A part of a cell having a specific function.

organic compound. A chemical compound that contains one or more carbon atoms.

osmoconformer. An organism that cannot osmoregulate; conforms to the salt concentration of its environment.

osmoregulator. An organism that can maintain an optimal internal concentration of salts, within a range of external salt concentrations.

osmosis. Passive movement (diffusion) of water through a semipermeable membrane.

ovary. In animals, the female gonad; in plants, the basal part of the pistil.

oviduct. A tube for conducting eggs.

oviparous. Egg-laying.

ovoviviparous. Producing eggs that are incubated and hatched within the female's body.

ovulation. The discharge of eggs from the follicles of the ovary.

ovule. An immature seed containing the embryo sac with egg.

oxytocin. A hormone produced by the posterior lobe of the pituitary gland, causing contraction of smooth muscles of the uterus and breasts.

P

palisade mesophyll. Column-shaped cells beneath the upper epidermis of leaves.

palmate. Arranged around one point like leaflets of Virginia creeper.

parasite. An organism living in or on a living individual of another species from which it obtains food, generally harming the host.

parathormone. A hormone produced by the parathyroid glands; regulates metabolism of calcium and phosphorus.

parenchyma. A simple plant tissue composed of thin-walled cells.

parthenogenesis. Asexual reproduction by an organism that is equipped to reproduce sexually. The egg is spontaneously activated, without contact by sperm.

parturition. The action or process of giving birth.

pedicel. The stalk of a single flower in a cluster.

peduncle. The stalk of a single flower or the main stalk of a cluster of flowers.

pelagic. Of the open sea.

pentose sugar. A monosaccharide with five carbon atoms; a part of a nucleotide.

pepsin. A gastric enzyme that acts upon proteins.

peptide bond. The covalent link between two amino acids; the carboxyl end of one amino acid bonds to the amino end of the other amino acid.

perfect flower. A flower having both kinds of essential parts, staminate and pistillate.

perianth. Sepals and petals collectively.

pericarp. The wall of a fruit.

pericycle. The outer layer of a vascular cylinder, especially in roots.

peristalsis. Wavelike muscular contractions of a tubular organ, such as an intestine.

petiole. The stalk of a leaf.

PGA, phosphoglyceric acid. A 3-carbon compound regarded as the first organic compound synthesized from carbon dioxide and water during photosynthesis.

PGAL, phosphoglyceraldehyde. A 3-carbon food, regarded as the end product of photosynthesis.

pH. A scale ranging from 0 to 14, used to indicate the degree of acidity or alkalinity. Number 7 indicates neutrality; 6–0 represent increasing acidity; 8–14, increasing alkalinity.

phagocytosis. A cell's act of engulfing particles.

pharynx. A part of the digestive tract of many animals; in humans, a passage common to the digestive and respiratory systems.

phenotype. Expressed hereditary characteristics.

phenotypic ratio. The proportion of phenotypes resulting from a specific cross.

pheromone. An animal secretion that influences other members of the same species.

photolysis. The splitting of water into hydrogen and oxygen during the first phase of photosynthesis.

photoperiodism. The relation between the blooming of plants and the length of exposure to darkness.

photosynthesis. The synthesis of simple foods from carbon dioxide and water, in which light is the source of energy.

phylum. A major category of classification in the animal kingdom, located between the kingdom and the class.

pinnate. Arranged along a longitudinal axis.

pinocytosis. A cell's intake of fluid by forming a vesicle, or discharge by moving a vesicle to the cell membrane.

pistil. The female part of a flower, composed of one or more megasporophylls.

placenta. An organ of exchange between embryo (or fetus) and mother; in plants, the place where an ovule is attached to the ovary.

placentals. Mammals whose females nurture their embryos in the uterus by means of placentas.

plankton. Organisms, larvae or adults, that float or weakly swim at or near the surface of water.

plasma. The fluid (noncellular) portion of blood.

plasma membrane. The outer boundary of the cytoplasm, sometimes called the *plasmalemma*.

plasmid. A circular DNA molecule that exists independent of a bacterium's chromosome; used in genetic engineering as a vehicle for addition of foreign DNA.

plasmolysis. The shrinking of protoplasm due to loss of water.

plastid. A plant organelle usually containing pigments or stored food.

platelet. A cell fragment concerned with the clotting of blood.

polar bodies. Vestigial eggs produced along with functional eggs during meiosis.

pollen. Male gametophytes of seed plants.

pollination. Transfer of pollen to the pistil.

polymorphism. The occurrence of two or more morphological forms within a species.

polyp. A form of cnidaria that is usually attached to the substratum.

polypeptide. A polymer of several to many amino acids, linked by peptide bonds.

polyploidy. The condition of having more than two complete sets of chromosomes per cell, in exact multiples of the haploid number (3N, 4N, etc.).

polysaccharide. Any compound carbohydrate that may be broken into molecules of monosaccharide sugars.

population. All individuals of a species or all members of the same species in a specific location.

prairie. A middle-latitude grassland, grasses tall.

primary oocyte. A diploid animal cell from which one egg and three polar bodies originate as a result of two consecutive divisions.

primary spermatocyte. A diploid animal cell from which four sperms originate as a result of two consecutive divisions.

primary tissues. Tissues produced by apical meristems of plants.

primitive. Unspecialized: in an early stage of evolution.

primitive streak. The center of growth for all three germ layers, located at the posterior end of the longitudinal axis of an early embryo.

producers. Organisms that can convert light energy to chemical form, by photosynthesis.

progesterone. A hormone secreted by the corpus luteum; the pregnancy hormone.

prokaryotes. Organisms whose cells have no membrane-bound nuclei or other organelles such as mitochondria and plastids; bacteria.

prophase. The earliest phase of mitosis during which chromosomes develop to their shortest and thickest form.

protein. A large polypeptide, usually at least 50 amino acids in length; may consist of more than one polypeptide.

prothallium. The gametophyte of ferns and related plants.

protonema. In mosses, a filamentous gametophytic structure arising from a spore and producing buds that grow into gametophytes.

protostome. An animal whose embryonic blastopore becomes a mouth, and whose anus is formed later.

pseudocoel. A body cavity not entirely lined by cells of mesodermal origin.

pseudopodium. A variable and temporary appendage extended from certain cells and used for locomotion or feeding.

punctuated equilibrium. A model featuring evolution occurring by relatively sudden and large changes, rather than a gradual accumulation of small changes.

Punnett square. A drawn grid whose blocks are used to record all possible gene combinations when gametes of parents of known genotypes are combined.

purine. A nitrogenous base of nucleic acids, either adenine or guanine.

putrefaction. The decay of proteins, accompanied by the production of foul-smelling compounds.

pyrimidine. A nitrogenous base of nucleic acids, either cytosine, thymine, or uracil.

R

radicle. The lower tip of an embryonic plant that grows into a primary root.

ray flowers. The outside flowers of a composite head, often mistaken for petals of a single flower.

receptacle. The crown of a peduncle or pedicel where floral parts are attached.

recessive. Unexpressed: used to describe a gene whose characteristic is hidden by the characteristic of a dominant allele.

recombinant DNA technology. Methods for the artificial placement of a gene into an organism that does not normally contain it.

referred pain. Pain felt in a part of the body remote from where it actually occurs.

reflex. An unconscious response to a stimulus.

reflex arc. The pathway of impulse transmission in a reflex.

regeneration. Growth of tissue to replace a lost portion in an adult organism.

regular flower. A flower with radial symmetry.

relic. A species, once more widely dispersed, now surviving in an isolated place or places.

renin. A kidney hormone affecting blood pressure.

rennin. A secretion of the stomach that curdles milk.

reproductive isolation. Inability of members of two species to reproduce successfully.

respiration. A metabolic process within cells that provides energy for cell activities.

respiratory quotient. The ratio of oxygen and carbon dioxide exchanged during respiration.

rhizoids. Rootlike structures of gametophytes, lacking conducting tissues.

rhizome. A horizontal underground stem.

ribose. A pentose sugar in RNA.

ribosome. An organelle found either free in the cytoplasm or attached to the endoplasmic reticulum; the site of protein synthesis.

RNA, ribonucleic acid. A polynucleotide whose 5-carbon sugar is ribose; three types are transfer RNA, ribosomal RNA, and messenger RNA.

rookery. A breeding place for congregating birds (also seals).

root hair. An epidermal outgrowth from the absorption zone of roots, used for absorbing water and other substances.

r-selected species. Those whose members use the reproductive strategy of producing offspring early in life, with the offspring being very large in number but rather poorly prepared to survive.

S

saprophyte. An organism depending on dead bodies for food; more specifically, a plant that lives on dead organic matter.

sarcomere. A section of a muscle myofibril located between two Z lines.

sarcoplasmic reticulum. The endoplasmic reticulum in muscle cells; acts as a reservoir for the calcium that triggers contraction.

savanna. A tropical grassland.

sclerenchyma. A simple plant tissue composed of cells with thickened walls, like fibers or stone cells.

secondary spermatocyte. A haploid cell resulting from the meiotic division of a primary spermatocyte.

secondary tissues. Tissues like cork, phloem, and xylem that are produced by cambium.

secretins. Hormones produced in the duodenum that cause the liver and pancreas to secrete enzymes.

seed. A mature ovule of a seed plant containing an embryonic plant and sometimes a food-storage tissue called endosperm.

semiconservative replication. The method used by organisms to duplicate DNA, whereby exactly half of each resulting DNA molecule came from the previously existing DNA molecule.

sensory neuron. A neuron transmitting a stimulus from a receptor toward the central nervous system.

sepal. A part of the outer whorl of most flowers.

sex chromosome. A chromosome containing genes that help determine sex; in humans, these are called X and Y.

short-day plant. A plant that flowers when exposed to long periods of darkness.

sieve tube. A conducting tube in phloem composed of a row of cells whose end walls are perforated by pores. Protoplasm is continuous throughout the tube.

simple fruit. A fruit derived from a single pistil of a single flower, e.g., tomato.

somatic. Pertaining to the wall of the body as distinguished from viscera in cavities; or nonreproductive cells.

sorus. A cluster of sporangia on the leaves of ferns.

species. A group of related organisms capable of interbreeding effectively.

spermatids. Cells resulting from the division of a secondary spermatocyte and destined to become sperms.

sphincter. A band of muscles encircling an opening or passage and controlling the flow of materials through it.

spicules. Simple or branching needles of calcareous or silicious materials giving support in sponges.

spinal ganglion. A concentration of sensory cell bodies in the dorsal root of the spinal nerve.

spindle. A biconical fibrous structure seen in a dividing cell; made of microtubules; may pull chromosomes to poles of cell during mitosis and meiosis.

spiracle. A pore opening to a trachea in insects and some other arthropods.

spirillum. A spiral-shaped bacterium.

sporangium. A spore container in plants.

spore. A reproductive plant cell not requiring fertilization; in life cycles, a haploid cell produced by the sporophyte.

spore mother cell. A diploid cell from which haploid spores are derived.

sporophyll. A spore-bearing leaf, sometimes

considerably modified as in the case of a stamen.

sporophyte. A spore-producing phase of a plant life cycle.

sporulation. Production of spores.

stamen. The male part of the flower; a microsporophyll.

steppe. A middle-latitude grassland, grasses short.

stigma. The part of a pistil receptive to pollen.

stoma. An epidermal pore in plants through which gases are exchanged with the environment.

suberin. The waterproofing substance in the walls of cork cells.

subspecies. A distinctly different subgroup within a species, with genetically determined characteristics setting it apart from another subgroup.

substrate. A chemical entity with which an enzyme can interact, fitting into the enzyme's active site.

succession. A series of replacements of communities of organisms due to their alteration of the environment, making it less suitable for themselves and more suitable for another. The final community of the series, called the climax, is self-perpetuating and stable under normal conditions.

sucrase. The sucrose-digesting enzyme.

sucrose. Table sugar, a disaccharide.

superior ovary. In plants, an ovary attached on top of the receptacle.

symbiosis. Dissimilar organisms living in a close relationship.

sympatric. An ecological term describing populations of related species that live in the same geographical area without interbreeding.

synapse. The gap between the axon of one neuron and the dendrite of another, or between a neuron and an effector.

synapsis. Pairing of homologous chromosomes during prophase I of meiosis.

syncytium. A multinucleate tissue; cells confluent, not separated by cell membranes.

synecology. The branch of ecology dealing with the study of communities of organisms.

syrinx. The voice box of birds, located at the base of the trachea.

T

tadpole. The larval stage of frogs and toads.

taiga. The boreal forest, a high-latitude coniferous forest.

taxis. Directional orientation of unattached animals or motile reproductive cells.

taxon. Any taxonomic category such as class, family, or species.

taxonomy. The branch of biology dealing with classification of organisms.

T cells. One of the two major types (with B cells) in an immune system; attack foreign substances or cells by phagocytosis.

teleology. The practice of ascribing purposeful direction to natural processes; using end results to explain why phenomena occur.

telophase. The last phase of mitosis when chromosomes reach the poles of the spindle and a new nucleus begins to form.

territoriality. Behavior of some animals, consisting of claiming and defending a specific geographical area.

testa. The seed coat.

test cross. The mating between an individual of the dominant phenotype with one of the homozygous recessive phenotype to determine whether the former is heterozygous or homozygous.

testosterone. A hormone responsible for masculine characteristics.

thallus. A simple plant body without conducting tissues.

thermocline. A layer in a deep lake between the upper warm stratum and the lower cold stratum, where the temperature decreases about 10 centigrade for every increase of meter in depth.

thorax. The chest.

threshold intensity. The minimum intensity of a stimulus required to start an impulse.

thylakoid. A flattened, saclike membraneous structure whose membranes contain chlorophyll and other pigments; when occurring in stacks within a chloroplast, they comprise the grana.

thymine. A nitrogenous base of the pyrimidine type that is a constituent of nucleotides.

thyroxin. The hormone secreted by the thyroid gland, influencing the speed of metabolism.

tissue. A group of cells that are morphologically and functionally similar.

tracheae. Conducting tubes such as air passages to lungs, air tubes in insects, or vessels in wood.

tracheophytes. Plants with conducting tissues, including ferns and seed plants; vascular plants.

transcription. The synthesis of messenger RNA from the DNA template.

transduction. The introduction of genes from one bacterium to another by an invading virus; the capacity of receptor cells to change stimuli into electrical impulses for transmission through neurons.

transfer RNA. Cytoplasmic RNA that holds specific amino acids, later carries them to messenger RNA aligned on the ribosomes.

translation. The production of a polypeptide under the direction of messenger RNA; occurs on ribosomes.

translocation. The movement of foods from one place to another in plants.

transpiration. The evaporation of water from the leaves of plants.

trisaccharide. A compound sugar that can be broken into three monosaccharide molecules.

trochophore. An early aquatic larval stage found in some brachiopods, bryozoans, nemerteans, flatworms, molluscs, and annelids.

tropism. A directional growth response in plants.

trypsin. A pancreatic enzyme that digests proteins.

T tubules. A system of membranous tubes in muscle; carry action potentials from muscle fiber surface to the site of contraction.

tube cell. A part of a pollen grain that grows to the vicinity of the egg.

tuber. The enlarged tip of a rhizome, e.g., Irish potato.

tundra. A frozen desert (where subsoil is permanently frozen).

typhlosole. The dorsal fold of the intestine of an earthworm, increasing food absorption.

U

uracil. A nitrogenous base of the pyrimidine type that is a constituent of nucleotides in RNA.

urea. A nitrogenous compound produced by the liver and excreted by kidneys; it is rather toxic and requires a considerable amount of water to flush it from the body.

ureter. The tube conducting urine from the kidney to the urinary bladder.

urethra. The tube conducting urine from the urinary bladder to the outside; in males, it is also a passage for semen.

uric acid. An insoluble nitrogenous compound excreted by the kidneys or comparable structures, especially eliminated by birds, terrestrial reptiles, and insects; in humans, overproduction or retention of uric acid can produce kidney stones and deposits in joints (gout).

uterus. The organ where the embryo or fetus develops; womb.

V

vacuole. A cytoplasmic cavity filled with water and other materials that are not part of the protoplasm.

valve. The half-shell of a bivalve mollusc such as a clam or oyster.

vascular bundle. In plants, a strand of conducting and supporting tissues.

vasopressin. A posterior pituitary hormone that causes increased blood pressure and water retention (also called antidiuretic hormone).

ventral root. The lower branch of a spinal nerve that connects to the spinal cord; the pathway of motor neurons.

ventricle. A compartment of the heart that pumps blood to the tissues.

venule. A small vein.

villus. A fingerlike projection from the inner wall of the small intestine that increases the surface area.

viroid. An infective particle consisting only of a piece of RNA.

virus. An infective particle consisting of a protein capsule enclosing nucleic acid.

visceral reflex. An unconscious response in the eye, internal organs, or blood vessels; its pathway is in the autonomic nervous system.

vitamin. An organic molecule functioning as (or being converted to) a cofactor or coenzyme; must be imported by the organism needing it.

viviparous. Giving birth to living offspring.

W

water-vascular system. A unique system in echinoderms used especially for locomotion, circulation, and food-getting.

wood. The tough cellulose-containing secondary xylem of certain plants.

X

xanthophyll. A class of yellow pigments found in plastids of plants.

xerophyte. A plant adapted for survival where water is scarce; a water-conserving plant.

xylem. A complex plant tissue used for conducting water and dissolved inorganic substances and for support; the wood of plants.

Y

yolk. A material stored with an animal embryo and acting as food for the embryo; consists largely of protein and lipid.

yolk sac. A sac extending from the ventral surface of an animal embryo, often filled with food.

Z

zooplankton. Nonphotosynthetic marine organisms of kingdom Protista, living near the ocean surface.

zygospore. A cell resulting from fertilization that undergoes meiosis before germinating.

zygote. The cell resulting from the uniting of two gametes.